Bayard Taylor del.

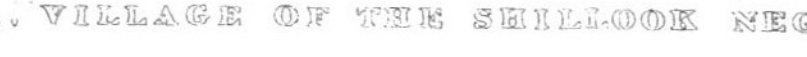

(The turning point.)

NEW YORK: G. P. PUTNAM.

CENTRAL AFRICA.

BAYARD TAYLOR.

The Ethiopian Nile.

NEW-YORK: G. P. PUTNAM.

A

JOURNEY TO CENTRAL AFRICA;

OR,

LIFE AND LANDSCAPES FROM EGYPT TO THE NEGRO KINGDOMS OF THE WHITE NILE.

BY

BAYARD TAYLOR.

With a Map and Illustrations by the Author.

ELEVENTH EDITION.

NEW YORK:
G. P. PUTNAM, 532 BROADWAY.
1862.

R. CRAIGHEAD,
Printer, Stereotyper, and Electrotyper,
Carton Building,
81, 83, and 85 Centre Street.

Dedicated to

A. B.

OF SAXE-COBURG-GOTHA,

BY

HIS FELLOW-TRAVELLER IN EGYPT.

B. T.

PREFACE.

THERE is an old Italian proverb, which says a man has lived to no purpose, unless he has either built a house, begotten a son, or written a book. As I have already complied more than once with the latter of these requisitions, I must seek to justify the present repetition thereof, on other grounds. My reasons for offering this volume to the public are, simply, that there is room for it. It is the record of a journey which led me, for the most part, over fresh fields, by paths which comparatively few had trodden before me. Although I cannot hope to add much to the general stock of information concerning Central Africa, I may serve, at least, as an additional witness, to confirm or illustrate the evidence of others. Hence, the preparation of this work has appeared to me rather in the light of a duty than a diversion, and I have endeavored to impart as much instruction as amusement to the reader. While seeking to give correct pictures of the rich, adventurous life into which I was thrown, I have resisted the temptation to yield myself up to its more subtle and poetic aspects. My aim has been to furnish a faithful narrative of my own experience, believing that none of those embellishments which the imagination so readily furnishes, can equal the charm of the unadorned truth.

There are a few words of further explanation which I wish to say. The journey was undertaken solely for the purpose of restoring a frame exhausted by severe mental labor. A previous experience of a tropical climate convinced me that I should best accomplish my object by a visit to Egypt, and as I had a whole winter before me, I determined to penetrate as far into the interior of Africa as the time would allow, attracted less by the historical and geographical interest of those regions than by the desire to participate in their free, vigorous, semi-barbaric life. If it had been my intention, as some of my friends supposed, to search for the undiscovered sources of the White Nile, I should not have turned back, until the aim was accomplished or all means had failed.

I am aware that, by including in this work my journey through Egypt, I have gone over much ground which is already familiar. Egypt, however, was the vestibule through which I passed to Ethiopia and the kingdoms beyond, and I have not been able to omit my impressions of that country without detracting from the completeness of the narrative. This book is the record of a single journey, which, both in its character and in the circumstances that suggested and accompanied it, occupies a separate place in my memory. Its performance was one uninterrupted enjoyment, for, whatever the privations to which it exposed me, they were neutralized by the physical delight of restored health and by a happy confidence in the successful issue of the journey, which never forsook me. It is therefore but just to say, that the pictures I have drawn may seem over-bright to others who may hereafter follow me; and I should warn all such that they must expect to encounter many troubles and annoyances.

Although I have described somewhat minutely the antiquities of Nubia and Ethiopia which I visited, and have not been insensible to the interest which every traveller in Egypt must feel in the remains of her ancient art, I have aimed at giving representations of the living races which inhabit those countries rather than the old ones which have passed away. I have taken it for granted that the reader will feel more interested—as I was—in a live Arab, than a dead

Pharaoh. I am indebted wholly to the works of Champollion, Wilkinson and Lepsius for whatever allusions I have made to the age and character of the Egyptian ruins.

B. T.

NEW YORK, July, 1854.

CONTENTS.

CHAPTER I.

Arrival at Alexandria—The Landing—My First Oriental Bath—The City—Preparations for Departure, ... 13

CHAPTER II.

Departure—The Kangia—The Egyptian Climate—The Mahmoudieh Canal—Entrance into the Nile—Pleasures of the Journey—Studying Arabic—Sight of the Pyramids—The Barrage—Approach to Cairo, ... 21

CHAPTER III.

Entrance—The Ezbekiyeh—Saracenic Houses—Donkeys—The Bazaars—The Streets—Processions—View from the Citadel—Mosque of Mohammed Ali—The Road to Suez—The Island of Rhoda, ... 34

CHAPTER IV.

Necessity of Leaving Immediately—Engaging a Boat—The Dragomen—Achmet el Saïdi—Funds—Information—Procuring an Outfit—Preparing for the Desert—The Lucky Day—Exertions to Leave—Off, ... 46

CHAPTER V.

Howling Dervishes—A Chicken Factory—Ride to the Pyramids—Quarrel with the Arabs—The Ascent—View from the Summit—Backsheesh—Effect of Pyramid-climbing—The Sphinx—Playing the Cadi—We obtain Justice—Visit to Sakkara and the Mummy Pits—The Exhumation of Memphis—Interview with M. Mariette—Account of his Discoveries—Statue of Remeses II.—Return to the Nile, . 55

CHAPTER VI.

Leaving the Pyramids—A Calm and a Breeze—A Coptic Visit—Minyet—The Grottoes of Beni-Hassan—Doum Palms and Crocodiles—Djebel Aboufayda—Entrance into Upper Egypt—Diversions of the Boatmen—Siout—Its Tombs—A Landscape—A Bath, ... 71

CHAPTER VII.

Independence of Nile Life—The Dahabiyeh—Our Servants—Our Residence—Our Manner of Living—The Climate—The Natives—Costume—Our Sunset Repose—My Friend—A Sensuous Life Defended, ... 85

CHAPTER VIII.

Calm—Mountains and Tombs—A Night Adventure in Ekhmin—Character of the Boatmen—Fair Wind—Pilgrims—Egyptian Agriculture—Sugar and Cotton—Grain—Sheep—Arrival at Kenneh—A Landscape—The Temple of Dendera—First Impressions of Egyptian Art—Portrait of Cleopatra—A Happy Meeting—We approach Thebes, ... 98

CHAPTER IX.

Arrival at Thebes—Ground-Plan of the Remains—We Cross to the Western Bank—Guides—The Temple of Goorneh—Valley of the Kings' Tombs—Belzoni's Tomb—The Races of Men—Vandalism of Antiquarians—Bruce's Tomb—Memnon—The Grandfather of Sesostris—The Head of Amunoph—The Colossi of the Plain—Memnonian Music—The Statue of Remeses—The Memnonium—Beauty of Egyptian Art—More Scrambles among the Tombs—The Bats of the Assasseef—Medeenet Abou—Sculptured Histories—The Great Court of the Temple—We return to Luxor, ... 113

CHAPTER X.

The Dancing Girls of Egypt—A Night Scene in Luxor—The Orange-Blossom and the Apple-Blossom—The Beautiful Bemba—The Dance—Performance of the Apple-Blossom—The Temple of Luxor—A Mohammedan School—Gallop to Karnak—View of the Ruins—The Great Hall of Pillars—Bedouin Diversions—A Night Ride—Karnak under the Full Moon—Farewell to Thebes, ... 131

CHAPTER XI.

The Temple of Hermontis—Esneh and its Temple—The Governor—El Kab by Torchlight—The Temple of Edfou—The Quarries of Djebel Silsileh—Ombos—Approach to Nubia—Change in the Scenery and Inhabitants—A Mirage—Arrival at Assouan, ... 145

CHAPTER XII.

An Official Visit—Achmet's Dexterity—The Island of Elephantine—Nubian Children—Trip to Philæ—Linant Bey—The Island of Philæ—Sculptures—The Negro Race—

Breakfast in a Ptolemaic Temple—The Island of Biggeh—Backsheesh—The Cataract—The Granite Quarries of Assouan—The Travellers separate, . . . 152

CHAPTER XIII.

Solitary Travel—Scenery of the Nubian Nile—Agriculture—The Inhabitants—Arrival at Korosko—The Governor—The Tent Pitched—Shekh Abou-Mohammed—Bargaining for Camels—A Drove of Giraffes—Visits—Preparations for the Desert—My Last Evening on the Nile, ... 162

CHAPTER XIV.

The Curve of the Nile—Routes across the Desert—Our Caravan starts—Riding on a Dromedary—The Guide and Camel-drivers—Hair-dressing—El Biban—Scenery—Dead Camels—An Unexpected Visit—The Guide makes my Grave—The River without Water—Characteristics of the Mirage—Desert Life—The Sun—The Desert Air—Infernal Scenery—The Wells of Mûrr-hàt—Christmas—Mountain Chains—Meeting Caravans—Plains of Gravel—The Story of Joseph—Djebel Mokràt—The Last Day in the Desert—We see the Nile again, ... 171

CHAPTER XV.

A Draught of Water—Abou-Hammed—The Island of Mokràt—Ethiopian Scenery—The People—An Ababdeh Apollo—Encampment on the Nile—Tomb of an Englishman—Eesa's Wedding—A White Arab—The Last Day of the Year—Abou-Hashym—Incidents—Loss of my Thermometer—The Valley of Wild Asses—The Eleventh Cataract—Approach to Berber—Vultures—Eyoub Outwitted—We reach El Mekheyref—The Caravan Broken up, ... 193

CHAPTER XVI.

A Wedding—My Reception by the Military Governor—Achmet—The Bridegroom—A Guard—I am an American Bey—Kèff—The Bey's Visit—The Civil Governor—About the Navy—The Priest's Visit—Riding in State—The Dongolese Stallion—A Merchant's House—The Town—Dinner at the Governor's—The Pains of Royalty—A Salute to the American Flag—Departure, ... 206

CHAPTER XVII.

Fortunate Travel—The America—Ethiopian Scenery—The Atbara River—Damer—A Melon Patch—Agriculture—The Inhabitants—Change of Scenery—The First Hippopotamus—Crocodiles—Effect of My Map—The Raïs and Sailors—Arabs in Ethiopia—Ornamental Scars—Beshir—The Slave Bakhita—We Approach Meroë, 219

CHAPTER XVIII.

Arrival at Bedjerowiyeh—The Ruins of Meroë—Walk Across the Plain—The Pyramids—Character of their Masonry—The Tower and Vault—Finding of the Treasure—The Second Group—More Ruins—Site of the City—Number of the Pyramids—The Antiquity of Meroë—Ethiopian and Egyptian Civilization—The Caucasian Race—Reflections, ... 229

CHAPTER XIX.

The Landscapes of Ethiopia—My Evenings beside the Nile—Experiences of the Arabian Nights—The Story of the Sultana Zobeide and the Wood-cutter—Character of the Arabian Tales—Religion. 238

CHAPTER XX.

Arrival at Shendy—Appearance of the Town—Shendy in Former Days—We Touch at El Metemma—The Nile beyond Shendy—Flesh Diet vs. Vegetables—We Escape Shipwreck—A Walk on Shore—The Rapids of Derreira—Djebel Gerri—The Twelfth Cataract—Night in the Mountain Gorge—Crocodiles—A Drink of Mareesa—My Birth-Day—Fair Wind—Approach to Khartoum—The Junction of the Two Niles—Appearance of the City—We Drop Anchor, ... 258

CHAPTER XXI.

The American Flag—A Rencontre—Search for a House—The Austrian Consular Agent—Description of his Residence—The Garden—The Menagerie—Barbaric Pomp and State—Picturesque Character of the Society of Khartoum—Foundation and Growth of the City—Its Appearance—The Population—Unhealthiness of the Climate—Assembly of Ethiopian Chieftains—Visit of Two Shekhs—Dinner and Fireworks, ... 270

CHAPTER XXII.

Visit to the Catholic Mission—Dr. Knoblecher, the Apostolic Vicar—Moussa Bey—Visit to Lattif Pasha—Reception—The Pasha's Palace—Lions—We Dine with the Pasha—Ceremonies upon the Occasion—Music—The Guests—The Franks in Khartoum—Dr. Péney—Visit to the Sultana Nasra—An Ethiopian Dinner—Character of the Sultana, ... 280

CHAPTER XXIII.

Recent Explorations of Soudân—Limit of the Tropical Rains—The Conquest of Ethiopia—Countries Tributary to Egypt—The District of Takka—Expedition of Moussa Bey—The Atbara River—The Abyssinian Frontier—Christian Ruins of Abou-Haràss—The Kingdom of Sennaar—Kordofan—Dar-Für—The Princess of Dar-Für in Khartoum—Her Visit to Dr. Reitz—The Unknown Countries of Central Africa, ... 297

CHAPTER XXIV.

Excursions around Khartoum—A Race into the Desert—Euphorbia Forest—The Banks of the Blue Nile—A Saint's Grave—The Confluence of the Two Niles—Magnitude of the Nile—Comparative Size of the Rivers—Their Names—Desire to penetrate further into Africa—Attractions of the White Nile—Engage the Boat *John Ledyard*—Former Restrictions against exploring the River—Visit to the Pasha—Despotic Hospitality—Achmet's Misgivings—We set sail, . . . 309

CHAPTER XXV.

Departure from Khartoum—We enter the White Nile—Mirage and Landscape—The Consul returns—Progress—Loss of the Flag-Scenery of the Shores—Territory of the Hassaniyehs—Curious Conjugal Custom—Multitudes of Water Fowls—Increased Richness of Vegetation—Apes—Sunset on the White Nile—We reach the Kingdom of the Shillook Negroes, ... 320

CHAPTER XXVI.

Morning—Magnificence of the Island Scenery—Birds and Hippopotami—Flight of the Natives—The Island of Aba—Signs of Population—A Band of Warriors—The Shekh and the Sultan—A Treaty of Peace—The Robe of Honor—Suspicions—We walk to the Village—Appearance of the Shillooks—The Village—The Sultan gives Audience—Women and Children—Ornaments of the Natives—My Watch—A Jar of Honey—Suspicion and Alarm—The Shillook and the Sultan's Black Wife—Character of the Shillooks—The Land of the Lotus—Population of the Shillook Kingdom—The Turning Point—A View from the Mast-Head, ... 329

CHAPTER XXVII.

Explorations of the White Nile—Dr. Knoblecher's Voyage in 1849-50—The Lands of the Shillooks and Dinkas—Intercourse with the Natives—Wild Elephants and Giraffes—The Sobat River—The Country of Marshes—The Gazelle Lake—The Nuehrs—Interview with the Chief of the Kyks—The Zhir Country—Land of the Baris—The Rapids Surmounted—Arrival at Logwek, in Lat. 4° 10′ North—Panorama from Mt. Logwek—Sources of the White Nile—Character of the Bari Nation—Return of the Expedition—Fascination of the Nile, ... 345

CHAPTER XXVIII.

We leave the Islands of the Shillooks—Tropical Jungles—A Whim and its Consequences—Lairs of Wild Beasts—Arrival among the Hassaniyehs—A Village—The Woman and the Sultan—A Dance of Salutation—My Arab Sailor—A Swarthy Cleopatra—Salutation of the Saint—Miraculous Fishing—Night View of a Hassaniyeh Village—Wad Shèllayeh—A Shekh's Residence—An Ebony Cherub—The Cook Attempts Suicide—Evening Landscape—The Natives and their Cattle—A Boyish Governor—We reach Khartoum at Midnight, ... 356

CHAPTER XXIX.

The Departure of Abd-el Kader Bey—An Illuminated Picture—The Breakfast on the Island—Horsemanship—The Pasha's Stories—Departure of Lattif Effendi's Expedition—A Night on the Sand—Abou-Sin, and his Shukoree Warriors—Change in the Climate—Intense Heat and its Effects—Preparations for Returning—A Money Transaction—Farewell Visits—A Dinner with Royal Guests—Jolly King Dyaab—A Shillook Dance—Reconciliation—Taking Leave of my Pets, . . . 372

*

CHAPTER XXX.

The Commerce of Soudân—Avenues of Trade—The Merchants—Character of the Imports—Speculation—The Gum Trade of Kordofan—The Ivory Trade—Abuses of the Government—The Traffic in Slaves—Prices of Slaves—Their Treatment, . 384

CHAPTER XXXI.

Farewell Breakfast—Departure from Khartoum—Parting with Dr. Reitz—A Prediction and its Fulfilment—Dreary Appearance of the Country—Lions—Burying-Grounds—The Natives—My Kababish Guide, Mohammed—Character of the Arabs—Habits of Deception—My Dromedary—Mutton and Mareesa—A Soudân Ditty—The Rowyàn—Akaba Gerri—Heat and Scenery—An Altercation with the Guide—A Mishap—A Landscape—Tedious Approach to El Metemma—Appearance of the Town—Preparations for the Desert—Meeting Old Acquaintances, . . 392

CHAPTER XXXII.

Entering the Desert—Character of the Scenery—Wells—Fear of the Arabs—The Laloom Tree—Effect of the Hot Wind—Mohammed overtakes us—Arab Endurance—An unpleasant Bedfellow—Comedy of the Crows—Gazelles—We encounter a Sand-storm—The Mountain of Thirst—The Wells of Djeekdud—A Mountain Pass—Desert Intoxication—Scenery of the Table-land—Bir Khannik—The Kababish Arabs—Gazelles again—Ruins of an Ancient Coptic Monastery—Distant View of the Nile Valley—Djebel Berkel—We come into Port, ... 406

CHAPTER XXXIII.

Our whereabouts—Shekh Mohammed Abd e'-Djebàl—My residence at Abdôm—Crossing the River—A Superb Landscape—The Town of Merawe—Ride to Djebel Berkel—The Temples of Napata—Ascent of the Mountain—Ethiopian Panorama—Lost and Found—The Pyramids—The Governor of Merawe—A Scene in the Divan—The Shekh and I—The Governor Dines with me—Ruins of the City of Napata—A Talk about Religions—Engaging Camels for Wadi-Halfa—The Shekh's Parting Blessing, ... 421

CHAPTER XXXIV.

Appearance of the Country—Korti—The Town of Ambukol—The Caravan reorganized—A Fiery Ride—We reach Edabbe—An Illuminated Landscape—A Torment—Nubian Agriculture—Old Dongola—The Palace-Mosque of the Nubian Kings—A Panorama of Desolation—The Old City—Nubian Gratitude—Another Sand-Storm—A Dreary Journey—The Approach to Handak—A House of Doubtful Character—The Inmates—Journey to El Ordee (New Dongola)—Khoorshid Bey—Appearance of the Town, ... 438

CHAPTER XXXV.

We start for Wadi-Halfa—The Plague of Black Gnats—Mohammed's Coffin—The Island of Argo—Market-Day—Scenery of the Nile—Entering Dar El-Màhass—

Ruined Fortresses—The Camel-Men—A Rocky Chaos—Fakir Bender—The Akabe of Mâhass—Camp in the Wilderness—The Charm of Desolation—The Nile again—Pilgrims from Dar-Für—The Struggle of the Nile—An Arcadian Landscape—The Temple of Soleb—Dar Sukkôt—The Land of Dates—The Island of Sai—A Sea of Sand—Camp by the River—A Hyena Barbecue, ... 457

CHAPTER XXXVI.

The Batn El-Hadjar, or Belly of Stone—Ancient Granite Quarries—The Village of Dal—A Ruined Fortress—A Wilderness of Stones—The Hot Springs of Ukmé—A Windy Night—A Dreary Day in the Desert—The Shekh's Camel Fails—Descent to Samneh—The Temple and Cataract—Meersheh—The Sale of Abou-Sin—We Emerge from the Belly of Stone—A Kababish Caravan—The Rock of Aben-Seer—View of the Second Cataract—We reach Wadi-Halfa—Selling my Dromedaries—Farewell to Abou-Sin—Thanksgiving on the Ferry-boat—Parting with the Camel-men, ... 471

CHAPTER XXXVII.

Wadi Halfa—A Boat for Assouan—We Embark on the Nile Again—An Egyptian Dream—The Temples of Abou-Simbel—The Smaller Temple—The Colossi of Remeses II.—Vulgarity of Travellers—Entering the Great Temple—My Impressions—Character of Abou-Simbel—The Smaller Chambers—The Races of Men—Remeses and the Captive Kings—Departure, ... 486

CHAPTER XXXVIII.

I Lose my Sunshine, and Regain it—Nubian Scenery—Derr—The Temple of Amada—Mysterious Rappings—Familiar Scenes—Halt at Korosko—Escape from Shipwreck—The Temple of Sebooa—Chasing other Boats—Temple of Djerf Hossayn—A Backsheesh Experiment—Kalabshee—Temple of Dabôd—We reach the Egyptian Frontier, ... 495

CHAPTER XXXIX.

Assouan—A Boat for Cairo—English Tourists—A Head-wind—Ophthalmia—Esneh—A Mummied Princess—Ali Effendi's Stories—A Donkey Afrite—Arrival at Luxor—The Egyptian Autumn—A Day at Thebes—Songs of the Sailors—Ali leaves me—Ride to Dendera—Head-winds again—Visit to Tahtah—The House of Rufaā Bey, ... 506

CHAPTER XL.

Siout in Harvest-time—A kind Englishwoman—A Slight Experience of Hasheesh—The Calm—Rapid Progress down the Nile—The Last Day of the Voyage—Arrival at Cairo—Tourists preparing for the Desert—Parting with Achmet—Conclusion, ... 517

JOURNEY TO CENTRAL AFRICA

CHAPTER I.

INTRODUCTION TO AFRICA.

Arrival at Alexandria—The Landing—My First Oriental Bath—The City—Preparations for Departure.

I LEFT Smyrna in the Lloyd steamer, *Contè Stürmer*, on the first day of November, 1851. We passed the blue Sporadic Isles—Cos, and Rhodes, and Karpathos—and crossing the breadth of the Eastern Mediterranean, favored all the way by unruffled seas, and skies of perfect azure, made the pharos of Alexandria on the evening of the 3d. The entrance to the harbor is a narrow and difficult passage through reefs, and no vessel dares to attempt it at night, but with the first streak of dawn we were boarded by an Egyptian pilot, and the rising sun lighted up for us the white walls of the city, the windmills of the Ras el-Tin, or Cape of Figs, and the low yellow sand-hills in which I recognized Africa—for they were prophetic of the desert behind them.

We entered the old harbor between the island of Pharos and the main land (now connected by a peninsular strip, on which the Frank quarter is built), soon after sunrise

The water swarmed with boats before the anchor dropped, and the Egyptian health officer had no sooner departed than we were boarded by a crowd of dragomen, hotel runners, and boatmen. A squinting Arab, who wore a white dress and red sash, accosted me in Italian, offering to conduct me to the Oriental Hotel. A German and a Smyrniote, whose acquaintance I had made during the voyage, joined me in accepting his services, and we were speedily boated ashore. We landed on a pile of stones, not far from a mean-looking edifice called the Custom-House. Many friends were there to welcome us, and I shall never forget the eagerness with which they dragged us ashore, and the zeal with which they pommelled one another in their generous efforts to take charge of our effects. True, we could have wished that their faces had been better washed, their baggy trousers less ragged and their red caps less greasy, and we were perhaps ungrateful in allowing our Arab to rate them soundly and cuff the ears of the more obstreperous, before our trunks and carpet-bags could be portioned among them. At the Custom-House we were visited by two dark gentlemen, in turbans and black flowing robes, who passed our baggage without scrutiny, gently whispering in our ears, "*backsheesh,*"—a word which we then heard for the first time, but which was to be the key-note of much of our future experience. The procession of porters was then set in motion, and we passed through several streets of whitewashed two story houses, to the great square of the Frank quarter, which opened before us warm and brilliant in the morning sunshine.

The principal hotels and consulates front on this square The architecture is Italian, with here and there a dash of Sar acenic, in the windows and doorways, especially in new buildings. A small obelisk of alabaster, a present from Mohammed Ali, stands in the centre, on a pedestal which was meant for a fountain, but has no water. All this I noted, as well as a crowd of donkeys and donkey-boys, and a string of laden camels, on our way to the hotel, which we found to be a long and not particularly clean edifice, on the northern side of the square. The English and French steamers had just arrived, and no rooms were to be had until after the departure of the afternoon boat for Cairo. Our dragoman, who called himself Ibrahim, suggested a bath as the most agreeable means of passing the intermediate time.

The clear sky, the temperature (like that of a mild July day at home), and the novel interest of the groups in the streets, were sufficient to compensate for any annoyance: but when we reached the square of the French Church, and saw a garden of palm-trees waving their coronals of glittering leaves every thing else was forgotten. My German friend, who had never seen palms, except as starveling exotics in Sorrento and Smyrna, lifted his hands in rapture, and even I, who had heard tens of thousands rustle in the hot winds of the Tropics, felt my heart leap as if their beauty were equally new to my eyes. For no amount of experience can deprive the traveller of that happy feeling of novelty which marks his first day on the soil of a new continent. I gave myself up wholly to its inebriation. *Et ego in Africâ*, was the sum of my thoughts, and I neither saw nor cared to know the fact (which we discovered in due time), that our friend Ibrahim was an arrant knave.

The bath to which he conducted us was pronounced to be

the finest in Alexandria, the most superb in all the Orient, but it did not at all accord with our ideas of Eastern luxury. Moreover, the bath-keeper was his intimate friend, and would bathe us as no Christians were ever bathed before. One fact Ibrahim kept to himself, which was, that his intimate friend and he shared the spoils of our inexperience. We were conducted to a one-story building, of very unprepossessing exterior. As we entered the low, vaulted entrance, my ears were saluted with a dolorous, groaning sound, which I at first conjectured to proceed from the persons undergoing the operation, but which I afterward ascertained was made by a wheel turned by a buffalo, employed in raising water from the well. In a sort of basement hall, smelling of soap-suds, and with a large tank of dirty water in the centre, we were received by the bath-keeper, who showed us into a room containing three low divans with pillows. Here we disrobed, and Ibrahim, who had procured a quantity of napkins, enveloped our heads in turbans and swathed our loins in a simple Adamite garment. Heavy wooden clogs were attached to our feet, and an animated bronze statue led the way through gloomy passages, sometimes hot and steamy, sometimes cold and soapy, and redolent of any thing but the spicy odors of Araby the Blest, to a small vaulted chamber, lighted by a few apertures in the ceiling. The moist heat was almost suffocating; hot water flowed over the stone floor, and the stone benches we sat upon were somewhat cooler than kitchen stoves. The bronze individual left us, and very soon, sweating at every pore, we began to think of the three Hebrews in the furnace. Our comfort was not increased by the groaning sound which we still heard and by seeing, through a hole in the door, five or six naked figures lying motionless along the edge of a steaming vat, in the outer room.

Presently our statue returned with a pair of coarse hair-gloves on his hands. He snatched off our turbans, and then, seizing one of my friends by the shoulder as if he had been a sheep, began a sort of rasping operation upon his back. This process, varied occasionally by a dash of scalding water, was extended to each of our three bodies, and we were then suffered to rest awhile. A course of soap-suds followed, which was softer and more pleasant in its effect, except when he took us by the hair, and holding back our heads, scrubbed our faces most lustily, as if there were no such things as eyes, noses and mouths. By this time we had reached such a salamandrine temperature that the final operation of a dozen pailfuls of hot water poured over the head, was really delightful After a plunge in a seething tank, we were led back to our chamber and enveloped in loose muslin robes. Turbans were bound on our heads and we lay on the divans to recover from the languor of the bath. The change produced by our new costume was astonishing. The stout German became a Turkish mollah, the young Smyrniote a picturesque Persian, and I—I scarcely know what, but, as my friends assured me, a much better Moslem than Frank. Cups of black coffee, and pipes of inferior tobacco completed the process, and in spite of the lack of cleanliness and superabundance of fleas, we went forth lighter in body, and filled with a calm content which nothing seemed able to disturb.

After a late breakfast at the hotel, we sallied out for a survey of the city. The door was beleaguered by the donkeys and their attendant drivers, who hailed us in all languages at once. "*Venez, Monsieur!*" "Take a ride, sir; here is a good donkey!" "*Schœner Esel!*" "*Prendete il mio burrico!*"—and you are made the vortex of a whirlpool of donkeys. The one-eyed donkey-boys fight, the donkeys kick, and there is no rest till you have bestridden one of the little beasts. The driver then gives his tail a twist and his rump a thwack, and you are carried off in triumph. The animal is so small that you seem the more silly of the two, when you have mounted, but after he has carried you for an hour in a rapid gallop, you recover your dignity in your respect for him.

The spotless blue of the sky and the delicious elasticity of the air were truly intoxicating, as we galloped between gardens of date-trees, laden with ripe fruit, to the city gate, and through it into a broad road, fringed with acacias, leading to the Mahmoudieh canal. But to the south, on a rise of dry, sandy soil, stood the Pillar of Diocletian—not of Pompey, whose name it bears. It is a simple column, ninety-eight feet in height, but the shaft is a single block of red granite, and stands superbly against the back-ground of such a sky and such a sea. It is the only relic of the ancient Alexandria worthy of its fame, but you could not wish for one more imposing and eloquent. The glowing white houses of the town, the minarets, the palms and the acacias fill the landscape, but it stands apart from them, in the sand, and looks only to the sea and the desert.

In the evening we took donkeys again and rode out of the town to a café on the banks of the canal. A sunset of burning rose and orange sank over the desert behind Pompey's Pillar, and the balmiest of breezes stole towards us from the sea, through palm gardens. A Swiss gentleman, M. de Gonzenbach, whose kindness I shall always gratefully remember accompanied us. As we sat under the acacias, sipping the black Turkish coffee, the steamer for Cairo passed, disturbing the serenity of the air with its foul smoke, and marring the delicious repose of the landscape in such wise, that we vowed we would have nothing to do with steam so long as we voyaged on the Nile. Our donkey-drivers patiently held the bridles of our long-eared chargers till we were ready to return. It was dark, and not seeing at first my attendant, a little one-eyed imp, I called at random: "Abdallah!" This, it happened, was actually his name, and he came trotting up, holding the stirrup ready for me to mount. The quickness with which these young Arabs pick up languages, is truly astonishing. "*Come vi chiamate?*" (what's your name?) I asked of Abdallah, as we rode homeward. The words were new to him, but I finally made him understand their meaning, whereupon he put his knowledge into practice by asking me: "*Come vi chiamate?*" "Abbas Pasha," I replied. "Oh, well," wäs his prompt rejoinder, "if you are Abbas Pasha, then I am Seyd Pasha." The next morning he was at the door with his donkey, which I fully intended to mount, but became entangled in a wilderness of donkeys, out of which Ibrahim extricated me by hoisting me on another animal. As I rode away, I caught a glimpse of the little fellow, crying lustily over his disappointment.

We three chance companions fraternized so agreeably that we determined to hire a boat for Cairo, in preference to waiting for the next steamer. We accordingly rode over to the Mahmoudieh Canal, accompanied by Ibrahim, to inspect the barks. Like all dragomen, Ibrahim had his private preferences, and conducted us on board a boat belonging to a friend of his, a grizzly raïs, or captain. The craft was a small *kangia*, with a large lateen sail at the bow and a little one at the stern. It was not very new, but looked clean, and the raïs demanded three hundred piastres for the voyage. The piastre is the current coin of the East. Its value is fluctuating, and always higher in Egypt than in Syria and Turkey, but may be assumed at about five cents, or twenty to the American dollar. Before closing the bargain, we asked the advice of M. de Gonzenbach, who immediately despatched his Egyptian servant and engaged a boat at two hundred and twenty-five piastres. Every thing was to be in readiness for our departure on the following evening.

CHAPTER II.

FIRST VOYAGE ON THE NILE.

Departure—The Kangia—The Egyptian Climate—The Mahmoudieh Canal—Entrance into the Nile—Pleasures of the Journey—Studying Arabic—Sight of the Pyramids—The Barrage—Approach to Cairo.

WE paid a most exorbitant bill at the Oriental Hotel, and started on donkeyback for our boat, at sunset. Our preparations for the voyage consisted of bread, rice, coffee, sugar, butter and a few other comestibles; an earthen furnace and charcoal; pots and stew-pans, plates, knives and forks, wooden spoons, coffee-cups and water-jars; three large mats of cane-leaves, for bedding; and for luxuries, a few bottles of claret, and a gazelle-skin stuffed with choice Latakieh tobacco. We were prudent enough to take a supper with us from the hotel, and not trust to our own cooking the first night on board.

We waited till dark on the banks of the Canal before our baggage appeared. There is a Custom-House on all sides of Alexandria, and goods going out must pay as well as goods coming in. The gate was closed, and nothing less than the silver oil of a dollar greased its hinges sufficiently for our cart to pass through. But what was our surprise on reaching the boat, to find the same *kangia* and the same grizzly raïs, who had previously demanded three hundred piastres. He seemed no less astonished than we, for the bargain had been made by a third party, and I believe he bore us a grudge during the rest of the voyage. The contract placed the boat at our disposition; so we went on board immediately, bade adieu to the kind friends who had accompanied us, and were rowed down the Canal in the full glow of African moonlight.

Some account of our vessel and crew will not be out of place here. The boat was about thirty-five feet in length, with a short upright mast in the bow, supporting a lateen sail fifty feet long. Against the mast stood a square wooden box, lined with clay, which served as a fireplace for cooking. The middle boards of the deck were loose and allowed entrance to the hold, where our baggage was stowed. The sailors also lifted them and sat on the cross-beams, with their feet on the shallow keel, when they used the oars. The cabin, which occupied the stern of the boat, was built above and below the deck, so that after stepping down into it we could stand upright. The first compartment contained two broad benches, with a smaller chamber in the rear, allowing just enough room, in all, for three persons to sleep. We spread our mats on the boards, placed carpet-bags for pillows (first taking out the books), and our beds were made. Ibrahim slept on the deck, against the cabin-door.

Our raïs, or captain, was an old Arab, with a black, wrinkled face, a grizzly beard and a tattered blue robe. There were five sailors—one with crooked eyes, one with a moustache, two copper-colored Fellahs, and one tall Nubian, black as the Egyptian darkness. The three latter were our favorites, and more cheerful and faithful creatures I never saw. One of the Fellahs sang nasal love-songs the whole day long, and was always foremost in the everlasting refrain of "*haylee-sah!*" and "*ya salaam!*" with which the Egyptian sailors row and tow and pole their boats against the current. Before we left the boat we had acquired a kind of affection for these three men, while the raïs, with his grim face and croaking voice, grew more repulsive every day.

We spread a mat on the deck, lighted our lantern and sat down to supper, while a gentle north wind slowly carried our boat along through shadows of palms and clear spaces of moonlight. Ibrahim filled the shebooks, and for four hours we sat in the open air, which seemed to grow sweeter and purer with every breath we inhaled. We were a triad—the sacred number—and it would have been difficult to find another triad so harmonious and yet differing so strongly in its parts. One was a *Landwirth* from Saxe-Coburg, a man of forty-five, tall, yet portly in person, and accustomed to the most comfortable living and the best society in Germany. Another was a Smyrniote merchant, a young man of thirty, to whom all parts of Europe were familiar, who spoke eight languages, and who within four months had visited Ispahan and the Caucasus. Of the third it behooves me not to speak, save that he was from the New World, and that he differed entirely from his friends in stature, features, station in life, and every thing else but mutual goodfellowship. "Ah," said the German in the fulness of his heart, as we basked in the moonlight, "what a heavenly air! what beautiful palms! and this wonderful repose in all Nature, which I never felt before!" "It is better than the gardens of Ispahan," added the Smyrniote. Nor did I deceive them when I said that for many months past I had known no mood of mind so peaceful and grateful.

We rose somewhat stiff from our hard beds, but a cup of coffee and the fresh morning air restored the amenity of the voyage. The banks of the Canal are flat and dull, and the country through which we passed, after leaving the marshy brink of Lake Mareotis, was in many places still too wet from the recent inundation to be ploughed for the winter crops. It is a dead level of rich black loam, and produces rice, maize, sugar-cane and millet. Here and there the sand has blown over it, and large spaces are given up to a sort of coarse, wiry grass. The villages are miserable collections of mud huts, but the date-palms which shadow them and the strings of camels that slowly pass to and fro, render even their unsightliness pictu resque. In two or three places we passed mud machines, driven by steam, for the purpose of cleaning the Canal. Ropes were stretched across the channel on both sides, and a large number of trading boats were obliged to halt, although the wind was very favorable. The barrier was withdrawn for us Franks, and the courteous engineer touched his tarboosh in reply to our salutations, as we shot through.

Towards noon we stopped at a village, and the Asian went ashore with Ibrahim to buy provisions, while the European walked ahead with his fowling-piece, to shoot wild ducks for dinner. The American stayed on board and studied an Arabic vocabulary. Presently Ibrahim appeared with two fowls, two pigeons, a pot of milk and a dozen eggs. The Asian set about preparing breakfast, and showed himself so skilful that our bark soon exhaled the most savory odors. When we picked up our European he had only two hawks to offer us, but we gave him in return a breakfast which he declared perfect. We ate on deck, seated on a mat; a pleasant wind filled our sails.

and myriads of swallows circled and twittered over our heads in the cloudless air. The calm, contemplative state produced by the coffee and pipes which Ibrahim brought us, lasted the whole afternoon, and the villages, the cane-fields, the Moslem oratories, the wide level of the Delta and the distant mounds of forgotten cities, passed before our eyes like the pictures of a dream. Only one of these pictures marred the serenity of our minds. It was an Arab burying-ground, on the banks of the Canal—a collection of heaps of mud, baked in the sun. At the head and foot of one of the most recent, sat two women—paid mourners—who howled and sobbed, in long, piteous, despairing cries, which were most painful to hear. I should never have imagined that any thing but the keenest grief could teach such heart-breaking sounds.

When I climbed the bank at sunset, for a walk, the minarets of Atfeh, on the Nile, were visible. Two rows of acacias, planted along the Canal, formed a pleasant arcade, through which we sailed, to the muddy excrescences of the town. The locks were closed for the night, and we were obliged to halt, which gave us an opportunity of witnessing an Arabic marriage procession. The noise of two wooden drums and a sort of fife announced the approach of the bride, who, attended by her relatives, came down the bank from the mud-ovens above. She was closely veiled, but the Arabs crowded around to get a peep at her face. No sooner had the three Franks approached, than she was doubly guarded and hurried off to the house of her intended husband. Some time afterwards I ascended the bank to have a nearer view of the miserable hovels, but was received with such outcries and menacing gestures, that I made a slow and dignified retreat. We visited, however, the house of the bridegroom's father, where twenty or thirty Arabs, seated on the ground, were singing an epithalamium, to which they kept time by clapping their hands.

Next morning, while our raïs was getting his permit to pass the locks (for which four official signatures and a fee of thirty piastres are necessary), we visited the bazaar, and purchased long tubes of jasmine-wood for our pipes, and vegetables for our kitchen. On all such occasions we detailed Seyd, the tall Nubian, whose ebony face shone resplendent under a snow-white turban, to be our attendant. The stately gravity with which he walked behind us, carrying bread and vegetables, was worthy the pipe-bearer of a Sultan. By this time we had installed the Asian as cook, and he very cheerfully undertook the service. We soon discovered that the skill of Ibrahim extended no further than to the making of a *pilaff* and the preparation of coffee. Moreover his habits and appearance were not calculated to make us relish his handiwork. The naïveté with which he took the wash-basin to make soup in, and wiped our knives and forks on his own baggy pantaloons, would have been very amusing if we had not been interested parties. The Asian was one day crumbling some loaf sugar with a hammer, when Ibrahim, who had been watching him, suddenly exclaimed in a tone of mingled pity and contempt, "that's not the way!" Thereupon he took up some of the lumps, and wrapped them in one corner of his long white shirt, which he thrust into his mouth, and after crushing the sugar between his teeth, emptied it into the bowl with an air of triumph.

A whole squadron of boats was waiting at the locks, but with Frankish impudence, we pushed through them, and took our place in the front rank. The sun was intensely hot, and we sweated and broiled for a full hour, in the midst of a horrible tumult of Arabs, before the clumsy officers closed the last gate on us and let us float forth on the Nile. It is the western, or Canopic branch of the river which flows past Atfeh. It is not broader than the Hudson at Albany, but was more muddy and slimy from its recent overflow than the Mississippi at New Orleans. Its water is no less sweet and wholesome than that of the latter river. After leaving the monotonous banks of the Canal, the aspect of its shores, fringed with groves of palm, was unspeakably cheerful and inspiring. On the opposite side, the slender white minarets of Fooah, once a rich manufacturing town, sparkled in the noonday sun. A fresh north wind from the Mediterranean slowly pressed our boat against the strong current, while the heavily-laden merchant vessels followed in our wake, their two immense lateen sails expanded like the wings of the Arabian roc. We drank to the glory of old Father Nile in a cup of his own brown current, and then called Ibrahim to replenish the empty shebooks. Those who object to tobacco under the form of cigars, or are nauseated by the fumes of a German meerschaum, should be told that the Turkish pipe, filled with Latakieh, is quite another thing. The aroma, which you inhale through a long jasmine tube, topped with a soft amber mouth-piece, is as fragrant as roses and refreshing as ripe dates. I have no doubt that the atmosphere of celestial musk and amber which surrounded Mahomet, according to the Persian Chronicles, was none other than genuine Latakieh, at twenty piastres the oka. One thing is certain, that without the capacity to smoke a shebook, no one can taste the true flavor of the Orient.

An hour or two after sunset the wind fell, and for the rest

of the night our men tracked the boat slowly forward, singing cheerily as they tugged at the long tow-rope. The Asian spread on the deck his Albanian capote, the European his ample travelling cloak, and the representatives of three Continents, travelling in the fourth, lay on their backs enjoying the moonlight, the palms, and more than all, the perfect silence and repose. With every day of our journey I felt more deeply and gratefully this sense of rest. Under such a glorious sky, no disturbance seemed possible. It was of little consequence whether the boat went forward or backward, whether we struck on a sand-bar or ploughed the water under a full head of wind; every thing was right. My conscience made me no reproach for such a lazy life. In America we live too fast and work too hard, I thought: shall I not know what Rest is, once before I die? The European said to me naïvely, one day: "I am a little surprised, but very glad, that no one of us has yet spoken of European politics." Europe! I had forgotten that such a land existed: and as for America, it seemed very dim and distant.

Sometimes I varied this repose by trying to pick up the language. Wilkinson's Vocabulary and Capt. Hayes's Grammar did me great service, and after I had tried a number of words with Ibrahim, to get the pronunciation, I made bolder essays. One day when the sailors were engaged in a most vociferous discussion, I broke upon them with: "What is all this noise about? stop instantly!" The effect was instantaneous; the men were silent, and Seyd, turning up his eyes in wonder, cried out: "*Wallah!* the Howadji talks Arabic!" The two copper-faced Fellahs thought it very amusing, and every new word I learned sufficed to set them laughing for half an hour. I called out to a fisherman, seated on the bank: "O Fisherman, have you any fish?" and he held up a string of them and made answer: "O Howadji, I have." This solemn form of address, which is universal in Arabic, makes the language very piquant to a student.

During our second night on the river, we passed the site of ancient Saïs, one of the most renowned of Egyptian cities, which has left nothing but a few shapeless mounds. The country was in many places still wet from the inundation, which was the largest that had occurred for many years. The Fellahs were ploughing for wheat, with a single buffalo geared to a sharp pole, which scratched up the soil to the depth of three inches. Fields of maize and sugar-cane were frequent, and I noticed also some plantations of tobacco, millet, and a species of lupin, which is cultivated for its beans. The only vegetables we found for sale in the villages, were onions, leeks and tomatoes. Milk, butter and eggs are abundant and very good, but the cheese of the country is detestable. The habitations resemble ant-hills, rather than human dwellings, and the villages are dépôts of filth and vermin, on the most magnificent scale. Our boat was fortunately free from the latter, except a few cockroaches. Except the palm and acacia, without which a Nile journey would lose half its attractions, I saw few trees. Here and there stood a group of superb plane-trees, and the banana sometimes appeared in the gardens, but there is nothing of that marvellous luxuriance and variety of vegetation which is elsewhere exhibited in the neighborhood of the Tropics.

On the evening of the third day we reached the town of Nadir, and, as there was no wind, went ashore for an hour or two. There was a café on the bank—a mud house, with two windows, adorned with wooden frames, carved in the Moorish style. A divan, built of clay and whitewashed, extended along one side of the room, and on this we seated ourselves cross-legged, while the host prepared the little coffee-cups and filled the pipes. Through the open door we saw the Nile, gleaming broadly under the full moon, and in the distance, two tall palm-trees stood clearly against the sky. Our boatmen, whom we had treated to *booza*, the Egyptian beer, sat before us, and joined in the chorus of a song, which was sung to entertain us. The performers were three women, and a man who played a coarse reed flute. One of the women had a tambourine, another a small wooden drum, and the third kept time by slapping the closed fingers of the right hand on the palm of the left. The song, which had a wild, rude harmony that pleased me, was followed by a dance, executed by one of the women. It was very similar to the fandango, as danced by the natives of the Isthmus of Panama, and was more lascivious than graceful. The women, however, were of the lowest class, and their performances were adapted to the taste of the boatmen and camel-drivers, by whom they are patronized.

The next day the yellow hills of the Libyan Desert, which in some places press the arable land of the Delta even to the brink of the Nile, appeared in the west. The sand appeared to be steadily advancing towards the river, and near Werdan had already buried a grove of acacias as high as their first branches. The tops were green and flourishing above the deluge, but another year or two would overwhelm them completely. We had a thick fog during the night, and the following day was exceedingly hot though the air was transparent as crystal. Our three faces were already of the color of new bronze, which was burned into the skin by the reflection from the water. While my friends were enjoying their usual afternoon repose, a secret presentiment made me climb to the roof of our cabin. I had not sat there long, before I descried two faint blue triangles on the horizon, far to the south. I rudely broke in upon their indolence with a shout of "the Pyramids!" which Seyd echoed with "*El-hàram Faraoon!*" I was as much impressed with the view as I expected to be, but I completely nullified the European's emotion by translating to him Thackeray's description of his first sight of those renowned monuments.

The same evening we reached the northern point of the Delta, where we were obliged to remain all night, as the wind was not sufficiently strong to allow us to pass the *Barrage* Singularly enough, this immense work, which is among the greatest undertakings of modern times, is scarcely heard of out of Egypt. It is nothing less than a damming of the Nile, which is to have the effect of producing two inundations a year, and doubling the crops throughout the Delta. Here, where the flood divides itself into two main branches, which find separate mouths at Damietta and Rosetta, an immense dam has not only been projected, but is far advanced toward completion. Each branch will be spanned by sixty-two arches, besides a central gateway ninety feet in breadth, and flanked by lofty stone towers. The point of the Delta, between the two dams, is protected by a curtain of solid masonry, and the abutments which it joins are fortified by towers sixty or seventy feet in height. The piers have curved breakwaters on the upper side, while the opposite parapet of the arches rises high above them, so that the dam consists of three successive terraces, and presents itself like a wedge, against the force of such an immense body of water. The material is brick, faced with stone. When complete, it is intended to close the side-arches during low water, leaving only the central gateway open. By this means sufficient water will be gained to fill all the irrigating canals, while a new channel, cut through the centre of the Delta, will render productive a vast tract of fertile land. The project is a grand one, and the only obstacle to its success is the light, porous character of the alluvial soil on which the piers are founded. The undertaking was planned and commenced by M. Linant, and has since been continued by other engineers.

The Egyptian boatmen have reason to complain of the Barrage. The main force of the river is poured through the narrow space wherein the piers have not yet been sunk, which cannot be passed without a strong north wind. Forty or fifty boats were lying along the shore, waiting the favorable moment. We obtained permission from the engineer to attach our boat to a large government barge, which was to be drawn up by a stationary windlass. As we put off, the wind freshened, and we were slowly urged against the current to the main rapid, where we were obliged to hold on to our big friend. Behind us the river was white with sails—craft of all kinds, pushed up by the wind, dragged down by the water, striking against each other, entangling their long sails and crowding into the narrow passage, amid shouts, cries and a bewildering profusion of Arabic gutturals. For half an hour, the scene was most exciting, but thanks to the windlass, we reached smoother water, and sailed off gayly for Cairo.

The true Nile expanded before us, nearly two miles in

width. To the south, the three Pyramids of Gizeh loomed up like isolated mountain-peaks on the verge of the Desert. On the right hand the Mokattam Hills lay red and bare in the sunshine, and ere long, over the distant gardens of Shoobra, we caught sight of the Citadel of Cairo, and the minarets of the mosque of Sultan Hassan. The north wind was faithful: at three o'clock we were anchored in Boulak, paid our raïs, gave the crew a backsheesh, for which they kissed our hands with many exclamations of "*taïb!*" (good!) and set out for Cairo.

CHAPTER III.

PICTURES OF CAIRO.

Entrance—The Ezbekiyeh—Saracenic Houses—Donkeys—The Bazaars—The Streets —Processions—View from the Citadel—Mosque of Mohammed Ali—The Road to Suez—The Island of Rhoda.

Our approach to and entrance into Cairo was the illuminated frontispiece to the volume of my Eastern life. From the Nile we had already seen the mosque of Sultan Hassan, the white domes, and long, pencil-like minarets of the new mosque of Mohammed Ali, and the massive masonry of the Citadel, crowning a projecting spur of the Mokattam Hills, which touches the city on the eastern side. But when, mounted on ambling donkeys, we followed the laden baggage-horses through the streets of Boulak, and entered the broad, shaded highway leading through gardens, grain-fields and groves of palm and banana, to the gate of the *Ezbekiyeh*—the great square of Cairo—the scene, which, at a distance, had been dimmed and softened by the filmy screen of the Egyptian air, now became so gay, picturesque and animated, so full of life and motion and color, that my dreams of the East were at once displaced by the vivid reality. The donkey-riding multitudes who passed continually to and fro, were wholly unlike the crowds of Smyrna and Alexandria, where the growing influence of European dress and customs is already visible. Here, every thing still exhaled the rich aroma of the Orient, as it had been wafted to me from the Thousand and One Nights, the Persian poets and the Arab chroniclers. I forgot that I still wore a Frank dress, and found myself wondering at the temerity of the few Europeans we met. I looked without surprise on the long processions of donkeys carrying water-skins, the heavily-laden camels, the women with white masks on their faces and black bags around their bodies, the stolid Nubian slaves, the grave Abyssinians, and all the other various characters that passed and repassed us. But because they were so familiar, they were none the less interesting, for all had been acquaintances, when, like Tennyson, "true Mussulman was I, and sworn," under the reign of the good Haroun Al-Raschid.

We entered the Ezbekiyeh, which is wholly overgrown with majestic acacias and plane-trees, and thickets of aromatic flowering shrubs. It is in the Frank quarter of the city, and was first laid out and planted by order of Mohammed Ali. All the principal hotels front upon it, and light, thatched cafés fill the space under the plane-trees, where the beau monde of Cairo promenade every Sunday evening. Nothing of the old City of the Caliphs, except a few tall minarets, can be seen from this quarter, but the bowery luxuriance of the foliage is all that the eye demands, and over the plain white walls, on every side, the palms—single, or in friendly groups—lift their feathery crowns. After installing our household gods in the chambers of the quiet and comfortable Hotel d'Europe, we went out to enjoy the sweet evening air in front of one of the cafés. I tried for the first time the narghileh, or Persian water-pipe The soft, velvety leaves of the tobacco of Shiraz are burned in a small cup, the tube of which enters a glass vase, half filled with rose-scented water. From the top of this vase issues a flexible tube, several feet in length, with a mouth-piece of wood or amber. At each inspiration, the smoke is drawn downward and rises through the water with a pleasant bubbling sound. It is deprived of all the essential oil of the weed, and is exceed ingly mild, cool and fragrant. But instead of being puffed out of the mouth in whiffs, it is breathed full into the lungs and out again, like the common air. This is not so difficult a matter as might be supposed; the sensation is pleasant and slightly exhilarating, and is not injurious to the lungs when moderately indulged in.

The Turkish quarter of Cairo still retains the picturesque Saracenic architecture of the times of the Caliphs. The houses are mostly three stories in height, each story projecting over the other, and the plain stone walls are either whitewashed or striped with horizontal red bars, in a manner which would be absurd under a northern sky, but which is here singularly harmonious and agreeable. The only signs of sculpture are occasional door-ways with richly carved arches, or the light marble gallery surrounding a fountained court. I saw a few of these in retired parts of the city. The traveller, however, has an exhaustless source of delight in the wooden balconies inclosing the upper windows. The extraordinary lightness, grace and delicate fragility of their workmanship, rendered still more striking by contrast with the naked solidity of the walls to which they cling, gave me a new idea of the skill and fancy of the Saracenic architects. The wood seems rather woven in the loom, than cut with the saw and chisel. Through these lattices of fine network, with borders worked in lace-like patterns, and sometimes topped with slender turrets and pinnacles, the wives of the Cairene merchants sit and watch the crowds passing softly to and fro in the twilight of the bazaars, themselves unseen. It needed no effort of the imagination to people the fairy watch-towers under which we rode daily, with forms as beautiful as those which live in the voluptuous melodies of Hafiz.

To see Cairo thoroughly, one must first accustom himself to the ways of those long-eared cabs, without the use of which I would advise no one to trust himself in the bazaars. Donkey-riding is universal, and no one thinks of going beyond the Frank quarter on foot. If he does, he must submit to be followed by not less than six donkeys with their drivers. A friend of mine, who was attended by such a cavalcade for two hours, was obliged to yield at last, and made no second attempt. When we first appeared in the gateway of our hotel, equipped for an excursion, the rush of men and animals was so great, that we were forced to retreat until our servant and the porter whipped us a path through the yelling and braying mob. After one or two trials, I found an intelligent Arab boy, named Kish, who, for five piastres a day, furnished strong and ambitious donkeys, which he kept ready at the door from morning till night. The other drivers respected Kish's privilege, and thenceforth I had no trouble. The donkeys are so small that my feet nearly touched the ground, but there is no end to their strength and endurance. Their gait, whether a pace or a gallop, is so easy and light that fatigue is impossible. The drivers take great pride in having high-cushioned red saddles, and in hanging bits of jingling brass to the bridles. They keep their donkeys close shorn, and frequently beautify them by painting them various colors. The first animal I rode had legs barred like a zebra's, and my friend's rejoiced in purple flanks and a yellow belly. The drivers run behind them with a short stick, punching them from time to time, or giving them a sharp pinch on the rump. Very few of them own their donkeys, and I understood their pertinacity when I learned that they frequently received a beating on returning home in the evening empty-handed.

The passage of the bazaars seems at first quite as hazardous on donkey-back as on foot, but it is the difference between knocking somebody down and being knocked down yourself, and one naturally prefers the former alternative. There is no use in attempting to guide the donkey, for he won't be guided. The driver shouts behind, and you are dashed at full speed into a confusion of other donkeys, camels, horses, carts, water-carriers and footmen. In vain you cry out: "*Bess!*" (enough!) "*Piano!*" and other desperate adjurations; the driver's only reply is: "Let the bridle hang loose!" You dodge your head under a camel-load of planks; your leg brushes the wheel of a dust-cart; you strike a fat Turk plump in the back; you miraculously escape upsetting a fruit-stand; you scatter a company of spectral, white-masked women, and at last reach some more quiet street, with the sensation of a man who has stormed a battery. At first this sort of riding made me very nervous, but finally I let the donkey go his own way, and took a curious interest in seeing how near a chance I ran of striking or being struck. Sometimes there seemed no hope of avoiding a violent collision, but by a series of the most remarkable dodges he generally carried me through in safety. The cries of the driver running behind, gave me no little amusement: "The Howadji comes! Take care on the right hand! take care on the left hand! O man, take care! O maiden, take care! O boy, get out of the way! The Howadji comes!" Kish had strong lungs and his donkey would let nothing pass him, and so, wherever we went, we contributed our full share to the universal noise and confusion.

Cairo is the cleanest of all oriental cities. The regulations established by Mohammed Ali are strictly carried out. Each man is obliged to sweep before his own door, and the dirt is carried away in carts every morning. Besides this, the streets are watered several times a day, and are nearly always cool and free from dust. The constant evaporation of the water, however, is said to be injurious to the eyes of the inhabitants, though in other respects the city is healthy. The quantity of sore-eyed, cross-eyed, one-eyed, and totally blind persons one meets every where, is surprising. There are some beggars, mostly old or deformed, but by no means so abundant or impertinent as in the Italian cities. A number of shabby policemen, in blue frock-coats and white pantaloons, parade the principal thoroughfares, but I never saw their services called into requisition. The soldiers, who wear a European dress of white cotton, are by far the most awkward and unpicturesque class. Even the Fellah, whose single brown garment hangs loose from his shoulders to his knees, has an air of dignity compared with these Frankish caricatures. The genuine Egyptian costume, which bears considerable resemblance to the Greek, and especially the Hydriote, is simple and graceful. The colors are dark—principally brown, blue, green and violet—relieved by a heavy silk sash of some gay pattern, and by the red slippers and tarboosh. But, as in Turkey, the Pashas and Beys, and many of the minor officers of the civil departments have adopted the Frank dress, retaining only the tarboosh,—a change which is by no means becoming to them. I went into an Egyptian barber-shop one day, to have my hair shorn, and enjoyed the preparatory pipe and coffee in company with two individuals, whom I supposed to be French or Italians of the vulgar order, until the barber combed out the long locks on the top of their head, by which Mussulmen expect to be lifted up into Paradise. When they had gone, the man informed me that one was Khalim Pasha, one of the grandsons of Mohammed Ali, and the other a Bey, of considerable notoriety. The Egyptians certainly do not gain any thing by adopting a costume which, in this climate, is neither so convenient nor so agreeable as their own.

Besides the animated life of the bazaars, which I had an opportunity of seeing, in making my outfit for the winter's journey, I rarely went out without witnessing some incident or ceremony illustrative of Egyptian character and customs. One morning I encountered a stately procession, with music and banners, accompanying a venerable personage, with a green turban on his head and a long white beard flowing over his breast. This, as Kish assured me, was the Shereef of Mecca. He was attended by officers in the richest Turkish and Egyptian costumes, mounted on splendid Arabian steeds, who were almost hidden under their broad housings of green and crimson velvet, embroidered with gold. The people on all sides, as he passed, laid their hands on their breasts and bowed low, which he answered by slowly lifting his hand. It was a simple motion, but nothing could have been more calm and majestic.

On another occasion, I met a bridal procession in the streets of Boulak. Three musicians, playing on piercing flutes, headed the march, followed by the parents of the bride, who, surrounded by her maids, walked under a crimson canopy. She was shrouded from head to foot in a red robe, over which a gilded diadem was fastened around her head. A large crowd of friends and relatives closed the procession, close behind which followed another, of very different character. The chief actors were four boys, of five or six years old, on their way to be circumcised. Each was mounted on a handsome horse, and wore the gala garments of a full-grown man, in which their little bodies were entirely lost. The proud parents marched by their sides, supporting them, and occasionally holding to their lips bottles of milk and sherbet. One was a jet black Nubian, who seemed particularly delighted with his situation, and grinned on all sides as he passed along. This procession was headed by a buffoon, who carried a laugh with him which opened a ready passage through the crowd. A man followed balancing on his chin a long pole crowned with a bunch of flowers. He came to me for backsheesh. His success brought me two swordsmen out of the procession, who cut at each other with scimitars and caught the blows on their shields. The coolness, swiftness and skill with which they parried the strokes was really admirable, and the concluding flourish was a masterpiece. One of them, striking with the full sweep of his arm, aimed directly at the face of the other, as if to divide his head into two parts; but without making a pause, the glittering weapon turned, and sliced the air within half an inch of his eyes. The man neither winked nor moved a muscle of his face, but after the scimitar had passed, dashed it up with his shield, which he then reversed.

and dropping on one knee, held to me for backsheesh. After these came a camel, with a tuft of ostrich feathers on his head and a boy on his back, who pounded vigorously on two wooden drums with one hand, while he stretched the other down to me for backsheesh. Luckily the little candidates for circumcision were too busily engaged with their milk bottles and sugar-plums, to join in the universal cry.

I had little time to devote to the sights of Cairo, and was obliged to omit the excursions to the Petrified Forest, to Heliopolis and Old Cairo, until my return. Besides the city itself, which was always full of interest, I saw little else except the Citadel and the Island of Rhoda. We took the early morning for our ride to the former place, and were fortunate enough to find our view of the Nile-plain unobscured by the mists customary at this season. The morning light is most favorable to the landscape, which lies wholly to the westward. The shadows of the Citadel and the crests of the Mokattam Hills then lie broad and cool over the city, but do not touch its minarets, which glitter in the air like shafts of white and rosy flame. The populace is up and stirring, and you can hear the cries of the donkeymen and water-carriers from under the sycamores and acacias that shade the road to Boulak. Over the rich palm-gardens, the blue streak of the river and the plain beyond, you see the phantoms of two pyramids in the haze which still cu tains the Libyan Desert. Northward, beyond the parks and palaces of Shoobra, the Nile stretches his two great arms toward the sea, dotted, far into the distance, with sails that flash in the sun. From no other point, and at no other time, is Cairo so grand and beautiful.

Within the walls of the Citadel is the *Bir Youssef*—Joseph's Well—as it is called by the Arabs, not from the virtuous Hebrew, but from Sultan Saladin, who dug it out and put it in operation. The well itself dates from the old Egyptian time, but was filled with sand and entirely lost for many centuries. It consists of an upper and lower shaft, cut through the solid rock, to the depth of two hundred and sixty feet. A winding gallery, lighted from the shaft, extends to the bottom of the first division, where, in a chamber cut in the rock, a mule turns the large wheel which brings up a continual string of buckets from the fountain below. The water is poured into a spacious basin, and carried thence to the top by another string of buckets set in motion at the surface. Attended by two Arabs with torches, we made the descent of the first shaft and took a drink of the fresh, cool fluid. This well, and the spot where the Mameluke Emin Bey jumped his horse over the wall and escaped the massacre of his comrades, are the only interesting historical points about the Citadel; and the new mosque of Mohammed Ali, which overlooks the city from the most projecting platform of the fortifications, is the only part which has any claim to architectural beauty. Although it has been in process of erection for many years, this mosque is not nearly completed internally. The exterior is finished, and its large, white, depressed dome, flanked by minarets so tall and reed-like that they seem ready to bend with every breeze, is the first signal of Cairo to travellers coming up or down the Nile. The interior walls are lined throughout with oriental alabaster, stained with the orange flush of Egyptian sunsets, and the three domes blaze with elaborate arabesques of green, blue, crimson and gold. In a temporary chamber, fitted up in one corner, rests the coffin of Mohammed Ali, covered with a heavy velvet pall, and under the marble arches before it, a company of priests, squatted on the green carpet covering the floor, bow their heads continually and recite prayers or fragments of the Koran.

Before descending into the city, I rode a little way into the Desert to the tombs of the Caliphs, on the road to Suez. They consist mostly of stone canopies raised on pillars, with mosques or oratories attached to them, exhibiting considerable variety in their design, but are more curious than impressive The track in the sand made by the pilgrims to Mecca and the overland passengers to Suez, had far more real interest in my eyes. The pilgrims are fewer, and the passengers more numerous, with each successive year. English-built omnibuses, whirled along by galloping post-horses, scatter the sand, and in the midst of the herbless Desert, the travellers regale themselves with beefsteak and ale, and growl if the accustomed Cheshire is found wanting. At this rate, how long will it be before there is a telegraph-station in Mecca, and the operator explodes with his wire a cannon on the Citadel of Cairo, to announce that the prayers on Mount Arafat have commenced ?

The Island of Rhoda, which I visited on a soft, golden afternoon, is but a reminiscence of what it was a few years ago. Since Ibrahim Pasha's death it has been wholly neglected, and though we found a few gardeners at work, digging up the sodden flower-beds and clipping the rank myrtle hedges, they only served to make the neglect more palpable. During the recent inundation, the Nilè had risen to within a few inches of covering the whole island, and the soil was still soft and clammy. Nearly all the growths of the tropics are nurtured here; the coffee, the Indian fig, the mango, and other trees alternate with the palm, orange, acacia, and the yellow mimosa, whose blossoms make the isle fragrant. I gathered a bunch of roses and jasmine-flowers from the unpruned vines. In the centre of the garden is an artificial grotto lined with shells, many of which have been broken off and carried away by ridiculous tourists. There is no limit to human silliness, as I have wisely concluded, after seeing Pompey's Pillar disfigured by "Isaac Jones" (or some equally classic name), in capitals of black paint, a yard long, and finding "Jenny Lind' equally prominent on the topmost stone of the great Pyramid (Of course, the enthusiastic artist chiselled his own name beside hers.) A mallet and chisel are often to be found in the outfits of English and American travellers, and to judge from the frequency of certain names, and the pains bestowed upon their inscription, the owners must have spent the most of their time in Upper Egypt, in leaving records of their vulgar vanity.

CHAPTER IV.

PREPARATIONS FOR THE JOURNEY INTO CENTRAL AFRICA.

Necessity of Leaving Immediately—Engaging a Boat—The Dragomen—Achmet el Saïdi—Funds—Information—Procuring an Outfit—Preparing for the Desert—The Lucky Day—Exertions to Leave—Off!

I DEVOTED but little time to seeing Cairo, for the travelling season had arrived, and a speedy departure from Cairo was absolutely necessary. The trip to Khartoum occupies at least two months and it is not safe to remain there later than the first of March, on account of the heat and the rainy season, which is very unhealthy for strangers. Dr. Knoblecher, the Catholic Apostolic Vicar for Central Africa, had left about a month previous, on his expedition to the sources of the White Nile. I therefore went zealously to work, and in five days my preparations were nearly completed. I prevailed upon the European of our triad, who had intended proceeding no further than Cairo, to join me for the voyage to Assouan, on the Nubian frontier, and our first care was to engage a good *dahabiyeh*, or Nile-boat. This arrangement gave me great joy, for nowhere is a congenial comrade so desirable as on the Nile. My friend appreciated the river, and without the prospect of seeing Thebes, Ombos and Philæ, would have cheerfully borne all the inconveniences and delays of the journey, for the Nile's sake alone. Commend me to such a man, for of the hundreds of tourists who visit the East, there are few such! On my arrival, I had found that the rumors I had heard on the road respecting the number of travellers and the rise in the price of boats, were partially true. Not more than a dozen boats had left for Upper Egypt, but the price had been raised in anticipation. The ship carpenters and painters were busily employed all along the shore at Boulak, in renovating the old barks or building new ones, and the Beys and Pashas who owned the craft were anticipating a good harvest. Some travellers paid forty-five pounds a month for their vessels, but I found little difficulty in getting a large and convenient boat, for two persons, at twenty pounds a month. This price, it should be understood, includes the services of ten men, who find their own provisions, and only receive a gratuity in case of good behavior. The American Consul, Mr. Kahil, had kindly obtained for me the promise of a bark from Ismail Pasha, before our arrival—a superb vessel, furnished with beds, tables, chairs and divans, in a very handsome style—which was offered at thirty pounds a month, but it was much larger than we needed. In the course of my inspection of the fleet of barks at Boulak, I found several which might be had at fifteen, and seventeen pounds a month, but they were old, inconvenient, and full of vermin. Our boat, which I named the Cleopatra, had been newly cleansed and painted, and contained, besides a spacious cabin, with beds and divans, a sort of portico on the outside, with cushioned seats, where we proposed to sit during the balmy twilights, and smoke our shebooks.

Without a tolerable knowledge of Arabic, a dragoman is indispensable. The few phrases I had picked up, on the way from Alexandria, availed me little, and would have been useless in Nubia, where either the Berberi language, or a different Arabic dialect is spoken; and I therefore engaged a dragoman for the journey. This class of persons always swarm in Cairo, and I had not been there a day before I was visited by half a dozen, who were anxious to make the trip to Khartoum. How they knew I was going there, I cannot imagine; but I found that they knew the plans of every traveller in Cairo as well. I endeavored to find one who had already made the journey, but of all who presented themselves, only two had been farther than the second Cataract. One of these was a Nubian, who had made a trip with the Sennaar merchants, as far as Shendy, in Ethiopia; but he had a sinister, treacherous face, and I refused him at once. The other was an old man, named Suleyman Ali, who had been for three years a servant of Champollion, whose certificate of his faithfulness and honesty he produced.

He had been three years in Sennaar, and in addition to Italian, (the only Frank tongue he knew), spoke several Ethiopian dialects. He was a fine, venerable figure, with an honest face, and I had almost decided to take him, when I learned that he was in feeble health and would scarcely be able to endure the hardships of the journey. I finally made choice of a dark Egyptian, born in the valley of Thebes. He was called Achmet el Saïdi, or Achmet of Upper Egypt, and when a boy had been for several years a servant in the house of the English Consul at Alexandria. He spoke English fluently, as well as a little Italian and Turkish. I was first attracted to him by his bold, manly face, and finding that his recommendations were excellent, and that he had sufficient spirit, courage and address to serve us both in case of peril, I engaged him, notwithstanding he had never travelled beyond Wadi Halfa (the Second Cataract). I judged, however, that I was quite as familiar with the geography of Central Africa as any dragoman I could procure, and that, in any case, I should find it best to form my own plans and choose my own paths. How far I was justified in my choice, will appear in the course of the narrative.

The next step was to procure a double outfit—for the Nile and the Desert—and herein Achmet, who had twice made the journey to Mount Sinai and Petra, rendered me good service. I had some general knowledge of what was necessary, but without the advantage of his practical experience, should have been very imperfectly prepared. As it was, many things were forgotten in the haste of departure, the need of which I felt when it was too late to procure them. I had been prudent enough, when in Vienna, to provide myself with Berghaus's great map of Arabia and the Valley of the Nile, which, with a stray volume of Russegger, were my only guides. In Khartoum, afterwards, I stumbled upon a copy of Hoskins's Ethiopia. The greater part of my funds I changed into Egyptian silver *medjids*, *colonnati*, or Spanish pillar-dollars, and the Austrian dollar of Maria Theresa, all of which are current as far as Sennaar and Abyssinia. I also procured five hundred piastres in copper pieces of five paràs (about half a cent) each, which were contained in a large palm-basket, and made nearly an ass's load. In addition to these supplies, I obtained from an Armenian merchant a letter of credit on his brother in Khartoum, for two thousand piastres, on which, he gave me to understand, I should be obliged to pay a discount of twenty per cent. I endeavored, but in vain, to procure some information relative to the cost of travelling in Nubia and the countries beyond The Frank merchants knew nothing, except that the expenses were vast, and predicted that the sum I took would prove insufficient and that I should certainly become involved in great difficulties and embarrassments. The native merchants who had made the journey were all jealous of a foreign traveller attempting to penetrate into their peculiar domain, and gave me no satisfactory information, while to the imagination of the Cairenes, Sennaar is the utmost verge of the world, and he who has been there and returned in safety, enjoys the special protection of Allah. Even Achmet, although he showed no signs of fear, and did not hesitate to accompany me, informed his family and friends that we were going no further than Wadi Halfa, for he said they would certainly detain him by force, should they learn the truth.

I did not think it necessary to obtain a firman from Abbas Pasha, which might readily have been procured. The American, English and Austrian Consuls kindly gave me letters to the principal Consular agents and merchants in Khartoum, besides which, Achmet professed to have some acquaintance with Lattif Pasha, who was then Pasha of Soudan. To the Hon. Mr. Murray, the English Consul-General, and Mr. Constantine Kahil, the American Vice-Consul at Cairo, I was especially indebted for favors. The former intrusted me with despatches for Khartoum and Obeid, in Kordofan, and the latter furnished me with letters to the Governors of Thebes, Assouan and Korosko, asking the latter to insure my safety on the journey through the Nubian Desert. Thus prepared, I anticipated no further trouble on the road than from hard-trotting camels, sand, brackish water, and the like privations, which are easily borne.

The furnishing of a Nile-boat requires considerable know ledge of housekeeping. The number of small articles required for this floating speck of civilization in a country of barbarians, is amazing to a bachelor. I had no idea that the art of cooking needed such a variety of tools and appliances, and for the first time in my life, conceived some respect for the fame of Ude and Soyer. There are frying-pans and stew-pans; coffee-pots and tea-pots; knives, forks, spoons, towels, cups, ladles and boxes; butter, lard, flour, rice, macaroni, oil, vinegar, mustard and pepper; and no end to the groceries. We must have a table and chairs, quilts and pillows, mats, carpets and napkins, and many other articles which I should never have thought of without the help of Achmet and of M. Pini, who keeps a general dépôt of supplies. His printed lists, in four languages, lighten the traveller's labor very greatly. His experience in regard to the quantity required, is also of much service; otherwise an inexperienced person would not know whether to take twelve or fifty pounds of rice, nor how much sugar belonged to so much coffee. The expense of our outfit, including bread, fowls, mutton, charcoal, and every other requisite, was about two thousand piastres—a little more than one hundred dollars. The calculation was made for one month's provisions for two persons.

For my further journey after leaving the Nile, I was recommended to take a large supply, on account of the scarcity and expense of many articles in Upper Nubia and Sennaar. I therefore purchased sufficient tea, coffee, flour, rice, biscuits, sugar, macaroni and dried fruit to last me two months, beside a complete *canteen*, or supply of articles necessary for life in the desert. I took an extra quantity of gunpowder, tobacco and coffee, for presents to the Arab shekhs. The entire cost of this outfit was about nine hundred piastres. In addition, I procured a good Turkish tent for two hundred and fifty piastres, to which I added a supply of tent-pins, lantern-poles, water-skins, and leathern water-flasks, all these articles being procured to better advantage in Cairo. I did not propose adopting the Egyptian costume until I had made some progress in the language, and therefore contented myself with purchasing a *bornous* of camel's hair, a sabre, a broad shawl of Tripoli silk, for the waist, and shoes of white leather, which are very cool and comfortable. I also followed the custom of the European residents, in having my hair shorn close to the head, and wearing a white cotton skull-cap. Over this was drawn the red tarboosh, or fez, and as a protection against the sun, I bound a large white shawl around it, which was my first lesson in turban-making.

Achmet, influenced by a superstition which is not peculiar to the East, begged me to hasten our preparations, in order that we might leave Boulak on Monday, which day, he averred, was the luckiest in the week, and would render our journey prosperous from beginning to end. Knowing from experience that half the success of the journey is in the start, and believing that it is better to have superstition with you than against you, I determined to gratify him. He was as zealous as I could wish, and we rested not from morning to night, until at last, from the spirit with which we labored, it seemed almost a matter of life and death, that the boat should leave on Monday. I had a clause inserted in our written contract with the captain, that he should forfeit a day's rent, in case he was not ready at the appointed hour; but, in spite of this precaution,

Achmet, who well knew the indifference of the Arab nature, was constantly on his track. Two or three times a day he galloped to Boulak, to hasten the enlistment of the men, the baking of bread for the voyage, the furbishing of the cabin, and the overhauling of the sails, oars and rigging. My European friends in Cairo smiled at our display of activity, saying that such a thing had never been known, as a boat sailing at the appointed time, and that I was fatiguing myself to no purpose.

Monday (Nov. 17th) came, and the Egyptian cook, Salame, whom we had engaged for the Nile voyage, was despatched to the markets to lay in a supply of fowls, eggs, butter and vegetables. My letters home—the last I expected to send, for months to come—were committed to the Post Office, and after an early dinner, we saw our baggage and stores laden upon carts and started for Boulak, under Achmet's guidance. We took leave of the few friends we had made in Cairo, and followed. The *Cleopatra* was still lying in the midst of a crowd of *dahabiyehs*, but the American flag, hoisted at the peak of her little mizzenmast, was our "cornet," proclaiming departure. We found Achmet unjacketed and unturbaned, stowing away the stores, with one eye on the raïs, and another (as it seemed to me) on each of the tardy sailors. There was still charcoal to be bought, and *bois gras* for kindling fires, and clubs for the men, to prevent invasions from the shore, with many more of those wants which are never remembered until the last moment. The afternoon wore away; the shadows of the feathery date-trees on the island of Rhoda stretched long and cool across the Nile; but before the sun had touched the tops of the Pyramids, we had squeezed out from the shipping of Boulak, and were slowly working up the Nile before a light wind, while our boatmen thumped the *tarabooka*, and sang their wild Arab songs of departure. The raïs came up to know whether he had not fulfilled his contract, and Achmet with a cheerful face, turned to me and said: "Praised be Allah, master! we shall have a lucky journey."

Achmet.

CHAPTER V.

THE PYRAMIDS AND MEMPHIS.

Howling Dervishes—A Chicken Factory—Ride to the Pyramids—Quarrel with the Arabs—The Ascent—View from the Summit—Backsheesh—Effect of Pyramid climbing—The Sphinx—Playing the Cadi—We obtain Justice—Visit to Sakkara and the Mummy Pits—The Exhumation of Memphis—Interview with M. Mariette—Account of his Discoveries—Statue of Remeses II.—Return to the Nile.

"And Morning opes in haste her lids,
To gaze upon the Pyramids."—EMERSON.

WE went no further than the village of Gizeh, three or four miles above Cairo, on the first evening, having engaged our donkeys and their drivers to meet us there and convey us to the Pyramids on the following morning. About dusk, the raïs moored our boat to the bank, beside a College of dervishes, whose unearthly chants, choruses and clapping of hands, were prolonged far into the night. Their wild cries, and deep, monotonous bass howlings so filled our ears that we could not choose but listen, and, in spite of our fatigue sleep was impossible. After performing for several hours, they gradually ceased, through sheer exhaustion, though there was one tough old dervish, who continued to gasp out, "*Allah! Allah!*" with such a spasmodic energy, that I suspected it was produced by the involuntary action of his larynx, and that he could not have stopped, even had he been so minded.

When we threw open the latticed blinds of our cabin, before sunrise, the next morning, the extraordinary purity of the air gave rise to an amusing optical delusion on the part of my friend. "See that wall!" said he, pointing to a space between two white houses; "what a brilliant color it is painted, and how those palms and these white houses are relieved against it!" He was obliged to look twice before he perceived that what he had taken for a wall close at hand, was really the sky, and rested upon a far-off horizon. Our donkeys were in readiness on the bank, and I bestrode the same faithful little gray who had for three days carried me through the bazaars of Cairo. We left orders for the raïs to go on to Bedracheyn, a village near the supposed site of Memphis, and taking Achmet with us, rode off gayly among the mud hovels and under the date-trees of Gizeh, on our way to the Pyramids. Near the extremity of the village, we entered one of the large chicken-hatching establishments for which the place is famed, but found it empty. We disturbed a numerous family of Fellahs, couched together on the clay floor, crept on our hands and knees through two small holes and inspected sundry ovens covered with a layer of chaff, and redolent of a mild, moist heat and a feathery smell. The owner informed us that for the first four or five days the eggs were exposed to smoke as well as heat, and that when the birds began to pick the shell, which generally took place in fifteen days, they were placed in another oven and carefully accouched.

The rising sun shone redly on the Pyramids, as we rode out on the broad harvest land of the Nile. The black, unctuous loam was still too moist from the inundation to be ploughed, except in spots, here and there, but even where the water had scarce evaporated, millions of germs were pushing their slender blades up to the sunshine. In that prolific soil, the growth of grain is visible from day to day. The Fellahs were at work on all sides, preparing for planting, and the ungainly buffaloes drew their long ploughs slowly through the soil. Where freshly turned, the earth had a rich, soft lustre, like dark-brown velvet, beside which the fields of young wheat, beans and lentils, glittered with the most brilliant green. The larks sang in the air and flocks of white pigeons clustered like blossoms on the tops of the sycamores. There, in November, it was the freshest and most animating picture of Spring. The direct road to the Pyramids was impassable, on account of the water, and we rode along the top of a dyke, intersected by canals, to the edge of the Libyan Desert—a distance of nearly ten miles. The ruptures in the dyke obliged us occasionally to dismount, and at the last canal, which cuts off the advancing sands from the bounteous plain on the other side, our donkeys were made to swim, while we were carried across on the shoulders of two naked Arabs. They had run out in advance to meet us, hailing us with many English and French phrases, while half a dozen boys, with earthen bottles which they had just filled from the slimy canal, crowded after them, insisting, in very good English, that we should drink at once and take them with us to the Pyramids.

Our donkeys' hoofs now sank deep in the Libyan sands and we looked up to the great stone-piles of Cheops, Cephrenes and Mycerinus, not more than half a mile distant Our sunrise view of the Pyramids on leaving Gizeh, was sufficient, had I gone no further, and I approached them, without the violent emotion which sentimental travellers experience, but with a quiet feeling of the most perfect satisfaction. The form of the pyramid is so simple and complete, that nothing is left to the imagination. Those vast, yellowish-gray masses, whose feet are wrapped in the silent sand, and whose tops lean against the serene blue heaven, enter the mind and remain in the memory with no shock of surprise, no stir of unexpected admiration. The impression they give and leave, is calm, grand and enduring as themselves.

The sun glared hot on the sand as we toiled up the ascent to the base of Cheops, whose sharp corners were now broken into zigzags by the layers of stone. As we dismounted in his shadow, at the foot of the path which leads up to the entrance, on the northern side, a dozen Arabs beset us. They belonged to the regular herd who have the Pyramids in charge, and are so renowned for their impudence that it is customary to employ the janissary of some Consulate in Cairo, as a protection. Before leaving Gizeh I gave Achmet my sabre, which I thought would be a sufficient show to secure us from their importunities. However, when we had mounted to the entrance and were preparing to climb to the summit, they demanded a dollar from each for their company on the way. This was just four times the usual fee, and we flatly refused the demand. My friend had in the mean time become so giddy from the few steps he had mounted, that he decided to return, and I ordered Achmet, who knew the way, to go on with me and leave the Arabs to their howlings. Their leader instantly sprang before him, and attempted to force him back. This was too much for Achmet, who thrust the man aside, whereupon he was instantly beset by three or four, and received several hard blows. The struggle took place just on the verge of the stones, and he was prudent enough to drag his assailants into the open space before the entrance of the Pyramid. My friend sprang towards the group with his cane, and I called to the donkey-driver to bring up my sabre, but by this time Achmet had released himself, with the loss of his turban.

The Arabs, who had threatened to treat us in the same manner, then reduced their demand to the regular fee of five piastres for each. I took three of them and commenced the ascent, leaving Achmet and my friend below. Two boys followed us, with bottles of water. At first, the way seemed hazardous, for the stones were covered with sand and fragments which had fallen from above, but after we had mounted twenty courses, the hard, smooth blocks of granite formed broader and more secure steps. Two Arabs went before, one holding each of my hands, while the third shoved me up from the rear. The assistance thus rendered was not slight, for few of the stones are less than four feet in height. The water-boys scampered up beside us with the agility of cats. We stopped a moment to take breath, at a sort of resting-place half-way up—an opening in the Pyramid, communicating with the uppermost of the interior chambers. I had no sooner sat down on the nearest stone, than the Arabs stretched themselves at my feet and entertained me with most absurd mixture of flattery and menace. One, patting the calves of my legs, cried out; "Oh, what fine, strong legs! how fast they came up: nobody ever went up the Pyramid so fast!" while the others added: "Here you must give us backsheesh: every body gives us a dollar here." My only answer was, to get up and begin climbing, and they did not cease pulling and pushing till they left me breathless on the summit. The whole ascent did not occupy more than ten minutes.

The view from Cheops has been often described. I cannot say that it increased my impression of the majesty and grandeur of the Pyramid, for that was already complete. My eyes wandered off from the courses of granite, broadening away below my feet, to contemplate the glorious green of the Nile-plain, barred with palm-trees and divided by the gleaming flood of the ancient river; the minarets of Cairo; the purple walls of the far Arabian mountains; the Pyramid groups of Sakkara and Dashoor, overlooking disinterred Memphis in the South; and the arid yellow waves of the Libyan Desert, which rolled unbroken to the western sky. The clear, open heaven above, which seemed to radiate light from its entire concave, clasped in its embrace and harmonized the different features of this wonderful landscape. There was too much warmth and brilliance for desolation. Every thing was alive and real; the Pyramids were not ruins, and the dead Pharaohs, the worshippers of Athor and Apis, did not once enter my mind.

My wild attendants did not long allow me to enjoy the view quietly. To escape from their importunities for backsheesh, I gave them two piastres in copper coin, which instantly turned their flatteries into the most bitter complaints. It was insulting to give so little, and they preferred having none ; if I would not give a dollar, I might take the money back. I took it without more ado, and put it into my pocket. This rather surprised them, and first one, and then another came to me and begged to have it again, on his own private account. I threw the coins high into the air, and as they clattered down on the stones, there ensued such a scramble as would have sent any but Arabs over the edge of the Pyramid. We then commenced the descent, two seizing my hands as before, and dragging me headlong after them. We went straight down the side, sliding and leaping from stone to stone without stopping to take breath, and reached the base in five or six minutes. I was so excited from the previous aggression of the Arabs, that I neither felt fatigue nor giddiness on the way up and down, and was not aware how violent had been my exertions. But when I touched the level sand, all my strength vanished in an instant. A black mist came over my eyes, and I sank down helpless and nearly insensible. I was scarcely able to speak, and it was an hour before I could sit upright on my donkey. I felt the Pyramid in all my bones, and for two or three days afterwards moved my joints with as much difficulty as a rheumatic patient.

The Arabs, who at first had threatened to kill Achmet, now came forward and kissed his hands, humbly entreating pardon. But his pride had been too severely touched by the blows he had received, and he repulsed them, spitting upon the ground, as the strongest mark of contempt. We considered it due to him, to ourselves, and to other travellers after us, to represent the matter to the Shekh of the Pyramids, who lives in a village called Kinnayseh, a mile distant, and ordered

Achmet to conduct us thither. We first rode along the base of the Pyramid of Cephrenes, and down the sand drifts to the majestic head of the Sphinx. I shall not attempt to describe this enormous relic of Egyptian art. There is nothing like it in the world. Those travellers who pronounce its features to be negro in their character, are certainly very hasty in their conclusions. That it is an Egyptian head is plainly evident, notwithstanding its mutilation. The type, however, is rather fuller and broader than is usual in Egyptian statues.

On reaching the village we found that the shekh was absent in Cairo, but were received by his son, who, after spelling out a few words of my Arabic passport and hearing Achmet's relation of the affair, courteously invited us to his house. We rode between the mud huts to a small court-yard, where we dismounted. A carpet was spread on the ground, under a canopy of palm-leaves, and the place of honor was given to us, the young shekh seating himself on the edge, while our donkey-drivers, water-boys and a number of villagers, stood respectfully around. A messenger was instantly despatched to the Pyramids, and in the mean time we lighted the pipe of peace. The shekh promised to judge the guilty parties and punish them in our presence. Coffee was ordered, but as the unlucky youth returned and indiscreetly cried out, "*Ma feesh!*" (there is none!) the shekh took him by the neck, and run him out of the court-yard, threatening him with all manner of penalties unless he brought it.

We found ourselves considered in the light of judges, and I thought involuntarily of the children playing Cadi, in the Arabian tale. But to play our Cadi with the necessary gravity of countenance was a difficult matter. It was rather em barrassing to sit cross-legged so long, and to look so severe. My face was of the color of a boiled lobster, from the sun, and in order to protect my eyes, I had taken off my cravat and bound it around the red tarboosh. My friend had swathed his felt hat in like manner, and when the shekh looked at us from time to time, while Achmet spoke of our friendship with all the Consuls in Cairo, it was almost too much to enjoy quietly. However, the shekh, who wore a red cap and a single cotton garment, treated us with much respect. His serene, impartial demeanor, as he heard the testimony of the various witnesses who were called up, was most admirable. After half an hour's delay, the messenger returned, and the guilty parties were brought into court, looking somewhat alarmed and very submissive. We identified the two ringleaders, and after considering the matter thoroughly, the shekh ordered that they should be instantly bastinadoed. We decided between ourselves to let the punishment commence, lest the matter should not be considered sufficiently serious, and then to show our mercy by pardoning the culprits.

One of the men was then thrown on the ground and held by the head and feet, while the shekh took a stout rod and began administering the blows. The victim had prepared himself by giving his bornous a double turn over his back, and as the end of the rod struck the ground each time, there was much sound with the veriest farce of punishment. After half a dozen strokes, he cried out, "*ya salaam!*" whereupon the crowd laughed heartily, and my friend ordered the shekh to stop. The latter cast the rod at our feet, and asked us to continue the infliction ourselves, until we were satisfied. We told him and the company in general, through Achmet, that we were convinced of his readiness to punish imposition; that we wished to show the Arabs that they must in future treat travellers with respect; that we should send word of the affair to Cairo, and they might rest assured that a second assault would be more severely dealt with. Since this had been demonstrated, we were willing that the punishment should now cease, and in conclusion returned our thanks to the shekh, for his readiness to do us justice. This decision was received with great favor; the two culprits came forward and kissed our hands and those of Achmet, and the villagers pronounced a unanimous sentence of "*taïb!*" (good!) The indiscreet youth again appeared, and this time with coffee, of which we partook with much relish, for this playing the Cadi was rather fatiguing. The shekh raised our hands to his forehead, and accompanied us to the end of the village, where we gave the coffee-bearer a backsheesh, dismissed our water-boys, and turned our donkeys' heads toward Abousir.

Achmet's dark skin was pale from his wounded pride, and I was faint from pyramid-climbing, but a cold fowl, eaten as we sat in the sun, on the border of the glowing Desert, comforted us. The dominion of the sand has here as distinct a bound as that of the sea; there is not thirty yards from the black, pregnant loam, to the fiery plain, where no spear of grass grows. Our path lay sometimes on one side of this border, sometimes on the other, for more than an hour and a half, till we reached the ruined pyramids of Abousir, where it turned southward into the Desert. After seeing Cheops and Cephrenes, these pyramids are only interesting on account of their dilapidated state and the peculiarity of their forms, some of their sides taking a more obtuse angle at half their height

They are buried deep in the sand, which has so drifted toward the plain, that from the broad hollow lying between them and the group of Sakkara, more than a mile distant, every sign of vegetation is shut out. Vast, sloping causeways of masonry lead up to two of them, and a large mound, occupying the space between, suggests the idea that a temple formerly stood there. The whole of the desert promontory, which seemed to have been gradually blown out on the plain, from the hills in the rear, exhibits traces here and there of ruins beneath the surface. My friend and I, as we walked over the hot sand, before our panting donkeys, came instinctively to the same conclusion—that a large city must have once occupied the space between, and to the southward of, the two groups of pyramids. It is not often that amateur antiquarians find such sudden and triumphant confirmation of their conjectures, as we did.

On the way, Achmet had told us of a Frenchman who had been all summer digging in the sand, near Sakkara. After we had crawled into the subterranean dépôt of mummied ibises, and nearly choked ourselves with dust in trying to find a pot not broken open; and after one of our donkeymen went into a human mummy pit and brought out the feet and legs of some withered old Egyptian, we saw before us the residence of this Frenchman; a mud hut on a high sand-bank. It was an unfortunate building, for nearly all the front wall had tumbled down, revealing the contents of his kitchen. One or two Arabs loitered about, but a large number were employed at the end of a long trench which extended to the hills.

Before reaching the house a number of deep pits barred our path, and the loose sand, stirred by our feet, slid back into the bottom, as if eager to hide the wonders they disclosed. Pavements, fresh as when first laid; basement-walls of white marble, steps, doorways, pedestals and fragments of pillars glittered in the sun, which, after the lapse of more than two thousand years, beheld them again. I slid down the side of the pit and walked in the streets of Memphis. The pavement of bitumen, which once covered the stone blocks, apparently to protect them and deaden the noise of horses and chariots, was entire in many places. Here a marble sphinx sat at the base of a temple, and stared abstractedly before her; there a sculptured cornice, with heavy mouldings, leaned against the walls of the chamber into which it had fallen, and over all were scattered fragments of glazed and painted tiles and sculptured alabaster. The principal street was narrow, and was apparently occupied by private dwellings, but at its extremity were the basement-walls of a spacious edifice. All the pits opened on pavements and walls, so fresh and cleanly cut, that they seemed rather the foundations of a new city, laid yesterday, than the remains of one of the oldest capitals of the world.

We approached the workmen, where we met the discoverer of Memphis, Mr. Auguste Mariette. On finding we were not Englishmen (of whose visits he appeared to be rather shy), he became very courteous and communicative. He apologized for the little he had to show us, since on account of the Vandalism of the Arabs, he was obliged to cover up all his discoveries, after making his drawings and measurements. The Egyptian authorities are worse than apathetic, for they would not hesitate to burn the sphinxes for lime, and build barracks for filthy soldiers with the marble blocks. Besides this, the French influence at Cairo was then entirely overshadowed by that of England, and although M. Mariette was supported in his labors by the French Academy, and a subscription headed by Louis Napoleon's name, he was forced to be content with the simple permission to dig out these remarkable ruins and describe them. He could neither protect them nor remove the portable sculptures and inscriptions, and therefore preferred giving them again into the safe keeping of the sand Here they will be secure from injury, until some more fortunate period, when, possibly, the lost Memphis may be entirely given to the world, as fresh as Pompeii, and far more grand and imposing.

I asked M. Mariette what first induced him to dig for Memphis in that spot, since antiquarians had fixed upon the mounds near Mitrahenny (a village in the plain below, and about four miles distant), as the former site of the city. He said that the tenor of an inscription which he found on one of the blocks quarried out of these mounds, induced him to believe that the principal part of the city lay to the westward, and therefore he commenced excavating in the nearest sand-hill in that direction. After sinking pits in various places he struck on an avenue of sphinxes, the clue to all his after discoveries. Following this, he came upon the remains of a temple (probably the *Serapeum*, or Temple of Serapis, mentioned by Strabo), and afterward upon streets, colonnades, public and private edifices, and all other signs of a great city. The number of sphinxes alone, buried under these high sand-drifts, amounted to two thousand, and he had frequently uncovered twenty or thirty in a day. He estimated the entire number of statues, inscriptions and reliefs, at between four and five thousand. The most remarkable discovery was that of eight colossal statues, which were evidently the product of Grecian art. During thirteen months of assiduous labor, with but one assistant, he had made drawings of all these objects and forwarded them to Paris. In order to be near at hand, he had built an Arab house of unburnt bricks, the walls of which had just tumbled down for the third time. His workmen were then engaged in clearing away the sand from the dwelling of some old Memphian, and he intended spreading his roof over the massive walls, and making his residence in the exhumed city.

The man's appearance showed what he had undergone, and gave me an idea of the extraordinary zeal and patience required to make a successful antiquarian. His face was as brown as an Arab's, his eyes severely inflamed, and his hands as rough as a bricklayer's. His manner with the native workmen was admirable, and they labored with a hearty good-will which almost supplied the want of the needful implements. All they had were straw baskets, which they filled with a sort of rude shovel, and then handed up to be carried off on the heads of others. One of the principal workmen was deaf and dumb, but the funniest Arab I ever saw. He was constantly playing off his jokes on those who were too slow or too negligent. An unlucky girl, stooping down at the wrong time to lift a basket of sand, received the contents of another on her head, and her indignant outcry was hailed by the rest with screams of laughter. I saw the same man pick out of the sand a glazed tile containing hieroglyphic characters. The gravity with which he held it before him, feigning to peruse it, occasionally nodding his head, as if to say, "Well done for old Pharaoh!" could not have been excelled by Burton himself.

Strabo states that Memphis had a circumference of seven

teen miles, and therefore both M. Mariette and the antiquarians are right. The mounds of Mitrahenny probably mark the eastern portion of the city, while its western limit extended beyond the Pyramids of Sakkara, and included in its suburbs those of Abousir and Dashoor. The space explored by M. Mariette is about a mile and a half in length, and somewhat more than half a mile in breadth. He was then continuing his excavations westward, and had almost reached the first ridge of the Libyan Hills, without finding the termination of the ruins. The magnitude of his discovery will be best known when his drawings and descriptions are given to the world. A few months after my visit, his labors were further rewarded by finding thirteen colossal sarcophagi of black marble, and he has recently added to his renown by discovering an entrance to the Sphinx. Yet at that time, the exhumation of the lost Memphis—second only in importance to that of Nineveh—was unknown in Europe, except to a few *savans* in Paris, and the first intimation which some of my friends in Cairo and Alexandria had of it, was my own account of my visit, in the newspapers they received from America. But M. Mariette is a young man, and will yet see his name inscribed beside those of Burckhardt, Belzoni and Layard.

We had still a long ride before us, and I took leave of Memphis and its discoverer, promising to revisit him on my return from Khartoum. As we passed the brick Pyramid of Sakkara, which is built in four terraces of equal height, the dark, grateful green of the palms and harvest-fields of the Nile appeared between two sand-hills—a genuine balm to our heated eyes. We rode through groves of the fragrant mimosa to a broad dike, the windings of which we were obliged to follow across the plain, as the soil was still wet and adhesive. It was too late to visit the beautiful Pyramids of Dashoor, the first of which is more than three hundred feet in height, and from a distance has almost as grand an effect as those of Gizeh. Our tired donkeys lagged slowly along to the palm-groves of Mitrahenny, where we saw mounds of earth, a few blocks of red granite and a colossal statue of Remeses II. (Sesostris)—which until now were supposed to be the only remains of Memphis. The statue lies on its face in a hole filled with water. The countenance is said to be very beautiful, but I could only see the top of Sesostris's back, which bore a faint resemblance to a crocodile.

Through fields of cotton in pod and beans in blossom, we rode to the Nile, dismissed our donkeys and their attendants, and lay down on some bundles of corn-stalks to wait the arrival of our boat. But there had been a south wind all day, and we had ridden much faster than our men could tow. We sat till long after sunset before the stars and stripes, floating from the mizzen of the *Cleopatra*, turned the corner below Bedrasheyn. When, at last, we sat at our cabin-table, weary and hungry, we were ready to confess that the works of art produced by our cook, Salame, were more marvellous and interesting than Memphis and the Pyramids.

CHAPTER VI.

FROM MEMPHIS TO SIOUT.

Leaving the Pyramids—A Calm and a Breeze—A Coptic Visit—Minyeh—The Grottoes of Beni-Hassan—Doum Palms and Crocodiles—Djebel Aboufayda—Entrance into Upper Egypt—Diversions of the Boatmen—Siout—Its Tombs—A Landscape—A Bath.

> "It flows through old hushed Egypt and its sands,
> Like some grave, mighty thought threading a dream."
>
> LEIGH HUNT'S SONNET TO THE NILE.

THE extent of my journey into Africa led me to reverse the usual plan pursued by travellers on the Nile, who sail to Assouan or Wadi-Halfa without pause, and visit the antiquities on their return. I have never been able to discern the philosophy of this plan. The voyage up is always longer, and more tedious (to those heathens who call the Nile tedious), than the return; besides which, two visits, though brief, with an interval between, leave a more complete and enduring image, than a single one. The mind has time to analyze and contrast, and can afterwards confirm or correct the first impressions. How any one can sail from Cairo to Siout, a voyage of two hundred and sixty miles, with but one or two points of interest, without taking the Pyramids with him in memory, I cannot imagine. Were it not for that recollection, I should have pronounced Modern Egypt more interesting than the

Egypt of the Pharaohs and the Ptolemies. I omitted seeing none of the important remains on my upward journey, so that I might be left free to choose another route homeward, if possible. It seemed like slighting Fortune to pass Dendera, and Karnak and Ombos, without notice. Opportunity is rare, and a wise man will never let it go by him. I knew not what dangers I might have to encounter, but I knew that it would be a satisfaction to me, even if speared by the Bedouins of the Lybian Desert, to think: "You rascals, you have killed me, but I have seen Thebes!"

The Pyramids of Dashoor followed us all the next day after leaving Memphis. Our sailors tugged us slowly along shore, against a mild south wind, but could not bring us out of the horizon of those red sandstone piles. Our patience was tried, that day and the next, by our slow and toilsome progress, hindered still more by running aground on sand-banks, but we were pledged to patience, and had our reward. On the morning of the fourth day, as we descried before us the minarets of Benisouef, the first large town after leaving Cairo, a timid breeze came rustling over the dourra-fields to the north, and puffed out the Cleopatra's languid sails. The tow-rope was hauled in, our Arabs jumped on board and produced the drum and tambourine, singing lustily as we moved out into the middle of the stream. The wind increased; the flag lifted itself from the mast and streamed toward Thebes, and Benisouef went by, almost before we had counted its minarets. I tried in vain to distinguish the Pyramid of Illahoon, which stands inland, at the base of the Libyan Hills and the entrance of the pass leading to the Lake of Fyoom, the ancient Mœris. Near the Pyramid are the foundations of the famous Labyrinth, lately excavated by Dr. Lepsius. The Province of Fyoom, surrounding the lake, is, with the exception of the Oases in the Libyan Desert, the only productive land west of the mountains bordering the Nile.

All afternoon, with both sails full and our vessel leaning against the current, we flew before the wind. At dusk, the town of Feshn appeared on our left; at midnight, we passed Abou-Girgeh and the Mounds of Behnesa, the ancient Oxyrinchus; and when the wind left us, at sunrise, we were seventy miles from Benisouef. The Arabian Mountains here approach the river, and at two points terminate in abrupt precipices of yellow calcareous rock. The bare cliffs of Djebel el Tayr (the Mountain of Birds), are crowned with the "Convent of the Pulley," so called from its inaccessible situation, and the fact that visitors are frequently drawn to the summit by a rope and windlass. While passing this convent, a cry came up from the muddy waters of the river: "We are Christians, O Howadji!" and presently two naked Coptic monks wriggled over the gunwale, and sat down, panting and dripping, on the deck. We gave them backsheesh, which they instantly clapped into their mouths, but their souls likewise devoutly yearned for brandy, which they did not get. They were large, lusty fellows, and whatever perfection of spirit they might have attained, their flesh certainly had never been unnecessarily mortified. After a breathing spell, they jumped into the river again, and we soon saw them straddling from point to point, as they crawled up the almost perpendicular cliff. At Djebel el Tayr, the birds of Egypt (according to an Arabic legend) assemble annually and choose one of their number to remain there for a year. My friend complained that the wild geese and ducks were not represented, and out of revenge fired at a company of huge pelicans, who were seated on a sand-bank.

The drum and tambourine kept lively time to the voices of our sailors, as we approached Minyeh, the second large town on the river, and the capital of a Province. But the song this time had a peculiar significance. After the long-drawn sound, something between a howl and a groan, which terminated it, we were waited upon by a deputation, who formally welcomed us to the city. We responded by a backsheesh of twenty-five piastres, and the drum rang louder than ever. We stayed in Minyeh long enough to buy a leg of mutton, and then sailed for the tombs of Beni-Hassan. The wind left us as we reached a superb palm-grove, which for several miles skirts the foot of Djebel Shekh Timay. The inhabitants are in bad odor, and in addition to our own guard, we were obliged to take two men from the village, who came armed with long sticks and built a fire on the bank, beside our vessel. This is a regulation of the Government, to which travellers usually conform, but I never saw much reason for it. We rose at dawn and wandered for hours through the palms, to the verge of the Desert. When within two or three miles of the mountain of Beni-Hassan, we provided ourselves with candles, water-flasks and weapons, and set off in advance of our boat. The Desert here reached the Nile, terminating in a bluff thirty to forty feet in height, which is composed of layers of pebbles and shelly sand, apparently the deposit of many successive floods. I should have attributed this to the action of the river, cutting a deeper channel from year to year, but I believe it is now acknowledged that the bed of the Nile is gradually rising, and that the yearly inun dation covers a much wider space than in the time of the Pharaohs. It is difficult to reconcile this fact with the very perceptible encroachments which the sand is making on the Libyan shore; but we may at least be satisfied that the glorious harvest-valley through which the river wanders can never be wholly effaced thereby.

We climbed to the glaring level of the Desert, carrying with us the plumes of a beautiful gray heron which my friend brought down. A solitary Arab horseman was slowly moving along the base of the arid hills, and we descried in the distance a light-footed gazelle, which leisurely kept aloof and mocked our efforts to surround it. At the foot of the mountain we passed two ruined villages, destroyed several years ago by Ibrahim Pasha, on account of the marauding propensities of the inhabitants. It has a cruel sound, when you are told that the people were driven away, and their dwellings razed to the ground, but the reality is a trifling matter. The Arabs take their water-skins and pottery, jump into the Nile, swim across to a safer place, and in three or four days their palaces of mud are drying in the sun. We came upon them the next morning, as thievishly inclined as ever, and this was the only place where I found the people otherwise than friendly.

A steep path, up a slope covered with rounded boulders of hard black rock, leads to the grottoes of Beni-Hassan. They are among the oldest in Egypt, dating from the reign of Osirtasen I, about 1750 years before the Christian Era, and are interesting from their encaustic paintings, representing Egyptian life and customs at that early date. The rock chambers extend for nearly half a mile along the side of the mountain. The most of them are plain and without particular interest, and they have all suffered from the great spoilers of Egypt—

the Persian, the Copt and the Saracen. Four only retain their hieroglyphics and paintings, and are adorned with columns hewn from the solid rock. The first we entered contained four plain, fluted columns, one of which had been shivered in the centre, leaving the architrave and capital suspended from the ceiling. The walls were covered with paintings, greatly faded and defaced, representing the culture and manufacture of flax, the sowing and reaping of grain, and the making of bread, besides a number of spirited hunting and fishing scenes. The occupant of the tomb appears to have been a severe master, for his servants are shown in many places, undergoing the punishment of the bastinado, which is even inflicted upon women. He was also wealthy, for we still see his stewards presenting him with tablets showing the revenues of his property. He was a great man in Joseph's day, but the pit in which he lay is now empty, and the Arabs have long since burned his mummy to boil their rice.

The second tomb is interesting, from a painting representing thirty men, of a foreign nation, who are brought before the deceased occupant. Some antiquarians suppose them to be the brethren of Joseph, but the tomb is that of a person named Nehophth, and the number of men does not correspond with the Bible account. Two of the southern tombs, which are supported by pillars formed of four budding locust-stalks bound together, are covered with paintings representing different trades and professions. The rear walls are entirely devoted to illustrations of gymnastic exercises, and the figures are drawn with remarkable freedom and skill. There are never more than two persons in a group, one being painted red and the other black, in order the better to show the position of each. In at least five hundred different groupings the same exercise is not repeated, showing a wonderful fertility of invention, either on the part of the artist or the wrestlers. The execution of these figures fully reached my ideas of Egyptian pictorial art, but the colors were much less vivid than some travellers represent. The tombs are not large, though numerous, and what is rather singular, there is not the least trace of a city in the neighborhood, to which they could have belonged.

The next day at noon we passed between the mounds of Antinoë and Hermopolis Magna, lying on opposite banks of the Nile. Antinoë, built by the Emperor Adrian in honor of his favorite, the glorious Antinous, who was here drowned in the river, has entirely disappeared, with the exception of its foundations. Twenty-five years ago, many interesting monuments were still standing, but as they were, unfortunately, of the white calcareous stone of the Arabian Hills, they have been long since burnt for lime. Before reaching Antinoë we had just come on board, after a long walk on the western bank, and the light wind which bore us toward the mountain of Shekh Abaddeh was too pleasant to be slighted; so we saw nothing of Adrian's city except some heaps of dirt. The splendid evening, however, which bathed the naked cliffs of the mountain in rosy flame, was worth more to us than any amount of marble blocks.

The guide book says, "hereabouts appears the doum palm, and crocodiles begin to be more frequently seen." The next morning we found one of the trees, but day after day we vainly sought a crocodile. My friend recalled a song of Geibel's, concerning a German musician who played his violin by the Nile till the crocodiles came out and danced around the Pyramids, and in his despair would also have purchased a violin, if any could have been found in Siout. I had seen alligators on the Mississippi, and took the disappointment more complacently. The doum palm differs from the columnar date-palm in the form of its leaves, which are fan-like, and in having a branching trunk. The main stem divides a few feet from the root, each of the branches again forming two, and each of these two more, till the tree receives a broad, rounded top. The fruit hangs below in clusters, resembling small cocoa-nuts, and has a sort of gingerbread flavor, which is not disagreeable. When fully dry and hard, it takes a polish like ivory, and is manufactured by the Arabs into beads, pipe bowls and other small articles.

We approached the mountain of Aboufayda with a strong and favorable wind. Here the Nile, for upward of ten miles, washes the foot of lofty precipices, whose many deep fissures and sharp angles give them the appearance of mountains in ruin. The afternoon sun shone full on the yellow rocks, and their jagged pinnacles were cut with wonderful distinctness against the perfect blue of the sky. This mountain is considered the most dangerous point on the Nile for boats, and the sailors always approach it with fear. Owing to its deep side-gorges, the wind sometimes shifts about without a moment's warning, and if the large lateen sail is caught aback, the vessel is instantly overturned. During the passage of this and other similar straits, two sailors sit on deck, holding the sail-rope, ready to let it fly in the wind on the slightest appearance of danger. The shifting of the sail is a delicate business, at such times, but I found it better to trust to our men, awkward as they were, than to confuse by attempting to direct them. At Djebel Shekh Saïd, the sailors have a custom of throwing two or three loaves of bread on the water, believing that it will be taken up by two large white birds and deposited on the tomb of the Shekh. The wind favored us in passing Aboufayda; the Cleopatra dashed the foam from the rough waves, and in two or three hours the southern corner of the mountain lay behind us, leaning away from the Nile like the shattered pylon of a temple.

Before sunset we passed the city of Manfalout, whose houses year by year topple into the mining flood. The side next the river shows only halves of buildings, the rest of which have been washed away. In a few years the tall and airy minarets will follow, and unless the inhabitants continue to shift their dwellings to the inland side, the city will entirely disappear. From this point, the plain of Siout, the garden of Upper Egypt, opened wide and far before us. The spur of the Libyan hills, at the foot of which the city is built, shot out in advance, not more than ten or twelve miles distant, but the Nile, loth to leave these beautiful fields and groves, winds hither and thither in such a devious, lingering track, that you must sail twenty-five miles to reach El Hamra, the port of Siout. The landscape, broader and more majestic than those of Lower Egypt, is even richer and more blooming. The Desert is kept within its proper bounds; it is no longer visible from the river, and the hills, whose long, level lines frame the view on either side, enhance by their terrible sterility the luxury of vegetation which covers the plain. It is a bounteous land, visited only by healthy airs, and free from the pestilence which sometimes scourges Cairo.

The wind fell at midnight, but came to us again the next morning at sunrise, and brought us to El Hamra before noon.

Our men were in high spirits at having a day c rest before them, the contracts for boats always stipulating for a halt of twenty-four hours at Siout and Esneh, in order that they may procure their supplies of provisions. They buy wheat and dourra, have it ground in one of the rude mills worked by buffaloes, and bake a sufficient quantity of loaves to last two or three weeks. Our men had also the inspiration of backsheesh in their song, and their dolorous love-melodies rang from shore to shore. The correctness with which these people sing is absolutely surprising. Wild and harsh as are their songs, their choruses are in perfect accord, and even when at the same time exerting all their strength at the poles and oars, they never fail in a note. The melodies are simple, but not without expression, and all are pervaded with a mournful monotony which seems to have been caught from the Desert. There is generally an improvisatore in each boat's crew, who supplies an endless number of lines to the regular chorus of "*hay-haylee sah!*" So far as I could understand our poet, there was not the least meaning or connection in his poetry, but he never failed in the rhythm. He sang, for instance: "O Alexandrian!"—then followed the chorus: "Hasten, three of you!"—chorus again: "Hail, Sidi Ibrahim!" and so on, for an hour at a time. On particular occasions, he added pantomime, and the scene on our forward deck resembled a war-dance of the Blackfeet. The favorite pantomime is that of a man running into a hornet's nest. He stamps and cries, improvising all the while, the chorus seeking to drown his voice. He then throws off his mantle, cap, and sometimes his last garment, slapping his body to drive off the hornets, and howling with pain. The song winds up with a prolonged cry, which only ceases when every lung is emptied. Even when most mirthfully inclined, and roaring in ecstasy over some silly joke, our men always laughed in accord. So sound and hearty were their cachinnatory choruses, that we involuntarily laughed with them.

A crowd of donkeys, ready saddled, awaited us on the bank, and the boys began to fight before our boat was moored. We chose three unpainted animals, so large that our feet were at least three inches from the ground, and set off on a gallop for Siout, which is about a mile and a half from the river. Its fifteen tall, white minarets rose before us, against the background of the mountain, and the handsome front of the palace of Ismail Pasha shone through the dark green of its embosoming acacias. The road follows the course of a dam, built to retain the waters of the inundation, and is shaded with palms, sycamores and mimosas. On either side we looked down upon fields of clover, so green, juicy and June-like that I was tempted to jump from my donkey and take a roll therein. Where the ground was still damp the Arabs were ploughing with camels, and sowing wheat on the moist, fat loam. We crossed a bridge and entered the court of justice, one of the most charmingly clean and shady spots in Egypt. The town, which is built of sun-dried bricks, whose muddy hue is somewhat relieved by the whitewashed mosques and minarets, is astonishingly clean in every part. The people themselves appeared to be orderly, intelligent and amiable.

The tombs of the City of Wolves, the ancient Lycopolis, are in the eastern front of the mountain overhanging the city. We rode to the *Stabl Antar*, the principal one, and then climbed to the summit. The tombs are much larger than those of Beni-Hassan, but have been almost ruined by the modern Egyptians. The enormous square pillars which filled their halls have been shattered down for lime, and only fragments of the capitals still hang from the ceilings of solid rock. The sculptures and hieroglyphics, which are here not painted but sculptured in intaglio, are also greatly defaced. The second tomb called by the Arabs *Stabl Hamam* (Pigeon Stable), retains its grand doorway, which has on each side the colossal figure of an ancient king. The sand around its mouth is filled with fragments of mummied wolves, and on our way up the mountain we scared one of their descendants from his lair in a solitary tomb. The *Stabl Hamam* is about sixty feet square by forty in height, and in its rough and ruined aspect is more impressive than the more chaste and elegant chambers of Beni-Hassan. The view of the plain of Siout, seen through its entrance, has a truly magical effect. From the gray twilight of the hall in which you stand, the green of the fields, the purple of the distant mountains, and the blue of the sky, dazzle your eye as if tinged with the broken rays of a prism.

From the summit of the mountain, which we reached by scaling a crevice in its white cliffs, we overlooked a more beautiful landscape than that seen from the Pyramid. In the north, beyond the spires of Manfalout and the crags of Aboufayda, we counted the long palm-groves, receding behind one another to the yellow shore of the Desert; in front, the winding Nile and the Arabian Mountains;. southward, a sea of wheat and clover here deepening into dark emerald, there paling into gold, according to the degree of moisture in the soil, and ceasing only because the eye refused to follow; while behind us, over the desert hills, wound the track of the yearly caravan from Dar-Fūr and Kordofàn. Our Arab guide pointed out a sandy plain, behind the cemetery of the Mamelukes, which lay at our feet, as the camping-ground of the caravan, and tried to tell us how many thousand camels were assembled there. As we looked upon the superb plain, teeming with its glory of vegetable life and enlivened by the songs of the Arab ploughmen, a funeral procession came from the city and passed slowly to the burying-ground, accompanied by the dismal howling of a band of women. We went below and rode between the whitewashed domes covering the graves of the Mamelukes. The place was bright, clean and cheerful, in comparison with the other Arab burying-grounds we had seen. The grove which shades its northern wall stretches for more than a mile along the edge of the Desert—a picturesque avenue of palms, sycamores, fragrant acacias, mimosas and acanthus. The air around Siout is pregnant with the rich odor of the yellow mimosa-flowers, and one becomes exhilarated by breathing it.

The city has handsome bazaars and a large bath, built by Mohammed Bey Defterdar, the savage son-in-law of Mohammed Ali. The halls are spacious, supported by granite columns, and paved with marble. Little threads of water, scarcely visible in the dim, steamy atmosphere, shoot upward from the stone tanks, around which a dozen brown figures lie stretched in the lazy beatitude of the bath. I was given over to two Arabs, who scrubbed me to desperation, plunged me twice over head and ears in a tank of scalding water, and then placed me under a cold *douche*. When the whole process, which occupied more than half an hour, was over, a cup of coffee and a pipe were brought to me as I lay stretched out on the divan, while another attendant commenced a course of dislocation, twisting and cracking all my joints and pressing violently with both hands on my breast. Singularly enough, this removed the languor occasioned by so much hot water, and gave a wonderful elasticity to the frame. I walked out as if shod with the wings of Mercury, and as I rode back to our boat, congratulated my donkey on the airy lightness of his load.

The Cleopatra.

CHAPTER VII.

LIFE ON THE NILE.

Independence of Nile Life—The Dahabiyeh—Our Servants—Our Residence—Our Manner of Living—The Climate—The Natives—Costume—Our Sunset Repose—My Friend—A Sensuous Life Defended.

> ———"The life thou seek'st
> Thou'lt find beside the Eternal Nile."—Moore's Alciphron.

We hear much said by tourists who have visited Egypt, concerning the comparative pains and pleasures of life on the Nile, and their decisions are as various as their individual characters. Four out of every five complain of the monotony and tedium of the voyage, and pour forth touching lamentations over the annoyance of rats and cockroaches, the impossibility of procuring beef-steak, or the difficulty of shooting crocodiles. Some of them are wholly impermeable to the influences of the climate, scenery and ruins of Egypt, and carry to the Nubian frontier the airs of Broadway or Bond-street. I have heard such a one say: "This seeing the Nile is a nice thing *to have gotten over*, but it is a great bore while you are about it." Such is the spirit of those travelling snobs (of all nations), by some of whom sacred Egypt is profaned every winter. They are unworthy to behold the glories of the Nile, and if I had the management of Society, they never should. A palm-tree is to them a good post to shoot a pigeon from; Dendera is a "rum old concern," and a crocodile is better than Karnak.

There are a few, however, who will acknowledge the truth of the picture which follows, and which was written in the cabin of the Cleopatra, immediately after our arrival in Upper Egypt. As it is a faithful transcript of my Nilotic life, I have deviated from the regular course of my narrative, in order to give it without change:—

The Nile is the Paradise of Travel. I thought I had already fathomed all the depths of enjoyment which the traveller's restless life could reach—enjoyment more varied and exciting, but far less serene and enduring than that of a quiet home—but here I have reached a fountain too pure and powerful to be exhausted. I never before experienced such a thorough deliverance from all the petty annoyances of travel in other lands, such perfect contentment of spirit, such entire abandonment to the best influences of nature. Every day opens with a *jubilate*, and closes with a thanksgiving. If such a balm and blessing as this life has been to me, thus far, can be felt twice in one's existence, there must be another Nile somewhere in the world.

Other travellers undoubtedly make other experiences and take away other impressions. I can even conceive circumstances which would almost destroy the pleasure of the journey. The same exquisitely sensitive temperament which in our case has not been disturbed by a single untoward incident, might easily be kept in a state of constant derangement by an unsympathetic companion, a cheating dragoman, or a fractious crew. There are also many trifling *desagrémens*, inseparable from life in Egypt, which some would consider a source of annoyance; but as we find fewer than we were prepared to meet, we are not troubled thereby. Our enjoyment springs from causes so few and simple, that I scarcely know how to make them suffice for the effect, to those who have never visited the Nile. It may be interesting to such to be made acquainted with our manner of living, in detail.

In the first place, we are as independent of all organized Governments as a ship on the open sea. (The Arabs call the Nile *El bahr*, "the sea.") We are on board our own chartered vessel, which must go where we list, the captain and sailors being strictly bound to obey us. We sail under national colors, make our own laws for the time being, are ourselves the only censors over our speech and conduct, and shall have no communication with the authorities on shore, unless our subjects rebel. Of this we have no fear, for we commenced by maintaining strict discipline, and as we make no unreasonable demands, are always cheerfully obeyed. Indeed, the most complete harmony exists between the rulers and the ruled, and though our government is the purest form of despotism, we flatter ourselves that it is better managed than that of the Model Republic.

Our territory, to be sure, is not very extensive. The *Cleopatra* is a *dahabiyeh*, seventy feet long by ten broad. She has two short masts in the bow and stern, the first upholding the *trinkeet*, a lateen sail nearly seventy feet in length. The latter carries the *belikôn*, a small sail, and the American colors. The narrow space around the foremast belongs to the crew, who cook their meals in a small brick furnace, and sit on the gunwale, beating a drum and tambourine and singing for hours in interminable choruses, when the wind blows fair. If there is no wind, half of them are on shore, tugging us slowly along the banks with a long tow-rope, and singing all day long: "*Ayà hamàm—ayà hamàm!*" If we strike on a sand-bank, they jump into the river and put their shoulders against the hull, singing: "*hay-haylee sah!*" If the current is slow, they ship the oars and pull us up stream, singing so complicated a refrain that it is impossible to write it with other than Arabic characters. There are eight men and a boy, besides our stately raïs, Hassan Abd el-Sadek, and the swarthy pilot, who greets us every morning with a whole round of Arabic salutations.

Against an upright pole which occupies the place of a mainmast, stands our kitchen, a high wooden box, with three furnaces. Here our cook, Salame, may be seen at all times, with the cowl of a blue capote drawn over his turban, preparing the marvellous dishes, wherein his delight is not less than ours. Salame, like a skilful artist, as he is, husbands his resources, and each day astonishes us with new preparations, so that, out of few materials, he has attained the grand climax of all art—variety in unity. Achmet, my faithful dragoman, has his station here, and keeps one eye on the vessel and one on the kitchen, while between the two he does not relax his protecting care for us. The approach to the cabin is flanked by our provision chests, which will also serve as a breastwork in case of foreign aggression. A huge filter-jar of porous earthenware stands against the back of the kitchen. We keep our fresh butter and vegetables in a box under it, where the sweet Nile-water drips cool and clear into an earthen basin. Our bread and vegetables, in an open basket of palm-blades, are suspended beside it, and the roof of the cabin supports our poultry-yard and pigeon-house. Sometimes (but not often) a leg of mutton may be seen hanging from the ridge-pole, which extends over the deck as a support to the awning.

The cabin, or Mansion of the Executive Powers, is about twenty-five feet long. Its floor is two feet below the deck, and its ceiling five feet above, so that we are not cramped or crowded in any particular. Before the entrance is a sort of portico, with a broad, cushioned seat on each side, and side-awnings to shut out the sun. This place is devoted to pipes and meditation. We throw up the awnings, let the light pour in on all sides, and look out on the desert mountains while we inhale the incense of the East. Our own main cabin is about ten feet long, and newly painted of a brilliant blue color. A broad divan, with cushions, extends along each side, serving as a sofa by day, and a bed by night. There are windows, blinds, and a canvas cover at the sides, so that we can regulate our light and air as we choose. In the middle of the cabin is our table and two camp stools, while shawls, capotes, pistols, sabre and gun are suspended from the walls. A little door at the further end opens into a wash-room, beyond which is a smaller cabin with beds, which we have alloted to Achmet's use. Our cook sleeps on deck, with his head against the provision chest. The raïs and pilot sleep on the roof of our cabin, where the latter sits all day, holding the long arm of the rudder, which projects forward over the cabin from the high end of the stern.

Our manner of life is simple, and might even be called monotonous, but we have never found the greatest variety of landscape and incident so thoroughly enjoyable. The scenery of the Nile, thus far, scarcely changes from day to day, in its forms and colors, but only in their disposition with regard to each other. The shores are either palm-groves, fields of cane and dourra, young wheat, or patches of bare sand, blown out from the desert. The villages are all the same agglomerations of mud-walls, the tombs of the Moslem saints are the same white ovens, and every individual camel and buffalo resembles its neighbor in picturesque ugliness. The Arabian and Libyan Mountains, now sweeping so far into the foreground that their yellow cliffs overhang the Nile, now receding into the violet haze of the horizon, exhibit little difference of height, hue, or geological formation. Every new scene is the turn of a kaleidoscope, in which the same objects are grouped in other relations, yet always characterized by the most perfect harmony. These slight, yet ever-renewing changes, are to us a source of endless delight. Either from the pure atmosphere, the healthy life we lead, or the accordant tone of our spirits, we find ourselves unusually sensitive to all the slightest touches, the most minute rays of that grace and harmony which bathes every landscape in cloudless sunshine. The various groupings of the palms, the shifting of the blue evening shadows on the rose-hued mountain walls, the green of the wheat and sugar-cane, the windings of the great river, the alternations of wind and calm—each of these is enough to content us, and to give every day a different charm from that which went before. We meet contrary winds, calms and sand-banks without losing our patience, and even our excitement in the swiftness and grace with which our vessel scuds before the north-wind is mingled with a regret that our journey is drawing so much the more swiftly to its close. A portion of the old Egyptian repose seems to be infused into our natures, and lately, when I saw my face in a mirror, I thought I perceived in its features something of the patience and resignation of the Sphinx.

Although, in order to enjoy this life as much as possible, we subject ourselves to no arbitrary rules, there is sufficient regularity in our manner of living. We rise before the sun, and after breathing the cool morning air half an hour, drink a cup of coffee and go ashore for a walk, unless the wind is very strong in our favor. My friend, who is an enthusiastic sportsman and an admirable shot, takes his fowling-piece, and I my sketch-book and pistols. We wander inland among the fields of wheat and dourra, course among the palms and acacias for game, or visit the villages of the Fellahs. The temperature, which is about 60° in the morning, rarely rises above 75°, so that we have every day three or four hours exercise in the mild and pure air. My friend always brings back from one to two dozen pigeons, while I, who practise with my pistol on such ignoble game as hawks and vultures, which are here hardly shy enough to shoot, can at the best but furnish a few wing feathers to clean our pipes.

It is advisable to go armed on these excursions, though there is no danger of open hostility on the part of the people. Certain neighborhoods, as that of Beni Hassan, are in bad repute, but the depredations of the inhabitants, who have been disarmed by the Government, are principally confined to thiev ing and other petty offences. On one occasion I fell in with a company of these people, who demanded my tarboosh, shoes and shawl, and would have taken them had I not been armed. In general, we have found the Fellahs very friendly and well disposed. They greet us on our morning walks with "*Salamàt!*" and "*Sàbah el Kheyr!*" and frequently accompany us for miles. My friend's fowling-piece often brings around him all the men and boys of a village, who follow him as long as a pigeon is to be found on the palm-trees. The certainty of his shot excites their wonder. "Wallah!" they cry; "every time the Howadji fires, the bird drops." The fact of my wearing a tarboosh and white turban brings upon me much Arabic conversation, which is somewhat embarrassing, with my imperfect knowledge of the language; but a few words go a great way. The first day I adopted this head-dress (which is convenient and agreeable in every respect), the people saluted me with "good morning, O Sidi!" (Sir, or Lord) instead of the usual "good morning, O Howadji!" (*i. e.* merchant, as the Franks are rather contemptuously designated by the Arabs).

For this climate and this way of life, the Egyptian costume is undoubtedly much better than the European. It is light, cool, and does not impede the motion of the limbs. The turban thoroughly protects the head against the sun, and shades the eyes, while it obstructs the vision much less than a hat-brim. The broad silk shawl which holds up the baggy trowsers, shields the abdomen against changes of temperature and tends to prevent diarrhœa, which, besides ophthalmia, is the only ailment the traveller need fear. The latter disease may be avoided by bathing the face in cold water after walking or any exercise which induces perspiration. I have followed this plan, and though my eyes are exposed daily to the full blaze of the sun.

find them growing stronger and clearer. In fact, since leaving the invigorating camp-life of California, I have not felt the sensation of health so purely as now. The other day, to the great delight of our sailors and the inexhaustible merriment of my friend, I donned one of Achmet's dresses. Though the short Theban's flowing trowsers and embroidered jacket gave me the appearance of a strapping Turk, who had grown too fast for his garments, they were so easy and convenient in every respect, that I have decided to un-Frank myself for the remainder of the journey.

But our day is not yet at an end. We come on board about eleven o'clock, and find our breakfast ready for the table. The dishes are few, but well cooked, and just what a hungry man would desire—fowls, pigeons, eggs, rice, vegetables, fruit, the coarse but nourishing bread of the country, and the sweet water of the Nile, brought to a blush by an infusion of claret After breakfast we seat ourselves on the airy divans in front of the cabin, and quietly indulge in the luxury of a shebook, filled by Achmet's experienced hand, and a *finjan* of Turkish coffee. Then comes an hour's exercise in Arabic, after which we read guide-books, consult our maps, write letters, and occupy ourselves with various mysteries of our household, till the noonday heat is over. Dinner, which is served between four and five o'clock, is of the same materials as our breakfast, but differently arranged, and with the addition of soup. My friend avers that he no longer wonders why Esau sold his birthright, now that he has tasted our pottage of Egyptian lentils. Coffee and pipes follow dinner, which is over with the first flush of sunset and the first premonition of the coolness and quiet of evening.

We seat ourselves on deck, and drink to its fulness the balm of this indescribable repose. The sun goes down behind the Libyan Desert in a broad glory of purple and rosy lights; the Nile is calm and unruffled, the palms stand as if sculptured in jasper and malachite, and the torn and ragged sides of the Arabian Mountains, pouring through a hundred fissures the sand of the plains above, burn with a deep crimson lustre, as if smouldering from some inward fire. The splendor soon passes off and they stand for some minutes in dead, ashy paleness. The sunset has now deepened into orange, in the midst of which a large planet shines whiter than the moon. A second glow falls upon the mountains, and this time of a pale, but intense yellow hue, which gives them the effect of a transparent painting. The palm-groves are dark below and the sky dark behind them; they alone, the symbols of perpetual desolation, are transfigured by the magical illumination. Scarcely a sound disturbs the solemn magnificence of the hour. Even our full-throated Arabs are silent, and if a wave gurgles against the prow, it slides softly back into the river, as if rebuked for the venture. We speak but little, and then mostly in echoes of each other's thoughts. "This is more than mere enjoyment of Nature," said my friend, on such an evening: "it is worship."

Speaking of my friend, it is no more than just that I should confess how much of the luck of this Nile voyage is owing to him, and therein may be the secret of my complete satisfaction and the secret of the disappointment of others. It is more easy and yet more difficult for persons to harmonize while travelling, than when at home. By this I mean, that men of kindred natures and aims find each other more readily and confide in each other more freely, while the least jarring element rapidly drives others further and further apart. No confessional so completely reveals the whole man as the companionship of travel. It is not possible to wear the conventional masks of Society, and one repulsive feature is often enough to neutralize many really good qualities. On the other hand, a congeniality of soul and temperament speedily ripens into the firmest friendship and doubles every pleasure which is mutually enjoyed. My companion widely differs from me in age, in station, and in his experiences of life; but to one of those open, honest and loving natures which are often found in his native Saxony, he unites a most warm and thorough appreciation of Beauty in Nature or Art. We harmonize to a miracle, and the parting with him at Assouan will be the sorest pang of my journey.

My friend, the Howadjî, in whose "Nile-Notes" the Egyptian atmosphere is so perfectly reproduced, says that "Conscience falls asleep on the Nile." If by this he means that artificial quality which bigots and sectarians call Conscience, I quite agree with him, and do not blame the Nile for its soporific powers. But that simple faculty of the soul, native to all men, which acts best when it acts unconsciously, and leads our passions and desires into right paths without seeming to lead them, is vastly strengthened by this quiet and healthy life. There is a cathedral-like solemnity in the air of Egypt; one feels the presence of the altar, and is a better man without his will. To those rendered misanthropic by disappointed ambition—mistrustful by betrayed confidence—despairing by unassuageable sorrow—let me repeat the motto which heads this chapter.

I have endeavored to picture our mode of life as faithfully and minutely as possible, because it bears no resemblance to travel in any other part of the world. Into the heart of a barbarous continent and a barbarous land, we carry with us every desirable comfort and luxury. In no part of Europe or America could we be so thoroughly independent, without undergoing considerable privations, and wholly losing that sense of rest which is the greatest enjoyment of this journey. We are cut off from all communication with the great world of politics, merchandise and usury, and remember it only through the heart, not through the brain. We go ashore in the delicious mornings, breathe the elastic air, and wander through the palm-groves, as happy and care-free as two Adams in a Paradise without Eves. It is an episode which will flow forward in the under-currents of our natures through the rest of our lives, soothing and refreshing us whenever it rises to the surface. I do not reproach myself for this passive and sensuous existence. I give myself up to it unreservedly, and if some angular-souled utilitarian should come along and recommend me to shake off my laziness, and learn the conjugations of Coptic verbs or the hieroglyphs of Kneph and Thoth, I should not take the pipe from my mouth to answer him. My friend sometimes laughingly addresses me with two lines of Hebel's quaint Allemanic poetry:

> "Ei solch a Leben, junges Bluat,
> Desh ish wohl für a Thierle guat."

(such a life, young blood, best befits an animal), but I tell him that the wisdom of the Black Forest won't answer for the Nile. If any one persists in forcing the application, I prefer being called an animal to changing my present habits. An entire life so spent would be wretchedly aimless, but a few months are in truth "sore labor's bath" to every wrung heart and overworked brain.

I could say much more, but it requires no little effort to write three hours in a cabin, when the palms are rustling their tops outside, the larks singing in the meadows, and the odor of mimosa flowers breathing through the windows. To travel and write, is like inhaling and exhaling one's breath at the same moment. You take in impressions at every pore of the mind, and the process is so pleasant, that you sweat them out again most reluctantly. Lest I should overtake the remedy with the disease, and make to-day Labor, which should be Rest, I shall throw down the pen, and mount yonder donkey, which stands patiently on the bank, waiting to carry me to Siout once more, before starting for Thebes.

CHAPTER VIII.

UPPER EGYPT.

Calm—Mountains and Tombs—A Night Adventure in Ekhmin—Character of the Boatmen—Fair Wind—Pilgrims—Egyptian Agriculture—Sugar and Cotton—Grain—Sheep—Arrival at Kenneh—A Landscape—The Temple of Dendera—First Impressions of Egyptian Art—Portrait of Cleopatra—A Happy Meeting—We approach Thebes.

Our men were ready at the appointed time, and precisely twenty-four hours after reaching the port of Siout we spread our sails for Kenneh, and exchanged a parting salute with the boat of a New York physician, which arrived some hours after us. The north wind, which had been blowing freshly during the whole of our stay, failed us almost within sight of the port, and was followed by three days of breathless calm, during which time we made about twelve miles a day, by towing. My friend and I spent half the time on shore, wandering inland through the fields and making acquaintances in the villages. We found such tours highly interesting and refreshing, but nevertheless always returned to our floating Castle of Indolence, doubly delighted with its home-like cabin and lazy divans. Many of the villages in this region are built among the mounds of ancient cities, the names whereof are faithfully enumerated in the guide-book, but as the cities themselves have wholly disappeared, we were spared the necessity of seeking for their ruins.

On the third night after leaving Siout, we passed the village of Gow el-Kebir, the ancient Antæopolis, whose beautiful temple has been entirely destroyed during the last twenty-five years, partly washed away by the Nile and partly pulled down to furnish materials for the Pasha's palace at Siout. Near this the famous battle between Hercules and Antæus is reported to have taken place. The fable of Antæus drawing strength from the earth appears quite natural, after one has seen the fatness of the soil of Upper Egypt. We ran the gauntlet of Djebel Shekh Hereedee, a mountain similar to Aboufayda in form, but much more lofty and imposing. It has also its legend: A miraculous serpent, say the Arabs, has lived for centuries in its caverns, and possesses the power of healing diseases. All these mountains, on the eastern bank of the Nile, are pierced with tombs, and the openings are sometimes so frequent and so near to each other as to resemble a colonnade along the rocky crests. They rarely contain inscriptions, and many of them were inhabited by hermits and holy men, during the early ages of Christianity. At the most accessible points the Egyptians have commenced limestone quarries, and as they are more concerned in preserving piastres than tombs, their venerable ancestors are dislodged without scruple. Whoever is interested in Egyptian antiquities, should not postpone his visit longer. Not only Turks, but Europeans are engaged in the work of demolition, and the very antiquarians who profess the greatest enthusiasm for these monuments, are ruthless Vandals towards them when they have the power.

We dashed past the mountain of Shekh Hereedee in gallant style, and the same night, after dusk, reached Ekhmin, the ancient Panopolis. This was one of the oldest cities in Egypt, and dedicated to the Phallic worship, whose first symbol, the obelisk, has now a purely monumental significance A few remnants of this singular ancient faith appear to be retained among the modern inhabitants of Ekhmin, but only in the grossest superstitions, and without reference to the abstract creative principle typified by the Phallic emblems. The early Egyptians surrounded with mystery and honored with all religious solemnity what they regarded as the highest human miracle wrought by the power of their gods, and in a philosophical point of view, there is no branch of their complex faith more interesting than this.

As we sat on the bank in the moonlight, quietly smoking our pipes, the howling of a company of dervishes sounded from the town, whose walls are a few hundred paces distant from the river. We inquired of the guard whether a Frank dare visit them. He could not tell, but offered to accompany me and try to procure an entrance. I took Achmet and two of our sailors, donned a Bedouin capote, and set out in search of the dervishes. The principal gate of the town was closed, and my men battered it vainly with their clubs, to rouse the guard We wandered for some time among the mounds of Panopolis, stumbling over blocks of marble and granite, under palms eighty feet high, standing clear and silvery in the moonlight. At last, the clamor of the wolfish dogs we waked up on the road, brought us one of the watchers outside of the walls, whom we requested to admit us into the city. He replied that this could not be done. "But," said Achmet, "here is an Effendi who has just arrived, and must visit the mollahs to-night; admit him and fear nothing." The men thereupon conducted us to another gate and threw a few pebbles against the window above it. A woman's voice replied, and presently the bolts were undrawn and we entered. By this time the dervishes had ceased their howlings, and every thing was as still as death. We walked for half an hour through the deserted streets, visited the mosques and public buildings, and heard no sound but our own steps. It was a strangely interesting promenade. The Arabs, armed with clubs, carried a paper lantern, which flickered redly on the arches and courts we passed through. My trusty Theban walked by my side, and took all possible trouble to find the retreat of the dervishes—but in vain. We passed out through the gate, which was instantly locked behind us, and had barely reached our vessel, when the unearthly song of the Moslem priests, louder and wilder than ever, came to our ears.

The prejudice of the Mohammedans against the Christians is wearing away with their familiarity with the Frank dress and their adoption of Frankish vices. The Prophet's injunction against wine is heeded by few of his followers, or avoided by drinking *arakee*, a liquor distilled from dates and often flavored with hemp. Their conscience is generally satisfied with a pilgrimage to Mecca and the daily performance of the prescribed prayers, though the latter is often neglected. All of my sailors were very punctual in this respect, spreading their carpets on the forward deck, and occupying an hour or two every day with genuflexions, prostrations, and salutations toward Mecca, the direction of which they never lost, notwithstanding the windings of the Nile. In the cathedrals of Christian Europe I have often seen pantomimes quite as unnecessary, performed with less apparent reverence. The people of Egypt are fully as honest and well-disposed as the greater part of the Italian peasantry. They sometimes deceive in small things, and are inclined to take trifling advantages, but that is the natural result of living under a government whose only rule is force, and which does not even hesitate to use fraud. Their good humor is inexhaustible. A single friendly word wins them, and even a little severity awakes no lasting feeling of revenge. I should much rather trust myself alone among the Egyptian Fellahs, than among the peasants of the Campagna, or the boors of Carinthia. Notwithstanding our men had daily opportunities of plundering us, we never missed a single article. We frequently went ashore with our dragoman, leaving every thing in the cabin exposed, and especially such articles as tobacco, shot, dates, &c., which would most tempt an Arab, yet our confidence was never betrayed. We often heard complaints from travellers in other boats, but I am satisfied that any one who will enforce obedience at the start, and thereafter give none but just and reasonable commands, need have no difficulty with his crew.

The next morning, the wind being light, we walked forward to El Menschieh, a town about nine miles distant from Ekhmin. It was market-day, and the bazaar was crowded with the countrymen, who had brought their stock of grain, sugar-cane and vegetables. The men were taller and more muscular than in Lower Egypt, and were evidently descended from a more intelligent and energetic stock. They looked at us curiously, but with a sort of friendly interest, and courteously made way for us as we passed through the narrow bazaar. In the afternoon the wind increased to a small gale, and bore us rapidly past Gebel Tookh to the city of Girgeh, so named in Coptic times from the Christian saint, George. Like Manfalout, it has been half washed away by the Nile, and two lofty minarets were hanging on the brink of the slippery bank, awaiting their turn to fall. About twelve miles from Girgeh, in the Libyan Desert, are the ruins of Abydus, now covered by the sand, except the top of the portico and roof of the temple-palace of Sesostris, and part of the temple of Osiris. We held a council whether we should waste the favorable wind or miss Abydus, and the testimony of Achmet, who had visited the ruins, having been taken, we chose the latter alternative. By this time Girgeh was nearly out of sight, and we comforted ourselves with the hope of soon seeing Dendera.

The pilgrims to Mecca, by the Kenneh and Kosseir route, were on their return, and we met a number of boats, crowded with them, on their way to Cairo from the former place. Most of the boats carried the red flag, with the star and crescent. On the morning after leaving Girgeh, we took a long stroll through the fields of Farshoot, which is, after Siout, the richest agricultural district of Upper Egypt. An excellent system of irrigation, by means of canals, is kept up, and the result shows what might be made of Egypt, were its great natural resources rightly employed. The Nile offers a perpetual fountain of plenty and prosperity, and its long valley, from Nubia to the sea, would become, in other hands, the garden of the world. So rich and pregnant a soil I have never seen. Here, side by side, flourish wheat, maize, cotton, sugar-cane, indigo, hemp, rice, dourra, tobacco, olives, dates, oranges, and the vegetables and fruits of nearly every climate. The wheat, which, in November, we found young and green, would in March be ripe for the sickle, and the people were cutting and threshing fields of dourra, which they had planted towards the end of summer. Except where the broad meadows are first reclaimed from the rank, tufted grass which has taken possession of them, the wheat is sowed upon the ground, and then ploughed in by a sort of crooked wooden beam, shod with iron, and drawn by two camels or buffaloes. I saw no instance in which the soil was manured. The yearly deposit made by the bountiful river seems to be sufficient. The natives, it is true, possess immense numbers of pigeons, and every village is adorned with towers, rising above the mud huts like the pylons of temples, and inhabited by these birds. The manure collected from them is said to be used, but probably only in the culture of melons, cucumbers, and other like vegetables with which the gardens are stocked.

The fields of sugar-cane about Farshoot were the richest I saw in Egypt. Near the village, which is three miles from the Nile, there is a steam sugar-refinery, established by Ibrahim Pasha, who seems to have devoted much attention to the culture of cane, with a view to his own profit. There are several of these manufactories along the Nile, and the most of them were in full operation, as we passed. At Radamoon, between Minyeh and Siout, there is a large manufactory, where the common coarse sugar made in the Fellah villages is refined and sent to Cairo. We made use of this sugar in our household and found it to be of excellent quality, though coarser than that of the American manufactories. The culture of cotton has not been so successful. The large and handsome manufactory built at Kenneh, is no longer in operation, and the fields which we saw there, had a forlorn, neglected appearance. The plants grow luxuriantly, and the cotton is of fine quality, but the pods are small and not very abundant. About Siout, and in Middle and Lower Egypt, we saw many fields of indigo, which is said to thrive well. Peas, beans and lentils are cultivated to a great extent, and form an important item of the food of the inhabitants. The only vegetables we could procure for our kitchen, were onions, radishes, lettuce and spinage. The Arabs are very fond of the tops of radishes, and eat them with as much relish as their donkeys.

One of the principal staples of Egypt is the dourra (*holcus sorghum*), which resembles the *zea* (maize) in many respects In appearance, it is very like broom-corn, but instead of the long, loose panicle of red seeds, is topped by a compact cone of grains, smaller than those of maize, but resembling them in form and taste. The stalks are from ten to fifteen feet high, and the heads frequently contain as much substance as two ears of maize. It is planted in close rows, and when ripe is cut by the hand with a short sickle, after which the heads are taken off and threshed separately. The grain is fed to horses, donkeys and fowls, and in Upper Egypt is used almost universally for bread. It is of course very imperfectly ground, and unbolted, and the bread is coarse and dark, though nourishing. In the Middle and Southern States of America this grain would thrive well and might be introduced with advantage.

The plains of coarse, wiry grass (*halfeh*), which in many points on the Nile show plainly the neglect of the inhabitants, who by a year's labor might convert them into blooming fields, are devoted to the pasturage of large herds of sheep, and goats, and sometimes droves of buffaloes. The sheep are all black or dark-brown, and their bushy heads remind one of terriers. The wool is rather coarse, and when roughly spun and woven by the Arabs, in its natural color, forms the mantle, something like a Spanish *poncho*, which is usually the Fellah's only garment. The mutton, almost the only meat to be found, is generally lean, and brings a high price, considering the abundance of sheep. The flesh of buffaloes is eaten by the Arabs, but is too tough, and has too rank a flavor, for Christian stomachs. The goats are beautiful animals, with heads as slender and delicate as those of gazelles. They have short, black horns, curving downward—long, silky ears, and a peculiarly mild and friendly expression of countenance. We had no difficulty in procuring milk in the villages, and sometimes fresh butter, which was more agreeable to the taste than the sight. The mode of churning is not calculated to excite one's appetite. The milk is tied up in a goat's skin, and suspended by a rope to the branch of a tree. One of the Arab housewives (who are all astonishingly ugly and filthy) then stations herself on one side, and propels it backward and forward till the process is completed. The cheese of the country resembles a mixture of sand and slacked lime, and has an abominable flavor.

Leaving Farshoot, we swept rapidly past Haou, the ancient *Diospolis parva*, or Little Thebes, of which nothing is left but some heaps of dirt, sculptured fragments, and the tomb of a certain Dionysius, son of a certain Ptolemy. The course of the mountains, which follow the Nile, is here nearly east and west, as the river makes a long curve to the eastward on approaching Kenneh. The valley is inclosed within narrower bounds, and the Arabian Mountains on the north, shooting out into bold promontories from the main chain, sometimes rise from the water's edge in bluffs many hundred feet in height. The good wind, which had so befriended us for three days, followed us all night, and when we awoke on the morning of December 4th, our vessel lay at anchor in the port of Kenneh, having beaten by four hours the boat of our American friend, which was reputed to be one of the swiftest on the river.

Kenneh, which lies about a mile east of the river, is celebrated for the manufacture of porous water-jars, and is an inferior mart of trade with Persia and India, by means of Kosseir, on the Red Sea, one hundred and twenty miles distant. The town is large, but mean in aspect, and does not offer a single object of interest. It lies in the centre of a broad plain. We rode through the bazaars, which were tolerably well stocked and crowded with *hadji*, or pilgrims of Mecca. My friend, who wished to make a flag of the Saxe-Coburg colors, for his return voyage, tried in vain to procure a piece of green cotton cloth. Every other color was to be had but green, which, as the sacred hue, worn only by the descendants of Mohammed, was nowhere to be found. He was finally obliged to buy a piece of white stuff and have it specially dyed. It came back the same evening, precisely the color of the Shereef of Mecca's turban.

On the western bank of the Nile, opposite Kenneh, is the site of the city of Tentyra, famed for its temple of Athor. It is now called Dendera, from the modern Arab village. After breakfast, we shipped ourselves and our donkeys across the Nile, and rode off in high excitement, to make our first acquaintance with Egyptian temples The path led through a palm grove, which in richness and beauty rivalled those of the

Mexican *tierra caliente.* The lofty shafts of the date and the vaulted foliage of the doum-palm, blended in the most picturesque groupage, contrasted with the lace-like texture of the flowering mimosa, and the cloudy boughs of a kind of gray cypress. The turf under the trees was soft and green, and between the slim trunks we looked over the plain, to the Libyan Mountains—a long train of rosy lights and violet shadows. Out of this lovely wood we passed between magnificent fields of dourra and the castor-oil bean, fifteen feet in height, to a dyke which crossed the meadows to Dendera. The leagues of rank grass on our right rolled away to the Desert in shining billows, and the fresh west-wind wrapped us in a bath of intoxicating odors. In the midst of this green and peaceful plain rose the earthy mounds of Tentyra, and the portico of the temple, almost buried beneath them, stood like a beacon, marking the boundary of the Desert.

We galloped our little animals along the dyke, over heaps of dirt and broken bricks, among which a number of Arabs were burrowing for nitrous earth, and dismounted at a small pylon, which stands two or three hundred paces in front of the temple. The huge jambs of sandstone, covered with sharply cut hieroglyphics and figures of the Egyptian gods, and surmounted by a single block, bearing the mysterious winged globe and serpent, detained us but a moment, and we hurried down what was once the dromos of the temple, now represented by a double wall of unburnt bricks. The portico, more than a hundred feet in length, and supported by six columns, united by screens of masonry, no stone of which, or of the columns themselves, is unsculptured, is massive and imposing, but struck me as being too depressed to produce a very grand effect. What was my astonishment, on arriving at the entrance, to find that I had approached the temple on a level with half its height, and that the pavement of the portico was as far below as the scrolls of its cornice were above me. The six columns I had seen covered three other rows, of six each, all adorned with the most elaborate sculpture and exhibiting traces of the brilliant coloring which they once possessed. The entire temple, which is in an excellent state of preservation, except where the hand of the Coptic Christian has defaced its sculptures, was cleaned out by order of Mohammed Ali, and as all its chambers, as well as the roof of enormous sand-stone blocks, are entire, it is considered one of the most complete relics of Egyptian art.

I find my pen at fault, when I attempt to describe the impression produced by the splendid portico. The twenty-four columns, each of which is sixty feet in height, and eight feet in diameter, crowded upon a surface of one hundred feet by seventy, are oppressive in their grandeur. The dim light, admitted through the half closed front, which faces the north, spreads a mysterious gloom around these mighty shafts, crowned with the fourfold visage of Athor, still rebuking the impious hands that have marred her solemn beauty. On the walls, between columns of hieroglyphics, and the cartouches of the Cæsars and the Ptolemies, appear the principal Egyptian deities—the rigid Osiris, the stately Isis and the hawk-headed Orus. Around the bases of the columns spring the leaves of the sacred lotus, and the dark-blue ceiling is spangled with stars, between the wings of the divine emblem. The sculptures are all in raised relief, and there is no stone in the temple without them. I cannot explain to myself the unusual emotion I felt while contemplating this wonderful combination of a simple and sublime architectural style with the utmost elaboration of ornament. My blood pulsed fast and warm on my first view of the Roman Forum, but in Dendera I was so saddened and oppressed, that I scarcely dared speak for fear of betraying an unmanly weakness. My friend walked silently between the columns, with a face as rigidly sad as if he had just looked on the coffin of his nearest relative. Though such a mood was more painful than agreeable, it required some effort to leave the place, and after a stay of two hours, we still lingered in the portico and walked through the inner halls, under the spell of a fascination which we had hardly power to break.

The portico opens into a hall, supported by six beautiful columns, of smaller proportions, and lighted by a square aperture in the solid roof. On either side are chambers connected with dim and lofty passages, and beyond is the sanctuary and various other apartments, which receive no light from without. We examined their sculptures by the aid of torches, and our Arab attendants kindled large fires of dry corn stalks, which cast a strong red light on the walls. The temple is devoted to Athor, the Egyptian Venus, and her image is everywhere seen, receiving the homage of her worshippers. Even the dark staircase, leading to the roof—up which we climbed over heaps of sand and rubbish—is decorated throughout with processions of symbolical figures. The drawing has little of that grotesque stiffness which I expected to find in Egyptian sculptures, and the execution is so admirable in its gradations of light and shade, as to resemble, at a little distance, a monochromatic painting. The antiquarians view these remains with little interest, as they date from the comparatively recent era of the Ptolemies, at which time sculpture and architecture were on the decline. We, who had seen nothing else of the kind, were charmed with the grace and elegance of this sumptuous mode of decoration. Part of the temple was built by Cleopatra, whose portrait, with that of her son Cæsarion, may still be seen on the exterior wall. The face of the colossal figure has been nearly destroyed, but there is a smaller one, whose soft, voluptuous outline is still sufficient evidence of the justness of her renown. The profile is exquisitely beautiful. The forehead and nose approach the Greek standard, but the mouth is more roundly and delicately curved, and the chin and cheek are fuller. Were such an outline made plastic, were the blank face colored with a pale olive hue, through which should blush a faint, rosy tinge, lighted with bold black eyes and irradiated with the lightning of a passionate nature, it would even now 'move the mighty hearts of captains and of kings."

Around the temple and over the mounds of the ancient city are scattered the ruins of an Arab village which the inhabitants suddenly deserted, without any apparent reason, two or three years previous to our visit. Behind it, stretches the yellow sand of the Desert. The silence and aspect of desertion harmonize well with the spirit of the place, which would be much disturbed were one beset, as is usual in the Arab towns, by a gang of naked beggars and barking wolf-dogs. Besides the temple, there are also the remains of a chapel of Isis, with a pylon, erected by Augustus Cæsar, and a small temple, nearly whelmed in the sand, supposed to be one of the *mammeisi*, or lying-in houses of the goddess Athor, who was honored in this form, on account of having given birth to the third member of the divine Triad.

At sunset, we rode back from Dendera and set sail for

Thebes. In the evening, as we were sweeping along by moonlight, with a full wind, a large *dahabiyeh* came floating down the stream. Achmet, who was on the look-out, saw the American flag, and we hailed her. My delight was unbounded, to hear in reply the voice of my friend, Mr. Degen, of New York, who, with his lady and two American and English gentlemen, were returning from a voyage to Assouan. Both boats instantly made for the shore, and for the first time since leaving Germany I had the pleasure of seeing familiar faces. For the space of three hours I forgot Thebes and the north wind, but towards midnight we exchanged a parting salute of four guns and shook out the broad sails of the Cleopatra, who leaned her cheek to the waves and shot off like a sea-gull. I am sure she must have looked beautiful to my friends, as they stood on deck in the moonlight.

CHAPTER IX.

THEBES—THE WESTERN BANK.

Arrival at Thebes—Ground-Plan of the Remains—We Cross to the Western Bank—Guides—The Temple of Goorneh—Valley of the Kings' Tombs—Belzoni's Tomb—The Races of Men—Vandalism of Antiquarians—Bruce's Tomb—Memnon—The Grandfather of Sesostris—The Head of Amunoph—The Colossi of the Plain—Memnonian Music—The Statue of Remeses—The Memnonium—Beauty of Egyptian Art—More Scrambles among the Tombs—The Bats of the Assasseef—Medeenet Abou—Sculptured Histories—The Great Court of the Temple—We return to Luxor.

On the following evening, about nine o'clock, as my friend and I were taking our customary evening pipe in the cabin, our vessel suddenly stopped. The wind was still blowing, and I called to Achmet to know what was the matter. "We have reached Luxor," answered the Theban. We dropped the she-books, dashed out, up the bank, and saw, facing us in the brilliant moonlight, the grand colonnade of the temple, the solid wedges of the pylon, and the brother-obelisk of that which stands in the Place de la Concorde, in Paris. The wide plain of Thebes stretched away on either hand, and the beautiful outlines of the three mountain ranges which inclose it, rose in the distance against the stars. We looked on the landscape a few moments, in silence. "Come," said my friend, at length, "this is enough for to-night. Let us not be too hasty to exhaust what is in store for us." So we returned to our cabin, closed the blinds, and arranged our plans for best seeing, and best enjoying the wonders of the great Diospolis.

Before commencing my recital, let me attempt to give an outline of the typography of Thebes. The course of the Nile is here nearly north, dividing the site of the ancient city into two almost equal parts. On approaching it from Kenneh, the mountain of Goorneh, which abuts on the river, marks the commencement of the western division. This mountain, a range of naked limestone crags, terminating in a pyramidal peak, gradually recedes to the distance of three miles from the Nile, which it again approaches further south. Nearly the whole of the curve, which might be called the western wall of the city, is pierced with tombs, among which are those of the queens, and the grand priestly vaults of the Assasseef. The Valley of the Kings' Tombs lies deep in the heart of the range seven or eight miles from the river. After passing the corner of the mountain, the first ruin on the western bank is that of the temple-palace of Goorneh. More than a mile further, at the base of the mountain, is the Memnonium, or temple of Remeses the Great, between which and the Nile the two Memnonian colossi are seated on the plain. Nearly two miles to the south of this is the great temple of Medeenet Abou, and the fragments of other edifices are met with, still further beyond. On the eastern bank, nearly opposite Goorneh, stands the temple of Karnak, about half a mile from the river. Eight miles eastward, at the foot of the Arabian Mountains, is the small temple of Medamot, which, however, does not appear to have been included in the limits of Thebes. Luxor is directly on the bank of the Nile, a mile and a half south of

Karnak, and the plain extends several miles beyond it, before reaching the isolated range, whose three conical peaks are the landmarks of Thebes to voyagers on the river.

These distances convey an idea of the extent of the ancient city, but fail to represent the grand proportions of the land scape, so well fitted, in its simple and majestic outlines, to inclose the most wonderful structures the world has ever seen. The green expanse of the plain; the airy coloring of the mountains; the mild, solemn blue of the cloudless Egyptian sky;—these are a part of Thebes, and inseparable from the remembrance of its ruins.

At sunrise we crossed to the western bank and moored our boat opposite Goorneh. It is advisable to commence with the Tombs, and close the inspection of that side with Medeenet Abou, reserving Karnak, the grandest of all, for the last. The most unimportant objects in Thebes are full of interest when seen first, whereas Karnak, once seen, fills one's thoughts to the exclusion of every thing else. There are Arab guides for each bank, who are quite familiar with all the principal points, and who have a quiet and unobtrusive way of directing the traveller, which I should be glad to see introduced into England and Italy. Our guide, old Achmet Gourgàr, was a tall, lean gray-beard, who wore a white turban and long brown robe, and was most conscientious in his endeavors to satisfy us. We found several horses on the bank, ready saddled, and choosing two of the most promising, set off on a stirring gallop for the temple of Goorneh and the Valley of the Kings' Tombs, leaving Achmet to follow with our breakfast, and the Arab boys with their water bottles.

The temple of Goorneh was built for the worship of Amun,

the Theban Jupiter, by Osirei and his son, Remeses the Great, the supposed Sesostris, nearly fourteen hundred years before the Christian era. It is small, compared with the other ruins, but interesting from its rude and massive style, a remnant of the early period of Egyptian architecture. The two pylons in front of it are shattered down, and the dromos of sphinxes has entirely disappeared. The portico is supported by a single row of ten columns, which neither resemble each other, nor are separated by equal spaces. What is most singular, is the fact that notwithstanding this disproportion, which is also observable in the doorways, the general effect is harmonious. We tried to fathom the secret of this, and found no other explanation than in the lowness of the building, and the rough granite blocks of which it is built. One seeks no proportion in a natural temple of rock, or a cirque of Druid stones. All that the eye requires is rude strength, with a certain approach to order. The effect produced by this temple is of a similar character, barring its historical interest. Its dimensions are too small to be imposing, and I found, after passing it several times, that I valued it more as a feature in the landscape, than for its own sake.

The sand and pebbles clattered under the hoofs of our horses, as we galloped up the gorge of *Biban el Molook*, the "Gates of the Kings." The sides are perpendicular cliffs of yellow rock, which increased in height, the further we advanced, and at last terminated in a sort of basin, shut in by precipices several hundred feet in height and broken into fantastic turrets, gables and pinnacles. The bottom is filled with huge heaps of sand and broken stones, left from the excavation of the tombs in the solid rock. There are twenty-one tombs in this valley, more than half of which are of great extent and richly adorned with paintings and sculptures. Some have been filled with sand or otherwise injured by the occasional rains which visit this region, while a few are too small and plain to need visiting. Sir Gardner Wilkinson has numbered them all in red chalk at the entrances, which is very convenient to those who use his work on Egypt as a guide. I visited ten of the principal tombs, to the great delight of the old guide, who complained that travellers are frequently satisfied with four or five. The general arrangement is the same in all, but they differ greatly in extent and in the character of their decoration.

The first we entered was the celebrated tomb of Remeses I., discovered by Belzoni. From the narrow entrance, a precipitous staircase, the walls of which are covered with columns of hieroglyphics, descends to a depth of forty feet, where it strikes a horizontal passage leading to an oblong chamber, in which was formerly a deep pit, which Belzoni filled. This pit protected the entrance to the royal chamber, which was also carefully walled up. In the grace and freedom of the drawings, and the richness of their coloring, this tomb surpasses all others. The subjects represented are the victories of the monarch, while in the sepulchral chamber he is received into the presence of the gods. The limestone rock is covered with a fine coating of plaster, on which the figures were first drawn with red chalk, and afterwards carefully finished in colors. The reds, yellows, greens and blues are very brilliant, but seem to have been employed at random, the gods having faces sometimes of one color, sometimes of another. In the furthest chamber, which was left unfinished, the subjects are only sketched in red chalk. Some of them have the loose and uncertain lines of a pupil's hand, over which one sees the bold and rapid corrections of the master. Many of the figures are remarkable for their strength and freedom of outline. I was greatly interested in a procession of men, representing the different nations of the earth. The physical peculiarities of the Persian, the Jew and the Ethiopian are therein as distinctly marked as at the present day. The blacks are perfect counterparts of those I saw daily upon the Nile, and the noses of the Jews seem newly painted from originals in New York. So little diversity in the distinguishing features of the race, after the lapse of more than three thousand years, is a strong argument in favor of the new ethnological theory of the separate origin of different races. Whatever objections may be urged against this theory, the fact that the races have not materially changed since the earliest historic times, is established by these Egyptian records, and we must either place the first appearance of Man upon the earth many thousands of years in advance of Bishop Usher's chronology, or adopt the conclusion of Morton and Agassiz.

The burial-vault, where Belzoni found the alabaster sarcophagus of the monarch, is a noble hall, thirty feet long by nearly twenty in breadth and height, with four massive pillars forming a corridor on one side. In addition to the light of our torches, the Arabs kindled a large bonfire in the centre, which brought out in strong relief the sepulchral figures on the ceiling, painted in white on a ground of dark indigo hue. The pillars and walls of the vault glowed with the vivid variety of their colors, and the general effect was unspeakably rich and gorgeous. This tomb has already fallen a prey to worse plunderers than the Medes and Persians. Belzoni carried off the sarcophagus, Champollion cut away the splendid jambs and architrave of the entrance to the lower chambers, and Lepsius has finished by splitting the pillars and appropriating their beautiful paintings for the Museum at Berlin. At one spot, where the latter has totally ruined a fine doorway, some indignant Frenchman has written in red chalk: "*Meurtre commis par Lepsius.*" In all the tombs of Thebes, wherever you see the most flagrant and shameless spoliations, the guide says, "Lepsius." Who can blame the Arabs for wantonly defacing these precious monuments, when such an example is set them by the vanity of European antiquarians?

Bruce's Tomb, which extends for four hundred and twenty feet into the rock, is larger than Belzoni's, but not so fresh and brilliant. The main entrance slopes with a very gradual descent, and has on each side a number of small chambers and niches, apparently for mummies. The illustrations in these chambers are somewhat defaced, but very curious, on account of the light which they throw upon the domestic life of the Ancient Egyptians. They represent the slaughtering of oxen, the preparation of fowls for the table, the kneading and baking of bread and cakes, as well as the implements and utensils of the kitchen. In other places the field laborers are employed in leading the water of the Nile into canals, cutting dourra, threshing and carrying the grain into magazines. One room is filled with furniture, and the row of chairs around the base of the walls would not be out of place in the most elegant modern drawing-room. The Illustrated Catalogue of the London Exhibition contains few richer and more graceful patterns. In a chamber nearer the royal vault, two old, blind minstrels are seen, playing the harp in the presence of the King, whence this is sometimes called the Harper's Tomb. The pillars of the grand hall, like those of all the other tombs we visited, represent the monarch, after death, received into the presence of the gods—stately figures, with a calm and serious aspect, and lips, which, like those of the Sphinx, seemed closed upon some awful mystery. The absurdity of the coloring does not destroy this effect, and a blue-faced Isis, whose hard, black eye-ball stares from a brilliant white socket, is not less impressive than the same figure, cut in sandstone or granite.

The delicacy and precision of the hieroglyphics, sculptured in intaglio, filled me with astonishment. In the tomb of Amunoph III., which I visited the next day, they resembled the ciphers engraved upon seals in their exquisite sharpness and regularity. Only the principal tombs, however, are thus beautified. In others the figures are either simply painted, or apparently sunken in the plaster, while it was yet fresh, by prepared patterns. The latter method accounts for the exact resemblance of long processions of figures, which would otherwise require a most marvellous skill on the part of the artist. In some unfinished chambers I detected plainly the traces of these patterns, where the outlines of the figures were blunt and the grain of the plaster bent, and not cut. The family likeness in the faces of the monarchs is also too striking, unfortunately, for us to accept them all as faithful portraits. They are all apparently of the same age, and their attributes do not materially differ. This was probably a flattery on the part of the artists, or the effect of a royal vanity, which required to be portrayed in the freshness of youth and the full vigor of body and mind. The first faces I learned to recognize were those of Remeses II., the supposed Sesostris, and Amunoph III.

The tomb of Memnon, as it was called by the Romans, is the most elegant of all, in its proportions, and is as symmetrical as a Grecian temple. On the walls of the entrance are several inscriptions of Greek tourists, who visited it in the era of the Ptolemies, and spent their time in carving their names, like Americans nowadays. The huge granite sarcophagus in which the monarch's mummy was deposited, is broken, as are those of the other tombs, with a single exception. This is the tomb of Osirei I., the grandfather of Sesostris, and the oldest in the valley. I visited it by crawling through a hole barely large enough to admit my body, after which I slid on my back down a passage nearly choked with sand, to another hole, opening into the burial chamber. Here no impious hand had defaced the walls, but the figures were as perfect and the coloring as brilliant as when first executed. In the centre stood an immense sarcophagus, of a single block of red granite, and the massive lid, which had been thrown off, lay beside it. The dust in the bottom gave out that peculiar mummy odor perceptible in all the tombs, and in fact long after one has left them, for the clothes become saturated with it. The guide, delighted with having dragged me into that chamber, buried deep in the dumb heart of the mountain, said not a word, and from the awful stillness of the place and the phantasmagoric gleam of the wonderful figures on the walls, I could have imagined myself a neophyte, on the threshold of the Osirian mysteries.

We rode to the Western Valley, a still deeper and wider glen, containing tombs of the kings of the foreign dynasty of Atin-Re. We entered the two principal ones, but found the paintings rude and insignificant. There are many lateral passages and chambers and in some places deep pits, along the edge of which we were obliged to craw.. In the last tomb a very long and steep staircase descends into the rock. As we were groping after the guide, I called to my friend to take care, as there was but a single step, after making a slip. The words were scarcely out of my mouth before I felt a tremendous thump, followed by a number of smaller ones, and found myself sitting in a heap of sand, at the bottom, some twenty or thirty feet below. Fortunately, I came off with but a few sligh bruises.

Returning to the temple of Goorneh, we took a path over the plain, through fields of wheat, lupins and lentils, to the two colossi, which we had already seen from a distance. These immense sitting figures, fifty-three feet above the plain, which has buried their pedestals, overlook the site of vanished Thebes and assert the grandeur of which they and Karnak are the most striking remains. They were erected by Amunoph III., and though the faces are totally disfigured, the full, round, beautiful proportions of the colossal arms, shoulders and thighs do not belie the marvellous sweetness of the features which we still see in his tomb. Except the head of Antinous, I know of no ancient portrait so beautiful as Amunoph. The long and luxuriant hair, flowing in a hundred ringlets, the soft grace of the forehead, the mild serenity of the eye, the fine thin lines of the nostrils and the feminine tenderness of the full lips, triumph over the cramped rigidity of Egyptian sculpture, and charm you with the lightness and harmony of Greek art. In looking on that head, I cannot help thinking that the subject overpowered the artist, and led him to the threshold of a truer art. Amunoph, or Memnon, was a poet in soul, and it was meet that his statue should salute the rising sun with a sound like that of a harp-string.

Modern research has wholly annihilated this beautiful fable. Memnon now sounds at all hours of the day, and at the command of all travellers who pay an Arab five piastres to climb into his lap. We engaged a vender of modern scarabei, who threw off his garments, hooked his fingers and toes into the cracks of the polished granite, and soon hailed us with "Salaam!" from the knee of the statue. There is a certain stone on Memnon's lap, which, when sharply struck, gives out a clear metallic ring. Behind it is a small square aperture, invisible from below, where one of the priests no doubt stationed himself to perform the daily miracle. Our Arab rapped on the arms and body of the statue, which had the usual dead sound of stone, and rendered the musical ring of the sun-smitten block more striking. An avenue of sphinxes once led from the colossi to a grand temple, the foundations of which we found about a quarter of a mile distant. On the way are the fragments of two other colossi, one of black granite. The enormous substructions of the temple and the pedestals of its columns have been sufficiently excavated to show what a superb edifice has been lost to the world. A crowd of troublesome Arabs, thrusting upon our attention newly baken cinerary urns newly roasted antique wheat, and images of all kinds fresh from the maker's hand, disturbed our quiet examination of the ruins, and in order to escape their importunities, we rode to the Memnonium.

This edifice, the temple-palace of Remeses the Great, is supposed to be the Memnonium, described by Strabo. It is built on a gentle rise of land at the foot of the mountain, and looks eastward to the Nile and Luxor. The grand stone pylon, which stands at the entrance of its former avenue of sphinxes has been half levelled by the fury of the Persian conquerors, and the colossal granite statue of Remeses, in the first court of the temple, now lies in enormous fragments around its pedestal. Mere dimensions give no idea of this immense mass, the weight of which, when entire, was nearly nine hundred tons. How poor and trifling appear the modern statues which we call colossal, when measured with this, one of whose toes is a yard in length; and how futile the appliances of modern art, when directed to its transportation for a distance of one hundred and fifty miles! The architrave at each end of the court was upheld by four caryatides, thirty feet in height. Though much defaced, they are still standing, but are dwarfed by the mighty limbs of Remeses. It is difficult to account for the means by which the colossus was broken. There are no marks of any instruments which could have forced such a mass asunder, and the only plausible conjecture I have heard is, that the stone must have been subjected to an intense heat and afterwards to the action of water. The statue, in its sitting position, must have been nearly sixty feet in height, and is the largest in the world, though not so high as the rock-hewn monoliths of Aboo-Simbel. The Turks and Arabs have cut several mill-stones out of its head, without any apparent diminution of its size.

The Memnonium differs from the other temples of Egypt in being almost faultless in its symmetry, even when measured by the strictest rules of art. I know of nothing so exquisite as the central colonnade of its grand hall—a double row of pillars, forty-five feet in height and twenty-three in circumference, crowned with capitals resembling the bell-shaped blossoms of the lotus. One must see them to comprehend how this simple form, whose expression is all sweetness and tenderness in the flower, softens and beautifies the solid majesty of the shaft. In spite of their colossal proportions, there is nothing massive or heavy in their aspect. The cup of the capital curves gently outward from the abacus on which the architrave rests, and seems the natural blossom of the columnar stem. On either side of this perfect colonnade are four rows of Osiride pillars, of smaller size, yet the variety of their form and proportions only enhances the harmony of the whole. This is one of those enigmas in architecture which puzzle one on his first acquaintance with Egyptian temples, and which he is often forced blindly to accept as new laws of art, because his feeling tells him they are true, and his reason cannot satisfactorily demonstrate that they are false.

We waited till the yellow rays of sunset fell on the capitals of the Memnonium, and they seemed, like the lotus flowers, to exhale a vapory light, before we rode home. All night we wandered in dreams through kingly vaults, with starry ceilings and illuminated walls; but on looking out of our windows at dawn, we saw the red saddle-cloths of our horses against the dark background of the palm grove, as they came down to the boat. No second nap was possible, after such a sight, and many minutes had not elapsed before we were tasting the cool morning air in the delight of a race up and down the shore. Our old guide, however, was on his donkey betimes, and called us off to our duty. We passed Goorneh, and ascended the eastern face of the mountain to the tombs of the priests and private citizens of Thebes. For miles along the mountain side, one sees nothing but heaps of sand and rubbish, with here and there an Arab hut, built against the face of a tomb whose chambers serve as pigeon-houses, and stalls for asses The earth is filled with fragments of mummies, and the bandages in which they were wrapped; for even the sanctity of death itself, is here neither respected by the Arabs nor the Europeans whom they imitate. I cannot conceive the passion which some travellers have, of carrying away withered hands and fleshless legs, and disfiguring the abodes of the dead with their insignificant names. I should as soon think of carving my initials on the back of a live Arab, as on these venerable monuments.

The first tomb we entered almost cured us of the desire to visit another. It was that called the Assasseef, built by a wealthy priest, and it is the largest in Thebes. Its outer court measures one hundred and three by seventy-six feet, and its passages extend between eight and nine hundred feet into the mountain. We groped our way between walls as black as ink, through long, labyrinthine suites of chambers, breathing a deathlike and oppressive odor. The stairways seemed tc lead into the bowels of the earth, and on either hand yawnea pits of uncertain depth. As we advanced, the ghostly vaults rumbled with a sound like thunder, and hundreds of noisome bats, scared by the light, dashed against the walls and dropped at our feet. We endured this for a little while, but on reaching the entrance to some darker and deeper mystery, were so surrounded by the animals, who struck their filthy wings against our faces, that not for ten kings' tombs would we have gone a step further. My friend was on the point of vowing never to set his foot in another tomb, but I persuaded him to wait until we had seen that of Amunoph. I followed the guide, who enticed me by flattering promises into a great many snakelike holes, and when he was tired with crawling in the dust, sent one of our water-carriers in advance, who dragged me in and out by the heels.

The temple of Medeenet Abou is almost concealed by the ruins of a Coptic village, among which it stands, and by which it is partially buried. The outer court, pylon and main hall of the smaller temple rise above the mounds and overlook the plain of Thebes, but scarcely satisfy the expectation of the traveller, as he approaches. You first enter an inclosure surrounded by a low stone wall, and standing in advance of the pylon. The rear wall, facing the entrance, contains two single pillars, with bell-shaped capitals, which rise above it and stand like guards before the doorway of the pylon. Here was another enigma for us. Who among modern architects would dare to plant two single pillars before a pyramidal gateway of solid masonry, and then inclose them in a plain wall, rising to half their height? Yet here the symmetry of the shafts is not injured by the wall in which they stand, nor oppressed by the ponderous bulk of the pylon. On the contrary, the light columns and spreading capitals, like a tuft of wild roses hanging from the crevice of a rock, brighten the rude strength of the masses of stone with a gleam of singular loveliness. What would otherwise only impress you by its size, now endears itself to you by its beauty. Is this the effect of chance, or the result of a finer art than that which flourishes in our day? I will not pretend to determine, but I must confess that Egypt, in whose ruins I had expected to find only a sort of barbaric grandeur, has given me a new insight into that vital Beauty which is the soul of true Art.

We devoted little time to the ruined court and sanctuaries

which follow the pylon, and to the lodges of the main temple standing beside them like watch-towers, three stories in height. The majestic pylon of the great temple of Remeses III. rose behind them, out of heaps of pottery and unburnt bricks, and the colossal figure of the monarch in his car, borne by two horses into the midst of the routed enemy, attracted us from a distance. We followed the exterior wall of the temple, for its whole length of more than six hundred feet, reading the sculptured history of his conquests. The entire outer wall of the temple presents a series of gigantic cartoons, cut in the blocks of sandstone, of which it is built. Remeses is always the central figure, distinguished from subjects and foes no less by his superior stature than by the royal emblems which accompany him. Here we see heralds sounding the trumpet in advance of his car, while his troops pass in review before him; there, with a lion walking by his side, he sets out on his work of conquest. His soldiers storm a town, and we see them climbing the wall with ladders, while a desperâte hand-to-hand conflict is going on below. In another place, he has alighted from his chariot and stands with his foot on the neck of a slaughtered king. Again, his vessels attack a hostile navy on the sea. One of the foreign craft becomes entangled and is capsized, yet while his spearmen hurl their weapons among the dismayed enemy, the sailors rescue those who are struggling in the flood. After we have passed through these stiange and stirring pictures, we find the monarch reposing on his throne, while his soldiers deposit before him the hands of the slaughtered, and his scribes present to him lists of their numbers, and his generals lead tc him long processions of fettered captives. Again, he is represented as offering a group of subject kings to Amun, the Theban Jupiter, who says to him: "Go, my cherished and chosen, make war on foreign nations, besiege their forts and carry off their people to live as captives." On the front wall, he holds in his grasp the hands of a dozen monarchs, while with the other hand he raises his sword to destroy them. Their faces express the very extreme of grief and misery, but he is cold and calm as Fate itself.

We slid down the piles of sand and entered by a side-door into the grand hall of the temple. Here, as at Dendera, a surprise awaited us. We stood on the pavement of a magnificent court, about one hundred and thirty feet square, around which ran a colonnade of pillars, eight feet square and forty feet high. On the western side is an inner row of circular columns, twenty-four feet in circumference, with capitals representing the papyrus blossom. The entire court, with its walls, pillars and doorways, is covered with splendid sculptures and traces of paint, and the ceiling is blue as the noonday sky, and studded with stars. Against each of the square columns facing the court once stood a colossal caryatid, upholding the architrave of another colonnade of granite shafts, nearly all of which have been thrown from their bases and lie shivered on the pavement. This court opens towards the pylon into another of similar dimensions, but buried almost to the capitals of its columns in heaps of rubbish. The character of the temple is totally different from that of every other in Egypt. Its height is small in proportion to its great extent, and it therefore loses the airy lightness of the Memnonium and the impressive grandeur of Dendera. Its expression is that of a massive magnificence, if I may use such a doubtful compound: no single epithet suffices to describe it.

With Medeenet Abou finished our survey of the western division of Thebes—two long days of such experience as the contemplation of a lifetime cannot exhaust. At sunset we took advantage of the wind, parted from our grooms and water-carriers, who wished to accompany me to Khartoum, and crossed the Nile to Luxor.

CHAPTER X.

THE ALMEHS, LUXOR AND KARNAK.

The Dancing Girls of Egypt—A Night Scene in Luxor—The Orange-Blossom and the Apple-Blossom—The Beautiful Bemba—The Dance—Performance of the Apple Blossom—The Temple of Luxor—A Mohammedan School—Gallop to Karnak—View of the Ruins—The Great Hall of Pillars—Bedouin Diversions—A Night Ride—Karnak under the Full Moon—Farewell to Thebes.

Two days in the tombs of the Kings and the temples of the Remesides and the Osirei exhausted us more thoroughly than a week of hard labor. In addition to the natural and exciting emotion, with which we contemplated those remains, and which we would not have repressed, if we could, we puzzled ourselves with the secrets of Egyptian architecture and the mysteries of Egyptian faith. Those pregnant days were followed by sleepless nights, and we reached Luxor at sunset with a certain dread of the morrow. Our mental nerves were too tensely strung, and we felt severely the want of some relaxation of an opposite character. The course which we adopted to freshen our minds for Karnak may strike a novice as singular, but it was most effectual, and can be explained on the truest philosophical principles.

In the afternoon Achmet had informed us that two of the celebrated Almehs, or dancing-women of the East, who had been banished to Esneh, were in Luxor, and recommended us to witness their performance. This was a welcome proposition, and the matter was soon arranged. Our raïs procured a large room, had it cleared, engaged the performers and musicians, and took the cushions of our cabin to make us a stately seat. If one should engage Castle Garden, and hire a company of ballet-dancers to perform for his special amusement, the fact would shake the pillars of New-York society, and as it was, I can think of some very good friends who will condemn our proceeding as indiscreet, and unworthy the serious aims of travel. As I have no apology to make to myself, I need make none to them, except to suggest that the first end of travel is instruction, and that the traveller is fully justified in pursuing this end, so long as he neither injures himself nor others.

About eight o'clock, accompanied by Achmet, our Theban guide, the raïs of our vessel, and our favorite sailor, Ali, we set out for the rendezvous. Ali was the most gentleman-like Fellah I ever saw. His appearance was always neat and orderly, but on this particular evening his white turban was sprucer than ever, and his blue mantle hung as gracefully on his shoulders as the cloak of a Spanish grandee. He followed behind us, rejoicingly bearing the shebooks, as we walked under the moonlit columns of Luxor. We passed around the corner of the temple and ascended a flight of stone steps, to one of the upper chambers. It was a room about thirty feet long by fifteen wide, with a roof of palm-logs, covered with thatch. The floor rested on the ceiling of the ancient sanctuary. Our boat-lanterns of oiled paper were already suspended from the roof, and a few candles, stuck in empty bottles, completed the illumination.

We were politely received and conducted to the divan

formed impromptu of a large *cafass*, or hen-coop, covered with a carpet and cushions. We seated ourselves upon it, with legs crossed Moslem-wise, while our attendants ranged themselves on the floor on the left, and Ali stood on the right, ready to replenish the pipes. Opposite to us sat the two Almehs, with four attendant dancers, and three female singers, and beside them the music, consisting of two drums, a tambourine, and a squeaking Arab violin. Our crew, shining in white turbans, were ranged near the door, with a number of invited guests, so that the whole company amounted to upwards of forty persons. On our entrance the Almehs rose, came forward and greeted us, touching our hands to the lips and forehead. They then sat down, drank each a small glass of *arakee*, and while the drum thumped and the violin drawled a monotonous prelude to the dance, we had leisure to scrutinize their dress and features.

The two famed danseuses bore Arabic names, which were translated to us as the Orange-Blossom and the Apple-Blossom. The first was of medium size, with an olive complexion, and regular, though not handsome features. She wore a white dress, fitting like a vest from the shoulders to the hips, with short, flowing sleeves, under which a fine blue gauze, confined at the wrist with bracelets, hung like a mist about her arms. Her head-dress was a small red cap, with a coronet of gold coins, under which her black hair escaped in two shining braids. The Apple-Blossom, who could not have been more than fifteen years old, was small and slightly formed, dark-skinned, and might have been called beautiful, but for a defect in one of her eyes. Her dress was of dark crimson silk, with trowsers and armlets of white gauze, and a red cap, so covered with coins that it nearly resembled a helmet of golden scales with a fringe falling on each side of her face. Three of the other assistants were dressed in white, with shawls of brilliant patterns bound around the waist. The fourth was a Nubian slave, named Zakhfara, whose shining black face looked wonderfully picturesque under the scarlet mantle which enveloped it like a turban, and fell in long folds almost to her feet. Among the singers was one named Bemba, who was almost the only really beautiful Egyptian woman I ever saw. Her features were large, but perfectly regular; and her long, thick, silky hair hung loose nearly to her shoulders before its gleaming mass was gathered into braids. Her teeth were even, and white as pearls, and the lids of her large black eyes were stained with *kohl*, which gave them a languishing, melancholy expression. She was a most consummate actress; for she no sooner saw that we noticed her face than she assumed the most indifferent air in the world and did not look at us again. But during the whole evening every movement was studied. The shawl was disposed in more graceful folds about her head; the hair was tossed back from her shoulders; the hand, tinged with henna, held the jasmine tube of her pipe in a hundred different attitudes, and only on leaving did she lift her eyes as if first aware of our presence and wish us "*buona sera*"—the only Italian words she knew—with the most musical accent of which an Arab voice is capable.

Meanwhile, the voices of the women mingled with the shrill, barbaric tones of the violin, and the prelude passed into a measured song of long, unvarying cadences, which the drums and tambourine accompanied with rapid beats. The Orange-Blossom and one of her companions took the floor, after drink ing another glass of arakee and tightening the shawls around their hips The dance commenced with a slow movement, both hands being lifted above the head, while the jingling bits of metal on their shawls and two miniature cymbals of brass, fastened to the thumb and middle finger, kept time to the music. As the dancers became animated, their motions were more rapid and violent, and the measure was marked, not in pirouettes and flying bounds, as on the boards of Frank theatres, but by a most wonderful command over the muscles of the chest and limbs. Their frames vibrated with the music like the strings of the violin, and as the song grew wild and stormy towards its close, the movements, had they not accorded with it, would have resembled those of a person seized with some violent nervous spasm. After this had continued for an incredible length of time, and I expected to see the Almehs fall exhausted to the earth, the music ceased, and they stood before us calm and cold, with their breathing not perceptibly hurried. The dance had a second part, of very different character. Still with their lifted hands striking the little cymbals, they marked a circle of springing bounds, in which their figures occasionally reminded me of the dancing nymphs of Greek sculpture. The instant before touching the floor, as they hung in the air with the head bent forward, one foot thrown behind, and both arms extended above the head, they were drawn on the background of the dark hall, like forms taken from the frieze of a temple to Bacchus or Pan.

Eastern politeness did not require us to cry "brava!" or "encore!" so we merely handed our pipes to Ali, to be filled a second time. Old Achmet Gourgàr, our Theban guide, however, was so enraptured that he several times ejaculated "*taïb keteer!*" (very good indeed!) and Raïs Hassan's dark face beamed all over with delight. The circle of white turbaned heads in the rear looked on complacently, and our guard, who stood in the moonlight before the open door, almost forgot his duty in his enjoyment of the spectacle. I shall never forget the wild, fantastic picture we saw that night in the ruins of Luxor.

The Apple-Blossom, who followed in a dance with one named Bakhita, pleased me far better. She added a thousand graceful embellishments to the monotonous soul of the music; and her dance, if barbaric, was as poetic as her native palm-tree. She was lithe as a serpent, and agile as a young panther, and some of her movements were most extraordinary, in the nerve and daring required to execute them, and to introduce them without neglecting the rhythm of the dance. More than once she sank slowly back, bending her knees forward, till her head and shoulders touched the floor, and then, quick as a flash, shot flying into the air, her foot alighting in exact time with the thump of the drum. She had the power of moving her body from side to side, so that it curved like a snake from the hips to the shoulders, and once I thought that, like Lamia, she was about to resume her ancient shape, and slip out of sight through some hole in the ruined walls. One of the dances was a sort of pantomime, which she and Bakhita accompanied with their voices—clear, shrill, ringing tones, which never faltered for a moment, or varied a hair's breadth from the melody, while every muscle was agitated with the exertion of her movements. The song was pervaded with a strange, passionate *tremolo*, unlike any thing I ever heard before. The burden was: "I am alone; my family and my friends are all dead; the plague has destroyed them. Come, then, to me, and be my beloved, for I have no other to love me." Her gestures exhibited a singular mixture of the abandonment of grief, and the longing of love. While her body swayed to and fro with the wild, sad rhythm of the words, she raised both arms before her till the long sleeves fell back and covered her face: then opening them in wistful entreaty, sang the last line of the chorus, and bringing her hands to her forehead, relapsed into grief again. Apparently the prayer is answered, for the concluding movement expressed a delirious joy.

We listened to the music and looked on the dances for more than two hours, but at length the twanging of the violin and the never-ending drum-thumps began to set our teeth on edge, and we unfolded our cramped legs and got down from the divan. The lantern was unswung, the candle-ends taken from the empty bottles, the Almehs received their fees and went off rejoicing, and we left the chambers of Luxor to the night-wind and the moon.

The guide of the Eastern bank, a wiry young Bedouin, was in attendance next morning, and a crowd of horses and asses awaited us on the shore. I chose a brown mare, with a small, slender head and keen eye, and soon accustomed myself to the Turkish saddle and broad shovel-stirrups. The temple of Luxor is imbedded in the modern village, and only the front of the pylon, facing towards Karnak, and part of the grand central colonnade, is free from its vile excrescences. For this reason its effect is less agreeable than that of the Memnonium, although of much grander proportions. Its plan is easily traced, nevertheless, and having been built by only two monarchs, Remeses the Great and Amunoph III.—or, tc use their more familiar titles, Sesostris and Memnon—it is less bewildering, in a historical point of view, to the unstudied tourist, than most of the other temples of Egypt. The sanctuary, which stands nearest the Nile, is still protected by the ancient stone quay, though the river has made rapid advances, and threatens finally to undermine Luxor as it has already undermined the temples of Antæopolis and Antinoë. I rode into what were once the sacred chambers, but the pillars and sculptures were covered with filth, and the Arabs had built in, around and upon them, like the clay nests of the cliff-sparrow. The peristyle of majestic Osiride pillars, in front of the portico, as well as the portico itself, are buried to half their depth, and so surrounded by hovels, that to get an idea of their arrangement you must make the tour of a number of hen-houses and asses' stalls. The pillars are now employed as drying-posts for the buffalo dung which the Arabs use as fuel.

Proceeding towards the entrance, the next court, which is tolerably free from incumbrances, contains a colonnade of two rows of lotus-crowned columns, twenty-eight feet in circumference. They still uphold their architraves of giant blocks of sandstone, and rising high above the miserable dwellings of the village, are visible from every part of the plain of Thebes. The English Vice-Consul, Mustapha Agha, occupies a house between two of these pillars. We returned the visit he had paid us on our arrival, and were regaled with the everlasting coffee and shebook, than which there is no more grateful refreshment. He gave us the agreeable news that Mr. Murray was endeavoring to persuade the Pasha to have Karnak cleared of its rubbish and preserved from further spoliation. If I possessed despotic power—and I then wished it for the first time

—I should certainly make despotic use of it, in tearing down some dozens of villages and setting some thousands of Copts and Fellahs at work in exhuming what their ancestors have mutilated and buried. The world cannot spare these remains. Tear down Roman ruins if you will; level Cyclopean walls, build bridges with the stones of Gothic abbeys and feudal fortresses; but lay no hand on the glory and grandeur of Egypt.

In order to ascend the great pylon of the temple, we were obliged to pass through a school, in which thirty or forty little Luxorians were conning their scraps of the Koran. They immediately surrounded us, holding up their tin slates, scribbled with Arabic characters, for our inspection, and demanded backsheesh for their proficiency. The gray-bearded pedagogue tried to quiet them, but could not prevent several from following us. The victories of Remeses are sculptured on the face of the towers of the pylon, but his colossi, solid figures of granite, which sit on either side of the entrance, have been much defaced. The lonely obelisk, which stands a little in advance, on the left hand, is more perfect than its Parisian mate. From this stately entrance, an avenue of colossal sphinxes once extended to the Ptolemaic pylon of Karnak, a distance of a mile and a half. The sphinxes have disappeared, but the modern Arab road leads over its site, through fields of waste grass.

And now we galloped forward, through a long procession of camels, donkeys, and Desert Arabs armed with spears, towards Karnak, the greatest ruin in the world, the crowning triumph of Egyptian power and Egyptian art. Except a broken stone here and there protruding through the soil, the plain is as desolate as if it had never been conscious of a human dwelling, and only on reaching the vicinity of the mud hamlet of Karnak, can the traveller realize that he is in Thebes. Here the camel-path drops into a broad excavated avenue lined with fragments of sphinxes and shaded by starveling acacias. As you advance, the sphinxes are better preserved and remain seated on their pedestals, but they have all been decapitated. Though of colossal proportions, they are seated so close to each other, that it must have required nearly two thousand to form the double row to Luxor. The avenue finally reaches a single pylon, of majestic proportions, built by one of the Ptolemies, and covered with profuse hieroglyphics. Passing through this, the sphinxes lead you to another pylon, followed by a pillared court and a temple built by the later Remesides. This, I thought, while my friend was measuring the girth of the pillars, is a good beginning for Karnak, but it is certainly much less than I expect. "*Tāăl min hennee!*" (come this way!) called the guide, as if reading my mind, and led me up the heaps of rubbish to the roof and pointed to the north.

Ah, there was Karnak! Had I been blind up to this time, or had the earth suddenly heaved out of her breast the remains of the glorious temple? From all parts of the plain of Thebes I had seen it in the distance—a huge propylon, a shattered portico, and an obelisk, rising above the palms. Whence this wilderness of ruins, spreading so far as to seem a city rather than a temple—pylon after pylon, tumbling into enormous cubes of stone, long colonnades, supporting fragments of Titanic roofs, obelisks of red granite, and endless walls and avenues, branching out to isolated portals? Yet they stood as silently amid the accumulated rubbish of nearly four thousand years, and the sunshine threw its yellow lustre as serenely over the despoiled sanctuaries, as if it had never been otherwise, since the world began. Figures are of no use, in describing a place like this, but since I must use them, I may say that the length of the ruins before us, from west to east, was twelve hundred feet, and that the total circumference of Karnak, including its numerous pylæ, or gateways, is a mile and a half.

We mounted and rode with fast-beating hearts to the western or main entrance, facing the Nile. The two towers of the propylon—pyramidal masses of solid stone—are three hundred and twenty-nine feet in length, and the one which is least ruined, is nearly one hundred feet in height. On each side of the sculptured portal connecting them, is a tablet left by the French army, recording the geographical position of the principal Egyptian temples. We passed through and entered an open court, more than three hundred feet square, with a corridor of immense pillars on each side, connecting it with the towers of a second pylon, nearly as gigantic as the first. A colonnade of lofty shafts, leading through the centre of the court, once united the two entrances, but they have all been hurled down and lay as they fell, in long lines of disjointed blocks, except one, which holds its solitary lotus-bell against the sky. Two mutilated colossi of red granite still guard the doorway, whose lintel-stones are forty feet in length. Climbing over the huge fragments which have fallen from above and almost blocked up the passage, we looked down into the grand hall of the temple.

I knew the dimensions of this hall, beforehand; I knew the number and size of the pillars, but I was no more prepared for the reality than those will be, who may read this account of it and afterwards visit Karnak for themselves. It is the great good-luck of travel that many things must be seen to be known.

Nothing could have compensated for the loss of that overwhelming confusion of awe, astonishment, and delight, which came upon me like a flood. I looked down an avenue of twelve pillars—six on each side—each of which was thirty-six feet in circumference and nearly eighty feet in height. Crushing as were these ponderous masses of sculptured stone, the spreading bell of the lotus-blossoms which crowned them, clothed them with an atmosphere of lightness and grace. In front, over the top of another pile of colossal blocks, two obelisks rose sharp and clear, with every emblem legible on their polished sides On each side of the main aisle are seven other rows of columns —*one hundred and twenty-two*, in all—each of which is about fifty feet high and twenty-seven in circumference. They have the Osiride form, without capitals, and do not range with the central shafts. In the efforts of the conquerors to overthrow them, two have been hurled from their places and thrown against the neighboring ones, where they still lean, as if weary with holding up the roof of massive sandstone. I walked alone through this hall, trying to bear the weight of its unutterable majesty and beauty. That I had been so oppressed by Dendera, seemed a weakness which I was resolved to conquer, and I finally succeeded in looking on Karnak with a calmness more commensurate with its sublime repose—but not by daylight.

My ride back to Luxor, towards evening, was the next best thing after Karnak. The little animal I rode had become excited by jumping over stones and sliding down sand-heaps; our guide began to show his Bedouin blood by dashing at full gallop toward the pylons and reining in his horse at a bound, and, to conclude, I became infected with a lawless spirit that could not easily be laid. The guide's eyes sparkled when I proposed a race. We left my friend and the water-carriers, bounded across the avenue of sphinxes, and took a smooth path leading toward the Desert. My mare needed but a word and a jog of the iron stirrup. Away we flew, our animals stretching themselves for a long heat, crashing the dry dourra-stalks, clearing the water-ditches, and scattering on all sides the Arab laborers we met. After a glorious gallop of two or three miles my antagonist was fairly distanced; but one race would not content him, so we had a second, and finally a third, on the beach of Luxor. The horses belonged to him, and it was a matter of indifference which was the swiftest; he raced merely for the delight of it, and so did I.

The same gallant mare was ready for me at night. It was precisely full moon, and I had determined on visiting Karnak again before leaving. There was no one but the guide and I, he armed with his long spear, and I with my pistols in my belt. There was a wan haze in the air, and a pale halo around the moon, on each side of which appeared two faint mock-moons. It was a ghostly light, and the fresh north-wind, coming up the Nile, rustled solemnly in the palm-trees. We trotted silently to Karnak, and leaped our horses over the fragments until we reached the foot of the first obelisk. Here we dismounted and entered the grand hall of pillars. There was no sound in all the temple, and the guide, who seemed to comprehend my wish, moved behind me as softly as a shadow, and spoke not a word. It needs this illumination to comprehend Karnak. The unsightly rubbish has disappeared: the rents in the roof are atoned for by the moonlight they admit; the fragments shivered from the lips of the mighty capitals are only the crumpled edges of the flower; a maze of shadows hides the desolation of the courts, but every pillar and obelisk, pylon and propylon is glorified by the moonlight. The soul of Karnak is soothed and tranquillized. Its halls look upon you no longer with an aspect of pain and humiliation. Every stone seems to say: "I am not fallen, for I have defied the ages. I am a part of that grandeur which has never seen its peer, and I shall endure for ever, for the world has need of me."

I climbed to the roof, and sat looking down into the hushed and awful colonnades, till I was thoroughly penetrated with their august and sublime expression. I should probably have remained all night, an amateur colossus, with my hands on my knees, had not the silence been disturbed by two arrivals of romantic tourists—an Englishman and two Frenchmen. We exchanged salutations, and I mounted the restless mare again, touched her side with the stirrup, and sped back to Luxor. The guide galloped beside me, occasionally hurling his spear into the air and catching it as it fell, delighted with my readiness to indulge his desert whims. I found the captain and sailors all ready and my friend smoking his pipe on deck. In half an hour we had left Thebes.

CHAPTER XI.

FROM THEBES TO THE NUBIAN FRONTIER.

The Temple of Hermontis—Esneh and its Temple—The Governor—El Kab by Torchlight—The Temple of Edfou—The Quarries of Djebel Silsileh—Ombos—Approach to Nubia—Change in the Scenery and Inhabitants—A Mirage—Arrival at Assouan.

Our journey from Thebes to Assouan occupied six days, including a halt of twenty-four hours at Esneh. We left Luxor on the night of December 8th, but the westward curve of the Nile brought us in opposition with the wind, and the next day at noon we had only reached Erment, the ancient Hermontis, in sight of the three peaks of the Theban hills. We left our men to tug the boat along shore, and wandered off to the mounds of the old city, still graced with a small temple, or lying-in house of the goddess Reto, who is here represented as giving birth to the god Hor-pire. The sculptures in the dark chambers, now used as stalls for asses, were evidently intended only for the priesthood of the temple, and are not repeated, as are those of other temples, in the halls open to the public. Notwithstanding the great license which the Egyptian faith assumed, its symbols are, in general, scrupulously guarded from all low and unworthy forms of representation.

The group of pillars in the outer court charmed us by the

richness and variety of their designs. No two capitals are of similar pattern, while in their combinations of the papyrus, the lotus and the palm-leaf, they harmonize one with another and as a whole. The abacus, between the capital and the architrave, is so high as almost to resemble a second shaft. In Karnak and the Memnonium it is narrow, and lifts the ponderous beam just enough to prevent its oppressing the lightness of the capital. I was so delighted with the pillars of Hermontis that I scarcely knew whether to call this peculiarity a grace or a defect. I have never seen it employed in modern architecture, and judge therefore that it has either been condemned by our rules or that our architects have not the skill and daring of the Egyptians.

We reached Esneh the same night, but were obliged to remain all the next day in order to allow our sailors to bake their bread. We employed the time in visiting the temple, the only remnant of the ancient Latopolis, and the palace of Abbas Pasha, on the bank of the Nile. The portico of the temple, half buried in rubbish, like that of Dendera, which it resembles in design, is exceedingly beautiful. Each of its twenty-four columns is crowned with a different capital, so chaste and elegant in their execution that it is impossible to give any one the preference. The designs are mostly copied from the doum-palm, the date-palm, and the lotus, but the cane, the vine, and various water-plants are also introduced. The building dates from the time of the Ptolemies, and its sculptures are uninteresting. We devoted all our time to the study of the capitals, a labyrinth of beauty, in which we were soon entangled. The Governor of Esneh, Ali Effendi, a most friendly and agreeable Arab, accompanied us through the temple, and pointed out all the fishes, birds and crocodiles he could find. To him they were evidently the most interesting things in it. He asked me how old the building was, and by whom it had been erected. On leaving, we accepted his invitation to partake of coffee and pipes. The visit took place in due form, with many grave salutations, which we conscientiously imitated. Achmet had returned to our boat, and my small stock of Arabic was soon exhausted, but we managed to exchange all the necessary common-places.

The day of leaving Esneh, we reached El Kab, the ancient Eleuthyas, whose rock-tombs are among the most curious in Egypt. We landed at twilight, provided with candles, and made our way through fields of wiry *halfeh* grass, and through a breach in the brick wall of the ancient town, to the Arabian Desert. It was already dark, but our guide, armed with his long spear, stalked vigorously forward, and brought us safely up the mountain path to the entrances of the sepulchres. There are a large number of these, but only two are worth visiting, on account of the light which they throw on the social life of the Egyptians. The owner of the tomb and his wife—a red man and a yellow woman—are here seen, receiving the delighted guests. Seats are given them, and each is presented with an aromatic flower, while the servants in the kitchen hasten to prepare savory dishes. In other compartments, all the most minute processes of agriculture are represented with wonderful fidelity. So little change has taken place in three thousand years, that they would answer, with scarcely a correction, as illustrations of the Fellah agriculture of Modern Egypt.

The next morning we walked ahead to the temple of Edfou,

shooting a few brace of fat partridges by the way, and scaring two large jackals from their lairs in the thick grass. The superb pylon of the temple rose above the earthy mounds of Apollinopolis like a double-truncated pyramid. It is in an entire state of preservation, with all its internal chambers, passages and stairways. The exterior is sculptured with colossal figures of the gods, thirty feet in height, and from the base of the portal to the scroll-like cornice of the pylon, is more than a hundred feet. Through the door we entered a large open court, surrounded by a colonnade. The grand portico of the temple, buried nearly to the tops of its pillars, faced us, and we could only judge, from the designs of the capitals and the girth of the shaft, the imposing effect which it must have produced on those who entered the court. The interior is totally filled with rubbish, and a whole village of Arab huts stands on the roof.

A strong wind carried us, before sunset, to the quarries of Djebel Silsileh, the "Mountain of the Chain," where the Nile is compressed between two rugged sandstone hills. The river is not more than three hundred yards broad, and the approach to this rocky gateway, after so many weeks of level alluvial plain, is very striking. Here are the sandstone quarries whence the huge blocks were cut, to build the temples and shape the colossi of Thebes. They lie on the eastern bank, close to the river, and the ways down which the stones were slid to the vessels that received them, are still to be seen. The stone is of a pale reddish-brown color, and a very fine and clear grain. It appears to have been divided into squares of the proper size, and cut from above downward. The shape of many of the enormous blocks may be easily traced. In one place the rock has been roughly hewn into a sort of temple, supported by pillars thirty feet square, and with an entrance as grand and rude as a work of the Titans.

In the morning we awoke in the shadow of Ombos, which stands on a hill overlooking the Nile, into which its temple to Isis has fallen. Little now remains of the great temple to Savak, the crocodile-headed god, the deity of Ombos, but its double portico, supported by thirteen pillars, buried nearly waist-deep in the sands. The aspect of these remains, seated on the lonely promontory commanding the course of the river and the harvest-land of the opposite shore, while the stealthy Desert approaches it from behind, and year by year heaps the sand higher against the shattered sanctuary, is sadly touching. We lingered and lingered around its columns, loth to leave the ruined grace which a very few years will obliterate. Two such foes as the Nile and the Desert make rapid progress, where no human hand is interposed to stay them. As we sailed away, a large crocodile, perhaps Savak himself, lay motionless on a sand-bank with his long snout raised in the air.

We were two days in sailing from Ombos to Assouan owing to a dead calm, the first in two weeks. The nights were very cool, and the mid-day temperature not too warm for comfort. One morning my thermometer stood at 40°; the Arabs complained bitterly of the cold, and, wrapped in their woolen mantles, crawled about the deck as languidly as benumbed flies. At noon the mercury did not often rise above 75° in the shade. As we approach Nubia, the scenery of the river undergoes a complete change. The rugged hills of black sandstone and granite usurp the place of the fields, and leave but a narrow strip of cultivable land on either side. The Arabs are darker and show the blood of the desert tribes in their features They are, however, exceedingly friendly. The day before reaching Assouan, we walked ahead of our boat and were obliged to wait two or three hours. We had a retinue of boys, who pummelled one another as to which should pick up the pigeons we shot. The successful one came bounding back with a face sparkling with delight, and kissed the bird and touched it to his forehead as he gave it to us. As we were resting under the palm-trees, my friend regretted that we had not brought our shebooks along with us. One of the Arabs, guessing his wish from the word "shebook," instantly ran off and scoured the dourra-fields until he found a laborer who owned a pipe. He brought the man back, with the sickle in his hand and a corn-stalk pipe of very indifferent tobacco, which he gravely presented to my friend. Before returning on board we saw a wonderful mirage. Two small lakes of blue water, glittering in the sun, lay spread in the yellow sands, apparently not more than a mile distant. There was not the least sign of vapor in the air, and as we were quite unacquainted with the appearance of the mirage, we decided that the lakes were Nile-water, left from the inundation. I pointed to them and asked the Arabs: "Is that water?" "No, no!" they all exclaimed: "that is no water—that is a *bahr Shaytan!*" (a river of the Devil).

The white tomb of a Moslem saint, sparkling in the noon day sun, on the summit of a hill overlooking the Nile, finally announced our arrival at the Nubian frontier. We now beheld the palms of Assouan and the granite cliffs beyond—which we had been so impatient to reach, a few hours before—with regret, almost with dread. This was our point of separation.

My pathway was through those desolate hills, intó the heart of Nubia, into the Desert, and the strange countries beyond, where so few had been before me. The vestibule was passed: Egypt lay behind me. The long landscape of the Nile was but the dromos to that temple of African life, whose adytum was still far in advance, deep in the fiery tropical silence of Ethiopia. While my blood thrilled at the prospect, and the thirst of adventure and discovery inspired me as the wind of the Desert inspires the Arab charger, I could not part with indifference from the man who had shared with me the first august impression, the sublime fascination of Egypt. Nor was the prospect of a solitary voyage back to Cairo at all cheering to him. Achmet would of course accompany me, and the cook, Salame, who knew barely twenty words of French and Italian, must perforce act as dragoman. My friend was therefore completely at the mercy of the captain and crew, and saw nothing but annoyance and embarrassment before him. I had much trust in Raïs Hassan's honesty and good faith, and was glad to learn, several months afterwards, that his conduct had confirmed it.

CHAPTER XII.

PHILÆ AND THE CATARACT.

An Official Visit—Achmet's Dexterity—The Island of Elephantine—Nubian Children—Trip to Philæ—Linant Bey—The Island of Philæ—Sculptures—The Negro Race—Breakfast in a Ptolemaic Temple—The Island of Biggeh—Backsheesh—The Cataract—The Granite Quarries of Assouan—The Travellers separate.

"Where Nile reflects the endless length
Of dark-red colonnades."—MACAULAY.

WE had scarcely moored our vessel to the beach at Assouan, before a messenger of the Governor arrived to ask if there was an American on board. He received the information, and we were occupied in preparing ourselves for an excursion to the island of Elephantine, when Achmet called to us: "The Governor is coming." We had no time to arrange our cabin for his reception; he was already at the door, with two attendants, and the most I could do was to clear sufficient space for a seat on my divan. His Excellency was a short, stout, broad-faced man, with large eyes, a gray beard and a flat nose. He wore a semi-European dress of brown cloth, and was blunt though cordial in his manners. His attendants, one of whom was the Captain of the Cataract, wore the Egyptian dress, with black turbans. They saluted us by touching their hands to the lips and forehead, and we responded in similar manner, after which the Governor inquired after our health and we inquired after his. I delivered my letter, and while he was occupied in reading it, Achmet prepared the coffee and pipes. Luckily, we had three shebooks, the best of which, having an amber mouth-piece, was presented to the Governor. I waited for the coffee with some trepidation, for I knew we had but two Turkish *finjans*, and a Frank cup was out of the question. However, Achmet was a skilful servant. He presented the cups at such intervals that one was sure to be empty while the other was full, and artfully drew away the attention of our guests by his ceremonious presentations; so that not only they but both of us partook twice of coffee, without the least embarrassment, and I believe, had there been ten persons instead of five, he would have given the two cups the effect of ten.

After the Governor had expressed his pleasure in flowing Oriental phrases, and promised to engage me a boat for Korosko, he took his leave and we crossed in a ferry barge to Elephantine. This is a small but fertile island, whose granite foundations are fast anchored in the Nile. It once was covered with extensive ruins, but they have all been destroyed except a single gateway and an altar to Amun, both of red granite, and a sitting statue of marble. The southern part is entirely covered with the ruins of a village of unburnt brick, from the topmost piles of which we enjoyed a fine view of the picturesque environs of Assouan. The bed of the Nile, to the south, was broken with isles of dark-red granite rock, the same formation which appears in the jagged crests of the mountains beyond the city. Scattered over them were the tombs of holy men, dating from the times of the Saracens. A thin palm grove somewhat concealed the barren aspect of the city, but our glances passed it, to rest on the distant hills, kindling in the setting sun.

The island is inhabited by Nubians, and some twenty or thirty children, of from six to ten years of age—the boys entirely naked, the girls wearing the *ràhad*, a narrow leathern girdle, around the loins—surrounded us, crying "*backsheesh!*" and offering for sale bits of agate, coins, and fragments of pottery. Some of them had cunning but none of them intelligent faces, and their large black eyes had an astonishingly precocious expression of sensuality. We bought a few trifles and tried to dismiss them, but their numbers increased, so that by the time we had made the tour of the island we had a retinue of fifty followers. I took the branches of henna they offered me and switched the most impudent of them, but they seemed then to consider that they had a rightful claim to the backsheesh, and were more importunate than ever. As we left, they gathered on the shore and sang us a farewell chorus, but a few five para pieces, thrown among them, changed the harmony into a scramble and a fight, in which occupation these lovely children of Nature were engaged until we lost sight of them.

The next day we visited Philæ. We took donkeys and a guide and threaded the dismal valley of Saracenic tombs south of the town, into a pass leading through the granite hills. The landscape was wintry in its bleakness and ruggedness. The path over which we rode was hard sand and gravel, and on both sides the dark rocks were piled in a thousand wonderful combinations. On the surface there is no appearance of regular strata, but rather of some terrible convulsion, which has broken the immense masses and thrown them confusedly together. Russegger noticed that the structure of the primitive strata of Assouan was exactly similar to that of Northern Lapland. The varieties of landscape, in different climates, depend therefore upon the difference of vegetation and of atmospheric effect, rather than that of geological forms, which always preserve their identity. Dr. Kane also found in the bleak hills of Greenland the same structure which he had observed in the Ghauts of tropical India.

After three or four miles of this travel the pass opened upon the Nile, just above the Cataract. At the termination of the portage is a Nubian village, whose plantations of doum and date-palms and acacias are dazzling in their greenness, from contrast with the bleak pyramids of rock and the tawny drifts of the Lybian sands on the western bank. We rode down to the port, where a dozen trading vessels lay at anchor, and took a large boat for Philæ. The Governor of Assouan was there, and His Excellency showed me the vessel he had engaged for me—a small and rather old *dahabiyeh*, but the best to be had. The price was one hundred and fifty piastres for the trip—about one hundred and twenty miles—besides something for the men. Achmet attributed this moderate demand to the effect of a timely present, which had been delicately conveyed into the Governor's hands the night before. There was a tall gentleman, in the official Egyptian costume, in company with the Governor. Achmet said he was a French engineer in the service of Abbas Pasha, and I afterwards learned that he was none other than M. Linant, or Linant Bey whose name is so well known through his connection with the exploration of Petra, and of the antiquities in Ethiopia. He was accompanied by his wife, a French lady, who greeted us courteously, and two daughters of semi-Abyssinian origin. The latter were dressed in Oriental costume, but unveiled. M. Linant is a tall, grave person, about fifty years of age. He wore a crescent of diamonds on his breast, and his features expressed all the dignity and repose of one who had become thoroughly naturalized in the East.

As the wind carried us out into the stream, we saw the towers of the temple of Isis, on Philæ, through a savage gorge of the river. The enormous masses of dark granite were piled on either side to a height of several hundred feet, taking in some places the forms of monoliths and sitting colossi, one of which appeared so lightly balanced on the loose summit that a strong gale might topple it down the steep. The current in the narrow channel was so violent that we could make no headway, but a Nubian boy, swimming on a palm-log, carried a rope to the shore, and we were at length towed with much labor into the more tranquil basin girdling Philæ. The four lofty towers of the two pylons, the side corridors of pillars and the exterior walls of the temple seem perfectly preserved, on approaching the island, the green turf of whose banks and the grouping of its palms quite conceal the ruins of a miserable mud village which surrounds the structures. Philæ is the jewel of the Nile, but these ruins are an unsightly blotch, which takes away half its lustre. The setting is nevertheless perfect. The basin of black, jagged mountains, folding on all sides, yet half-disclosing the avenues to Egypt and Nubia; the hem of emerald turf at their feet, sprinkled with clusters of palm, and here and there the pillar or wall of a temple the ring of the bright river, no longer turbid as in Lower

Egypt: of these it is the centre, as it was once the radiant focus of their beauty.

The temple, which belongs to the era of the Ptolemies, and is little more than two thousand years old, was built by various monarchs, and is very irregular in its plan. Instead of preserving a fixed direction, it follows the curve of the island, and its various corridors and pylons have been added to each other with so little regard to proportion, that the building is much more agreeable when viewed as a collection of detached parts, than as a whole. From its locality, it has suffered comparatively little from the ravages of man, and might be restored to almost its original condition. The mud which Coptic Christians plastered over the walls of its sanctuaries has concealed, but not defaced, their richly-colored sculptures, and the palm-leaf and lotus capitals of its portico retain the first brilliancy of their green and blue tints. The double corridor of thirty-six columns, in front of the temple, reaching to the southern end of the island, has never been finished, some of the capitals last erected being unsculptured, and others exhibiting various stages of completion. In Egypt one so accustoms himself to looking back four thousand years, that Philæ seems but of yesterday. The Gothic Cathedrals of the Middle Ages are like antediluvian remains, compared with its apparent newness and freshness.

We examined the interior chambers with the aid of a torch, and I also explored several secret passages, inclosed in the thickness of the walls. The sculptures are raised on the face of the stone, and painted in light and brilliant colors. They represent Isis and Osiris, with their offspring, the god Horus, which three constituted the Trinity worshipped in Philæ. In one place Isis is seen giving suck to the infant god—a group which bore a singular resemblance to some painting I have seen of the Virgin and Child. The gods are here painted of fair, Greek complexion, and not, as in the oldest tombs and temples, of a light red. Their profiles are symmetrical and even beautiful, and the emblems by which they are surrounded, are drawn and colored in admirable taste. Those friends of the African Race, who point to Egypt as a proof of what that race has accomplished, are wholly mistaken. The only negro features represented in Egyptian sculpture are those of slaves and captives taken in the Ethiopian wars of the Pharaohs. The temples and pyramids throughout Nubia, as far as the frontiers of Dar-Fūr and Abyssinia, all bear the hieroglyphs of these monarchs, and there is no evidence in all the valley of the Nile that the Negro Race ever attained a higher degree of civilization than is at present exhibited in Congo and Ashantee.

East of the great temple is a square, open building, whose four sides are rows of columns, supporting an architrave, and united, at about half their height, by screens of stone. The capitals are all of different design, yet exhibit the same exquisite harmony which charmed us in Hermontis and Esneh. The screens and pillars were evidently intended to have been covered with sculpture, and a roof of sandstone blocks was to have been added, which would have made the structure as perfect as it is unique. The square block, or abacus, interposed between the capital and architrave, is even higher than in the pillars of Hermontis, and I was equally puzzled whether to call it a grace or a defect. There was one thing, however, which certainly did give a grace to the building, and that was our breakfast, which we ate on a block large enough to have made an altar for the Theban Jupiter, surrounded by a crowd of silent Arabs. They contemplated the ruins of our cold fowls with no less interest than did we those of the temples of Philæ.

Before returning, we crossed to the island of Biggeh, where two pillars of a temple to Athor stand sentry before the door of a mud hut, and a red granite colossus is lucky in having no head, since it is spared the sight of such desecration. The children of Biggeh fairly drove us away with the cries of "*backsheesh!*" The hideous word had been rung in our ears since leaving Assouan, and when we were again saluted with it, on landing at the head of the Cataract, patience ceased to be a virtue. My friend took his cane and I the stick of my donkey-driver, and since the naked pests dared not approach near enough to get the backsheesh, they finally ceased to demand it. The word is in every Nubian mouth, and the very boatmen and camel-drivers as they passed us said "*backsheesh*" instead of "good morning." As it was impossible to avoid hearing it, I used the word in the same way, and cordially returned the greeting. A few days previous, as we were walking on shore near Esneh, a company of laborers in a dourra-field began the cry. I responded, holding out my hand, whereupon one of the men pulled off his white cotton cap (his only garment), and offered it to me, saying: "If you are poor, take it."

We walked down to the edge of the Cataract and climbed a rock, which commanded a view of the principal rapid There is nothing like a fall, and the passage up and down is attended with little peril. The bed of the Nile is filled with granite masses, around which the swift current roars and foams, and I can imagine that the descent must be very exciting, though perhaps less so than that of the Rapids of the St. Lawrence. Boats are towed up, under the superintendence of one of the raïs, or captains of the Cataract. There are four of these officers, with a body of about two hundred men. The fee varies from two to four hundred piastres, according to the size of the boat. One third of the money is divided among the captains, and the remainder falls to the portion of the men. This also includes the descent, and travellers going to the Second Cataract and back, pay half the fee on returning.

On the following morning we visited the ancient granite quarries of Assouan. They lie in the hills, south of the town, and more than a mile from the river. I never saw a more magnificent bed of rock. Its color is a light red, flecked with green, and its grain is very fine and nearly as solid as porphyry. An obelisk, one hundred feet long and twelve feet square at the base, still lies in the quarry, having been abandoned on account of a slight fissure near its summit. Grooves were afterward cut, for the purpose of separating it into blocks, but for some reason or other the design was not carried out. In many parts of the quarry the method employed by the Egyptians to detach the enormous masses, is plainly to be seen. A shallow groove was first sunk along the line of fracture, after which mortices about three inches wide and four deep, were cut at short intervals, for the purpose of receiving wooden wedges. These having been driven firmly into their sockets, were saturated with water, and by their expansion forced the solid grain asunder.

We rode back to the *Cleopatra* with heavy hearts. Every

thing had been prepared for our departure, my friend for Cairo and Germany, and I for the Nubian Desert and White Nile. The Governor of Assouan had despatched a letter to the Governor of Korosko, asking him to have camels ready for the Desert, on my arrival, my own letters to my friends were finished, my equipage had been transferred to the shore, and camels had arrived to transport it around the Cataract to the Nubian village, where my boat was in readiness. Our handsome sailor, Ali, begged so hard to be allowed to accompany me, that I finally agreed to take him as a servant, and he was already on duty. Achmet was nearly as cheerful as he, notwithstanding he had just written to his family to say that he was going to Soudân, and had given up, as he afterwards informed me, all hopes of ever seeing Egypt again. The American flag was run down, and the Saxe-Coburg colors—green and white—hoisted in its stead. We had a parting visit from the Governor, who gave me another letter to Korosko, and we then sat down to a breakfast for which we had no appetite. The camels were loaded and sent off in advance, under Ali's charge, but I waited until every man was on board the good old vessel and ready to push off for Cairo. The large mainsail was unshipped and laid over the cabin, and the stern-sail, only to be used when the south-wind blows, hoisted in its place. The tow-rope was wound up and stowed away, and the large oars hung in the rowlocks. Finally, every sailor was at his post; the moment came, and we parted, as two men seldom part, who were strangers six weeks before. I goaded my donkey desperately over the sands, hastened the loading of my effects, and was speedily afloat and alone on the Nubian Nile.

Ali.

CHAPTER XIII.

THE NUBIAN NILE.

Solitary Travel—Scenery of the Nubian Nile—Agriculture—The Inhabitants—Arrival at Korosko—The Governor—The Tent Pitched—Shekh Abou-Mohammed—Bargaining for Camels—A Drove of Giraffes—Visits—Preparations for the Desert—My Last Evening on the Nile.

We passed to the west of the island of Biggeh, where the current is less rapid, and a gentle north wind soon carried us away from Philæ. Dark mountains of porphyry rock inclosed the river, and the solitude of the shores, broken only by the creaking of an occasional *sakia*, or irrigating wheel, made me feel keenly the loneliness of my situation. Achmet, who now became cook as well as dragoman, served me up three fowls cooked in different styles, for dinner—partly as an earnest of his skill, and partly to dispel my want of spirits. But the fragrant pipe which followed dinner was the true promoter of patience, and "Patience," says the Arab poet, "is the key of Content." My boat was a small, slow craft, and Raïs Hereedee, the captain, the most indolent of Nubians. His weak, feminine face showed a lack of character, which Achmet soon turned to advantage, by taking the command into his own hands. The wind was barely strong enough to obviate the necessity of towing, and my three sailors sat on the bow all day, singing: "*andèrbuddee! andèrbuddee!*" as we lazily ascended the river.

Those who do not go beyond Thebes are only half acquainted with the Nile. Above Esneh, it is no longer a broad, lazy current, watering endless fields of wheat and groves of palm, bounded in the distance by level lines of yellow mountain-walls. It is narrower, clearer and more rapid, and its valley, after the first scanty field of wheat or dourra, strikes the foot of broken and rocky ranges, through the gaps in which the winds of the Desert have spilled its sands. There is not the same pale, beautiful monotony of color, but the landscapes are full of striking contrasts, and strongly accented lights and shadows. Here, in Nubia, these characteristics are increased, and the Nile becomes a river of the North under a Southern sun. The mountains rise on either hand from the water's edge; piles of dark sandstone or porphyry rock, sometimes a thousand feet in height, where a blade of grass never grew, every notch and jag on their crests, every fissure on their sides, revealed in an atmosphere so pure and crystalline, that nothing but one of our cloudless mid-winter days can equal it. Their hue near at hand is a glowing brown; in the distance an intense violet. On the western bank they are lower; and the sand of that vast Desert, which stretches unbroken to the Atlantic, has heaped itself over their shoulders and poured long drifts and rills even to the water. In color it is a tawny gold, almost approaching a salmon tint, and its glow at sunrise equals that of the snow-fields of the Alps.

The arable land is a mere hem, a few yards in breadth on either side of the river. It supports a few scattering date-palms, which are the principal dependence of the Nubians. They are taxed at the rate of a piastre and a half each, annually, the trees being counted every five years by a Government officer appointed for that purpose. If half of them should die in the mean time, the tax remains the same until the next count. The trees are seven years in coming to maturity, after which they produce dates for seven years, and then gradually decay. They are male and female, and are generally planted so that the pollen may be blown from the male to the female flowers. In some parts of Egypt this impregnation is artificially produced. The banks are planted with wheat, beans and a species of lupin, from which bread is made, and wherever a little shelf of soil is found along the base of the mountains, the creaking sakias turn day and night to give life to patches of dourra and cotton. In a rough shed, protected from the sun by palm-mats, a cow or buffalo walks a weary round, raising the water, which is conveyed in small channels, built of clay, to all the numerous beds into which the field is divided. These are filled, in regular succession to the depth of two inches, and then left to stand until dried by the sun. The process is continued until the grain is nearly ripe. The sakias pay a tax of three hundred piastres a year, levied in lieu of a ground tax, which the Egyptians pay. With all their labor, the inhabitants scarcely produce enough to support themselves, and the children are sent to Cairo at an early age, where they become house-servants, and like the Swiss and Savoyards, send home a portion of their earnings. This part of Nubia is inhabited by the Kenoos tribe, who speak a language of their own. They and their language are designated by the general name of *Barăbra* (nearly equivalent to "barbarians") by the Arabs. They are more stupid than the Egyptian Fellahs, but their character for truth and honesty is superior. In my walks on shore, I found them very friendly, and much less impudent than the Nubians about Assouan.

The northern part of Nubia is rich in Egyptian remains, but I hastened on without visiting them, passing the temples of Dabôd, Kalabshee, Dakkeh, Dendoor and Sebooa, which looked at me invitingly from the western bank. Near Dendoor I crossed the Tropic of Cancer, and on the fourth afternoon after leaving Assouan, Raïs Hereedee pointed out in the distance the mountain of Korosko, the goal of the voyage. I was charmed with the near prospect of desert life, but I fancied Achmet was rather grave, since all beyond was an unknown region to him. The sharp peak of the mountain gradually drew nearer, and at dusk my boat was moored to a palm-tree, in front of the village of Korosko.

In less than half an hour, I received a visit from the Governor, Moussa Effendi, who brought me good news. A caravan had just arrived from Sennaar, and camels were in readiness for the journey to Berber, in Ethiopia. This was very lucky, for merchants are frequently detained at Korosko twenty or thirty days, and I had anticipated a delay of at least a week I also learned that Dr. Knoblecher, the Apostolic Vicar of the Catholic Missions in Central Africa, had left for Khartoum about twenty days previous. The Governor was profuse in his offers of assistance, stating that as Shekh Abou-Mohammed, a chief of the Ababdeh tribe, through whose territories my road lay, was then in Korosko, he would be enabled to make every arrangement for my safety and convenience.

Early the next morning my equipage was taken ashore, and my tent pitched for the first time, under a clump of palm-trees, overlooking the Nile. Leaving Ali to act as guard, I took Achmet and walked up to the village of Korosko, which is about a quarter of a mile from the shore, at the foot of the lofty Djebel Korosko. The Governor's mansion was a mud hut, differing from the other huts in size only. His Excellency received me cordially, and immediately sent for Shekh Abou-Mohammed, with whom the contract for camels must be made. The Shekh was a tall, imposing personage, with a dark-brown complexion, but perfectly straight and regular features. He was accompanied by a superb attendant—an Ababdeh, six feet two inches in height, with sharp, symmetrical features, and a fine, fierce eye. His hair was raised perpendicularly from his forehead, but on each side hung down in a great number of little twists, smeared with mutton-fat and castor-oil. His long cotton mantle was wrapped around him like a Greek chlamys, and his bearing was as manly and majestic as that of an Ajax or a Diomed. There was some controversy about the number of camels; Achmet and I had decided that we should not require more than five, and the Shekh insisted that we should take more, but finally agreed to furnish us with six, including one for the guide, at the price paid by officers of the Government—ninety piastres (four dollars and fifty cents) each, to El Mekheyref, the capital of Dar Berber, a journey of fourteen days. This included the services of camel-drivers, and all other expenses, except the hire of the guide, whose fee was that of a camel—ninety piastres. Merchants who travel this route, pay according to the weight of their loads, and frequently from one hundred and twenty to one hundred and fifty piastres.

Soon after returning to my tent, I was again visited by the Governor, who found my choice Latakieh very acceptable to his taste. I therefore presented him with two or three pounds of it, and some gunpowder, which he received in a way that made me sure of his good offices. Shekh Abou-Mohammed also came down, inspected my baggage, and was satisfied that the camels would not be overloaded. He declared, however, that the four *geerbehs*, or water-skins, which I had brought from Cairo, would not be sufficient, and as none were to be purchased in Korosko, loaned me four more for the journey, on my agreeing to pay him half their value. I also paid him for the camels, he giving a formal receipt therefor, which was intrusted to the guide, to be delivered to the Governor of Berber, on our arrival there. Three short, black Arabs of the Bishàree tribe, with immense bushy heads of twisted and greased hair, were presented to me as the camel-drivers. After receiving their share of the money (for the camels belonged to them), they squatted down together and occupied an hour or two in counting and dividing it. One of them then took a long palm-rope, and went into the desert to catch the animals, while the others remained to assist in arranging the baggage into separate loads.

The caravan from Sennaar brought twelve giraffes, which had been captured in the forests of the Blue Nile, as a present from Lattif Pasha, Governor of Soudân, to Abbas Pasha. They were in good condition, notwithstanding the toilsome march across the Nubian Desert. The officer who had them in charge informed me that they made frequent efforts to escape, and one of them, which broke from its keeper's hold, was only recaptured after a chase of several hours. Four large trading-boats were in readiness, to convey them to Assouan, and the graceful creatures stood on the bank, with their heads almost touching the crowns of the date-trees, looking with wonder on the busy scene below. For a long time they refused to enter the unsteady barges, but at last, trembling with fear, they were forced on board and floated away, their slim necks towering like masts in the distance.

There was a small tent on the bank, pitched not far from mine. Its occupant, a one-eyed, olive-faced young man, in Egyptian costume, came to pay me a visit, and I found that he was a son of M. Linant, by a former Abyssinian wife. He was then making his second trip to Soudân, as a merchant, on a capital of twenty-five thousand piastres, which his father had given him. Although he only required twelve camels, he had been eight days in Korosko waiting for them, and was still waiting when I left. He was accompanied by a young Frenchman, who was one of the grandest liars I ever met. He told me with a grave face, that he had travelled from Algiers to Egypt through the Great Sahara, and had on one occasion gone eight days without water, and the thermometer one hundred and twenty-five degrees in the shade! The son of the former Mek (king) of Shendy—the same fierce old savage who burned to death Ismail Pasha and his soldiers—was also in Korosko, and visited me during the day. He held some office under Government, which made him responsible for the security of travellers and merchandise in the Desert, and his presence probably facilitated my arrangements. He was a strikingly handsome man, and wore a superb Cashmere shawl twisted around his head as a turban.

The water-skins were soaked in the Nile all day, to prepare them for use. Achmet, backed by the Governor's authority, ransacked the village for further supplies of provisions, but the place was miserably poor, and he only succeeded in procuring two pounds of butter, a few fowls, and some bread. There were pigeons in abundance, however, and he cooked a sufficient number to last us two or three days. The fowls were placed in a light *cafass*, or coop, to be carried on the top of the baggage. Ali, proud of his new station, worked faithfully, and before night all our preparations were completed I then sent for a barber, had my hair shorn close to the skin, and assumed the complete Egyptian costume. I was already accustomed to the turban and shawl around the waist, and the addition of a light silk *sidree*, or shirt, and trowsers which contained eighteen yards of muslin, completed the dress, which in its grace, convenience, and adaptation to the climate and habits of the East, is immeasurably superior to the Frank costume. It allows complete freedom of the limbs, while the most sensitive parts of the body are thoroughly protected from changes of temperature. The legs, especially, are even less fettered by the wide Turkish trowsers than by a Highland kilt, and they fold themselves under you naturally and comfortably, in the characteristic attitude of the Orientals. The turban, which appears so hot and cumbrous, is in reality cool, and impervious to the fiercest sun that ever blazed.

After dinner, I seated myself at the tent door, wrapped in my capote, and gave myself up to the pipe of meditation. It was a splendid starlit evening. Not a blade of the palm-leaves was stirring, and the only sounds I heard were the melancholy drone of *sakias* along the river, and the cry of the jackal among the hills. The Nile had already become my home, endeared to me not more by the grand associations of its eldest human history than by the rest and the patience which I had breathed in its calm atmosphere. Now I was to leave it for the untried Desert, and the strange regions beyond, where I should find its aspect changed. Would it still give me the same health of body, the same peace and contentment of soul? "Achmet," said I to the Theban, who was sitting not far off, silently smoking, "we are going into strange countries—have you no fear?" "You remember, master," he answered, "that we left Cairo on a lucky day, and why should I fear, since all things are in the hands of Allah?"

Eyoub, the Ababdah Guide.

CHAPTER XIV.

THE GREAT NUBIAN DESERT.

The Curve of the Nile—Routes across the Desert—Our Caravan starts—Riding on a Dromedary—The Guide and Camel-drivers—Hair-dressing—El Biban—Scenery—Dead Camels—An Unexpected Visit—The Guide makes my Grave—The River without Water—Characteristics of the Mirage—Desert Life—The Sun—The Desert Air—Infernal Scenery—The Wells of Mûrr-hât—Christmas—Mountain Chains—Meeting Caravans—Plains of Gravel—The Story of Joseph—Djebel Mokrât—The Last Day in the Desert—We see the Nile again.

> "He sees the snake-like caravan crawl
> O'er the edge of the Desert, black and small,
> And nearer and nearer, till, one by one,
> He can count its camels in the sun."—Lowell.

A glance at the map will explain the necessity of my Desert journey. The Nile, at Korosko (which is in lat. 22° 38′), makes a sharp bend to the west, and in ascending his current, one travels in a south-westerly direction nearly to Dongola, thence south to Edabbe, in lat. 18°, after which his course is north-east as far as lat. 19° 30′, where he again resumes the general southern direction. The termini of this immense curve, called by the ancients the "elbows" of the Nile, are Korosko and Abou-Hammed, in southern Nubia. About ninety miles above the former place, at Wadi Halfa, is the second cataract of the Nile, the Southern Thule of Egyptian tourists. The river, between that point and Dongola, is so broken by rapids, that vessels can only pass during the inundation, and then with great difficulty and danger. The exigencies of trade have established, no doubt since the earliest times, the shorter route through the Desert. The distance between Korosko and Abou-Hammed, by the river, is more than six hundred miles, while by the Desert, it is, according to my reckoning, only two hundred and forty-seven miles. The former caravan route led directly from Assouan to Berber and Shendy, and lay some distance to the eastward of that from Korosko. It is the same travelled by Bruce and Burckhardt, but is now almost entirely abandoned, since the countries of Soudân have been made tributary to Egypt. It lies through a chain of valleys, inhabited by the Ababdeh Arabs, and according to Burckhardt, there are trees and water, at short intervals, for the greater part of the way. The same traveller thus describes the route from Korosko: "On that road the traveller finds only a single well, which is situated midway, four long days distant from Berber and as many from Sebooa [near Korosko]. A great inconvenience on that road is that neither trees nor shrubs are anywhere found, whence the camels are much distressed for food, and passengers are obliged to carry wood with them to dress their meals."

On the morning of the 21st of December, the water-skins were filled from the Nile, the baggage carefully divided into separate loads, the unwilling camels received their burdens, and I mounted a dromedary for the first time. My little caravan consisted of six camels, including that of the guide. As it was put in motion, the Governor and Shekh Abou-Mohammed wished me a safe journey and the protection of Allah. We passed the miserable hamlet of Korosko, turned a corner of the mountain-chain into a narrow stony valley, and in a few minutes lost sight of the Nile and his belt of palms. Thenceforth, for many days, the only green thing to be seen in all the wilderness was myself. After two or three hours' travel, we passed an encampment of Arabs, where my Bishàrees added another camel for their own supplies, and two Nubians, mounted on donkeys, joined us for the march to Berber. The first day's journey lay among rugged hills, thrown together confusedly, with no apparent system or direction. They were of jet black sandstone, and resembled immense piles of coke and anthracite. The small glens and basins inclosed in this chaos were filled with glowing yellow sand, which in many places streamed down the crevices of the black rocks, like rivulets of fire. The path was strewn with hollow globes of hard, black stones, precisely resembling cannon-balls. The guide gave me one of the size of a rifle-bullet, with a seam around the centre, as if cast in a mould. The thermometer showed a temperature of eighty degrees at two P. M., but the heat was tempered by a pure, fresh breeze. After eight hours' travel, I made my first camp at sunset, in a little hollow inclosed by mountains, where a gray jackal, after being twice shot at, came and looked into the door of the tent.

I found dromedary-riding not at all difficult. One sits on a very lofty seat, with his feet crossed over the animal's shoulders or resting on his neck. The body is obliged to rock backward and forward, on account of the long, swinging gait, and as there is no stay or fulcrum except a blunt pommel, around which the legs are crossed, some little power of equilibrium is necessary. My dromedary was a strong, stately beast, of a light cream color, and so even a gait, that it would bear the Arab test: that is, one might drink a cup of coffee, while going on a full trot, without spilling a drop. I found a great advantage in the use of the Oriental costume. My trowsers allowed the legs perfect freedom of motion, and I soon learned so many different modes of crossing those members, that no day was sufficient to exhaust them. The rising and kneeling of the animal is hazardous at first, as his long legs double together like a carpenter's rule, and you are thrown backwards and then forwards, and then backwards again, but the trick of it is soon learned. The soreness and fatigue of which many travellers complain, I never felt, and I attribute much of it to the Frank dress. I rode from eight to ten hours a day, read and even dreamed in the saddle, and was at night as fresh and unwearied as when I mounted in the morning.

My caravan was accompanied by four Arabs. The guide, Eyoub, was an old Ababdeh, who knew all the Desert between the Red Sea and the Nile, as far south as Abyssinia. The camel-drivers were of the great Bishàree tribe, which extends from Shendy, in Ethiopia, through the eastern portion of the Nubian Desert, to the frontiers of Egypt. They owned the burden camels, which they urged along with the cry of "Yo-ho! Shekh Abd-el Kader!" and a shrill barbaric song, the refrain of which was: "O Prophet of God, help the camels and bring us safely to our journey's end!" They were very susceptible to cold, and a temperature of 50°, which we frequently had in the morning, made them tremble like aspen leaves and they were sometimes so benumbed that they could scarcely load the camels. They were proud of their enormous heads of hair, which they wore parted on both temples, the middle portion being drawn into an upright mass, six inches in height, while the side divisions hung over the ears in a multitude of little twists. These love-locks they anointed every morning with suet, and looked as if they had slept in a hard frost, until the heat had melted the fat. I thought to flatter one of them as he performed the operation, by exclaiming "Beautiful!"—but he answered coolly: "You speak truth: it is very beautiful." Through the central mass of hair a wooden skewer was stuck, in order to scratch the head without disturbing the arrangement. They wore long swords, carried in a leathern scabbard over the left shoulder, and sometimes favored us with a war-dance, which consisted merely in springing into the air with a brandished sword and turning around once before coming down. Their names were El Emeem, Hossayn and Ali. We called the latter Shekh Ali, on account of his hair. He wore nothing but a ragged cotton clout, yet owned two camels, had a tent in the Desert, and gave Achmet a bag of dollars to carry for him. I gave to El Emeem, on account of his shrill voice, the nickname of *Wiz* (wild goose), by which he was thenceforth called. They were all very devout, retiring a short distance from the road to say their prayers, at the usual hours, and performing the prescribed ablutions with sand, instead of water.

On the second morning we passed through a gorge in the black hills, and entered a region called *El Biban*, or "The Gates." Here the mountains, though still grouped in the same disorder, were more open and gave room to plains of sand several miles in length. The narrow openings, through which the road passes from one plain to another, gave rise to the name. The mountains are higher than on the Nile, and present the most wonderful configurations—towers, fortresses, walls, pyramids, temples in ruin, of an inky blackness near at hand, but tinged of a deep, glowing violet hue in the distance. Towards noon I saw a mirage—a lake in which the broken peaks were reflected with great distinctness. One of the Nubians who was with us, pointed out a spot where he was obliged to climb the rocks, the previous summer, to avoid being drowned. During the heavy tropical rains which sometimes fall here, the hundreds of pyramidal hills pour down such floods that the sand cannot immediately drink them up, and the valleys are turned into lakes. The man described the roaring of the waters, down the clefts of the rocks, as something terrible. In summer the passage of the Desert is much more arduous than in winter, and many men and camels perish. The road was strewn with bones and carcasses, and I frequently counted twenty dead camels within a stone's throw. The stone-heaps which are seen on all the spurs of the hills, as landmarks for caravans, have become useless, since one could find his way by the bones in the sand. My guide, who was a great believer in afrites and devils, said that formerly many persons lost the way and perished from thirst, all of which was the work of evil spirits.

My next camp was in the midst of a high circular plain,

surrounded by hundreds of black peaks. Here I had an unexpected visit. I was sitting in my tent, about eight o clock, when I heard the tramp of dromedaries outside, and a strange voice saying: *ana wahed Ingleez* (I am an Englishman). It proved to be Capt. Peel, of the British Navy, (son of the late Sir Robert Peel), who was returning from a journey to Khartoum and Kordofan. He was attended by a single guide, and carried only a water-skin and a basket of bread. He had travelled nearly day and night since leaving Berber, and would finish the journey from that place to Korosko—a distance of four hundred miles—in seven days. He spent an hour with me, and then pushed onward through "The Gates" towards the Nile. It had been his intention to penetrate into Dar-Fûr, a country yet unvisited by any European, but on reaching Obeid, the Capital of Kordofan, his companion, a Syrian Arab, fell sick, and he was himself attacked with the ague This decided him to return, and he had left his baggage and servants to follow, and was making for England with all speed. He was provided with all the necessary instruments to make his travel useful in a scientific point of view, and the failure of his plans is much to be regretted. I was afterwards informed by M. Linant that he met Capt. Peel on the following day, and supplied him with water enough to reach the Nile.

Towards noon, on the third day, we passed the last of the "Gates," and entered the *Bahr bela Ma* (River without Water), a broad plain of burning yellow sand. The gateway is very imposing, especially on the eastern side, where it is broken by a valley or gorge of Tartarean blackness. As we passed the last peak, my guide, who had ridden in advance, dismounted beside what seemed to be a collection of graves—

little ridges of sand, with rough head and foot stones. He sat by one which he had just made. As I came up he informed me that all travellers who crossed the Nubian Desert, for the first time, are here expected to pay a toll, or fee to the guide and camel-men. "But what if I do not choose to pay?" I asked. "Then you will immediately perish, and be buried here. The graves are those of persons who refused to pay." As I had no wish to occupy the beautiful mound he had heaped for me, with the thigh-bones of a camel at the head and foot, I gave the men a few piastres, and passed the place. He then plucked up the bones and threw them away, and restored the sand to its original level.*

The *Bahr bela Ma* spread out before us, glittering in the hot sun. About a mile to the eastward lay (apparently) a lake of blue water. Reeds and water-plants grew on its margin, and its smooth surface reflected the rugged outline of the hills beyond. The Waterless River is about two miles in breadth, and appears to have been at one time the bed of a large stream.

* Burckhardt gives the following account of the same custom, in his travels in Nubia: "In two hours and a half we came to a plain on the top of the mountain called *Akabet el Benat,* the Rocks of the Girls. Here the Arabs who serve as guides through these mountains have devised a singular mode of extorting presents from the traveller; they alight at certain spots in the Akabet el Benat, and beg a present; if it is refused, they collect a heap of sand, and mould it into the form of a diminutive tomb, and then placing a stone at each of the extremities, they apprise the traveller that his tomb is made; meaning, that henceforward, there will be no security for him, in this rocky wilderness. Most persons pay a trifling contribution, rather than have their graves made before their eyes; there were, however, several tombs of this description dispersed over the plain."

It crosses all the caravan routes in the desert, and is supposed to extend from the Nile to the Red Sea. It may have been the outlet for the river, before its waters forced a passage through the primitive chains which cross its bed at Assouan and Kalabshee. A geological exploration of this part of Africa could not fail to produce very interesting results. Beyond the *Bahr bela Ma* extends the broad central plateau of the Desert, fifteen hundred feet above the sea. It is a vast reach of yellow sand, dotted with low, isolated hills, which in some places are based on large beds of light-gray sandstone of an unusually fine and even grain. Small towers of stone have been erected on the hills nearest the road, in order to guide the couriers who travel by night. Near one of them the guide pointed out the grave of a merchant, who had been murdered there two years previous, by his three slaves. The latter escaped into the Desert, but probably perished, as they were never heard of afterwards. In the smooth, loose sand, I had an opportunity of reviving my forgotten knowledge of trackography, and soon learned to distinguish the feet of hyenas, foxes, ostriches, lame camels and other animals. The guide assured me that there were devils in the Desert, but one only sees them when he travels alone.

On this plain the mirage, which first appeared in the *Biban*, presented itself under a variety of wonderful aspects. Thenceforth, I saw it every day, for hours together, and tried to deduce some rules from the character of its phenomena. It appears on all sides, except that directly opposite to the sun, but rarely before nine A. M. or after three P. M. The color of the apparent water is always precisely that of the sky, and this is a good test to distinguish it from real water, which is invariably of a deeper hue. It is seen on a gravelly as well as a sandy surface, and often fills with shining pools the slight depressions in the soil at the bases of the hills. Where it extends to the horizon there is no apparent line, and it then becomes an inlet of the sky, as if the walls of heaven were melting down and flowing in upon the earth. Sometimes a whole mountain chain is lifted from the horizon and hung in the air, with its reflected image joined to it, base to base. I frequently saw, during the forenoon, lakes of sparkling blue water, apparently not a quarter of a mile distant. The waves ripple in the wind; tall reeds and water-plants grow on the margin, and the Desert rocks behind cast their shadows on the surface. It is impossible to believe it a delusion. You advance nearer, and suddenly, you know not how, the lake vanishes. There is a grayish film over the spot, but before you have decided whether the film is in the air or in your eyes, that too disappears, and you see only the naked sand. What you took to be reeds and water-plants probably shows itself as a streak of dark gravel. The most probable explanation of the mirage which I could think of, was, that it was actually a reflection of the sky upon a stratum of heated air, next the sand.

I found the Desert life not only endurable but very agreeable. No matter how warm it might be at mid-day, the nights were always fresh and cool, and the wind blew strong from the north-west, during the greater part of the time. The temperature varied from 50°—55° at 6 A. M. to 80°—85° at 2 P. M. The extremes were 47° and 100°. So great a change of temperature every day was not so unpleasant as might be supposed. In my case, Nature seemed to make a special provision in order to keep the balance right. During the hot hours of the day I never suffered inconvenience from the heat, but up to 85° felt sufficiently cool. I seemed to absorb the rays of the sun, and as night came on and the temperature of the air fell, that of my skin rose, till at last I glowed through and through, like a live coal. It was a peculiar sensation, which I never experienced before, but was rather pleasant than otherwise. My face, however, which was alternately exposed to the heat radiated from the sand, and the keen morning wind, could not accommodate itself to so much contraction and expansion. The skin cracked and peeled off more than once, and I was obliged to rub it daily with butter. I mounted my dromedary with a "shining morning face," until, from alternate buttering and burning, it attained the hue and crispness of a well-basted partridge.

I soon fell into a regular daily routine of travel, which, during all my later experiences of the Desert, never became monotonous. I rose at dawn every morning, bathed my eyes with a handful of the precious water, and drank a cup of coffee. After the tent had been struck and the camels laden, I walked ahead for two hours, often so far in advance that I lost sight and hearing of the caravan. I found an unspeakable fascination in the sublime solitude of the Desert. I often beheld the sun rise, when, within the wide ring of the horizon, there was no other living creature to be seen. He came up like a god, in awful glory, and it would have been a natural act, had I cast myself upon the sand and worshipped him. The sudden change in the coloring of the landscape, on his appearance—the lighting up of the dull sand into a warm golden hue, and the tintings of purple and violet on the distant porphyry hills—was a morning miracle, which I never beheld without awe. The richness of this coloring made the Desert beautiful; it was too brilliant for desolation. The scenery, so far from depressing, inspired and exhilarated me. I never felt the sensation of physical health and strength in such perfection, and was ready to shout from morning till night, from the overflow of happy spirits. The air is an elixir of life—as sweet and pure and refreshing as that which the first Man breathed, on the morning of Creation. You inhale the unadulterated elements of the atmosphere, for there are no exhalations from moist earth, vegetable matter, or the smokes and steams which arise from the abodes of men, to stain its purity. This air, even more than its silence and solitude, is the secret of one's attachment to the Desert. It is a beautiful illustration of the compensating care of that Providence, which leaves none of the waste places of the earth without some atoning glory. Where all the pleasant aspects of Nature are wanting —where there is no green thing, no fount for the thirsty lip, scarcely the shadow of a rock to shield the wanderer in the blazing noon—God has breathed upon the wilderness his sweetest and tenderest breath, giving clearness to the eye, strength to the frame, and the most joyous exhilaration to the spirits.

Achmet always insisted on my taking a sabre as a protection against the hyenas, but I was never so fortunate as to see more than their tracks, which crossed the path at every step. I saw occasionally the footprints of ostriches, but they, as well as the giraffe, are scarce in this Desert. Towards noon, Achmet and I made a halt in the shadow of a rock, or if no rock was at hand, on the bare sand, and took our breakfast. One's daily bread is never sweeter than in the Desert. The rest of the day I jogged along patiently beside the baggage camels, and at sunset halted for the night. A divan on the sand, and a well-filled pipe, gave me patience while dinner was preparing, and afterwards I made the necessary entries in my journal. I had no need to court sleep, after being rocked all day on the dromedary.

At the close of the third day, we encamped opposite a mountain which Eyoub called *Djebel Khattab* (the Mountain of Wood). The *Bahr Khattab*, a river of sand, similar to the Bahr bela Ma, and probably a branch of it, crossed our path. I here discovered that the water-skins I had hired from Shekh Abou-Mohammed were leaky, and that our eight skins were already reduced to four, while the Arabs had entirely exhausted their supply. This rendered strict economy necessary, as there was but a single well on the road. Until noon the next day we journeyed over a vast plain of sand, interrupted by low reefs of black rock. To the south-east it stretched unbroken to the sky, and looking in that direction, I saw two hemispheres of yellow and blue, sparkling all over with light and heat, so that the eye winked to behold them. The colocynth (called by the Arabs *murràr*), grew in many places in the dry, hot sand. The fruit resembles a melon, and is so intensely bitter that no animal will eat it. I made breakfast under the lee of an isolated rock, crowned with a beacon of camel-bones. We here met three Ababdehs, armed with long spears, on their way to Korosko. Soon after mid day the plain was broken by low ranges of hills, and we saw in front and to the east of us many blue mountain-chains. Our road approached one of them—a range, several miles in length, the highest peak of which reached an altitude of a thousand feet. The sides were precipitous and formed of vertical strata but the crests were agglomerations of loose stones, as if shaken out of some enormous coal-scuttle. The glens and gorges were black as ink; no speck of any other color relieved the terrible gloom of this singular group of hills. Their aspect was much more than sterile: it was infernal. The name given to them by the guide was *Djìlet e' Djìndee*, the meaning of which I could not learn. At their foot I found a few thorny shrubs, the first sign of vegetation since leaving Korosko.

We encamped half an hour before sunset on a gravelly plain, between two spurs of the savage hills, in order that our camels might browse on the shrubs, and they were only too ready to take advantage of the permission. They snapped off the hard, dry twigs, studded with cruel thorns, and devoured them as if their tongues were made of cast-iron. We were now in the haunts of the gazelle and the ostrich, but saw nothing of them. Shekh Ali taught me a few words of the Bishàree language, asking for the English words in return, and was greatly delighted when I translated *okàm* (camel), into "O camel!" "Wallah!" said he, "your language is the same as ours." The Bishàree tongue abounds with vowels, and is not unmusical. Many of the substantives commence with *o*—as *omek*, a donkey; *oshà*, a cow; *ogana*, a gazelle. The plural changes *o* into *a*, as *akam*, camels; *amek*, donkeys, &c. The language of the Ababdehs is different from that of the Bishàrees, but probably sprang from the same original stock. Lepsius considers that the Kenoos dialect of Nubia is an original African tongue, having no affinity with any of the Shemitic languages.

On the fifth day we left the plain, and entered a country

of broken mountain-ranges. In one place the road passed through a long, low hill of slate rock, by a gap which had been purposely broken. The strata were vertical, the laminæ varying from one to four inches in thickness, and of as fine a quality and smooth a surface as I ever saw. A long wady, or valley, which appeared to be the outlet of some mountain-basin, was crossed by a double row of stunted doum-palms, marking a water-course made by the summer rains. Eyoub pointed it out to me, as the half-way station between Korosko and Abou-Hammed. For two hours longer we threaded the dry wadys, shut in by black, chaotic hills. It was now noonday, I was very hungry, and the time allotted by Eyoub for reaching *Bir Mûrr-hàt* had passed. He saw my impatience and urged his dromedary into a trot, calling out to me to follow him. We bent to the west, turned the flank of a high range, and after half an hour's steady trotting, reached a side-valley or cul-de-sac, branching off from the main wady. A herd of loose camels, a few goats, two black camel's-hair tents, and half a dozen half-naked Ababdehs, showed that we had reached the wells. A few shallow pits, dug in the centre of the valley, furnished an abundance of bitter, greenish water, which the camels drank, but which I could not drink. The wells are called by the Arabs *el morra*, "the bitter." Fortunately, I had two skins of Nile-water left, which, with care, would last to Abou-Hammed. The water was always cool and fresh, though in color and taste it resembled a decoction of old shoes.

We found at the wells Capt. Peel's Syrian friend, Churi, who was on his way to Korosko with five camels, carrying the Captain's baggage. He left immediately after my arrival, or I might have sent by him a Christmas greeting to friends at home. During the afternoon three slave-merchants arrived, in four days from Abou-Hammed. Their caravan of a hundred and fifty slaves was on the way. They were tall, strong, handsome men, dark-brown in complexion, but with regular fea-

The Wells of Murr-Hat.

tures. They were greatly pleased with my sketch-book, but retreated hastily when I proposed making a drawing of them. I then called Eyoub into my tent, who willingly enough sat for the rough sketch which heads this chapter. Achmet did his best to give me a good Christmas dinner, but the pigeons were all gone, and the few fowls which remained were so spiritless from the heat and jolting of the camel, that their slaughter anticipated their natural death by a very short time Nevertheless, I produced a cheery illumination by the tent-lanterns, and made Eyoub and the Bishàrees happy with a bottle of arakee and some handfulls of tobacco. The wind whistled drearily around my tent, but I glowed like fire from the oozing out of the heat I had absorbed, and the Arabs without, squatted around their fire of camel's dung, sang the wild, monotonous songs of the Desert.

We left Mûrr-hàt at sunrise, on the morning of the sixth day. I walked ahead, through the foldings of the black mountains, singing as I went, from the inspiration of the brilliant sky and the pure air. In an hour and a half the pass opened on a broad plain of sand, and I waited for my caravan, as the day was growing hot. On either side, as we continued our journey, the blue lakes of the mirage glittered in the sun. Several isolated pyramids rose above the horizon, far to the East, and a purple mountain-range in front, apparently two or three hours distant, stretched from east to west. "We will breakfast in the shade of those mountains," I said to Achmet, but breakfast-time came and they seemed no nearer, so I sat down in the sand and made my meal. Towards noon we met large caravans of camels, coming from Berber. Some were laden with gum, but the greater part were without burdens, as they were to be sold in Egypt. In the course of the day upwards of a thousand passed us. Among the persons we met was Capt. Peel's *cáwass*, or janissary (whom he had left in Khartoum), on his return, with five camels and three slaves which he had purchased on speculation. He gave such a dismal account of Soudân, that Achmet was quite gloomy for the rest of the day.

The afternoon was intensely hot, the thermometer standing at 100°, but I felt little annoyance from the heat, and used no protection against it. The sand was deep and the road a weary one for the camels, but the mountains which seemed so near at hand in the morning were not yet reached. We pushed forward; the sun went down, and the twilight was over before we encamped at their base. The tent was pitched by the light of the crescent moon, which hung over a pitchy-black peak. I had dinner at the fashionable hour of seven. Achmet was obliged to make soup of the water of Mûrr-hàt, which had an abominable taste. I was so drowsy that before my pipe was finished, I tumbled upon my mattress, and was unconscious until midnight, when I awoke with the sensation of swimming in a river of lava. Eyoub called the mountain *Kab el Kafass* —an absurd name, without meaning—but I suspect it is the same ridge which crosses the caravan route from Shendy to Assouan, and which is called Djebel Shigre by Bruce and Burckhardt.

The tent was struck in the morning starlight, at which time the thermometer stood at 55°. I walked alone through the mountains, which rose in conical peaks to the height of near a thousand feet. The path was rough and stony until I reached the outlet of the pass. When the caravan came up, I found that the post-courier who left Korosko two days after us, had joined it. He was a jet-black, bare-headed and bare-legged Bishàree, mounted on a dromedary. He remained with us all day, and liked our company so well that he encamped with us, in preference to continuing his journey. On leaving the mountain, we entered a plain of coarse gravel, abounding with pebbles of agate and jasper. Another range, which Eyoub called Djebel Dighlee, appeared in front, and we reached it about noon. The day was again hot, the mercury rising to 95°. It took us nearly an hour to pass Djebel Dighlee, beyond which the plain stretched away to the Nile, interrupted here and there by a distant peak. Far in advance of us lay Djebel Mokràt, the limit of the next day's journey. From its top, said Eyoub, one may see the palm-groves along the Nile. We encamped on the open plain, not far from two black pyramidal hills, in the flush of a superb sunset. The ground was traversed by broad strata of gray granite, which lay on the surface in huge boulders. Our camels here found a few bunches of dry, yellow grass, which had pierced the gravelly soil. To the south-east was a mountain called by the Arabs *Djebel Nogàra* (the Mountain of the Drum), because, as Eyoub declared, a devil who had his residence among its rocks, frequently beat a drum at night, to scare the passing caravans.

The stars were sparkling freshly and clearly when I rose, on the morning of the eighth day, and Djebel Mokràt lay like a faint shadow on the southern horizon. The sun revealed a few isolated peaks to the right and left, but merely distant isles on the vast, smooth ocean of the Desert. It was a rapture to breathe air of such transcendent purity and sweetness. I breakfasted on the immense floor, sitting in the sun, and then jogged on all day, in a heat of 90°, towards Djebel Mokràt, which seemed as far off as ever. The sun went down, and it was still ahead of us. "That is a *Djebel Shaytan*," I said to Eyoub; "or rather, it is no mountain; it is an afrite." "O Effendi!" said the old man, "don't speak of afrites here. There are many in this part of the Desert, and if a man travels alone here at night, one of them walks behind him and forces him to go forward and forward, until he has lost his path." We rode on by the light of the moon and stars—silently at first, but presently Shekh Ali began to sing his favorite song of "*Yallah salaàmeh, el-hamdu lillàh fôk belàmeh*," and one of the Kenoos, to beguile the way, recited in a chanting tone copious passages from the Koran. Among other things, he related the history of Joseph, which Achmet translated to me The whole story would be too long to repeat, but portions of it are interesting.

"After Joseph had been thrown into the well," continued the Kenoos, "a caravan of Arabs came along, and began to draw water for the camels, when one of the men said: 'O Shekh, there is something in the well.' 'Well,' said the Shekh, 'if it be a man, he belongs to me, but if it be goods, you may have them.' So they drew it up, and it was Joseph, and the Shekh took him to Cairo and sold him to Azeez (Potiphar). [I omit his account of Potiphar's wife, which could not well be repeated.] When Joseph was in prison, he told what was the meaning of the dreams of Sultan Faraoon's baker and butler who were imprisoned with him. The Sultan himself soon afterwards had a dream about seven fat cows eating seven lean ones, which nobody could explain. Then the jailer went to Faraoon, and said: 'Here is Joseph, in jail—he can tell you all about it.' Faraoon said: 'Bring him here, then.' So they put Joseph in a bath, washed him, shaved his head, gave him a new white turban, and took him to the Sultan, who said to him: 'Can you explain my dream?' 'To be sure I can,' said Joseph, 'but if I tell you, you must make me keeper of your magazines.' 'Very well:' said Faraoon. Then Joseph told how the seven fat cows meant seven years when the Nile would have two inundations a year, and the seven lean cows, seven years afterwards when it would have no inundation at all; and he said to Faraoon that since he was now magazine-keeper, he should take from all the country as far as Assouan, during the seven fat years, enough wheat and dourra and beans, to last during the seven lean ones." The narrator might have added that the breed of fat kine has never been restored, all the cattle of Egypt being undoubted descendants of the lean stock.

Two hours after sunset, we *killed* Djebel Mokràt, as the Arabs say: that is, turned its corner. The weary camels were let loose among some clumps of dry, rustling reeds, and I stretched myself out on the sand, after twelve hours in the saddle. Our water was nearly exhausted by this time, and the provisions were reduced to hermits' fare—bread, rice and dates. I had, however, the spice of a savage appetite, which was no sooner appeased, than I fell into a profound sleep. I could not but admire the indomitable pluck of the little donkeys owned by the Kenoos. These animals not only carried provisions and water for themselves and their masters, the whole distance, but the latter rode them the greater part of the way; yet they kept up with the camels, plying their little legs as ambitiously the last day as the first. I doubt whether a horse would have accomplished as much under similar circumstances.

The next morning we started joyfully, in hope of seeing the Nile, and even Eyoub, for the first time since leaving Korosko, helped to load the camels. In an hour we passed the mountain of Mokràt, but the same endless plain of yellow gravel extended before us to the horizon. Eyoub had promised that we should reach Abou-Hammed in half a day, and even pointed out some distant blue mountains in the south, as being beyond the Nile. Nevertheless, we travelled nearly till noon without any change of scenery, and no more appearance of river than the abundant streams of the mirage, on all sides. I drank my last cup of water for breakfast, and then continued my march in the burning sun, with rather dismal spirits. Finally, the Desert, which had been rising since we left the mountain, began to descend, and I saw something like round granite boulders lying on the edge of the horizon. "Effendi, see the doum trees!" cried Eyoub. I looked again: they *were* doum-palms, and so broad and green that they must certainly stand near water. Soon we descended into a hollow in the plain, looking down which I saw to the south a thick grove of trees, and over their tops the shining surface of the Nile. "Ali," I called to my sailor-servant, "look at that great *bahr shaytan!*" The son of the Nile, who had never before, in all his life, been more than a day out of sight of its current, was almost beside himself with joy. "Wallah, master," he cried, "that is no river of the Devil: it is the real Nile—the water of Paradise." It did my heart good to see his extravagant delight. "If you were to give me five piastres, master," said he, "I would not drink the bitter water of Mûrr-hàt." The guide made me a salutation, in his dry way, and the two Nubians greeted me with "a great welcome to you, O, Effendi!" With every step the valley unfolded before me—such rich deeps of fanlike foliage, such a glory in the green of the beans and lupins, such radiance beyond description in the dance of the sunbeams on the water! The landscape was balm to my burning eyes, and the mere sight of the glorious green herbage was a sensuous delight, in which I rioted for the rest of the day.

The Tent-Door, at Abou Hammed

CHAPTER XV

THE ETHIOPIAN FRONTIER.

A Draught of Water—Abou-Hammed—The Island of Mokràt—Ethiopian Scenery—The People—An Ababdeh Apollo—Encampment on the Nile—Tomb of an Englishman—Eesa's Wedding—A White Arab—The Last Day of the Year—Abou-Hashym—Incidents—Loss of my Thermometer—The Valley of Wild Asses—The Eleventh Cataract—Approach to Berber—Vultures—Eyoub Outwitted—We reach El Mekheyref—The Caravan Broken up.

Achmet and I began to feel thirst, so we hurried on in advance, to the mud hamlet of Abou-Hammed. We dismounted on the bank of the river, where we were received by a dark Ababdeh, who was officiating in place of the Governor, and invited me to take possession of the latter's house. Achmet gave him a large wooden bowl and told him to fill it from the Nile, and we would talk to him afterwards. I shall never forget the luxury of that long, deep draught. My body absorbed the water as rapidly as the hot sand of the Desert, and I drank at least a quart without feeling satisfied. I preferred my tent to the Governor's house, and had it pitched where I could look out on the river and the palms. Abou-Hammed is a miserable village, inhabited by a few hundred Ababdehs and Bisharees. The Desert here extended to the water's edge, while the opposite banks were as green as emerald. There was a large mud fortress, with round bastions at the corners, to the west of the village. It formerly belonged to an Ababdeh Shekh, but was then deserted.

In the afternoon I crossed to the island of Mokrât, which lies opposite. The vessel was a sort of a canoe, made of pieces of the doum-palm, tied together with ropes and plastered with mud. My oarsmen were two boys of fifteen, half-naked fellows with long, wild hair, yet very strong and symmetrical limbs and handsome features. I landed in the shade of the palms, and walked for half an hour along the shore, through patches of dourra and cotton, watered by the creaking mills. The whole island, which is upwards of twenty miles long, is level and might be made productive, but the natives only cultivate a narrow strip along the water. The trees were doum and date palm and acacia, and I saw in the distance others of a rich, dark green, which appeared to be sycamore. The hippopotamus is found here, and the boatmen showed me the enormous tracks of three, which had made havoc among their bean-patches the day before. As I was returning to the boat I met three natives, tall, strong, stately men. I greeted them with "Peace be with you!" and they answered "Peace be with you," at the same time offering their hands. We talked for some time in broken Arabic, and I have rarely seen such good-will expressed in savage features. In fact, all the faces I now saw were of a superior stamp to that of the Egyptians. They expressed not only more strength and independence, but more kindness and gentleness.

I procured a lean sheep for eight piastres, and after Achmet had chosen the best parts for my dinner, I gave the remainder to Eyoub and the Bishàrees. The camels were driven down to the river, but only three drank out of the six. I took my seat in the shade of the tent, and looked at the broad blue current of the Nile for hours, without being wearied of the scene. Groups of tall Bishàrees stood at a respectable distance, gazing upon me, for a Frank traveller was no common sight. In the evening I attempted to reduce my desert temperature by a bath in the river, but I had become so sensitive to cold that the water made me shudder in every nerve, and it required a double portion of pipes and coffee to restore my natural warmth.

I left Abou-Hammed at noon the next day, having been detained by some government tax on camels, which my Bishàrees were called upon to pay. Our road followed the river, occasionally taking to the Desert for a short distance, to cut off a bend, but never losing sight of the dark clumps of palms and the vivid coloring of the grain on the western bank. The scenery bore a very different stamp from that of Egypt. The colors were darker, richer and stronger, the light more intense and glowing, and all forms of vegetable and animal life penetrated with a more full and impassioned expression of life. The green of the fields actually seemed to throb under the fiery gush of sunshine, and the palm leaves to thrill and tremble in the hot blue air. The people were glorious barbarians—

large, tall, full-limbed, with open, warm, intelligent faces and lustrous black eyes. They dress with more neatness than the Egyptian Fellahs, and their long hair, though profusely smeared with suet, is arranged with some taste and clothes their heads better than the dirty cotton skull-cap. Among those I saw at Abou-Hammed were two youths of about seventeen, who were wonderfully beautiful. One of them played a sort of coarse reed flute, and the other a rude stringed instrument, which he called a *tambour*. He was a superb fellow, with the purest straight Egyptian features, and large, brilliant, melting black eyes. Every posture of his body expressed a grace the most striking because it was wholly unstudied. I have never seen human forms superior to these two. The first, whom I named the Apollo Ababdese, joined my caravan, for the journey to Berber. He carried with him all his wealth—a flute, a sword, and a heavy shield of hippopotamus hide. His features were as perfectly regular as the Greek, but softer and rounder in outline. His limbs were without a fault, and the light poise of his head on the slender neck, the fine play of his shoulder-blades and the muscles of his back, as he walked before me, wearing only a narrow cloth around his loins, would have charmed a sculptor's eye. He walked among my camel-drivers as Apollo might have walked among the other shepherds of King Admetus. Like the god, his implement was the flute; he was a wandering minstrel, and earned his livelihood by playing at the festivals of the Ababdehs. His name was Eesa, the Arabic for Jesus. I should have been willing to take several shades of his complexion if I could have had with them his perfect ripeness, roundness and symmetry of body and limb. He told me that he smoked no tobacco and drank no ara kee, but only water and milk—a true offshoot of the golden age!

Abebdeh Flute and Tambour Players.

We encamped for the night in a cluster of doum-palms, near the Nile. The soil, even to the edge of the millet-patches which covered the bank, was a loose white sand, and shone like snow under the moon, while the doum-leaves rustled with as dry and sharp a sound as bare boughs under a northern sky. The wind blew fresh, but we were sheltered by a little rise of land, and the tent stood firm. The temperature (72°) was delicious; the stars sparkled radiantly, and the song of crickets among the millet reminded me of home. No sooner had we encamped than Eesa ran off to some huts which he spied in the distance, and told the natives that they must immediately bring all their sheep and fowls to the Effendi. The poor people came to inquire whether they must part with their stock, and were very glad when they found that we wanted nothing. I took only two cucumbers which an old man brought and humbly placed at my feet

The next morning I walked ahead, following the river bank but the camels took a shorter road through the Desert, and passed me unobserved. After walking two hours, I sought for them in every direction, and finally came upon Ali, who was doing his best to hold my dromedary down. No sooner had I straddled the beast than he rose and set off on a swinging gallop to rejoin the caravan. During the day our road led along the edge of the Desert, sometimes in the sand and sometimes over gravelly soil, covered with patches of thorny shrubs. Until I reached the village of Abou-Hashym, in the evening, there was no mark of cultivation on the eastern bank, though I saw in places the signs of fields which had long since been deserted. I passed several burying grounds, in one of which the guide showed me the grave of Mr. Melly, an English gentleman who died there about a year previous, on his return to Egypt with his family, after a journey to Khartoum. His tomb was merely an oblong mound of unburnt brick, with a rough stone at the head and foot. It had been strictly respected by the natives, who informed me that large sums were given to them to keep it in order and watch it at night. They also told me that after his death there was great difficulty in procuring a shroud. The only muslin in the neighborhood was a piece belonging to an old Shekh, who had kept it many years, in anticipation of his own death. It was sacred, having been sent to Mecca and dipped in the holy well of Zemzem. In this the body was wrapped and laid in the earth. The grave was in a dreary spot, out of sight of the river and surrounded by desert thorns.

We had a strong north-wind all day. The sky was cloudless, but a fine white film filled the air, and the distant mountains had the pale, blue-gray tint of an English landscape. The Bishàrees wrapped themselves closely in their mantles as they walked, but Eesa only tightened the cloth around his loins, and allowed free play to his glorious limbs. He informed me that he was on his way to Berber to make preparations for his marriage, which was to take place in another moon. He and Hossayn explained to me how the Ababdehs would then come together, feast on camel's flesh, and dance their sword-dances. "I shall go to your wedding, too," I said to Eesa. "Will you indeed, O Effendi!" he cried, with delight: "then I shall kill my she-camel, and give you the best piece." I asked whether I should be kindly received among the Ababdehs, and Eyoub declared that the men would be glad to see me, but that the women were afraid of Franks. "But," said Achmet, "the Effendi is no Frank." "How is this?" said Eyoub, turning to me. "Achmet is right," I answered; "I am a white Arab, from India." "But do you not speak the Frank language, when you talk with each other?" "No," said Achmet, "we talk Hindustanee." "O, praised be Allah!" cried Hossayn, clapping his hands with joy: "praised be Allah, that you are an Arab, like ourselves!" and there was such pleasure in the faces of all, that I immediately repented of having deceived them. They assured me, however, that the Ababdehs would not only admit me into their tribe, but that I might have the handsomest *Ababdiyeh* that could be found, for a wife. Hossayn had already asked Achmet to marry the eldest of his two daughters, who was then eleven years old.

I passed the last evening of the year 1851 on the bank of the Nile, near Abou-Hashym. There was a wild, green island in the stream, and reefs of black rock, which broke the current into rapids. The opposite shore was green and lovely, crowned with groups of palms, between whose stems I had glimpses of blue mountains far to the south and west. The temperature was mild, and the air full of the aroma of mimosa blossoms. When night came on I enjoyed the splendid moon and starlight of the tropics, and watched the Southern Cross rise above the horizon. The inhabitants of the village beat their wooden drums lustily all night, to scare the hippopotami away from their bean-fields. My dream before waking was of an immense lion, which I had tamed, and which walked beside me—a propitious omen, said the Arabs.

The morning was so cold that the Bishàrees were very languid in their movements, and even I was obliged to don my capote. Eesa helped the men in all the freedom of his naked limbs, and showed no signs of numbness. The village of Abou-Hashym extends for three or four miles along the river, and looked charming in the morning sunshine, with its bright fields of wheat, cotton and dourra spread out in front of the tidy clay houses. The men were at work among the grain, directing the course of the water, and shy children tended the herds of black goats that browsed on the thorns skirting the Desert. The people greeted me very cordially, and when I stopped to wait for the camels an old man came running up to inquire if I had lost the way. The western bank of the river is still richer and more thickly populated, and the large town of Bedjem, capital of the Beyooda country, lies just opposite Abou-Hashym. After leaving the latter place our road swerved still more from the Nile, and took a straight course over a rolling desert tract of stones and thorns, to avoid a very long curve of the stream. The air was still strong from the north, and the same gray vapor tempered the sunshine and toned down the brilliant tints of the landscape.

We passed several small burying-grounds, in which many of the graves were decked with small white flags stuck on poles, and others had bowls of water placed at the head—a custom for which I could get no explanation. Near El Bagh-eyr, where we struck the river again, we met two Bedouins, who had turned merchants and were taking a drove of camels to Egypt. One of them had the body of a gazelle which he had shot two days before, hanging at his saddle, and offered to sell to me, but the flesh had become too dry and hard for my teeth. Ali succeeded in buying a pair of fowls for three piastres, and brought me, besides, some doum-nuts, of the last year's growth. I could make no impression on them until the rind had been pounded with stones. The taste was like that of dry gingerbread, and when fresh, must be very agreeable. In the fields I noticed a new kind of grain, the heads of which resembled rice. The natives called it *dookhn*, and said that it was even more nutritious than wheat or dourra, though not so palatable.

I signalized New-Year's Day, 1852, by breaking my thermometer, which fell out of my pocket as I was mounting my dromedary. It was impossible to replace it, and one point wherein my journey might have been useful was thus lost. The variations of temperature at different hours of the day were very remarkable, and on leaving Korosko I had commenced a record which I intended to keep during the whole of my stay in Central Africa.* In the evening I found in the

* The following record of the temperature, from the time of leaving Korosko to the date of the accident which deprived me of the thermom-

Nile a fish about four feet long, which had just been killed by a crocodile. It was lying near the water's edge, and as I descended the bank to examine it, two slender black serpents slid away from before my feet.

We struck the tent early the next morning, and entered on the *akaba*, or pass of the *Wady el-homar.* (Valley of Asses.) It was a barren, stony tract, intersected with long hollows, which produced a growth of thorns and a hard, dry grass, the blades of which cut the fingers that attempted to pluck it. We passed two short ranges of low hills, which showed the same strata of coal-black shale, as in the Nubian Desert. The *akaba* takes its name from the numbers of wild asses which are found in it. These beasts are remarkably shy and fleet, but are sometimes killed and eaten by the Arabs. We kept a sharp look-out, but saw nothing more than their tracks in the sand. We met several companies of the village

eter, is interesting, as it shows a variation fully equal to that of our own climate:

		7 A. M.	12 M.	2 P. M.
Korosko,	Dec. 21st	59°	75°	80°
Desert,	" 22	50°	74°	80°
"	" 23	55°	75° (Bahr bela Ma)	85°
"	" 24	51°	70°	78°
"	" 25	54°	78°	85°
"	" 26	60°	91°	100°
"	" 27	55°	—	95°
"	" 28	59°	—	90°
Abou Hammed	" 29	61°	—	90°
The Nile	" 30	59°	—	85°
"	" 31	52°	78°	84°
"	Jan. 1st, 1852	47°	70°	68°

Arabs, travelling on foot or on donkeys. The women were unveiled, and wore the same cotton mantle as the men, reaching from the waist to the knees. They were all tolerably old, and, unlike the men, were excessively ugly. An Ababdeh, riding on his dromedary, joined company with us. He was naked to the loins, strongly and gracefully built, and sat erect on his high, narrow saddle, as if he and his animal were one—a sort of camel-centaur. His hair was profuse and bushy, but of a fine, silky texture, and "short Numidian curl," very different from the crisp wool of the genuine negro.

In the afternoon we reached the Nile again, at his Eleventh Cataract. For a space of two or three miles his bed is filled with masses of black rock, in some places forming dams, over which the current roars in its swift descent. The eastern bank is desert and uninhabited, but the western delighted the eye with the green brilliance of its fields. In a patch of desert grass we started a large and beautiful gazelle, spotted like a fallow-deer. I rode towards it and approached within thirty yards before it moved away. At sunset we reached a village called Ginnaynetoo, the commencement of the Berber country The inhabitants, who dwelt mostly in tents of palm-matting, were very friendly. As I was lying in my tent, in the evening, two, who appeared to be the principal persons of the place, came in, saluted me with "Peace be with you!" and asked for my health, to which I replied: "Very good, Allah be praised!" Each of them then took my hand in his, pressed it to his lips and forehead, and quietly retired.

We resumed our march through a dry, rolling country, grown with thorns, acacias in flower, and occasional doum-trees. Beyond the Nile, whose current was no longer to be seen, stretched the long mountain of Berber, which we first discerned the day previous, when crossing the rise of the Wady el-homar. The opposite bank was a sea of vivid green, as far as the eye could reach. Near the water the bean and lupin flourished in thick clusters; behind them extended fields of cotton, of a rich, dark foliage; and still beyond, tall ranks of dourra, heavy with ripening heads. Island-like groups of date-trees and doum-palms studded this rich bed of vegetation, and the long, blue slope of the mountain gave a crowning charm to the landscape. As we approached the capital of Berber, the villages on our right became more frequent, but our path still lay over the dry plain, shimmering with the lakes of the mirage. We passed a score of huge vultures, which had so gorged themselves with the carcase of a camel, that they could scarcely move out of our way. Among them were several white hawks, a company of crows, and one tall black stork, nearly five feet in height, which walked about with the deliberate pace of a staid clergyman. Flocks of quail rose before our very feet, and a large gray dove, with a peculiar cooing note, was very abundant on the trees.

My *shaytan* of a guide, Eyoub, wanted to stop at a village called El Khassa, which we reached at two o'clock. El Mekheyref, he said, was far ahead, and we could not get there; he would give us a sheep for our dinner; the Effendi must prove his hospitality (but all at the Effendi's expense), and many other weighty reasons—but it would not do. I pushed on ahead, made inquiries of the natives, and in two hours saw before me the mud fortress of El Mekheyref. The camel-men, who were very tired, from the long walk from Korosko, would willingly have stopped at El Khassa, but when I pointed out

Berber, and Achmet told them they could not deceive me, for I had the truth written in a book, they said not a word.

We entered the town, which was larger, cleaner and handsomer than any place I had seen since leaving Siout. Arnaout soldiers were mixed with the Arabs in the streets, and we met a harem of Cairene ladies taking a walk, under the escort of two eunuchs. One of them stopped and greeted us, and her large black eyes sparkled between the folds of her veil as she exclaimed, in great apparent delight: "Ah, I know you come from Cairo!" I passed through the streets, found a good place for my tent on the high bank above the water, and by an hour before sunset was comfortably encamped. I gave the men their backsheesh—forty-seven piastres in all, with which they were well satisfied, and they then left for the tents of their tribe, about two hours distant. I gave Eesa some trinkets for his bride, which he took with "God reward you!" pressed my hand to his lips, and then went with them.

CHAPTER XVI.

MY RECEPTION IN BERBER.

A Wedding—My Reception by the Military Governor—Achmet—The Bridegroom—A Guard—I am an American Bey—Kêff—The Bey's Visit—The Civil Governor—About the Navy—The Priest's Visit—Riding in State—The Dongolese Stallion—A Merchant's House—The Town—Dinner at the Governor's—The Pains of Royalty—A Salute to the American Flag—Departure.

I WAS sitting at my tent-door at dusk, after a luxurious dinner of fowls and melons, when we suddenly heard a great sound of drums and Arab singing, with repeated discharges of musketry. The people told us that a marriage was being celebrated, and proposed that I should go and take part in the festivities. I therefore partly resumed my Frank dress, and told Achmet that he must no longer represent me as a Turk, since, in the conquered countries of Soudân the ruling race is even more unpopular than the Franks. "Well, master," said he; "but I must at least make you an American Bey, because some rank is necessary in these countries." He took a lantern, and we set out, in the direction of the noises.

As we passed the mosque, a priest informed us that the wedding was at the Governor's house, and that the bridegroom was the son of a former Governor's *wekeel*, or deputy. The drums guided us to a spacious court-yard, at the door of which stood guards in festive dresses. The court was lighted by a large open brazier of charcoal, fastened on the end of a high pole, and by various colored lanterns. Long benches were ranged across the central space, facing the Governor's mansion, and upon them sat many of the inhabitants of the town, listening to the music. The Arnaout soldiers, in their picturesque dresses, were squatted around the walls, their yataghans and long guns gleaming in the moonlight. The musicians sat on a raised platform, beside the steps leading to the door. There were half a dozen drums, some Arab flutes, and a chorus of strong-lunged singers, who chanted a wild, barbaric epithalamium, in perfect time and accord. The people all saluted us respectfully, and invited us to enter. The Albanian guards ushered us into a lofty room, roofed with palm-logs, which were carefully chosen for their size and straightness. A broad, cushioned divan ran around two sides of the apartment. Here sat the military Governor, with his principal officers, while richly-dressed soldiers stood in waiting. An immense glass lantern gave light to this striking picture.

The Governor, who was called Yagheshir Bey (although he held the lower rank of a *Sanjak*), was an Albanian, and commander of the Egyptian troops in Berber and Shendy. He received me with great kindness, and made room for me beside him on the divan. He was a tall, stately man, about fifty years of age; his face was remarkably handsome, with a mild, benevolent expression, and he had the manners of a finished gentleman. On my left hand was one of his officers, also a tall, fur-capped Albanian. I presented both of the dignitaries with cigars, for which they seemed to have a great relish. Coffee soon appeared, served by negro slaves, in rich blue dresses, and then the Bey's shebook, with a mouth-piece studded with diamonds, was filled for me. The slaves presently returned, with large glass cups filled with delicious sherbet, which they offered upon gold-fringed napkins. Achmet, being seated on the other side of the Governor, was mistaken by the attendants for the American Bey, notwithstanding his dark complexion, and served first. I could not but admire the courtly ease of his manners, which belonged rather to the born son of a Pasha, than to the poor orphan boy of Luxor, indebted only to his honesty, quick sense, and the kindness of an English lady, for a better fate than that of the common Fellahs of Egypt. Yet with all the respect which he knew so well how to command, his devotion to me, as a servant, was unchanged, and he was as unremitting in his attentions as if soul and body had been given him expressly for my use.

The Bey, learning that I was bound for Khartoum, sent a soldier for the shekh of the harbor, whom he commanded, in my presence, to procure a boat for me, and see that it was ready to sail the next day. The only boats in this region are rough, open crafts, but the shekh promised to erect a tent of palm-mats on the poop, to serve as a cabin. Soon after he left the bridegroom appeared, led by an attendant, as he was totally blind. He was a handsome youth of eighteen, and in his air there was a charming mixture of the bridegroom's dignity and the boy's bashfulness. He was simply, but very tastefully dressed, in a blue embroidered jacket, white silk shirt, white shawl fringed with gold, full white trowsers and red slippers. He was led to the Governor, kissed his hand, and begged him to ask me if he might not be allowed to have dinner prepared for me. The officers asked me whether I knew of any remedy for his blindness, but as I found that the sight had been destroyed by cataract, I told them there was no help for him nearer than Cairo. The ceremonies were all over, and the bride, after the entire consummation of the nuptials, had gone to her father's house, to remain four days.

The Bey, finding that I was not a merchant, asked Achmet what rank I held, and the latter answered that in my own country it was something between a Bey and a Pasha. Before we left, three soldiers were sent down to the river, and, as I afterwards learned, remained all night, standing with whips over the poor sailors who were employed in removing the cargo from the hold of the vessel, which the shekh of the harbor had selected for me. The raïs was threatened with a hundred lashes, unless he had every thing ready by the next day. On leaving, I gave a *medjid* to the servants, as a gratuity is expected on such occasions. The Bey sent me one of his Arnaouts to carry the lantern, and insisted on stationing a guard near my tent. Two soldiers came soon afterwards, who sat upon my camp-chests and smoked my tobacco until morning. Many of the soldiers were slaves, who received only fifteen piastres a month, beside their rations. The Arnaouts were paid one hundred and twenty-five piastres, and thirty-five piastres additional, provided they furnished their own equipments. As I pulled off my turban and threw myself on my mattress, I involuntarily contrasted my position with that of the previous evening. Then, I slept in the midst of a cluster of Arab huts, a simple Howadji, among camel-drivers. Now, I was an American Bey, in my tent overlooking the Nile, watched by a guard of honor sent me by the commander of the military forces in Berber and Shendy. Al. honor to Ethiopian hospitality! For here was at last the true Ethiopia, beyond the confines of Nubia; beyond the ancient Capital of Queen Candace; beyond, not only the first and second, but the eleventh cataract of the Nile, and not far distant from "the steep of utmost Axumè."

The morning brought with it no less pleasant experiences. Seated at the door of my tent, indolently smoking, lulled by the murmuring of the Nile and cheered by the brightness of the green sea that bathed his western shore, I enjoyed the first complete *kèff* since leaving Egypt. The temperature was like that of an American June, and my pulse beat so full and warm, my whole body was so filled with a sense of health, of strength in repose, of pure physical satisfaction, that I could not be otherwise than happy. My pleasure was disturbed by an old Arab, who came up with two beautiful goats, which I supposed he wanted to sell, but when Achmet returned from the bazaar, I found that they were a present from the Bey.

As I was sitting at breakfast, an hour later, I heard Achmet talking loudly with some one on the outside of the tent, and called to him to know what was the matter. He stated that an officer had just arrived to announce the Bey's approach, but that he had ordered him to go back and say that I was at breakfast, and the Bey must not come for half an hour. "You have done a very rude thing," I said; for I felt annoyed that the Bey should receive such a message, as coming from me. "Don't be alarmed, master," he coolly replied; "the Bey is now certain that you are of higher rank than he." Fortunately, I had a handsome tent, the best of tobacco and pure Mocha coffee, so that I could comply with the requisites of Eastern hospitality in a manner worthy of my supposed rank. The tent was put in order, and I arranged a divan on one side, made of my carpet, mattress and capote. The two lantern-poles, bound together, formed a mast, which I planted at the door, and then run up the American flag. The preparations were scarcely completed before the Bey appeared, galloping up on a superb, jet-black stallion, with half a dozen officers in attendance. As he dismounted, I advanced to receive him. According to Arab etiquette, the highest in rank enters first, and true to Achmet's prediction, the Bey, after taking my hand, requested me to precede him. I declined, out of courtesy to him, and after a polite controversy on the subject, he passed his arm affectionately around my waist, and we went in side by side. Achmet had excellent coffee and sherbet in readiness, but the Bey preferred my cigars to the shebook. As he sat beside me on the divan, I thought I had rarely seen a nobler countenance. He had an unusually clear, large hazel eye, a long but not prominent nose, and the lines of fifty years had softened and subdued an expression which may have been fierce and fearless in his younger days. He was from a village near Parga, in Albania, and was delighted when I told him that not long previous, I had sailed past the shores of his native land.

He had no sooner taken his leave than the Civil Governor, *ad interim*, Mustapha Kashif, arrived, attended by his chief secretary, Mahmoud Effendi. Mustapha was an Anatolian, small in stature and quite withered and wasted by the torrid climate of Berber. His skin had a dark unhealthy hue, and his eyes a filmy glare, which I attributed to other causes than the diseased liver of which he complained. He immediately asked for arakee, and when I told him that it was bad for the liver, said it was the only thing which did him good. Mahmoud Effendi, who was a good-humored Turk, made himself quite at home. I showed them my sketches, with which they were greatly diverted. A remark of the Governor gratified me exceedingly, as it showed that all the attention I received was paid me, not on account of my supposed rank, but from the fact of my being the first American who had ever visited the place. "I have been in this country twenty-four years," said he, "and in all that time only some French and two or three German and English travellers have passed through. You are the first I have seen from *Yenkee-Doonea.* [This sounds very much like Yankee-Doodledom, but is in reality the Turkish for "New World."] You must not go home with an unfavorable account of us." He had once, when in Alexandria, visited an American man-of-war, which, it appeared, had left a strong impression upon his mind. After mentioning the circumstance, he asked me how many vessels there were in our Navy. I had mastered the Arabic language sufficiently to know the necessity of exaggeration, and answered, without hesitation, that there were one hundred. "Oh no!" said Mustapha, turning to Mahmoud, the Secretary: "His Excellency is entirely too modest. I know very well that there are *six hundred* vessels in the American Navy!" I had fallen far below the proper mark; but Achmet tried to straighten the matter by saying that I meant one hundred ships-of-the-line, and did not include the frigates, sloops-of-war, brigs and corvettes.

Before the Governor had finished his visit, there was a stir outside of the tent, and presently the Chief Mollah—the high priest of the mosque of Berber—made his appearance. He was a tall, dark-skinned Arab of between fifty and sixty years of age, and wore a long robe of the color sacred to Mahomet, with a turban of the same, under which the ends of a scarf of white gauze, embroidered with Arabic characters in gold, hung on both sides of his face. His manner was quiet and dignified, to a degree which I never saw excelled by any Christian divine. He refused the pipe, but took coffee and sherbet, holding the former two or three times alternately to each eye, while he murmured a form of prayer. He was very much delighted with my sketches, and I was beginning to feel interested in his remarks, when the Governor's servant appeared, leading a splendid chesnut stallion, with a bridle of scarlet silk cord, and trappings of cloth of the same royal color. He was brought in order that I might take a ride through the city. "But," said I to Achmet, "I cannot go until this priest has left." "You forget your high rank, O master!" said the cunning dragoman; "go without fear, and I will take charge of the priest." Without more ado, I took a hasty leave of the mollah, and swung myself into the saddle. The animal shot off like a bolt from a cross-bow, leaving the Governor to follow in my wake, on his favorite gray ass. On reaching the mosque, I waited for him, and we entered the bazaars together. He insisted on my preceding him, and at his command all the merchants rose and remained standing until we passed. All eyes were of course fixed upon me, and I had some difficulty in preserving a serious and dignified countenance, as I thought of my cracked nose and Abyssinian complexion. Two of the Governor's slaves attended me, and one of them, who had a remarkably insolent and scornful expres sion, was the only person who did not seem impressed by my presence. The fellow's face was disagreeable to me; he was the death's-head at my banquet.

The stallion was a noble beast, so full of blood and fire that it was worth a month's journey through the Desert to bestride him. He was small, and his limbs were scarcely long enough for the breadth of his chest and the fulness of his flanks. He had, however, the slender head and brilliant eye of the Arab breed, and his powerful neck expressed a fine disdain of other horses. He was of the best Dongolese stock, but resembled in many points the famed Anatolian breed of Asia Minor. He pranced and caracoled impatiently as I forced him to accommodate his pace to that of the ignoble ass. "Let him run!" said the Governor, as we reached a broad open square near the outskirts of the city. I slackened the rein, and he dashed away with a swiftness that almost stopped my breath. I am but an ordinary rider, but owing to the Turkish saddle, had no difficulty in keeping a firm seat and controlling the powerful steed. We visited the mud fortress of Berber, which is a square structure, with a bastion at each corner, having embrasures for three cannon, and the Governor gave me to understand that they made a mighty sound, every time they were fired. He then took me to the house of a French merchant, with a name something like D'Arfou. The merchant was absent in Cairo, but a black slave gave us admittance. We took seats in a cool portico, admired the Frenchman's handsome gray donkey and his choice cows, looked out the windows upon his garden, planted with fig, orange, banana and pomegranate trees, and were finally served with coffee, presented in heavy silver *zerfs*. A slave then appeared, bringing his child, a pretty boy of two years old, born of an Abyssinian mother. He refused to be taken into the Governor's arms, and contemplated me, his Frank relative, with much more satisfaction. M. D'Arfou's house—although the walls were mud, the floors gravel and the roof palm-logs—was cool, roomy and pleasant; and for that region, where one cannot easily have marble pavements and jasper fountains, was even luxurious.

We mounted again, and the Governor took me through the city, to its southern extremity. It is more than a mile in length, and contains about twenty thousand inhabitants. The houses are all of mud, which, though unsightly in appearance, is there as good as granite, and the streets are broad, clean, and unmolested by dogs. I was well pleased with the appearance of the place. The inhabitants are mostly Nubians, of the different tribes between Berber and Dongola, mixed with a few Ababdehs, Bisharees, and other Desert Arabs. Though scantily dressed, they seemed contented, if not with their masters, at least with their condition. Among the crowd that gathered to see us, I recognized Eesa, arrayed in a new, snow-white garment, and looking like a bronze Ganymede. He gazed at me wistfully, as if uncertain whether he should dare to speak, but I hailed him at once with: "*Salaamàt, ya Eesa!*" and he replied proudly and joyfully. After our tour was over, the Governor took me to his house, which, after that of the Pasha, was the finest one in the place. His reception-room was cool, with a broad divan, upon which we stretched ourselves at ease, sharing the single pillow between us. The attendants were dressing in an adjoining room, and presently appeared in all the splendor of snow-white turbans and trow sors. I was presented with a pipe, and as a great treat, a bottle of the mastic cordial of Scio was brought. The Governor insisted on my drinking three small glasses of it, three being the fortunate number. At this juncture Achmet appeared, to my great relief, for my whole stock of Arabic was exhausted.

We were about to leave, but the Governor declared that it was impossible. It would be disgraceful to him, should we not take dinner in his house, and in order that we might not be delayed, he ordered it to be served at once. I was willing enough to make use of this opportunity of partaking of an Arab dinner. First, a slave appeared, and gave each of us a napkin, which we spread over our knees. He was followed by another, who bore a brass ewer, and a pitcher from which he poured water over our hands. A small stand upholding a large circular piece of tin, was then placed before us. A covered dish stood in the centre, and a rampart of thin wheaten cakes, resembling Mexican tortillas, adorned the circumference. The cover was removed, disclosing a thick soup, with balls of dough and meat. We took the ebony spoons, and now behold the Governor, Achmet and I dipping fraternally into the same bowl, and politely stirring the choice lumps into each other's spoons. Mustapha was in the most hilarious humor, but his four dark attendants stood before us as solemn as Death. I thought then, and still think, that they hated him cordially. The soup was followed by a dish of *kibābs*, or small pieces of meat, fried in grease. These we picked out with our fingers, and then, tearing the wheat cakes into slices, sopped up the sauce. About ten different compounds of meat and vegetables followed, each unlike any thing I ever tasted before, but all quite palatable. The only articles I was able to detect in the whole dinner, were mutton-cutlets, egg-plants and sour milk Each dish was brought on separately, and we all three ate therefrom, either with spoons or fingers. When the repast was finished, water was brought again, and we washed our hands and quietly awaited the pipes and coffee. When we arose to leave, Achmet was about to give the customary medjid to the servants, but the Governor prevented him. Nevertheless, he found an opportunity as I was mounting, to slip it into the hand of the scornful slave, who took it without relaxing the scowl upon his features. I pranced back to my tent upon the chestnut stallion, from which I parted with more regret than from its owner.

By this time, every thing was in readiness for my departure. The sailors, who had worked all night with the whips of the Albanian soldiers hung over their backs (unknown to me, or I should not have permitted it), had brought the vessel to the bank below my tent, and the Bey had sent me his promised letter to the Governor of Shendy. The pleasures of royalty were now over, and I had to deal with some of its pains. All the officers and servants who had been employed for my benefit expected backsheesh, and every beggar in the place came to taste the bounty of the foreign king. When Achmet went to the bazaars to purchase a few necessaries, he overheard the people saying to one another, "That is the interpreter of the strange king," and many of them rose and remained standing until he had passed. Ali, who had spent the whole day apparently in hunting for chickens and pigeons, but Eblis knew for what in reality, was assailed on all sides with inquiries: "Who is this that has come among us? What high rank does he possess, that he receives such honor?"

Ali, who had known me merely as a Howadji, was somewhat perplexed how to explain the matter, but got out of his difficulty by declaring that I was the son of the great king of all the Franks.

I shall not soon forget that noble old Albanian, Yagheshir Bey. Achmet, who paid him a parting visit, and was received with the greatest kindness, conceived a strong affection for him. The Bey, on learning that I was ready to leave, sent word to me that he would bring a company of his Arnaouts down to the bank of the Nile, and salute my flag. "It is the first time that flag has been seen here," said he to Achmet, "and I must have it properly honored." And truly enough, when we were all embarked, and I had given the stars and stripes to the Ethiopian winds, a company of about fifty soldiers ranged themselves along the high bank, and saluted the flag with a dozen rattling volleys.

As I sailed away I returned the salute with my pistols, and the soldiers fired a parting volley after me for good luck on the voyage, but so recklessly that I heard the sharp whistle of the bullets quite close to the vessel. I felt more grateful to the Bey for this courtesy than for his kindness to myself. But Berber was soon left behind; for the wind was fair, and bore me southward, deeper into Africa.

CHAPTER XVII.

THE ETHIOPIAN NILE.

Fortunate Travel—The America—Ethiopian Scenery—The Atbara River—Damer—A Melon Patch—Agriculture—The Inhabitants—Change of Scenery—The First Hippopotamus—Crocodiles—Effect of My Map—The Raïs and Sailors—Arabs in Ethiopia—Ornamental Scars—Beshir—The Slave Bakhita—We Approach Meroë.

"Fair is that land as evening skies,
And cool—though in the depth it lies
Of burning Africa."—WORDSWORTH.

THE voyage from Berber to Khartoum was another link in my chain of fortunate travel. The Ethiopian Nile seemed to me more beautiful than the Egyptian; at least, the vegetation was richer, the air milder and sweeter, the water purer, and to crown all, the north-wind unfailing. Day and night there was a fresh, steady breeze, carrying us smoothly against the current, at the precise rate of speed which is most pleasant in a sailing craft—three to four miles an hour. The temperature was that of an American June, the nights deliciously mild and sweet, and the full moon shone with a splendor unknown in northern latitudes. I was in perfect health of body, and suffered no apprehension or anxiety for the future to disturb my happy frame of mind.

El Mekheyref looked very picturesque in the soft clear

light of the last afternoon hour, as I sailed away from it. The Bey's mansion and the mosque rose conspicuously above the long lines of clay walls, and groups of luxuriant date-trees in the gardens supplied the place of minarets and spires. Both shores, above the city, were in a high state of cultivation, and I passed many thriving villages before dusk. Even under the moon, the corn-fields on either hand were green and bright. I was installed in a temporary cabin, formed of my tent-canvas, stretched over a frame of palm-sticks, erected on the narrow poop-deck. Achmet and Ali took possession of the hold, which they occupied as kitchen and store-room. The raïs, sailors, and the two beautiful sheep which the Bey gave me, were grouped on the forecastle. On this first evening, the men, fatigued by their extra labors on my account, were silent, and I was left to the full enjoyment of the scene. The waves rippled pleasantly against the prow of the *America;* the frogs and crickets kept up a concert along the shore, and the *zikzak*, or crocodile-bird, uttered his sharp, twittering note at intervals. Hours passed thus, before I was willing to close my eyes.

The landscapes next morning were still more beautiful. The Nile was as broad as in Lower Egypt, flowing between banks of the most brilliant green. Long groves of palms behind the shore, shut out from view the desert tracts beyond, and my voyage all day was a panorama of the richest summer scenery. Early in the forenoon I passed the mouth of the Atbara, the ancient Astaboras, and the first tributary stream which the traveller meets on his journey from the Mediterranean. Its breadth is about one-third that of the main river but the volume of water must be in a much smaller proportion. The water is a clear, bright green, and its junction with the darker Nile is distinctly marked. I could look up the Atbara for about a mile, to where it curved out of sight between high green banks covered with flowering mimosas. It was a charming piece of river scenery, and I longed to follow the stream upward through the wild domains of the Hallengas and Hadendoas, through the forests and jungles of Takka and Schangalla, to where, an impetuous torrent, it foams through the Alpine highlands of Samen, under the eternal snows of Abba-Jaret and Amba-Hai. In Abyssinia it bears the name of Tacazze, but afterwards through the greater part of its course, is called the Atbara (and the country it waters, Dar Atbara), except at its junction with the Nile, where the natives name it El-bahr Mogran.

Two or three hours later we reached the large town of Damer, which gives its name to the point of land between the two rivers. It is a quarter of a mile from the shore, and is a collection of mud buildings, scattered through a grove of sont trees. My sailors stopped to get some mats, and I climbed the bank to look at the place, but there was nothing in the view to tempt me to enter. During the day we stopped at an island in the river, to buy some vegetables. Two men were guarding a large patch of ripe melons and cucumbers, behind which extended fields of dourra, divided by hedges of a kind of shrub cypress, all overgrown with a purple convolvulus in flower, and a wild gourd-vine, with bright yellow blossoms. In wandering through the luxuriant mazes of vegetation, I came upon a dwelling of the natives—a nest or arbor, scooped out of a thick clump of shrubs, and covered with dry branches. It resembled the *milpas*, or brush-huts of the Mexican rancheros. The only furniture was a frame of palm-sticks, serving as a divan, and four stones, arranged so as to form a fire-place On returning to the shore, I found Achmet in dispute with the two men. He had taken some melons, for which he offered them two and a half piastres. They demanded more, but as he had purchased melons for less in El Mekheyref, he refused, and giving them the money, took the melons perforce. "Well," said they, "you are our masters, and we must submit;" but they would sell no more to my sailors. The latter, however, procured a bowl of treacle, made of dates, and some sour milk, at another hut, and were contented therewith. The bean-fields along the shore had just been trampled down by a hippopotamus, whose huge foot-prints we saw in the soft mud near the water.

All day, we sailed between shores of vegetation, of the ripest green. Both banks of the river, through this region, are studded with water-wheels, whose creaking ceases not by day nor by night. It was pleasant to see the strings of jars ascending and descending, and to hear the cool plashing of the precious blood of the Nile, as it poured into the branching veins which are the life of that teeming soil. The wheels were turned by oxen, driven by Dinka slaves, who sang vociferous melodies the while, and the water was conveyed to fields distant from the river in the hollow trunks of the doum-tree.

There, where I expected to sail through a wilderness, I found a garden. Ethiopia might become, in other hands, the richest and most productive part of Africa. The people are industrious and peaceable, and deserve better masters. Their dread of the Turks is extreme, and so is their hatred. I stopped one evening at a little village on the western bank The sailors were sent to the houses to procure fowls and eggs, and after a long time two men appeared, bringing, as they said, the only chicken in the place. They came up slowly, stooped and touched the ground, and then laid their hands on their heads, signifying that they were as dust before my feet. Achmet paid them the thirty paras they demanded, and when they saw that the supposed Turks had no disposition to cheat them, they went back and brought more fowls. Travellers who go by the land routes give the people an excellent character for hospitality. I was informed that it is almost impossible to buy anything, even when double the value of the article is tendered, but by asking for it as a favor, they will cheerfully give whatever they have.

When I crept out of my tent on the third morning, the features of the scenery were somewhat changed. A blue chain of hills, which we had passed in the night, lay behind us, and a long, graceful mountain range rose on the right, broken by a pass which was cut through it at right angles to its course. The mountains retreated out of my horizon during the forenoon, but in the afternoon again approached nearly to the water's edge, on the eastern bank. They were of a dark-red color, exhibiting a broken, mound-like formation. We passed several islands during the day—beds of glorious vegetation. The sakias were turning at intervals of a hundred yards or less, and the rustling fields of wheat and dourra seemed bursting with the fulness of their juices. I now began to notice that warm vermilion tinge of the clouds, which is frequently exhibited near the Equator, but is nowhere so striking as in Central Africa. Lying heavily along the horizon, in the warm hours of the day, they appeared to glow with a dead, smouldering fire, like brands which are soft white ashes on the out side, but living coals within.

On the same day I saw the first hippopotamus. The men discerned him about a quarter of a mile off, as he came up to breathe, and called my attention to him. Our vessel was run towards him, and the sailors shouted, to draw his attention: "How is your wife, old boy?" "Is your son married yet?" and other like exclamations. They insisted upon it that his curiosity would be excited by this means, and he would allow us to approach. I saw him at last within a hundred yards, but only the enormous head, which was more than three feet in breadth across the ears. He raised it with a tremendous snort, opening his huge mouth at the same time, and I thought I had never seen a more frightful-looking monster. He came up in our wake, after we had passed, and followed us for some time. Directly afterwards we spied five crocodiles on a sand-bank. One of them was of a grayish-yellow color, and upward of twenty feet in length. We approached quietly to within a few yards of them, when my men raised their poles and shouted. The beasts started from their sleep and dashed quickly into the water, the big yellow one striking so violently against our hull, that I am sure he went off with a head-ache. The natives have many superstitions concerning the hippopotamus, and related to me some astonishing examples of his cunning and sagacity. Among others, they asserted that an Arab woman, at Abou-Hammed, went down to the river to wash some clothes, once upon a time. She laid the garments upon some smooth stones, and was engaged in trampling them with her feet, when a huge hippopotamus thrust his head out of the river, and after watching her for some time, made for the shore. The woman fled in terror, leaving the clothes behind her; whereupon the beast immediately took her place, and pounded away so vigorously with his feet, that in a short time there was not left a fragment as big as your hand.

On making inquiries for the ruins of Meroë, which we were then approaching, the raïs only knew that there were some "*beioot kadeem*" (ancient houses) near the village of Bedjerowiyeh, which we would probably reach that night. As I found on my map a name which nearly corresponded to that of the village, I had no doubt that this was Meroë, and gave orders that the boat should halt until the next day. The raïs was greatly surprised at my knowing the names of all the towns along the river, seeing that I had never been there before. I showed him my map, and told him that I knew from it, the name of every mountain, every village, and every river, from Cairo to Abyssinia. The men crowded around and inspected it with the utmost astonishment, and when I pointed out to them the location of Mecca, and read them the names of all the villages as far as Khartoum, they regarded it with an expression of reverential awe. "Wallah!" exclaimed the raïs: "this is truly a wonderful Frank!"

My raïs, whose name was Bakhid, belonged, with his men, to the Nubian tribe of Màhass, below Dongola. They were tall, well-formed men, with straight features and high cheekbones, but the lips were thicker than those of the Arab tribes of Ethiopia. The latter are of almost pure Shemitic blood, and are descended from families which emigrated into Africa from the Hedjaz, seven or eight centuries ago. This accounts for the prevalence and purity of the Arab language in these regions. The descendants of the Djaaleyn, or tribe of Beni

Koreish, of Yemen, are still to be found in the country of the Atbara, and there are those in Ethiopia, who claim to be descendants from the line of the Abbasides and the Ommiades. There has been very little intermixture with the negro races beyond Sennaar, who are looked upon as little better than wild beasts. The Arabic language is spoken from the Red Sea to the borders of Dar-Fūr and Bornou, and according to Burckhardt, the prevalent idioms are those of Hedjaz, in Arabia. The distinction between the descendants of the old Arab stock, and those who, like the Ababdehs and Bishàrees, belong to the native African races, is obvious to the most careless observer. The latter, however, must not be confounded with the Negro race, from which they differ still more widely.

Raïs Bakhid had with him a son named Ibrahim—a boy of twelve. His head was shaven so as to leave a circular tuft of hair on the crown; large silver rings hung from his ears, and each cheek was adorned with four broad scars—three horizontal, and one vertical,—which were produced by gashing the skin with a knife, and then raising the flesh so as to prevent the edges from uniting. All the Nubian tribes are scarred in the same way, frequently upon the breast and back as well as the face, and the number and position of the marks is generally a token of the particular tribe to which the person belongs. The slaves brought from the mountains of Fazogl, on the Abyssinian frontier, have a still greater profusion of these barbaric ornaments. I had another Mahassee on board—a fellow of five and twenty, named Beshir, who kept all the others in a continual laugh with his droll sayings. He spoke the dialect of his tribe, not a word of which I could understand, but his face and voice were so comical, that I laughed involuntarily whenever he spoke. He was a graceless fellow, given to all sorts of debauchery, and was never so happy as when he could drink his fill of *om bilbil*, (the "mother of nightingales,") as the beer of the country is called, because he who drinks it, sings.

Another curious character was an old woman named Bakhita, a slave of the owner of the vessel, who acted as cook for the sailors. She sat squatted on the forward deck all day hideously and nakedly ugly, but performed her duties so regularly and with such a contented face, laughing heartily at all the jokes which the men made at her expense, that I soon learned to tolerate her presence, which was at first disgusting. She was a native of the mountains of Dar-Für, but had been captured by the slave-hunters when a child. She was in Shendy on the night when Ismaïl Pasha and his soldiers were burned to death by Mek Nemr, in the year 1822. But with all my questioning, she could give no account of the scene, and it was a marvel that she remembered it at all. Life was to her a blank page, and what one day might write upon it, the next day erased. She sat from morning till night, grinding the dourra between two flat stones, precisely as the Mexican women grind their maize, occasionally rubbing her hands upon her woolly head to rid them of the paste. Her only trouble was my white sheep, which, in its search after food, would deliberately seize her mealy top-knots and begin to chew them. Her yells, at such times, were the signal for a fresh attack of Beshir's drollery. Yet old, and ugly, and imbruted as she was, no Frankish belle, whose bloom is beginning to wane, could have been more sensitive about her age. I was delighted to find this touch of vanity in her; it was the only trace of feminine nature she ever betrayed. Beshir's declaration that she was a hundred and fifty years old, roused her to fury. She rose up, turned to me with a face so hideously distorted that I could not laugh at it, and yelled out: "Look at me, O my lord! and tell me if this son of a dog speaks the truth!" "He lies, Bakhita," I answered; "I should say that you were not more than thirty years old." The fury of her face was instantly replaced by a simper of vanity which made it even more hideous; but from that time Bakhita considered me as her friend. Beshir, who never missed an opportunity of hailing the people on shore, called out one day to a damsel who came down to the river for water: "Here is your sister on board" The amiable maiden, not at all pleased with the comparison, rejoined "Am I sister to a hyena?"—a compliment, over which the old woman chuckled for a long time.

The wind fell at sunset, when we were about seven miles from Meroë, and while the sailors moored the boat to the shore and built a fire to cook the head and ribs of my sheep, I climbed the bank, to get a sight of the country. As far as I could see, the soil was cultivated, principally with cotton and dourra. The cotton was both in flower and pod, and was of excellent quality. Achmet and I visited a water-mill, under the charge of a Dinka slave, who came up humbly and kissed our hands We commanded him to go on with his work, when he took his seat on the beam of the wheel and drove his cows around, to the accompaniment of a loud, shrill song, which, at a distance harmonized strangely with the cry of the jackal, in the deserts away beyond the river.

CHAPTER XVIII.

THE RUINS OF MEROE.

Arrival at Bedjerowiyeh—The Ruins of Meroë—Walk Across the Plain—The Pyramids—Character of their Masonry—The Tower and Vault—Finding of the Treasure—The Second Group—More Ruins—Site of the City—Number of the Pyramids—The Antiquity of Meroë—Ethiopian and Egyptian Civilization—The Caucasian Race—Reflections.

A LIGHT breeze sprang up soon after midnight, and when I arose, at sunrise, we were approaching the village of Bedjerowiyeh. By the time coffee was ready, the America was moored at the landing-place, and Raïs Bakhid, who was familiar with all the localities, stood in waiting. Achmet, with Beshir and another sailor, also accompanied me. We crossed some fields of cotton and dookhn to the village, which was a cluster of *tokuls*, or circular huts of mud and sticks, in a grove of sont trees. The raïs tried to procure a donkey for me, but the people, who took me for an Egyptian, and appeared very timorous and humble, denied having any, although I saw two half-starved beasts among the trees. We therefore set out on foot, toward a range of mountains, about five miles distant.

The discovery of the ruins of Meroë is of comparatively recent date, and it is only within a very short time that their true character and place in Ethiopian history have been satisfactorily established. Hoskins, Cailliaud and Ferlini were the first to direct the attention of antiquarians to this quarter, and the later and more complete researches of Lepsius leave room for little more to be discovered concerning them. It is remarkable that both Bruce and Burckhardt, who travelled by land from Berber to Shendy, failed to see the ruins, which must have been visible from the road they followed. The former, in fact, speaks of the broken pedestals, carved stones and pottery which are scattered over the plain, and sagely says: "It is impossible to avoid risking a guess that this is the ancient city of Meroë"—but he does not mention the groups of pyramids which are so conspicuous a feature in the landscape.

Our path led over a plain covered with thorny shrubs at first, but afterwards hard black gravel, and we had not gone more than a mile before the raïs pointed out the pyramids of the ancient Ethiopian city. I knew it only from its mention in history, and had never read any description of its remains; consequently I was surprised to see before me, in the vapory morning air, what appeared to be the ruins of pylæ and porticos, as grand and lofty as those of Karnak. Rising between us and the mountains, they had an imposing effect, and I approached them with excited anticipations. As we advanced, however, and the morning vapors melted away, I found that they derived much of their apparent height from the hill upon which they are built, and that, instead of being the shattered parts of one immense temple, they were a group of separate pyramids, standing amid the ruins of others which have been completely destroyed.

We reached them after a walk of about four miles. They

stand upon a narrow, crescent-shaped hill, which rises forty or fifty feet from the plain, presenting its convex front to the Nile, while toward the east its hollow curve embraces a small valley lying between it and the mountain range. Its ridge is crowned with a long line of pyramids, standing so close to each other that their bases almost meet, but presenting no regular plan or association, except in the direction of their faces. None of them retains its apex, and they are all more or less ruined, though two are perfect to within a few courses of the top. I climbed one of the highest, from which I could overlook the whole group, as well as another cluster, which crowned the summit of a low ridge at the foot of the mountains opposite. Of those among which I stood, there were sixteen, in different degrees of ruin, besides the shapeless stone-heaps of many more. They are all built of fine red sandstone, in regular courses of masonry, the spaces of which are not filled, or cased, as in the Egyptian pyramids, except at the corners, which are covered with a narrow hem or moulding, in order to give a smooth outline. The stones are about eighteen inches high, and the recession of each course varies from two to four inches, so that the height of the structure is always much greater than the breadth of the base. A peculiarity of these pyramids is, that the sides are not straight but curved lines, of different degrees of convexity, and the breadth of the courses of stone is adjusted with the utmost nicety, so as to produce this form. They are small, compared with the enormous piles of Gizeh and Dashoor, but singularly graceful and elegant in appearance. Not one of the group is more than seventy feet in height, nor when complete could have exceeded one hundred.

All or nearly all have a small chamber attached to the exterior, exactly against the centre of their eastern sides, but nc passage leading into the interior; and from the traces of Dr Lepsius's labors, by which I plainly saw that he had attempted in vain to find an entrance, it is evident that they are merely solid piles of masonry, and that, if they were intended as tombs, the bodies were deposited in the outer chambers. Some of these chambers are entire, except the roof, and their walls are profusely sculptured with hieroglyphics, somewhat blurred and worn down, from the effect of the summer rains. Their entrances resembled the doorways of temples, on a miniature scale, and the central stones of two of them were sculptured with the sacred winged globe. I saw on the jamb of another a figure of the god Horus. The chambers were quite small, and not high enough to allow me to stand upright. The sculptures have a very different character from those in the tombs of Thebes, and their resemblance to those of the Ptolemaic period was evident at the first glance. The only cartouches of monarchs which I found were so obliterated that I could not identify them, but the figure of one of the kings, grasping in one hand the hair of a group of captives, while with the other he lifts a sword to slay them, bears a striking resemblance to that of Ptolemy Euergetes, on the pylon of the temple at Edfou. Many of the stones in the vast heaps which lie scattered over the hills, are covered with sculptures. I found on some the winged globe and scarabeüs, while others retained the scroll or fillet which usually covers the sloping corners of a pylon. On the northern part of the hill I found several blocks of limestone, which exhibited a procession of sculptured figures brilliantly colored.

The last structure on the southern extremity of the hill is

rather a tower than a pyramid, consisting of a high base or foundation, upon which is raised a square building, the corners presenting a very slight slope towards the top, which is covered with ruins, indicating that there was originally another and narrower story upon it. When complete, it must have borne considerable resemblance to the Assyrian towers, the remains of which are found at Nineveh. On this part of the hill there are many small detached chambers, all facing the east, and the remains of a large building. Here Lepsius appears to have expended most of his labors, and the heaps of stone and rubbish he has left behind him prevent one from getting a very clear idea of the original disposition of the buildings. He has quarried one of the pyramids down to its base, without finding any chamber within or pit beneath it. My raïs, who was at a loss to comprehend the object of my visit, spoke of Lepsius as a great Frank astrologer, who had kept hundreds of the people at work for many days, and at last found in the earth a multitude of chickens and pigeons, all of solid gold. He then gave the people a great deal of backsheesh and went away, taking the golden fowls with him. The most interesting object he has revealed is a vaulted room, about twenty feet long, which the raïs pointed out as the place where the treasures were found. It is possible that he here referred to the discoveries made about twenty years ago by Ferlini, who excavated a great quantity of rings and other ornaments—Greek and Roman, as well as Ethiopian—which are now in the Museum at Berlin. The ceiling of this vault is on the true principle of the arch, with a keystone in the centre, which circumstance, as well as the character of the sculptures, would seem to fix the age of the pyramids at a little more than two thousand years.

I took a sketch of this remarkable cluster of ruins from their northern end, and afterwards another from the valley below, whence each pyramid appears distinct and separate, no one covering the other. The raïs and sailors were puzzled what to make of my inspection of the place, but finally concluded that I hoped to find a few golden pigeons, which the Frank astrologer had not carried away. I next visited the eastern group, which consists of ten pyramids, more or less dilapidated, and the ruined foundations of six or eight more. The largest, which I ascended, consists of thirty-five courses of stone, and is about fifty-three feet in height, eight or ten feet of the apex having been hurled down. Each side of the apex is seventeen paces, or about forty-two feet long, and the angle of ascent is consequently much greater than in the pyramids of Egypt. On the slope of the hill are the substructions of two or three large buildings, of which sufficient remains to show the disposition of the chambers and the location of the doorways. Towards the south, near where the valley inclosed between the two groups opens upon the plain, are the remains of other pyramids and buildings, and some large, fortress-like ruins are seen on the summits of the mountains to the East. I would willingly have visited them, but the wind was blowing fresh, and the raïs was impatient to get back to his vessel. Many of the stones of the pyramids are covered with rude attempts at sculpturing camels and horses; no doubt by the Arabs, for they resemble a school-boy's first drawings on a slate—straight sticks for legs, squares for bodies, and triangles for humps.

Leaving the ruins to the company of the black goats that were browsing on the dry grass, growing in bunches at their eastern base, I walked to another group of pyramids, which lay a mile and a half to the south-west, towards the Nile. As we approached them, a herd of beautiful gray gazelles started from among the stones and bounded away into the Desert. "These were the tents of the poor people," said the raïs, pointing to the pyramids: "the Frank found no golden pigeons here." They were, in fact, smaller and more dilapidated than the others. Some had plain burial chambers attached to their eastern sides, but the sculptures were few and insignificant. There were sixteen in all, more or less ruined. Scattering mounds, abounding with fragments of bricks and building-stones, extended from these ruins nearly to the river's bank, a distance of more than two miles; and the foundations of many other pyramids might be seen among them. The total number of pyramids in a partial state of preservation—some being nearly perfect, while a few retained only two or three of the lower courses—which I counted on the site of Meroë, was *forty-two.* Besides these, I noticed the traces of forty or fifty others, which had been wholly demolished. The entire number, however, of which Meroë could boast, in its prime, was *one hundred and ninety-six.* The mounds near the river, which cover an extent of between one and two miles, point out the site of the city, the capital of the old Hierarchy of Meroë, and the pyramids are no doubt the tombs of its kings and priests. It is rather singular that the city has been so completely destroyed, as the principal spoilers of Egypt, the Persians, never penetrated into Ethiopia, and there is no evidence of the stones having been used to any extent by the Arabs, as building materials.

The examination of Meroë has solved the doubtful question of an Ethiopian civilization anterior to that of Egypt Hoskins and Cailliaud, who attributed a great antiquity to the ruins, were misled by the fact, discovered by Lepsius, that the Ethiopian monarchs adopted as their own, and placed upon their tombs the nomens of the earlier Pharaohs. It is now established beyond a doubt, that, so far from being the oldest, these are the latest remains of Egyptian art; their inferiority displays its decadence, and not the rude, original type, whence it sprang. Starting from Memphis, where not only the oldest Egyptian, but the oldest human records yet discovered, are found, the era of civilization becomes later, as you ascend the Nile. In Nubia, there are traces of Thothmes and Amunoph III., or about fifteen centuries before the Christian era; at Napata, the ancient capital of Ethiopia, we cannot get beyond King Tirhaka, eight centuries later; while at Meroë, there is no evidence which can fix the date of the pyramids earlier than the first, or at furthest, the second century before Christ. Egypt, therefore, was not civilized from Ethiopia, but Ethiopia from Egypt.

The sculptures at Meroë also establish the important fact that the ancient Ethiopians, though of a darker complexion than the Egyptians (as they are in fact represented, in *Egyptian* sculpture), were, like them, an offshoot of the great Caucasian race.* Whether they were originally emigrants from

* In the Letters of Lepsius, which were not published until after my return from Africa, I find the following passage, the truth of which is supported by all the evidence we possess: 'The Ethiopian name comprehended much that was dissimilar, among the ancients. The ancient population of the whole Nile Valley as far as Khartoum, and perhaps, also, along the Blue River, as well as the tribes of the Desert to

Northern India and the regions about Cashmere, as the Egyptians are supposed to have been, or, like the Beni Koreish at a later period, crossed over from the Arabian Peninsula, is not so easily determined. The theory of Pococke and other scholars, based on the presumed antiquity of Meroë, that here was the first dawning on African soil of that earliest Indian Civilization, which afterwards culminated at Memphis and Thebes, is overthrown; but we have what is of still greater significance—the knowledge that the highest Civilization, in every age of the world, has been developed by the race to which we belong.

I walked slowly back to the boat, over the desolate plain, striving to create from those shapeless piles of ruin the splendor of which they were once a part. The sun, and the wind, and the mountains, and the Nile, were what they had ever been; but where the kings and priests of Meroë walked in the pomp of their triumphal processions, a poor, submissive peasant knelt before me with a gourd full of goat's milk; and if I had asked him when that plain had been inhabited, he would have answered me, like Chidhar, the Prophet: "As thou seest it now, so has it been for ever!"

the east of the Nile, and the Abyssinian nations, were in former times probably even more distinctly separated from the negroes than now, and belonged to the Caucasian Race."

Moonlight on the Ethiopian Nile.

CHAPTER XIX.

ETHIOPIAN NIGHTS' ENTERTAINMENTS.

The Landscapes of Ethiopia—My Evenings beside the Nile—Experiences of the Arabian Nights—The Story of the Sultana Zobeide and the Wood-cutter—Character of the Arabian Tales—Religion.

"For it was in the golden prime
Of good Haroun Al-Raschid."—TENNYSON.

WITH my voyage on the Ethiopian Nile a thread of romance was woven, which, in the Oriental mood that had now become native to me, greatly added to the charm of the journey. My nights' entertainments were better than the Arabian. The moon was at the full, and although, during the day, a light north-wind filled my sails, it invariably fell calm at sunset, and remained so for two or three hours. During the afternoon, I lay stretched on my carpet on the deck, looking through half-closed eyes on the glittering river and his banks. The western shore was one long bower of Paradise—so green, so bright, so heaped with the deep, cool foliage of majestic sycamores and endless clusters of palms. I had seen no such beautiful palms since leaving Minyeh, in Lower Egypt. There they were taller, but had not the exceeding richness and glory of these. The sun shone hot in a cloudless blue heaven, and the air was of a glassy, burning clearness, like that which dwells in the inmost heart of fire. The colors of the landscape were as if enamelled on gold, so intense, so glowing in their intoxicating depth and splendor. When, at last, the wind fell—except a breeze just strong enough to shake the creamy odor out of the purple bean-blossoms—and the sun went down in a bed of pale orange light, the moon came up the other side of heaven, a broad disc of yellow fire, and bridged the glassy Nile with her beams.

At such times, I selected a pleasant spot on the western bank of the river, where the palms were loftiest and most thickly clustered, and had the boat moored to the shore. Achmet then spread my carpet and piled my cushions on the shelving bank of white sand, at the foot of the trees, where, as I lay, I could see the long, feathery leaves high above my head, and at the same time look upon the broad wake of the moon, as she rose beyond the Nile. The sand was as fine and soft as a bed of down, and retained an agreeable warmth from the sunshine which had lain upon it all day. As we rarely halted near a village, there was no sound to disturb the balmy repose of the scene, except, now and then, the whine of a jackal prowling along the edge of the Desert. Achmet crossed his legs beside me on the sand, and Ali, who at such times had special charge of my pipe, sat at my feet, ready to replenish it as often as occasion required. My boatmen, after gathering dry palm-leaves and the resinous branches of the mimosa, kindled a fire beside some neighboring patch of *dookhn*, and squatted around it, smoking and chatting in subdued tones, that their gossip might not disturb my meditations. Their white turbans and lean dark faces were brought out in strong relief by the red fire-light, and completed the reality of a picture which was more beautiful than dreams.

On the first of these evenings, after my pipe had been filled for the third time, Achmet, finding that I showed no disposition to break the silence, and rightly judging that I would rather listen than talk, addressed me. "Master," said he, "I know many stories, such as the story-tellers relate in the coffee-houses of Cairo. If you will give me permission, I will tell you some which I think you will find diverting." "Excellent!" said I; "nothing will please me better, provided you tell them in Arabic. This will be more agreeable to both of us, and whenever I cannot understand your words I will interrupt you, and you shall explain them as well as you can, in English." He immediately commenced, and while those evening calms lasted, I had such a living experience of the Arabian Nights, as would have seemed to me a greater marvel than any they describe, had it been foreshown to my boyish vision, when I first hung over the charmed pages. There, in my African mood, the most marvellous particulars seemed quite real and natural, and I enjoyed those flowers of Eastern romance with a zest unknown before. After my recent reception, as a king of the Franks, in the capital of Berber, it was not difficult to imagine myself Shahriar, the Sultan of the Indies, especially as the moon showed me my turbaned shadow on the sand. If the amber mouth-piece of my pipe was not studded with jewels, and if the zerf which held my coffee-cup was brass instead of gold, it was all the same by moonlight. Achmet, seated on the sand, a little below my throne, was Sheherazade, and Ali, kneeling at my feet, her sister, Dinarzade; though, to speak candidly, my imagination could not stretch quite so far. In this respect, Shahriar had greatly the advantage of me. I bitterly felt the difference between my dusky vizier, and his vizier's daughter. Nor did Ali, who listened to the stories with great interest, expressing his satisfaction occasionally by a deep guttural chuckle, ever surprise me by saying: "If you are not asleep, my sister, I beg of you to recount to me one of those delightful stories you know."

Nevertheless, those nights possessed a charm which separates them from all other nights I have known. The stories resembled those of the Arabian tale in being sometimes prolonged from one day to another. One of them, in fact, was "Ganem, the Slave of Love," but, as told by Achmet, differing slightly from the English version. The principal story, however, was new to me, and as I am not aware that it has ever been translated, I may be pardoned for telling it as it was told to me, taking the liberty to substitute my own words for Achmet's mixture of Arabic and English. I was too thoroughly given up to the pleasant illusion, to note down the story at the time, and I regret that many peculiarities of expression have escaped me, which then led me to consider it a genuine product of the age which produced the Thousand and One Nights.

"You already know, my Master," Achmet began, "that many hundred years ago all the people of Islam were governed by a caliph, whose capital was Baghdad, and I doubt not that you have heard of the great Caliph, Haroun Al-Raschid, who certainly was not only the wisest man of his day, but the wisest that has been known since the days of our Prophet, Mohammed, whose name be exalted! It rarely happens that a wise and great man ever finds a wife, whose wisdom is any match for his own; for as the wise men whom Allah sends upon the earth are few, so are the wise women still fewer. But herein was the Caliph favored of Heaven. Since the days of Balkis, the Queen of Sheba, whom even the prophet Solomon could not help but honor, there was no woman equal in virtue or in wisdom to the Sultana Zubeydeh (Zobeide). The Caliph never failed to consult her on all important matters, and her prudence and intelligence were united with his, in the government of his great empire, even as the sun and moon are sometimes seen shining in the heavens at the same time.

"But do not imagine that Haroun Al-Raschid and the Sultana Zubeydeh were destitute of faults. None except the Prophets of God—may their names be extolled for ever!—were ever entirely just, or wise, or prudent. The Caliph was subject to fits of jealousy and mistrust, which frequently led him to commit acts that obliged him, afterwards, to eat of the bitter fruit of repentance; and as for Zubeydeh, with all her wisdom she had a sharp tongue in her head, and was often so little discreet as to say things which brought upon her the displeasure of the Commander of the Faithful.

"It chanced that, once upon a time, they were both seated in a window of the *hareem*, which overlooked one of the streets of Baghdad. The Caliph was in an ill-humor, for a beautiful Georgian slave whom his vizier had recently brought him, had disappeared from the harem, and he saw in this the work of Zubeydeh, who was always jealous of any rival to her beauty. Now as they were sitting there, looking down into the street, a poor wood-cutter came along, with a bundle of sticks upon his head. His body was lean with poverty, and his only clothing was a tattered cloth, bound around his waist. But the most wonderful thing was, that in passing through the wood where he had collected his load, a serpent had seized him by the heel, but his feet were so hardened by toil that they resembled the hoofs of a camel, and he neither felt the teeth of the serpent, nor knew that he was still dragging it after him as he walked. The Caliph marvelled when he beheld this, but Zubeydeh exclaimed: 'See, O Commander of the Faithful! there is the man's wife!' 'What!' exclaimed Haroun, with sudden wrath: 'Is the wife then a serpent to the man, which stings him none the less because he does not feel it? Thou serpent, because thou hast stung me, and because thou hast made sport of the honest poverty of that poor creature, thou shalt take the serpent's place!' Zubeydeh answered not a word, for she knew that to speak would but increase the Caliph's anger. Haroun clapped his hands thrice, and presently Mesrour, his chief eunuch, appeared. 'Here Mesrour!' said he, 'take this woman with thee, follow yonder wood-cutter, and present her to him as his wife, whom the Caliph hath ordered him to accept.'

"Mesrour laid his hands upon his breast and bowed his head, in token of obedience. He then beckoned to Zubeydeh, who rose, covered herself with a veil and a feridjee, such as is worn by the wives of the poor, and followed him. When they had overtaken the wood-cutter, Mesrour delivered to him the message of the Caliph, and presented to him the veiled Zubeydeh. 'There is no God but God!' said the poor man; 'but how can I support a wife—I, who can scarcely live by my own labors?' 'Dost thou dare to disobey the Commander of the Faithful?' cried Mesrour, in such a savage tone, that the man trembled from head to foot; but Zubeydeh, speaking for the first time, said: 'Take me with thee, O Man! since it is the Caliph's will. I will serve thee faithfully, and perhaps the burden of thy poverty may be lightened through me.' The man thereupon obeyed, and they proceeded together to his house, which was in a remote part of the city. There were but two miserable rooms, with a roof which was beginning to fall in, from decay. The wood-cutter, having thrown down his bundle, went out to the bazaar, purchased some rice and a little salt, and brought a jar of water from the fountain. This was all he could afford, and Zubeydeh, who had kindled a fire in the mean time, cooked it and placed it before him. But when he would have had her raise her veil and sit down to eat with him, she refused, saying: 'I have promised that I shall not increase the burden of thy poverty. Promise me, in return, that thou wilt never seek to look upon my face, nor to enter that room, which I have chosen for my apartment. I am not without learning, O Man! and if thou wilt respect my wishes, it shall be well for thee.'

"The wood-cutter, who was not naturally deficient in intelligence, perceived from the words of Zubeydeh that she was a superior person, and, judging that he could not do better than to follow her counsel, promised at once all that she desired

She then declared, that as she intended to take charge of his household, he must give to her, every evening, all the money he had received for his wood during the day. The man consented to this likewise, produced a handful of copper coins, which altogether amounted to only one piastre—but you must know, my master, that a piastre, in the days of Haroun Al-Raschid, was four or five times as much as it is now-a-days Thus they lived together for several weeks, the wood-cutter going to the forest every day, and paying his gains every night into the hands of Zubeydeh, who kept his miserable house clean and comfortable and prepared his food. She managed things with so much economy that she was enabled to save two paras every day, out of the piastre which he gave her. When she had amassed twenty piastres in this way, she gave them to the wood-cutter, saying: 'Go now to the market and buy thee an ass with this money. Thou canst thus bring home thrice as much wood as before, and the ass can subsist upon the grass which he finds in the forest, and which costs thee nothing.' 'By Allah!' exclaimed the wood-cutter; 'thou art a wonderful woman, and I will obey thee in every thing.'

"He forthwith did as Zubeydeh ordered, and was now enabled to give her three or four piastres every evening. She presented him with a more decent garment, and added butter to his pillau of rice, but still preserved such a strict economy, that in a short time he was master of three asses instead of one, and was obliged to hire a man to assist him in cutting wood. One evening, as the asses came home with their loads, Zubeydeh remarked that the wood gave out a grateful fragrance, like that of musk or ambergris, and upon examining it more closely, she found that it was a most precious article—

in fact, that it had been cut from one of those spicy trees which sprang up where the tears of Adam fell upon the Earth, as he bewailed his expulsion from Paradise. For at that time the juices of the fruits of Paradise still remained in his body, and his tears were flavored by them—which was the cause of all the spices that grow in the lands of Serendib and India. Zubeydeh asked of the wood-cutter: 'To whom dost thou sell this wood?' and from his answer she found that it was all purchased by some Jewish merchants, who gave him no more for it than for the common wood with which she cooked his rice. 'The accursed Jews!' she exclaimed: 'Go thou to them immediately, and threaten to accuse them before the Cadi of defrauding a son of the Faith, unless they agree to pay thee for this wood henceforth, twelve times as much as they have paid before!'

"The man lost no time in visiting the Jewish merchants, who, when they saw that their fraud had been discovered, were greatly alarmed, and immediately agreed to pay him all that he demanded. The wood-cutter now brought home every night three donkey-loads of the precious wood, and paid to Zubeydeh from one to two hundred piastres. She was soon able to purchase a better house, where she not only gave the man more nourishing food, but sent for a teacher to instruct him how to read and write. He had so improved in appearance by this time, and had profited so well by the wise conversation of Zubeydeh, that he was quite like another person, and those who had known him in his poverty no longer recognized him. For this reason, the Caliph, who soon repented of his anger towards Zubeydeh and made every effort to recover her, was unable to find any trace of him. Mesrour sought day and night through the streets of Baghdad, but as Zubeydeh never left the wood-cutter's house, all his search was in vain, and the Caliph was like one distracted.

"One day, as the wood-cutter was on his way to the forest he was met by three persons, who desired to hire his asses for the day. 'But,' said he, 'I make my living from the wood which the asses carry to the city.' 'What profit do you make upon each load?' asked one of the men. 'If it is a good load, I often make fifty piastres,' answered the wood-cutter. 'Well,' said the men, 'we will give you two hundred piastres as the hire of each ass, for one day.' The wood-cutter, who had not expected such an extraordinary offer, was about to accept it at once, when he reflected that he had obeyed in all things the advice of Zubeydeh, and ought not to take such a step without her consent. He thereupon requested the men to wait while he returned home and consulted his wife. 'You have done right, O my lord!' said Zubeydeh: 'I commend your prudence, and am quite willing that you should accept the offer of the men, as the money will purchase other asses and repay you for the loss of the day's profit, if the persons should not return.'

"Now the three men were three celebrated robbers, who had amassed a vast treasure, which they kept concealed in a cave in one of the neighboring mountains. They hired the donkeys in order to transport this treasure to a barque in which they had taken passage to Bassora, where they intended to establish themselves as rich foreign merchants. But Allah, who governs all things, allows the plans of the wicked to prosper for a time, only that he may throw them into more utter ruin at the last. The robbers went to their secret cave with the donkeys and loaded them with all their spoils—great sacks of gold, of rubies, diamonds and emeralds, which the beasts were scarcely strong enough to carry. On their way to the river below Baghdad, where the boat was waiting for them, two of them stopped to drink at a well, while the other went on with the asses. Said one of the twain to the other: "Let us kill our comrade, that we may have the greater treasure." He at once agreed, and they had no sooner overtaken the third robber, than the first, with one stroke of his sabre, made his head fly from his body. The two then proceeded together for a short distance, when the murderer said: 'I must have more than half of the treasure, because I killed our comrade.' 'If you begin by claiming more than half, you will in the end claim the whole,' said the other robber, who refused to agree. They presently set upon each other with their swords, and after fighting for some time, both of them received so many wounds that they fell dead in the road.

"The asses, finding that no one was driving them any longer, took, from habit, the road to the wood-cutter's house, where they arrived safely, with the treasure upon their backs Great was the amazement of their master, who, at Zubeydeh's command, carried the heavy sacks into the house. But when he had opened one of them, and the splendor of the jewels filled the whole room, Zubeydeh exclaimed: 'God is great! Now, indeed, I see that my conduct is acceptable to Him, and that His hand hurries my design more swiftly to its completion.' But, as she knew not what had happened to the robbers, and supposed that the owner of the treasure would have his loss proclaimed in the bazaars, she determined to keep the sacks closed for the space of a moon, after which, according to the law, they would become her property, if they had not been claimed in the mean time. Of course, no proclamation of the loss was made, and at the end of the moon, she considered that she had a just right to the treasure, which, upon computation, proved to be even greater than that of the Caliph Haroun Al-Raschid.

"She commanded the wood-cutter to send her at once the most renowned architect of Baghdad, whom she directed to build, exactly opposite to the Caliph's Palace, another palace which should surpass in splendor any thing that had ever been beheld. For the purchase of the materials and the hire of the workmen, she gave him a hundred thousand pieces of gold. 'If men ask,' said she, 'for whom you are building the palace, tell them it is for the son of a foreign king.' The architect employed all the workmen in Baghdad, and followed her instructions so well, that in two months the palace was finished. The like of it had never been seen, and the Caliph's palace faded before its magnificence as the face of the moon fades when the sun has risen above the horizon. The walls were of marble, white as snow; the gates of ivory, inlaid with pearl; the domes were gilded, so that when the sun shone, the eye could not look upon them; and from a great fountain of silver, in the court-yard, a jet of rose-colored water, which diffused an agreeable odor, leaped into air. Of this palace it might be said, in the words of the poet: 'Truly it resembles Paradise; or is it the lost House of Irem, built from the treasures of King Sheddad? May kindness dwell upon the lips of the lord of this palace, and charity find refuge in his heart, that he be adjudged worthy to enjoy such splendor!'

"During the building of the palace, Zubeydeh employed

the best masters in teaching the wood-cutter all the accomplishments which his present condition required that he should possess. In a short time he was a very pattern of elegance in his manner; his words were choice and spoken with dignity and propriety, and his demeanor was that of one born to command rather than to obey. When she had succeeded to the full extent of her wishes, she commenced teaching him to play chess, and spent several hours a day in this manner, until he finally played with a skill equal to her own. By this time, the palace was completed, and after having purchased horses and slaves, and every thing necessary to the maintenance of a princely household, Zubeydeh and the wood-cutter took possession of it during the night, in order that they might not be observed by the Caliph. Zubeydeh bade the wood-cutter remember the promise he had made her. She still retained her own apartments, with a number of female slaves to attend her, and she now presented to him, as a harem becoming a prince, twenty Circassian girls, each one fairer than the morning-star.

"The next morning she called the wood-cutter, and addressed him thus: 'You see, my lord! what I have done for you. You remember in what misery I found you, and how, by your following my advice, every thing was changed. I intend to exalt you still higher, and in order that my plans may not be frustrated, I now ask you to promise that you will obey me in all things, for a month from this time.' Zubeydeh made this demand, for she knew how quickly a change of fortune may change a man's character, and how he will soon come to look upon that as a right which Allah granted him as a boon. But the wood-cutter threw himself at her feet, and said: 'O Queen! it is for you to command, and it is for me to obey

You have taught me understanding and wisdom; you have given me the wealth of kings. May Allah forget me, if I forget to give you, in return, gratitude and obedience.' 'Go, then,' continued Zubeydeh, 'mount this horse, and attended by twenty slaves on horseback, visit the coffee-house in the great bazaar. Take with thee a purse of three thousand pieces of gold, and as thou goest on thy way, scatter a handful occasionally among the beggars. Take thy seat in the coffee-house, where thou wilt see the Vizier's son, who is a skilful player of chess. He will challenge the multitude to play with him, and when no one accepts, do thou engage him for a thousand pieces of gold. Thou wilt win; but pay him the thousand pieces as if thou hadst lost, give two hundred pieces to the master of the coffee-house, divide two hundred pieces among the attendants, and scatter the remainder among the beggars.'

"The wood-cutter performed all that Zubeydeh commanded. He accepted the challenge of the Vizier's son, won the game, yet paid him a thousand pieces of gold as if he had lost, and then rode back to the palace, followed by the acclamations of the multitude, who were loud in their praises of his beauty, the elegance of his speech, his unbounded munificence, and the splendor of his attendance. Every day he visited the coffee house, gave two hundred pieces of gold to the master, two hundred to the servants, and distributed six hundred among the beggars. But the Vizier's son, overcome with chagrin at his defeat, remained at home, where, in a few days, he sickened and died. These things coming to the Vizier's ear, he felt a great desire to see the foreign prince, whose wealth and generosity were the talk of all Baghdad; and as he believed himself to be the greatest chess-player in the world, he determined to challenge him to a game. He thereupon visited the coffee-house, where he had not remained long when the wood-cutter made his appearance, in even greater splendor than before. This was in accordance with the instructions of Zubeydeh, who was informed of all that had taken place. He at once accepted the Vizier's challenge to play, for a stake of two thousand pieces of gold. After a hard-fought battle, the Vizier was fairly beaten, but the wood-cutter paid him the two thousand pieces of gold, as if he had lost the game, gave away another thousand as usual, and retired to his palace.

"The Vizier took his defeat so much to heart, that his chagrin, combined with grief for the loss of his son, carried him off in a few days. This circumstance brought the whole history to the ears of Haroun Al-Raschid himself, who was immediately seized with a strong desire to play chess with the foreign prince, not doubting but that, as he had always beaten his Vizier, he would be more than a match for the new antagonist. Accordingly he sent an officer to the palace of the wood-cutter, with a message that the Commander of the Faithful desired to offer his hospitality to the son of the foreign king. By Zubeydeh's advice, the invitation was accepted, and the officer speedily returned to Haroun Al-Raschid, to whom he gave such a description of the magnificence of the new palace, that the Caliph's mouth began to water, and he exclaimed: 'By Allah! I must look to this. No man, who has not the ring of Solomon on his finger, shall surpass me in my own capital!" In a short time the wood-cutter arrived, attired in such splendor that the day seemed brighter for his appearance, and attended by forty black slaves, in dresses of crimson silk with turbans of white and gold, and golden swords by their sides. They formed a double row from the court-yard tc the throne-hall where the Caliph sat, and up the avenue thus formed the wood-cutter advanced, preceded by two slaves in dresses of cloth-of-silver, who placed at the Caliph's feet two crystal goblets filled with rubies and emeralds of immense size. The Caliph, delighted with this superb present, rose, embraced the supposed prince, and seated him by his side. From the great wealth displayed by the wood-cutter, and the perfect grace and propriety of his manners, the Caliph suspected that he was no less a personage than the son of the King of Cathay.

"After a handsome repast had been served, the Caliph proposed a game of chess, stating that he had heard much of the prince's skill in playing. 'After I shall have played with you, O Commander of the Faithful!' said the wood-cutter, 'you will hear no more of my skill.' The Caliph was charmed with the modesty of this speech, and the compliment to himself, and they immediately began to play. The wood-cutter, although he might easily have beaten the Caliph, suffered the latter to win the first game, which put him into the best humor possible. But when the second game had been played, and the wood-cutter was the victor, he perceived that the Caliph's face became dark, and his good-humor was gone. 'You are too generous to your servant, O Caliph!' said he; 'had you not given me this success as an encouragement, I should have lost a second time.' At these words Haroun smiled, and they played a third game, which the wood-cutter purposely allowed him to win. Such was the counsel given to him by Zubeydeh, who said: 'If thou permittest him to win the first game, he will be so well pleased, that thou mayest venture to defeat him on the second game. Then, when he has won the third game, thy having been once victorious will magnify his opinion of his own skill; for where we never suffer defeat, we at last regard our conquests with indifference.'

"The result was precisely as Zubeydeh had predicted. The Caliph was charmed with the foreign prince, and in a few days made him his Vizier. The wood-cutter filled his exalted station with dignity and judgment, and became at once a great favorite with the people of Baghdad. The month of obedience which he promised to Zubeydeh was now drawing to a close when she said to him: 'Cease to visit the Caliph, and do not leave thy palace for two or three days. When the Caliph sends for thee, return for answer that thou art ill.' She foresaw that the Caliph would then come to see his Vizier, and gave the wood-cutter complete instructions, concerning what he should say and do.

"Haroun Al-Raschid no sooner heard of the illness of his Vizier, than he went personally to his palace, to see him. He was amazed at the size and splendor of the edifice. 'Truly,' said he, striking his hands together, 'this man hath found the ring of Solomon, which compels the assistance of the genii. In all my life I have never seen such a palace as this.' He found the Vizier reclining on a couch of cloth-of-gold, in a chamber, the walls whereof were of mother-of-pearl, and the floor of ivory. There was a fountain of perfumed water in the centre, and beside it stood a jasmine-tree, growing in a vase of crystal. 'How is this?' said the Caliph, seating himself on one end of the couch; 'a man whom the genii serve, should have the secrets of health in his hands.' 'It is no fever,' said the Vizier; 'but the other day as I was washing myself in the fountain, before the evening prayer, I stooped too near the jas mine tree, and one of its thorns scratched my left arm. 'What!' cried the Caliph, in amazement; 'the scratch of a blunt jasmine-thorn has made you ill!' 'You wonder at it, no doubt, O Commander of the Faithful!' said the Vizier; 'because, only a few months ago, you saw that I was insensible to the fangs of a serpent, which had fastened upon my heel.' 'There is no God but God!' exclaimed Haroun Al-Raschid, as by these words he recognized the poor wood-cutter, who had passed under the window of his palace—'hast thou indeed found the ring of Solomon?—and where is the woman whom Mesrour, at my command, brought to thee?'

"'She is here!' said Zubeydeh, entering the door. She turned towards the Caliph, and slightly lifting her veil, showed him her face, more beautiful than ever. Haroun, with a cry of joy, was on the point of clasping her in his arms, when he stopped suddenly, and said: 'But thou art now the wife of that man.' 'Not so, great Caliph!' exclaimed the Vizier who rose to his feet, now that there was no longer any need to affect illness; 'from the day that she entered my house, I have never seen her face. By the beard of the Prophet, she is not less pure than she is wise. It is she who has made me all that I am. Obedience to her was the seed from which the tree of my fortune has grown.' Zubeydeh then knelt at the Caliph's feet, and said: 'O Commander of the Faithful, restore me to the light of your favor. I swear to you that I am not less your wife than when the cloud of your anger overshadowed me. This honorable man has never ceased to respect me. My thoughtless words led you to send me forth to take the place of the serpent, but I have now shown you that a wife may also be to her husband as the staff, whereon he leans for support; as the camel, which bringeth him riches as the tent, which shelters and protects him; as the bath, which maketh him comely, and as the lamp, whereby his steps *are enlightened.*'

"Haroun Al-Raschid had long since bitterly repented of his rashness and cruelty. He now saw in what had happened, the hand of Allah, who had turned that which he had intended as a punishment, into a triumph. He restored Zubeydeh at once to his favor, and to the wood-cutter, whom he still retained as Vizier, he gave his eldest daughter in marriage. All the citizens of Baghdad took part in the festivities, which lasted two weeks, and the Caliph, to commemorate his gratitude, built a superb mosque, which is called the Mosque of the Restoration to this very day. The Vizier nobly requited all the pains which the Sultana Zubeydeh had taken with his education, and showed so much wisdom and justice in his administration of the laws, that the Caliph never had occasion to be dissatisfied with him. Thus they all lived together in the utmost happiness and concord, until they were each, in turn, visited by the Terminator of Delights and the Separator of Companions."

So ended Achmet's story; but without the moonlight, the tall Ethiopian palms and the soothing pipe, as accessories, I fear that this reproduction of it retains little of the charm which I found in the original. It was followed by other and wilder tales, stamped in every part with the unmistakable signet of the Orient. They were all characterized by the belief in an inevitable Destiny, which seems to be the informing soul of all Oriental literature. This belief affords every liberty to the poet and romancer, and the Arabic authors have not scrupled to make liberal use of it. There is no hazard in surrounding your hero with all sorts of real and imaginary dangers, or in heaping up obstacles in the path of his designs, when you know that his destiny obliges him to overcome them. He becomes, for the time, the impersonation of Fate, and circumstances yield before him. You see, plainly, that he was chosen, in the beginning, to do the very thing which he accomplishes, in the end. If a miracle is needed for his success, it is not withheld. Difficulties crowd upon him to the last, only that the final triumph may be more complete and striking. Yet with all these violations of probability, the Oriental tales exhibit a great fertility of invention and sparkle with touches of genuine human nature. The deep and absorbing interest with which the unlettered Arabs listen to their recital—the hold which they have upon the popular heart of the East—attests their value, as illustrations of Eastern life.

From Poetry we frequently passed to Religion, and Achmet was astonished to find me familiar not only with Mohammed, but with Ali and Abdullah and Abu-talib, and with many incidents of the Prophet's life, which were new to him. The Persian chronicles were fresh in my memory, and all the wonders related of Mohammed by that solemn old biographer, Mohammed Bekr, came up again as vividly as when I first read them. We compared notes, he repeated passages of the Koran, and so the Giaour and the True Believer discussed the nature of their faith, but always ended by passing beyond Prophet and Apostle, to the one great and good God, who is equally merciful to all men. I could sincerely adopt the first article of his faith: "*La illah il' Allah!*" "There is no God but God," while he was equally ready to accept the first commandment of mine.

CHAPTER XX.

FROM SHENDY TO KHARTOUM.

Arrival at Shendy—Appearance of the Town—Shendy in Former Days—We Touch at El Metemma—The Nile beyond Shendy—Flesh Diet vs. Vegetables—We Escape Shipwreck—A Walk on Shore—The Rapids of Derreira—Djebel Gerri—The Twelfth Cataract—Night in the Mountain Gorge—Crocodiles—A Drink of Mareesa—My Birth-Day—Fair Wind—Approach to Khartoum—The Junction of the Two Niles—Appearance of the City—We Drop Anchor.

The morning after visiting the ruins of Meroë I reached the old Ethiopian town of Shendy. It lies about half a mile from the river, but the massive fort and palace of the Governor are built on the water's edge. Several spreading sycamore trees gave a grace to the shore, which would otherwise have been dull and tame. Naked Ethiopians were fishing or washing their clothes in the water, and some of them, as they held their long, scarlet-edged mantles above their heads, to dry in the wind and sun, showed fine, muscular figures. The women had hideous faces, but symmetrical and well developed forms. A group of Egyptian soldiers watched us from the bank before the palace, and several personages on horseback, one of whom appeared to be the Governor himself, were hailing the ferry boat, which was just about putting off with a heavy load of natives.

We ran the boat to the shore, at a landing-place just above the palace. The banks of the river were covered with fields of cucumbers and beans, the latter brilliant with white and purple blossoms and filled with the murmuring sound of bees. Achmet, the raïs and I walked up to the capital—the famous Shendy, once the great mart of trade for the regions between the Red Sea and Dar-Fûr. On the way we met numbers of women with water-jars. They wore no veils, but certainly needed them, for their faces were of a broad, semi-negro character, and repulsively plain. The town is built in a straggling manner, along a low, sandy ridge, and is upwards of a mile in length, though it probably does not contain more than ten thousand inhabitants. The houses are mud, of course, but rough and filthy, and many of them are the same circular *tokuls* of mats and palm-sticks as I had already noticed in the smaller villages. The only decent dwelling which I saw had been just erected by a Dongolese merchant. There was a mosque, with a low mud minaret, but neither in this nor in any other respect did the place compare with El Mekheyref. The bazaar resembled a stable, having a passage through the centre, shaded with mats, and stalls on either side, some of which contained donkeys and others merchants. The goods displayed were principally blue and white cotton stuffs of coarse quality, beads, trinkets and the like. It was market-day, but the people had not yet assembled. A few screens of matting, erected on sticks, were the only preparations which had been made. The whole appearance of the place was that of poverty and desertion. Beyond the clusters of huts, and a mud wall which ran along the eastern side of the town, the Desert extended to the horizon—a hot, white plain, dotted with clumps of thorns. On our return to the boat, the raïs pointed out the spot where, in 1822, Ismail Pasha and his soldiers were burned to death by Mek Nemr (King Leopard), the last monarch of Shendy. The bloody revenge taken by Mohammed Bey Defterdar (son-in-law of Mohammed Ali), for that act, sealed the fate of the kingdom. The seat of the Egyptian government in Soudân was fixed at Khartoum, which in a few years became also the centre of trade, and now flourishes at the expense of Shendy and El Metemma.

Burckhardt, who visited Shendy during the reign of King Leopard, devotes much space to a description of the trade of the town at that time. It was then in the height of its prosperity, and the resort of merchants from Arabia, Abyssinia, Egypt, and even Syria and Asia Minor. It was also one of the chief slave-marts of Central Africa, in which respect it has since been superseded by Obeid, in Kordofan. The only commerce which has been left to Shendy is that with Djidda and the other Arabian ports, by way of Sowakin, on the Red Sea—a caravan journey of fourteen days, through the country of Takka, infested by the wild tribes of the Hallengas and Hadendoas. Mek Nemr, according to Burckhardt, was of the Djaaleyn tribe, who are descendants of the Beni Koreish, of Yemen, and still retain the pure Arabian features. I was afterwards, during my stay in Khartoum, enabled to verify the declaration of the same traveller, that all the tribes of Ethiopia between the Nile and the Red Sea are of unmixed Arab stock.

The palace of the Governor, which was a building of con

siderable extent, had heavy circular bastions, which were defended by cannon. Its position, on the bank of the Nile, was much more agreeable than that of the city, and the garrison had settled around it, forming a small village on its eastern side. The white walls and latticed windows of the palace reminded me of Cairo, and I anticipated a pleasant residence within its walls, on my return to Shendy. As I wished to reach Khartoum as soon as possible I did not call upon the Governor, but sent him the letter of recommendation from Yagheshir Bey. From Shendy, one sees the group of palms which serves as a landmark to El Metemma, the capital of a former Ethiopian Kingdom, further up the Nile, on its opposite bank. This is the starting point for caravans to Merawe and Dongola through the Beyooda Desert. We passed its port about noon, and stopped a few minutes to let the raïs pay his compliments to the owner of our vessel, who was on shore. He was a little old man, with a long staff, and dressed like the meanest Arab, although he was shekh of half a dozen villages, and had a servant leading a fine Dongolese horse behind him. The boat of Khalim Bey, agent of the Governor of Berber and Shendy, was at the landing place, and we saw the Bey, a tall, handsome Turk in a rich blue and crimson dress, who sent a servant to ask my name and character.

The scenery of the Nile, southward from Shendy, is again changed. The tropical rains which fall occasionally at Abou-Hammed and scantily at Berber, are here periodical, and there is no longer the same striking contrast between desert and garden land. The plains extending inward from the river are covered with a growth of bushes and coarse grass, which also appears in patches on the sides of the mountains. The inhabitants cultivate but a narrow strip of beans and dourra along the river, but own immense flocks of sheep and goats, which afford their principal sustenance. I noticed many fields of the grain called *dookhn*, of which they plant a larger quantity than of dourra. Mutton, however, is the Ethiopian's greatest delicacy. Notwithstanding this is one of the warmest climates in the world, the people eat meat whenever they can get it, and greatly prefer it to vegetable food. The sailors and camel-drivers, whose principal food is dourra, are, notwithstanding a certain quality of endurance, as weak as children, when compared with an able-bodied European, and they universally attribute this weakness to their diet. This is a fact for the lank vegetarians to explain. My experience coincided with that of the Ethiopians, and I ascribed no small share of my personal health and strength, which the violent alternations of heat and cold during the journey had not shaken in the least, to the fact of my having fared sumptuously every day.

After leaving Shendy, the Nile makes a bend to the west, and we went along slowly all the afternoon, with a side-wind. The shores were not so highly cultivated as those we had passed and low hills of yellow sand began to show themselves on either hand. The villages were groups of mud *tokuls*, with high, conical roofs, and the negro type of face appeared much more frequently among the inhabitants—the result of amalgamation with slaves. We saw numbers of young crocodiles which my sailors delighted to frighten by shouting and throwing sticks at them, as they sunned themselves on the sand. Wild geese and ducks were abundant, and the quiet little coves along the shore were filled with their young brood. During the day a large hawk or vulture dashed down to within a yard of the deck in the attempt to snatch a piece of my black ram which Beshir had just killed.

The next morning we had a narrow escape from shipwreck. The wind blew strong from the north, as we reached a twist in the river, where our course for several miles lay to the north-west, obliging the men to take in sail and tow the vessel. They had reached the turning-point and the sail was blowing loose, while two sailors lay out on the long, limber yard, trying to reef, when a violent gust pulled the rope out of the hands of the man on shore, and we were carried into the stream. The steersman put the helm hard up, and made for the point of an island which lay opposite, but the current was so strong that we could not reach it. It blew a gale, and the Nile was rough with waves. Between the island and the southern shore lay a cluster of sharp, black rocks, and for a few minutes we appeared to be driving directly upon them. The raïs and sailors, with many cries of "O Prophet! O Apostle!" gave themselves up to their fate; but the strength of the current saved us. Our bow just grazed the edge of the last rock, and we were blown across to the opposite shore, where we struck hard upon the sand and were obliged to remain two hours, until the wind abated. I was vexed and impatient at first, but remembering the effect of a pipe upon a similar occasion, I took one, and soon became calm enough to exclaim: "it is the will of Allah!"

While the boat was making such slow headway, I went ashore and walked an hour or two among the fields of beans and dourra. The plains for several miles inland were covered with dry grass and thorn-trees, and only needed irrigation to bloom as a garden. The sun was warm, the bean-fields alive with bees, and the wind took a rich summer fragrance from the white and purple blossoms. Near one of the huts, I accosted a woman who was weeding among the dourra. She told me that her husband had deserted her and taken another wife, leaving her the charge of their two children. He had also taken her three cows and given them to his new wife, so that her only means of support was to gather the dry grass and sell it in the villages. I gave her a few piastres, which she received gratefully. In the afternoon we passed the main bend of the river, and were able to make use of the wind, which by this time was light. The sailor who had been left ashore during the gale overtook us, by walking a distance of eight or ten miles and swimming one of the smaller arms of the river. The western bank of the river now became broken and hilly, occasionally overhung by bluffs of gravelly soil, of a dark red color. On the top of one of the hills there was a wall, which the raïs pointed out to me as *kadeem* (ancient), but it appeared too dilapidated to repay the trouble of a visit.

On the following day, the scenery became remarkably wild and picturesque. After passing the village of Derreira, on the right bank, the Nile was studded with islands of various sizes, rising like hillocks from the water, and all covered with the most luxuriant vegetation. The mimosa, the acacia, the palm, the sycamore and the *nebbuk* flourished together in rank growth, with a profusion of smaller shrubs, and all were matted together with wild green creepers, which dropped their long streamers of pink and purple blossoms into the water. Reefs of black rock, over which the waves foamed impetuously, made the navigation intricate and dangerous. The banks of the river were high and steep, and covered with bushes and rank grass, above which the rustling blades of the dourra glittered in the sun. The country was thickly populated, and the inhabitants were mostly of the Shygheean tribe—from Dar Shygheea, the region between Dongola and Berber. The sakias were tended by Dinka slaves, as black as ebony, and with coarse, brutish faces. At one point on the eastern shore, opposite the island of Bendi, the natives had collected all their live stock, but for what purpose I could not learn. The shore was covered with hundreds of camels, donkeys, sheep, cows and goats, carefully kept in separate herds.

After threading ten miles of those island bowers, we approached Djebel Gerri, which we had seen all day, ahead of us. The Nile, instead of turning westward around the flank of the mountain, as I had anticipated from the features of the landscape, made a sudden bend to the south, between a thick cluster of islands, and entered the hills. At this point there was a rapid, extending half-way across the river. The natives call it a *shellàl* (cataract), although it deserves the name no more than the cataracts of Assouan and Wadi-Halfa. Adopting the term, however, which has been sanctioned by long usage, this is the Twelfth Cataract of the Nile, and the last one which the traveller meets before reaching the mountains of Abyssinia. The stream is very narrow, compressed between high hills of naked red sandstone rock. At sunset we were completely shut in the savage solitude, and there we seemed likely to remain, for the wind came from all quarters by turns, and jammed the vessel against the rocks, more than once.

The narrow terraces of soil on the sides of the mountains were covered with dense beds of long, dry grass, and as we lay moored to the rocks, I climbed up to one of these, in spite of the raïs's warnings that I should fall in with lions and ser pents. I lay down in the warm grass, and watched the shadows deepen in the black gorge, as the twilight died away. The *zikzak* or crocodile-bird twittered along the shore, and, after it became quite dark, the stillness was occasionally broken by the snort of a hippopotamus, as he thrust his huge head above water, or by the yell of a hyena prowling among the hills. Talk of the pleasure of *reading* a traveller's adventures in strange lands! There is no pleasure equal to that of *living* them: neither the anticipation nor the memory of such a scene as I witnessed that evening, can approach the fascination of the reality. I was awakened after midnight by the motion of the vessel, and looking out of my shelter as I lay, could see that we were slowly gliding through the foldings of the stony mountains. The moon rode high and bright, over the top of a peak in front, and the sound of my prow, as it occasionally grated against the rocks, alone disturbed the stillness of the wild pass. Once the wind fell, and the men were obliged to make fast to a rock, but before morning we had emerged from the mountains and were moored to the bank, to await daylight for the passage of the last rapid.

In the mouth of the pass lies an island, which rises into a remarkable conical peak, about seven hundred feet in height. It is called the *Rowyàn* (thirst assuaged), while a lofty summit of the range of Gerri bears the name of *Djebel Attshàn* (the Mountain of Thirst). The latter stands on a basis of arid sand, whence its name, but the Rowyàn is encircled by the arms of the Nile. In the Wady Beit-Naga, some three or four hours' journey eastward from the river, are the ruined temples of Naga and Mesowuràt, described by Hoskins. The date of their erection has been ascertained by Lepsius to be coeval with that of Meroë. We here saw many crocodiles basking on the warm sand-banks. One group of five were enormous monsters, three of them being at least fifteen, and the other two twenty feet in length. They lazily dragged their long bodies into the water as we approached, but returned after we had passed. The zikzaks were hopping familiarly about them, on the sand, and I have no doubt that they do service to the crocodiles in the manner related by the Arabs.

The river was still studded with islands—some mere fragments of rock covered with bushes, and some large level tracts, flourishing with rich fields of cotton and dourra. About noon, we passed a village on the eastern bank, and I sent Ali and Beshir ashore to procure supplies, for my ram was finished. Ali found only one fowl, which the people did not wish to sell, but, Turk-like, he took it forcibly and gave them the usual price. Beshir found some *mareesa*, a fermented drink made of dourra, and for two piastres procured two jars of it, holding two gallons each, which were brought down to the boat by a pair of sturdy Dinka women, whose beauty was almost a match for Bakhita. The mareesa had an agreeable flavor and very little intoxicating property. I noticed, however, that after Beshir had drunk nearly a gallon, he sang and danced rather more than usual, and had much to say of a sweetheart of his, who lived in El-Metemma, and who bore the charming name of Gammerò-Betahadjerò. Bakhita, after drinking an equal portion, complained to me bitterly of my white sheep, which had nibbed off the ends of the woolly twists adorning her head, but I comforted her by the present of half a piastre, for the purpose of buying mutton-fat.

As the wind fell, at sunset, we reached a long slope of

snowy sand, on the island of Aüssee. Achmet went to the huts of the inhabitants, where he was kindly received and furnished with milk. I walked for an hour up and down the beautiful beach, breathing the mild, cool evening air, heavy with delicious odors. The glassy Nile beside me reflected the last orange-red hues of sunset, and the evening star, burning with a white, sparry lustre, made a long track of light across his breast. I remembered that it was my birth-day—the fourth time I had spent my natal anniversary in a foreign land. The first had been in Germany, the second in Italy, the third in Mexico, and now the last, in the wild heart of Africa. They were all pleasant, but this was the best of all.

When I returned to the vessel, I found my carpet and cushions spread on the sand, and Ali waiting with my pipe. The evening entertainment commenced: I was listening to an Arabian tale, and watching the figures of the boatmen, grouped around a fire they had kindled in a field of dookhn, when the wind came up with a sudden gust and blew out the folds of my idle flag. Instantly the sand was kicked over the brands, the carpet taken up, all hands called on board, and we dashed away on the dark river with light hearts. I rose before sunrise the next morning and found the wind unchanged. We were sailing between low shores covered with grain-fields, and a sandy island lay in front. The raïs no sooner saw me than he called my attention to the tops of some palm-trees that appeared on the horizon, probably six or eight miles distant. They grew in the gardens of Khartoum! We reached the point of the broad, level island that divides the waters of the two Niles, and could soon distinguish the single minaret and buildings of the city A boat, coming down from the White Nile, passed us on the right, and another, bound for Khartoum, led us up the Blue Nile. The proper division between the two rivers is the point of land upon which Khartoum is built, but the channel separating it from the island opposite is very narrow, and the streams do not fully meet and mingle their waters till the island is passed.

The city presented a picturesque—and to my eyes, accustomed to the mud huts of the Ethiopian villages—a really stately appearance, as we drew near. The line of buildings extended for more than a mile along the river, and many of the houses were embowered in gardens of palm, acacia, orange and tamarind trees. The Palace of the Pasha had a certain appearance of dignity, though its walls were only unburnt brick, and his *hareem*, a white, two-story building, looked cool and elegant amid the palms that shaded it. Egyptian soldiers, in their awkward, half-Frank costume, were lounging on the bank before the Palace, and slaves of inky blackness, resplendent in white and red livery, were departing on donkeys on their various errands. The slope of the bank was broken at short intervals by water-mills, and files of men with skins, and women with huge earthen jars on their heads, passed up and down between the water's edge and the openings of the narrow lanes leading between the gardens into the city. The boat of the Governor of Berber, rowed by twelve black slaves, put off from shore, and moved slowly down stream, against the north wind, as we drew up and moored the America below the garden of the Catholic Mission. It was the twelfth of January. I had made the journey from Assouan to Khartoum in twenty six days, and from Cairo in fifty-seven.

CHAPTER XXI.

LIFE IN KHARTOUM.

The American Flag—A Rencontre—Search for a House—The Austrian Consular Agent—Description of his Residence—The Garden—The Menagerie—Barbaric Pomp and State—Picturesque Character of the Society of Khartoum—Foundation and Growth of the City—Its Appearance—The Population—Unhealthiness of the Climate—Assembly of Ethiopian Chieftains—Visit of Two Shekhs—Dinner and Fireworks.

At the time of my arrival in Khartoum, there were not more than a dozen vessels in port, and the only one which would pass for respectable in Egypt was the Pasha's dahabiyeh. I had but an open merchant-boat, yet my green tent and flag gave it quite a showy air, and I saw that it created some little sensation among the spectators. The people looked at the flag with astonishment, for the stars and stripes had never before been seen in Khartoum. At the earnest prayer of the raïs, who was afraid the boat would be forcibly impressed into the service of the Government, and was anxious to get back to his sick family in El Metemma, I left the flag flying until he was ready to leave. Old Bakhita, in her dumb, ignorant way, expressed great surprise and grief when she learned that Achmet and I were going to desert the vessel. She had an indefinite idea that we had become part and parcel of it, and would remain on board for the rest of our lives.

I took Achmet and started immediately in search of a house, as in those lands a traveller who wishes to be respectable, must take a residence on arriving at a city, even if he only intends to stay two or three days. Over the mud walls on either side of the lane leading up from the water, I could look into wildernesses of orange, date, fig and pomegranate trees, oleanders in bloom and trailing vines. We entered a tolerable street, cleanly swept, and soon came to a coffee-house Two or three persons were standing at the door, one of whom —a fat, contented-looking Turk—eyed Achmet sharply. The two looked at each other a moment in mutual doubt and astonishment, and then fell into each other's arms. It was a Syrian merchant, whom Achmet had known in Cairo and Beyrout. "O master!" said he, his dark face radiant with delight, as he clasped the hand of the Syrian: "there never was such a lucky journey as this!"

The merchant, who had been two years in Khartoum, accompanied us in our search. We went first to the residence of the shekh of the quarter, who was not at home. Two small boys, the sons of one of a detachment of Egyptian physicians, who had recently arrived, received me. They complained bitterly of Soudân, and longed to get back again to Cairo. We then went to the Governor of the city, but he was absent in Kordofan. Finally, in wandering about the streets, we met a certain Ali Effendi, who took us to a house which would be vacant the next day. It was a large mud palace, containing an outer and inner divan, two sleeping rooms, a kitchen, store-rooms, apartments for servants, and an inclosed court-yard and stables, all of which were to be had at one hundred piastres a month—an exorbitant price, as I afterwards learned. Before engaging it, I decided to ask the advice of the Austrian Consular Agent, Dr. Reitz, for whom I had letters from the English and Austrian Consuls in Cairo. He received me with true German cordiality, and would hear of nothing else but that I should immediately take possession of an unoccupied room in his house. Accordingly the same day of my arrival beheld me installed in luxurious quarters, with one of the most brave, generous and independent of men as my associate.

As the Consul's residence was the type of a house of the best class in Khartoum, a description of it may give some idea of life in the place, under the most agreeable circumstances. The ground-plot was one hundred and thirty paces square, and surrounded by a high mud wall. Inside of this stood the dwelling, which was about half that length, and separated from it by a narrow garden and court-yard. Entering the court by the gate, a flight of steps conducted to the divan, or reception-room, in the second story. From the open ante-chamber one might look to the south over the gray wastes of Sennaar, or, if the sun was near his setting, see a reach in the White Nile, flashing like the point of an Arab spear. The divan had a cushioned seat around three sides and matting on the floor, and was really a handsome room, although its walls were mud, covered with a thin coating of lime, and its roof palm-logs overlaid with coarse matting, on which rested a layer of mud a foot thick. In the second story were also the Consular Office and a sleeping room. The basement contained the kitchen, store-rooms, and servants' rooms. The remainder of the house was only one story in height, and had a balcony looking on the garden, and completely embowered in flowering vines. The only rooms were the dining hall, with cushioned divans on each side and a drapery of the Austrian colors at the end, and my apartment, which overlooked a small garden-court, wherein two large ostriches paced up and down, and a company of wild geese and wild swine made continual discord. The court at the entrance communicated with the stables, which contained the Consul's horses—a white steed, of the pure Arabian blood of Nedjid, and the red stallion appropriated to my use, which was sent by the King of Dar-Für to Lattif Pasha, and presented by him to the Consul. A *hejin*, or trained dromedary, of unusual size, stood in the court, and a tame lioness was tied to a stake in the corner. She was a beautiful and powerful beast, and I never passed her without taking her head between my knees, or stroking her tawny hide until she leaned against me like a cat and licked my hand.

Passing through a side-door into the garden, we came upon a whole menagerie of animals. Under the long arbors, covered with luxuriant grape-vines, stood two surly hyenas, a wild ass from the mountains of the Atbara, and an Abyssinian mule. A tall marabout (a bird of the crane species, with a pouch-bill), stalked about the garden, occasionally bending a hinge in the middle of his long legs, and doubling them backwards, so that he used half of them for a seat. Adjoining the stable was a large sheep-yard, in which were gathered together gazelles, strange varieties of sheep and goats from the countries of the White Nile, a virgin-crane, and a large *antilopus leucoryx*, from Kordofan, with curved horns four feet in length. My favorite, however, was the leopard, which was a most playful and affectionate creature, except at meal-time He was not more than half grown, and had all the wiles of an intelligent kitten, climbing his post and springing upon me, or creeping up slyly and seizing my ankle in his mouth. The garden, which was watered by a well and string of buckets turned by an ox, had a rich variety of fruit trees. The grape season was just over, though I had a few of the last bunches; figs were ripening from day to day, oranges and lemons were in fruit and flower, bananas blooming for another crop, and the pomegranate and *kishteh*, or custard-apple, hung heavy on the branches. There was also a plantation of date-trees and sugar-cane, and a great number of ornamental shrubs.

In all these picturesque features of my residence in Khartoum, I fully realized that I had at last reached Central Africa. In our mode of life, also, there was a rich flavor of that barbaric pomp and state which one involuntarily associates with the name of Soudân. We arose at dawn, and at sunrise were in the saddle. Sometimes I mounted the red stallion, of the wild breed of Dar-Fūr, and sometimes one of the Consul's tall and fleet dromedaries. Six dark attendants, in white and scarlet dresses, followed us on dromedaries, and two grooms on foot ran before us, to clear a way through the streets. After passing through Khartoum, we frequently made long excursions up the banks of the two Niles, or out upon the boundless plain between them. In this way, I speedily became familiar with the city and its vicinity, and as, on our return, I always accompanied the Consul on all his visits to the various dignitaries, I had every opportunity of studying the peculiar life of the place, and gaining some idea of its governing principles. As the only city of Central Africa which has a regular communication with the Mediterranean (by which it occasionally receives a ray of light from the civilized world beyond), it has become a capital on a small scale, and its society is a curious compound of Christian, Turk and Barbarian. On the same day, I have had a whole sheep set before me, in the house of an Ethiopian Princess, who wore a ring in her nose; taken coffee and sherbet with the Pasha; and drank tea, prepared in the true English style, in the parlor of a European. When to these remarkable contrasts is added the motley character of its native population, embracing representatives from almost every tribe between Dar-Fūr and the Red Sea, between Egypt and the Negro kingdoms of the White Nile, it will readily be seen how rich a field of observation Khartoum offers to the traveller. Nevertheless, those who reside there, almost without exception, bestow upon the city and country all possible maledictions. Considered as a place of residence, other questions come into play, and they are perhaps not far wrong.

Khartoum is the most remarkable—I had almost said the only example of physical progress in Africa, in this century. Where, thirty years ago, there was not even a dwelling, unless it might be the miserable *tokul*, or straw hut of the Ethiopian Fellah, now stands a city of some thirty or forty thousand inhabitants, daily increasing in size and importance, and gradually drawing into its mart the commerce of the immense regions of Central Africa. Its foundation, I believe, is due to Ismail Pasha (son of Mohammed Ali), who, during his conquests of the kingdoms of Shendy and Sennaar, in the years 1821 and 1822, recognized the importance, in a military and commercial sense, of establishing a post at the confluence of the two Niles. Mohammed Bey Defterdar, who succeeded him, seconded the plan, and ere long it was determined to make Khartoum, on account of its central position, the capital of the Egyptian pashalik of Soudân. Standing at the mouth of the Blue Nile which flows down from the gold and iron mountains of Abyssinia, and of the White Nile, the only avenue to a dozen Negro kingdoms, rich in ivory and gum, and being nearly equidistant from the conquered provinces of Sennaar, Kordofan, Shendy and Berber, it speedily outgrew the old Ethiopian cities, and drew to itself the greater part of their wealth and commercial activity. Now it is the metropolis of all the eastern part of Soudân, and the people speak of it in much the same style as the Egyptians speak of their beloved Cairo.

The town is larger, cleaner and better built than any of the cities of Upper Egypt, except perhaps Siout. It extends for about a mile along the bank of the Blue Nile, facing the north, and is three-quarters of a mile in its greatest breadth. The part next the river is mostly taken up with the gardens and dwellings of Beys and other government officers, and wealthy merchants. The gardens of the Pasha, of Moussa Bey, Musakar Bey and the Catholic Mission are all large and beautiful, and towards evening, when the north wind rises, shower the fragrance of their orange and mimosa blossoms over the whole town. The dwellings, which stand in them, cover a large space of ground, but are, for the most part, only one story in height, as the heavy summer rains would speedily beat down mud walls of greater height. The Pasha's palace, which was built during the year previous to my visit, is of burnt brick, much of which was taken from the ancient Christian ruins of Abou-Haràss, on the Blue Nile. It is a quadrangular building, three hundred feet square, with a large open court in the centre. Its front formed one side of a square, which when complete, will be surrounded by other offices of government. For Soudân, it is a building of some pretension, and the Pasha took great pride in exhibiting it. He told me that the Arab shekhs who visited him would not believe that it was the work of man alone. Allah must have helped him to raise such a wonderful structure. It has an inclosed arched corridor in front, in the Italian style, and a square tower over the entrance. At the time of my visit Abdallah Effendi was building a very handsome two-story house of burnt brick, and the Catholic priests intended erecting another, as soon as they should have established themselves permanently. Within a few months, large additions had been made to the bazaar, while the houses of the slaves, on the outskirts of the city, were constantly springing up like ant-hills.

There is no plan whatever in the disposition of the buildings. Each man surrounds his property with a mud wall, regardless of its location with respect to others, and in going from one point to another, one is obliged to make the most perplexing zigzags. I rarely ventured far on foot, as I soon became bewildered in the labyrinth of blank walls. When mounted on the Consul's tallest dromedary, I looked down on the roofs of the native houses, and could take my bearings without difficulty. All the mysteries of the lower life of Khartoum were revealed to me, from such a lofty post. On each side I looked into pent yards where the miserable Arab and Negro families lazily basked in the sun during the day, or into the filthy nests where they crawled at night. The swarms of children which they bred in those dens sat naked in the dust, playing with vile yellow dogs, and sometimes a lean burden camel stood in the corner. The only furniture to be seen was a water-skin, a few pots and jars, a basket or two, and sometimes an *angareb*, or coarse wooden frame covered with a netting of ropes, and serving as seat and bed. Nearly half the population of the place are slaves, brought from the mountains above Fazogl, or from the land of the Dinkas, on the White Nile. One's commiseration of these degraded races is almost overcome by his disgust with their appearance and habits, and I found even the waste plain that stretches towards Sennaar a relief after threading the lanes of the quarters where they live.

Notwithstanding the nature of its population, Khartoum is kept commendably neat and clean. It will be a lucky day for Rome and Florence when their streets exhibit no more filth than those of this African city. The bazaars only, are swept every morning, but the wind performs this office for the remainder of the streets. The *soog*, or market, is held in a free space, opening upon the inland plain, where the country people bring their sheep, fowls, camels, dourra, vegetables and other common products. The slaughtering of animals takes place every morning on the banks of the Blue Nile, east of the city, which is thus entirely free from the effluvia arising therefrom. Here the sheep, cows, goats and camels are killed, skinned and quartered in the open air, and it is no unusual thing to see thirty or forty butchers at work on as many different animals, each surrounded by an attendant group of vultures, hawks, cranes, crows and other carnivorous birds. They are never molested by the people, and we sometimes rode through thousands of them, which had so gorged themselves that they scarcely took the trouble to move out of our way.

The place labors under the disadvantage of being the most unhealthy part of one of the most unhealthy regions in the world. From the southern frontier of Nubia, where the tropical rains begin to fall, to the table-land of Abyssinia on the south, and as far up the White Nile as has yet been explored, Soudân is devastated by fevers of the most malignant character. The summers are fatal to at least one-half of the Turks, Egyptians and Europeans who make their residence there, and the natives themselves, though the mortality is not so great among them, rarely pass through the year without an attack of fever. I arrived during the most healthy part of the year, and yet of all the persons I saw, three-fourths were complaining of some derangement of the system. The military hospital, which I visited, was filled with cases of fever, dysentery and small-pox. I was in such good bodily condition from my journey through the Desert that I could scarcely conceive the sensation of sickness, and the generous diet and invigorating exercise I enjoyed secured me from all fear of an attack. Travellers are not agreed as to the cause of this mortality in Soudân. Some attribute it to the presence of infusoriæ in the water; yet we drank the pure, mountain-born flood of the Blue Nile, and filtered it beforehand. I am disposed to side with Russegger, who accounts for it entirely by the miasma arising from decayed vegetation, during the intense heats. The country around Khartoum is a dead level; the only mountain to be seen is the long ridge of Djebel Gerrari, twelve miles to the north. Behind the town, the White Nile curves to the east, and during the inundation his waters extend even to the suburbs, almost insulating the place. The unusual sickness of the winter of 1852 might be accounted for by the inundation of the previous summer, which was so much higher than ordinary that the people were obliged to erect dykes to keep the water out of the streets. The opposite bank of the river is considered more healthy; and in the town of Halfay, only ten miles distant, the average mortality is much less.

I was fortunate in reaching Khartoum at a very interesting period. All the principal shekhs of the different tribes between the Nile and the Red Sea were then collected there, and as Dr. Reitz was on friendly terms with all of them, I had the opportunity of making their acquaintance, and could have readily procured a safe-conduct through their territories, if I had been disposed to make explorations in that direction.

During the summer there had been trouble in the neighborhood of Sennaar, and a general movement against the Egyptian rule was feared. In October and November, however, Moussa Bey made a campaign in the regions about and beyond the Atbara, and returned with the chief malcontents in chains. They were afterwards liberated, but had been retained in Khartoum until some disputed questions should be settled. On the night of my arrival, the consul received a visit of ceremony from the two principal ones: Hamed, the chief shekh of the Bishârees, and Owd-el-Kerim, son of the great shekh of the Shukorees, which inhabit the wide territory between the Atbara and the Blue Nile. They were accompanied by several attendants, and by Mohammed Kheyr, the commander of the Shygheean cavalry employed in the late expedition. The latter was a fierce-looking black in rich Turkish costume.

Hamed was a man of middle size, black, but with straight features and a mild, serious expression of face. He was dressed in white, as well as his attendant whose bushy hair was twisted into countless strings and pierced with a new wooden skewer. The Shukoree shekh arrived last. We were seated on the divan, and all rose when he entered. He was a tall, powerful man, with large, jet-black eyes and a bold, fierce face. He wore a white turban and flowing robes of the same color with a fringe and stripe of crimson around the border. The Consul advanced to the edge of the carpet to meet him, when the shekh opened his arms and the two fell upon each other's necks. Coffee and pipes were then served, and water was brought for the washing preparatory to dinner. Hamed and the Shygheean captain washed only their hands, but the great Owd-el-Kerim washed his hands, face and feet, and occupied nearly a quarter of an hour at his devotions, bowing his head many times to the earth and repeating the name of Allah with deep emphasis. We passed through the garden to the dining-room, where the shekhs were greatly amazed at seeing a table set in European style. They all failed in managing the knives and forks, except Owd-el-Kerim, who watched the Consul and myself, and did his part with dignity. Achmet had made a vermicelli soup, which they eyed very suspiciously, and did not venture to take more than a few mouthfuls. They no doubt went away with the full belief that the Franks devour worms. They were at a loss how to attack the roast mutton, until I carved it for them, but did such execution with their fingers among the stews and salads that the dishes were soon emptied.

After they had again partaken of coffee and pipes in the divan, the Consul ordered two or three rockets, which had been left from his Christmas celebration, to be sent up in order to satisfy the curiosity of his guests, who had heard much of those wonderful fires, which had amazed all Khartoum, three weeks before. The shekhs and attendants were grouped on the balcony, when the first rocket shot hissing into the air drew its fiery curve through the darkness, and burst into a rain of yellow stars. "*Wallah!*" and "*Mashallah!*" were echoed from mouth to mouth, and the desert chiefs could scarcely contain themselves, from astonishment and delight. The second rocket went up quite near to us, and sooner than was expected. Hamed, the Bishàree shekh, was so startled that he threw both his arms around the Consul and held fast for dear life, and even the great Owd-el-Kerim drew a long breath and ejaculated, "God is great!" They then took their leave, deeply impressed with the knowledge and wisdom of the Franks.

CHAPTER XXII.

VISITS IN KHARTOUM.

Visit to the Catholic Mission—Dr. Knoblecher, the Apostolic Vicar—Moussa Bey—Visit to Lattif Pasha—Reception—The Pasha's Palace—Lions—We Dine with the Pasha—Ceremonies upon the Occasion—Music—The Guests—The Franks in Khartoum—Dr. Péney—Visit to the Sultana Nasra—An Ethiopian Dinner—Character of the Sultana.

On the day of my arrival, Dr. Reitz proposed a visit to Dr. Knoblecher, the Apostolic Vicar of the Catholic Missions in Central Africa, who had returned to Khartoum about twenty days previous. The Vicar's name was already familiar to me, from the account of his voyage up the White Nile in 1850, which was published in the German journals during his visit to Europe, and it had been my design to propose joining his party, in case he had carried out his plan of making a second voyage in the winter of 1852. He ascended as far as lat. 4° north, or about sixty miles beyond the point reached by D'Arnaud and Werne, and therefore stands at the head of Nilotic explorers.

Preceded by two attendants, we walked through the town to the Catholic Mission, a spacious one-story building in a large garden near the river. Entering a court, in the centre of which grew a tall tamarind tree, we were received by an Italian monk, in flowing robes, who conducted us into a second court, inclosed by the residence of the Vicar. Here we met two other priests, a German and a Hungarian, dressed in flowing Oriental garments. They ushered us into a large room, carpeted with matting, and with a comfortable divan around the sides. The windows looked into a garden, which was filled with orange, fig and banana trees, and fragrant with jasmine and mimosa blossoms. We had scarcely seated ourselves, when the monks rose and remained standing, while Dr. Knoblecher entered. He was a small man, slightly and rather delicately built, and not more than thirty-five years of age. His complexion was fair, his eyes a grayish blue, and his beard, which he wore flowing upon his breast, a very decided auburn. His face was one of those which wins not only kindness but confidence from all the world. His dress consisted of a white turban, and a flowing robe of dark purple cloth. He is a man of thorough cultivation, conversant with several languages, and possesses an amount of scientific knowledge which will make his future explorations valuable to the world. During my stay in Khartoum I visited him frequently, and derived from him much information concerning the countries of Soudân and their inhabitants.

On our return we called upon Moussa Bey, the commander of the expedition sent into the lands of the Shukorees and the Hallengas, the foregoing summer. He was then ill of a fever and confined to his bed, but we entered the room without ceremony, and found with him the new Governor of Berber and Abd-el-Kader Bey, the Governor of Kordofan, besides several secretaries and attendants Moussa Bey was a Turk, perhaps fifty years of age, and had a strong, sturdy, energetic face. Several Arab shekhs, some of whom had been taken prisoners in the late expedition, were lounging about the court-yards.

The day after my arrival, Dr. Reitz presented me to Lattif Pasha, the Governor of Soudân. The Egyptian officials in Khartoum generally consider themselves as exiles, and a station in Soudân carries with it a certain impression of disgrace. For the Pasha, however, it is an office of great importance and responsibility, and its duties are fully as arduous as those of the Viceroy of Egypt himself. The provinces under his rule constitute a territory of greater extent than France, and there are as many factions among the native tribes as parties among the French politicians. It is moreover, in many respects, an independent sovereignty. Its great distance from the seat of authority, and the absence of any regular means of communication except the government post, gives the Pasha of Soudân opportunities of which he never fails to avail himself. Achmet Pasha at one time so strengthened himself here that he defied even Mohammed Ali, and it is still whispered that foul means were used to get rid of him. Since then, rotation in office is found to be good policy, and the Egyptian Government is careful to remove a Pasha before he has made himself dangerous. From the Turks and Europeans in Khartoum, I heard little good of Lattif Pasha. His character was said to be violent and arbitrary, and several most savage acts were attributed to him. One thing, however, was said in favor of him, and it was a great redeeming trait in those lands: he did not enrich himself by cheating the government. At the time of my visit it was understood that he had been recalled, and was to be superseded by Rustum Pasha.

We found the Pasha seated on his divan, with a secretary before him, reading a file of documents. The guards at the door presented arms as we entered, and the Pasha no sooner saw us than he rose, and remained standing till we came up. The Consul presented me, and we seated ourselves on the divan, separated from him by a pair of cushions. Pipes were brought to us by black slaves, and after a few common-places, he turned again to his business. The Secretary was reading despatches to the different provinces of Soudân. As fast as each was approved and laid aside, a Memlook slave of fifteen, who appeared to fill the office of page, stamped them with the Pasha's seal, in lieu of signature. When the affairs were concluded, the Pasha turned to us and entered into conversation. He was a man of forty-five years of age, of medium height, but stoutly built, and with regular and handsome features. His complexion was a pale olive, his eyes large and dark, and he wore a black beard and moustaches, very neatly trimmed. His mouth was full, and when he smiled, showed a perfect set of strong white teeth, which gave a certain grimness to his expression. His manner was refined, but had that feline smoothness which invariably covers sharp claws. If I had met him in London or Paris, in Frank costume, I should have set him down as the *primo basso* of the Italian Opera. He was plainly dressed in a suit of dark-blue cloth, and wore a small tarboosh on his head.

Our conversation first turned upon America, and finally upon steam navigation and maritime affairs in general. He took an interest in such subjects, as he was formerly Admiral in the navy of Mohammed Ali. An engraving of the Turkish frigate *Sultan Mahmoud*, which was built by the American

Eckford, hung on the wall opposite me. Over the divan was a portrait of Sultan Abdul-Medjid, and on each side two Arabic sentences, emblazoned on a ground of blue and crimson. The apartment was spacious and lofty; the ceiling was of smooth palm-logs, and the floor of cement, beaten hard and polished with the trowel. I expressed my surprise to the Pasha that he had erected such a stately building in the short space of nine months, and he thereupon proposed to show it to me more in detail. He conducted us to a reception-room, covered with fine carpets, and furnished with mirrors and luxurious divans; then the dining-room, more plainly furnished, the bath with Moorish arches glimmering in steamy twilight, and his private armory, the walls of which were hung with a small but rich assortment of Turkish and European weapons. The doors of the apartments were made of a dark red wood, of very fine grain, closely resembling mahogany. It is found in the mountains of Fazogl, on the south-western border of Abyssinia. It is susceptible of a fine polish, and the Pasha showed me a large and handsome table made from it.

The Pasha then led us into the court-yard, where the workmen were still busy, plastering the interior of the corridors surrounding it. A large leopard and a lion-whelp of six months old, were chained to two of the pillars. A younger whelp ran loose about the court, and gave great diversion to the Pasha, by lying in wait behind the pillars, whence he pounced out upon any young boy-slave, who might pass that way. The little fellow would take to his heels in great terror, and scamper across the court, followed by the whelp, who no sooner overtook him than he sprang with his fore-paws against the boy's back, threw him down, and then ran off, apparently very much delighted with the sport. He had the free range of the palace, but spent the most of his time in the kitchen, where he would leap upon a table, deliberately lie down, and watch the movements of the cooks with great interest. The Pasha told us that this whelp had on one occasion found his way to the harem, where his presence was first proclaimed by the screams of the terrified women. The leopard was a large and fierce animal, but the other lion was a rough, good-humored fellow, turning over on his back to be played with, and roaring frequently, with a voice that resembled the low notes of a melancholy trombone. From this court we passed into the outer corridor fronting the square, when the jewelled shebooks were again brought, and the Pasha discoursed for some time on the necessity of controlling one's passions and preserving a quiet temperament under all circumstances. When we rose to depart, he invited us to return and dine with him next day.

Towards sunset the horses were got ready; Dr. Reitz donned his uniform, and I dressed myself in Frank costume, with the exception of the tarboosh, shawl and red slippers. We called at the Catholic Mission on our way to the Palace, and while conversing with the monks in the garden, a message came from the Pasha requesting Aboona Suleyman—(Padre Solomon, as Dr. Knoblecher was called by the Copts and Mussulmen in Khartoum)—to accompany us. We therefore set out on foot with the Vicar, with the grooms leading the horses behind us. The Pasha received us at the entrance of his reception-room, and then retired to pray, before further conversation. The divan at the further end of the room was divided in the centre by a pile of cushions, the space on the right hand being reserved for the Pasha alone. The Consul, being the second independent power, seated himself on the left hand, Dr. Knoblecher modestly took the corner, and I drew up my legs beside him, on the side divan. After a short absence—during which, we also were supposed to have said our prayers—the Pasha returned, saluted us a second time, and seated himself. Four slaves appeared at the same moment, with four pipes, which they presented to us in the order of our rank, commencing with the Pasha.

When the aroma of the delicate Djebeli tobacco had diffused a certain amount of harmony among us, the conversation became more animated. The principal subject we discussed was the *coup d'étât* of Louis Napoleon, the news of which had just arrived by dromedary post, in twenty-four days from Cairo. The Pasha said it was precisely the thing which he had long ago predicted would come to pass. Louis Napoleon, he said, would behead Thiers, Cavaignac, Lamoricière and the others whom he had imprisoned, and make, if necessary, twenty coups d'étât, after which, France would begin to prosper. The French, he said, must be well beaten, or it is impossible to govern them. The conversation had hardly commenced, when a slave appeared, bearing a silver tray, upon which were four tiny glasses of mastic cordial, a single glass of water, and saucers which contained bits of orange and pomegranate. The Pasha was always served first. He drank the cordial, took a sip of water, and then each of us in turn, drinking from the same glass. At intervals of about five minutes the same refreshment appeared, and was served at least ten times before dinner was announced.

Presently there came a band of musicians—five Egyptian boys whom the Pasha had brought with him from Cairo. We had also two additions to the company of guests: Rufaä Bey an intelligent Egyptian, who was educated in France, and haa been principal of a native college in Cairo, under Mohammed Ali, and Ali Bey Khasib, the late Governor of Berber, who had been deposed on account of alleged mal-practices. The latter was the son of a water carrier in Cairo, but was adopted by the widow of Ismaïl Pasha, who gave him a superior education. Other accounts represented him to be the illegitimate son of either Ismaïl or Ibrahim Pasha, and this surmise was probably correct. He was a bold, handsome man of thirty, and was said to be the most intelligent of all the officials in Soudân.

After some little prelude, the musicians commenced. The instruments were a *zumarra*, or reed flute, a dulcimer, the wires of which were struck with a wooden plectrum, held between the first and middle fingers, and a tamborine, two of the boys officiating only as singers. The airs were Arabic and Persian, and had the character of improvisations, compared with the classic music of Europe. The rhythm was perfect, and the parts sustained by the different instruments arranged with considerable skill. The Egyptian officers were greatly moved by the melodies, which, in their wild, passionate, barbaric cadences, had a singular charm for my ear. The songs were principally of love, but of a higher character than the common songs of the people. The Pasha translated a brace for us. One related to the loves of a boy and maiden, the former of whom was humble, the latter the daughter of a Bey They saw and loved each other, but the difference in their stations prevented the fulfilment of their hopes. One day, as the girl was seated at her window, a funeral passed through the street below. She asked the name of the dead person, and they answered "Leyl," the name of her beloved, whom the violence of his passion had deprived of life. Her lamentations formed the theme of a separate song, in which the name of Leyl was repeated in one long, continued outcry of grief and love. The second song was of a widow who had many wooers, by whom she was so beset, that she finally appointed a day to give them her decision. The same day her son died, yet, because she had given her word, she mastered her grief by a heroic resolution, arrayed herself in her finest garments, received her suitors, and sang to her lute the song which would best entertain them. At the close of the festival she announced her loss in a song, and concluded by refusing all their offers

At last, dinner was announced. The Pasha led the way into the dining-room, stopping in an ante-chamber, where a group of slaves were ready with pitchers, ewers and napkins, and we performed the customary washing of hands. The Pasha then took his seat at the round table, and pointed out his place to each guest. Dr. Knoblecher and myself sat on his right, Dr. Reitz and Rufaā Bey on his left, and Ali Bey Khasib opposite. There were no plates, but each of us had a silver knife, spoon and fork, and the arrangement was so far in Frank style that we sat upon chairs instead of the floor. The only ceremony observed was, that the Pasha first tasted each dish as it was brought upon the table, after which the rest of us followed. We all ate soup from the same tureen, and buried our several right hands to the knuckles in the fat flesh of the sheep which was afterwards set before us. Claret was poured out for the Franks and Rufaā Bey (whose Moslem principles had been damaged by ten years residence in Paris), the Pasha and

Ali Bey alone abstaining. There were twenty courses in all, and the cookery was excellent. Besides the delicate Turkish compounds of meat and vegetables, delicious fish from the White Nile and fruits from the Pasha's garden, we had blanc mange and several varieties of French *patisserie.* At the close of the repast, a glass bowl containing a cool drink made from dried figs, quinces and apricots, was placed upon the table. The best possible humor prevailed, and I enjoyed the dinner exceedingly, the more so because I had not expected to find such a high degree of civilization in Soudân.

We had afterwards coffee and pipes in the reception-room, and about ten in the evening took leave of the Pasha and walked home, preceded by attendants carrying large glass lanterns. After accompanying Dr. Knoblecher to the gate of the Mission, Ali Bey Khasib took my hand, Rufaă Bey that of the Consul, and we walked to the residence of the Bey, who detained us an hour by the narration of the injuries and indignities which had been inflicted upon him by order of Abbas Pasha. The latter, on coming into power, took especial care to remove all those officers who had been favorites of Mohammed Ali. Many of them were men of high attainments and pure character, who had taken an active part in carrying out the old Pasha's measures of reform. Among them was Rufaă Bey, who, with several of his associates, was sent to Khartoum, ostensibly for the purpose of founding a College there, but in reality as a banishment from Egypt. He had been there a year and a half at the time of my visit, yet no order had been received from Cairo relative to the College. This state of inaction and uncertainty, combined with the effect of the climate, had already terminated the lives of two of his fellow-professors, and it was no doubt the design of Abbas Pasha to relieve himself of all of them by the same means. When I heard this story, the truth of which Dr. Reitz confirmed, I could readily account for the bitterness of the curses which the venerable old Bey heaped upon the head of his tyrannical ruler.

The Frank population of Khartoum was not large, consisting, besides Dr. Reitz and the priests of the Catholic Mission, of Dr. Péney, a French physician, Dr. Vierthaler, a German, and an Italian apothecary, the two former of whom were in the Egyptian service. Dr. Péney had been ten years in Soudân, and knew the whole country, from the mountains of Fazogl to the plains of Takka, on the Atbara River, and the Shangalla forests on the Abyssinian frontier. He was an exceedingly intelligent and courteous person, and gave me much interesting information, concerning the regions he had visited and the habits of the different tribes of Soudân. I had afterwards personal opportunity of verifying the correctness of many of his statements. There were a few Coptic merchants in the place, and on the second day after my arrival I had an opportunity of witnessing the New-Year ceremonies of their Church, which, like the Greek, still retains the old style. The service, which was very similar to a Catholic mass, was chanted in musical Arabic, and at its close we were presented with small cakes of unleavened flour, stamped with a cross. At the conclusion of the ceremonies coffee was given to us in an outer court, with the cordial "*Haneean!*" (a wish equivalent to the Latin *prosit*, or "may it benefit you!")—to which we replied: "*Allah Haneek!*" (may God give you benefit!)

Dr. Reitz took me one day to visit the celebrated Sitteh (Lady) Nasra, the daughter of the last King of Sennaar and brother of the present Shekh of that province. She is a woman of almost masculine talent and energy, and may be said to govern Sennaar at present. All the Arab shekhs, as well as the population at large, have the greatest respect for her, and invariably ask her advice, in any crisis of affairs. Her brother Idris Wed Adlan, notwithstanding his nominal subjection to Egypt, still possesses absolute sway over several hundred villages, and is called King of Kulle. The Lady Nasra retains the title of Sultana, on account of her descent from the ancient royal house of Sennaar. She has a palace at Soriba, on the Blue Nile, which, according to Lepsius, exhibits a degree of wealth and state very rare in Soudân. She was then in Khartoum on a visit, with her husband, Mohammed Defalleh, the son of a former Vizier of her father, King Adlan.

We found the Lady Nasra at home, seated on a carpet in her audience-hall, her husband and Shekh Abd-el-Kader—the Shekh of Khartoum, who married her daughter by a former husband—occupying an adjacent carpet. She gave the Consul her hand, saluted me, as a stranger, with an inclination of her head, and we seated ourselves on the floor opposite to her. She was about forty-five years old, but appeared younger, and still retained the traces of her former beauty. Her skin was a pale bronze color, her eyes large and expressive, and her face remarkable for its intelligence and energy. All her motions were graceful and dignified, and under more favorable circumstances she might have become a sort of Ethiopian Zenobia. She wore a single robe of very fine white muslin, which she sometimes folded so as nearly to conceal her features, and sometimes allowed to fall to her waist, revealing the somewhat over-ripe charms of her bosom. A heavy ring of the native gold of Kasan hung from her nose, and others adorned her fingers. Dr. Reitz explained to her that I was not a Frank, but came from a great country on the other side of the world. She spoke of the visit of Dr. Lepsius, at Soriba, and said that he was the only far-travelled stranger she had seen, except myself. I took occasion to say that I had frequently heard of her in my native land; that her name was well-known all over the world; and that the principal reason of my visit to Soudân, was the hope of seeing her. She was not in the least flattered by these exaggerated compliments, but received them as quietly as if they were her right. She was a born queen, and I doubt whether any thing upon the earth would have been able to shake her royal indifference.

Her slaves were all girls of twelve to fourteen years of age, naked except the *ràhad*, or girdle of leathern fringe about the loins. They had evidently been chosen for their beauty, and two of them, although as black as cast-iron statues, were incomparable for the symmetry of their forms and the grace of their movements. They brought us pipes and coffee, and when not employed, stood in a row at the bottom of the room, with their hands folded upon their breasts. Dinner was just ready, and we were invited to partake of it. The Sultana had already dined in solitary state, so her husband, Shekh Abd-el-Kader, the Consul and I, seated ourselves cross-legged on the floor, around the huge bowl containing an entire sheep stuffed with rice. We buried our fingers in the hot and smoking flesh and picked the choicest pieces from the ribs and flank, occasionally taking a handful of rice from the interior The only additional dish was a basket of raw onions and radishes. Before each of us stood a slave with a napkin and a large glass of *om bilbil*—the "mother of nightingales." After drinking, we returned the glass to the slave's hand, she standing all the while immovable as a statue. After we had eaten our fill of roast mutton and raw onions, they brought a dish of prepared dourra, called *abri*, which strongly resembles the *pinole* of Mexico. The grain is pounded very fine, sifted, mixed with a little sugar and water, and made into thin, dry leaves, as white and delicate as cambric. It is considered very nourishing, especially on a journey, for which purpose it is used by the rich shekhs of Soudân.

As we took our leave, the Sultana, observing that our cane batons, which we had just purchased in the bazaar, were of very indifferent quality, ordered two others to be brought, of a fine yellow wood, resembling box, which is found in the mountains on the Abyssinian frontier, and gave them to us.

CHAPTER XXIII.

THE COUNTRIES OF SOUDAN.

Recent Explorations of Soudân—Limit of the Tropical Rains—The Conquest of Ethiopia--Countries Tributary to Egypt—The District of Takka—Expedition of Moussa Bey—The Atbara River—The Abyssinian Frontier—Christian Ruins of Abou-Harâss—The Kingdom of Sennaar—Kordofan—Dar-Fûr—The Princess of Dar-Fûr in Khartoum—Her Visit to Dr. Reitz—The Unknown Countries of Central Africa.

UNTIL within a recent period, but little has been known of the geography and topography of the eastern portion of Central Africa. Few English travellers have made these regions the subject of their investigation, their attention having been principally directed towards the countries on the western coast The Niger, in fact, has been for them a more interesting problem than the Nile. The German travellers Rüppell and Russegger, however, by their explorations within the last twenty-five years, have made important contributions to our knowledge of Eastern Soudân, while D'Arnaud, Werne, and more than all, Dr. Knoblecher, have carried our vision far into the heart of the mysterious regions beyond. Still, the results of these explorations are far from being generally known, or even represented upon our maps. Geographical charts are still issued, in which the conjectured Mountains of the Moon continue to stretch their ridges across the middle of Africa, in latitudes where the latest travellers find a plain as level as the sea. A few words, therefore, concerning the character and relative position of the different countries of which I have occasion to speak, may make these sketches of African life and landscapes more intelligible to many readers.

As far as southern Nubia, with the exception of the Oases in the Libyan Desert, the Nile is the only agent of productiveness. Beyond the narrow limits of his bounteous valley, there is little except red sand and naked rock, from the Red Sea tc the Atlantic. On reaching lat. 19°, however, a change takes place in the desert landscapes. Here the tropical rains, which are unknown in Egypt and Northern Nubia, fall every summer, though in diminished quantity. The dry, gravelly plains, nevertheless, exhibit a scattering growth of grass and thorny shrubs, and springs are frequently found among the mountain ranges. As we proceed southward, the vegetation increases in quantity; the grass no longer keeps the level of the plain, but climbs the mountain-sides, and before reaching Khartoum, in lat. 15° 40′ north, we have passed the limit of the Desert The wide plains stretching thence eastward to the Atbara, and westward beyond Kordofan, are savannas of rank grass, crossed here and there by belts of the thorny mimosa, and differing little in aspect from the plains of California during the dry season. The Arabs who inhabit them are herdsmen, and own vast flocks of camels and sheep. The Nile here is no longer the sole river, and loses his title of "The Sea," which he owns in Egypt. The Atbara, which flows down to him from the Abyssinian Alps, has many tributaries of its own, the Blue Nile, between Khartoum and Sennaar, receives the large streams of the Ràhad and the Dender; and the White Nile, though flowing for the greater part of his known course through an immense plain, boasts two important affluents—the Sobat and the Bahr el-Ghazal. The soil, climate, productions and character of the scenery of this region are therefore very different from Egypt.

Before the conquest of Soudân by Mohammed Ali, little was known of the country between the Ethiopian Nile and the Red Sea, or of Central Africa south of the latitude of Kordofan and Sennaar. The White Nile, it is true, was known to exist, but was considered as a tributary stream. It was extremely difficult and dangerous to proceed beyond Nubia, and then only in company with the yearly caravans which passed between Assouan and Sennaar. Ibrahim Pasha, Ismaïl Pasha, and Mohammed Bey Defterdar, between the years 1820 and 1825, gradually subjugated and attached to the rule of Egypt the countries of Berber, Shendy and Sennaar, as far as the mountains of Fazogl, in lat. 11°, on the south-western frontier of Abyssinia, the wild domains of the Shukorees, the Bishàrees, the Hallengas and Hadendoas, extending to the Red Sea, and embracing the seaport of Sowakin, and the kingdom of Kordofan, west of the Nile, and bounded by the large and powerful negro kingdom of Dar-Fūr. The Egyptian possessions in Soudân are nearly as extensive as all Egypt, Nubia not included, and might become even richer and more flourishing under a just and liberal policy of government. The plains on both sides of the Nile might be irrigated to a much greater extent than in Egypt, and many vast tracts of territory given up to the nomadic tribes, could readily be reclaimed from the wilderness. The native inhabitants are infinitely more stupid and degraded than the Fellahs of Egypt, but that they are capable of great improvement is shown by the success attending the efforts of the Catholic priests in Khartoum, in educating children. The terrible climate of Soudân will always be a drawback to its physical prosperity, yet even this would be mitigated, in some measure, were the soil under cultivation.

As I followed the course of the Nile, from the northern limit of the tropical rains to Khartoum, my narrative will have given some idea of the country along his banks. The territory to the east, towards and beyond the Atbara, is still in a great measure unexplored. Burckhardt was the first European who visited it, but his route lay among the mountain-ranges near and parallel to the coast of the Red Sea. The long chain of Djebel Langay, which he crossed, is three to five thousand feet in height, and, like the mountain-spine of the island of Ceylon, never has the same season on both sides at once. When it rains on the eastern slopes, the western are dry, and the contrary. There is another and still higher chain near the coast, but the greater part of this region consists of vast plains, tenanted by the Arab herdsmen, and rising gradually towards the south into the first terraces of the table-land of Abyssinia. The land of the Shukorees and the Hallengas, lying on both sides of the Atbara, is called *Belad el Takka.* Dr. Reitz visited it during the summer of 1851, in company with the military expedition under Moussa Bey, and travelled for three or four weeks through regions where no European had been before him.

Leaving the town of Shendy, he travelled eastward for nine days over unbroken plains of grass, abounding with gazelles and hyenas, to a village called Goz Radjeb, on the Atbara River. This belongs to the Shukorees, against whom the expedition was in part directed. He then crossed the river, and travelled for two or three weeks through a broken mountain country, inhabited by the wandering races of the Hallenges and Hadendoas. The mountains, which were from two to three thousand feet in height, were crested with walls of naked porphyry rock, but their lower slopes were covered with grass and bushes, and peopled by myriads of apes. Between the ranges were many broad and beautiful valleys, some of which were inhabited. Here the vegetable and animal world was far richer than on the Nile. The Consul was obliged to follow the movements of the expedition, and therefore could not trace out any regular plan of exploration. After seeing just enough to whet his curiosity to penetrate further, Moussa Bey returned to Goz Radjeb. His route then followed the course of the Atbara, for a distance of one hundred and twenty miles, to the town of Sofie, on the Abyssinian frontier. The river, which is a clear and beautiful stream, has a narrow border of trees and underwood, and flows in a winding course through a region of low, grassy hills. By using the water for irrigation, the country, which is now entirely uncultivated, might be made very productive. The Shukorees possess immense herds of camels, and a *hegin*, or trained dromedary, which the Consul purchased from them, was one of the strongest and fleetest which I saw in Africa.

Near Sofie the savannas of grass give place to dense tropical forests, with a rank undergrowth which is often impenetrable. Here, in addition to the lion and leopard, which are common to all Soudân, the expedition saw large herds of the elephant and rhinoceros. The woods were filled with birds of brilliant plumage, and the vegetable world was rich and gorgeous beyond description. The Consul remained but a short time here, and then travelled westward to the town of Abou-Haràss on the Blue Nile, visiting on the way a curious isolated mountain, called Djebel Attesh. Near Abou-Haràss are the ruins of an ancient Christian town, probably dating from the fourth or fifth century, about which time Christianity, previously planted in Abyssinia, began to advance northward towards Nubia. The Consul obtained from the Governor of Abou-Haràss three iron crosses of a peculiar form, a number of beads which had belonged to a rosary, and a piece of incense—all of which were found in removing the bricks used to build the Pasha's palace and other edifices in Khartoum. The room which I occupied during my stay in Khartoum was paved with the same bricks. These remains are in curious contrast with the pyramids of Meroë and the temples of Mesowuràt. The Christian and Egyptian Faiths, advancing towards each other, almost met on these far fields.

The former kingdom of Sennaar included the country between the two Niles—except the territory of the Shillooks—as far south as lat. 12°. It is bounded by Abyssinia on the east, and by the mountains of the savage Galla tribes, on the south. The *Djezeereh* (Island) *el Hoye*, as the country between the rivers is called, is for the most part a plain of grass. Towards the south, there are some low ranges of hills, followed by other plains, which extend to the unknown mountain region, and abound with elephants and lions. The town of Sennaar, once the capital of this region and the residence of its Meks or Kings, is now of little importance. It was described to me as a collection of mud huts, resembling Shendy. The Egyptian rule extends ten days' journey further, to Fazogl, where the fine timber in the mountains and the gold-bearing sands of Kasan have given rise to the establishment of a military post Sennaar, as well as Kordofan, Berber and Dongola, is governed by a Bey, appointed by the Pasha of Soudân. It is only two weeks' journey thence to Gondar, the capital of Amhara, the principal Abyssinian kingdom. I was told that it is not difficult for merchants to visit the latter place, but that any one suspected of being a person of consequence is detained there and not allowed to leave again. I had a strong curiosity to see something of Abyssinia, and had I been quite sure that I should not be taken for a person of consequence, might have made the attempt to reach Gondar.

Kordofan lies west of the White Nile, and consists entirely of great plains of grass and thorns, except in the southern part, where there is a mountain range called Djebel Dyer, inhabited by emigrants from Dongola. It is not more than two hundred miles in breadth, from east to west. Its capital, Obeid, lies in lat. 13° 12′ north, and is a mere collection of mud huts. Mr. Peterick, the English Vice-Consul for Soudân, to whom I had letters from Mr. Murray, the English Consul-General in Cairo, had taken up his residence in Obeid. The soil of Kordofan is sterile, and the water is considered very unhealthy for foreigners. Capt. Peel gave me such a description of its endless thickets of thorns, its miserable population and its devastating fevers, that I lost all desire to visit it. The Governor, Abd-el-Kader Bey, was in Khartoum, and Dr. Reitz intended making a journey through the country in company with him. There is a caravan route of twenty days between Obeid and Dongola, through a wild region called the Beyooda, or Bedjûda. A few degrees further north, it would be a barren desert, but here it is an alternation of *wadys*, or valleys with ranges of porphyry mountains, affording water, trees, and sufficient grass for the herds of the wandering Arabs. It is inhabited by two tribes—the Kababish and the Howoweet, who differ strongly from the Arabs east of the Nile, in their appearance and habits. The latter, by their superior intelligence and their remarkable personal beauty, still attest their descent from the tribes of Hedjaz and Yemen. The tribes in the western desert are more allied to the Tibboos, and other tenants of the Great Zahara. The caravans on this road are exposed to the danger of attacks from the negroes of Dar-Für, who frequently waylay small parties, murder the individuals and carry off the camels and goods.

The great kingdom of Dar-Für offers a rich field for some future explorer. The extensive regions it incloses are supposed to furnish the key to the system of rivers and mountain-chains of Central Africa. Through the fear and jealousy of its rulers, no stranger has been allowed to pass its borders, since the visit of Mr. Browne, half a century ago. Of late, however, the relations between the Egyptian rulers in Soudân and the Sultan of Dar-Für have been quite amicable, and if nothing occurs to disturb this harmony there is some hope that the ban will be removed. Lattif Pasha informed me that he had written to the Sultan on behalf of Capt. Peel, who wished to pass through Dar-Für and reach Bornou. He had at that time received no answer, but it had been intimated, unofficially, that the Sultan would reply, giving Capt. Peel permission to enter the country and travel in it, but not to pass beyond it. There is an almost continual war between the Sultans of Bornou and Dar-Fūr, and the Pasha was of the opinion that it would be impossible to traverse Africa from east to west, in the line of those states.

A circumstance occurred lately, which may help to open Dar-Fūr to Europeans. The Sitteh (Lady) Sowakin, the aunt of Sultan Adah, the present monarch of that kingdom, is a zealous Moslem, and lately determined to make a pilgrimage to the grave of the Prophet. She arrived in Khartoum in August, 1851, attended by a large retinue of officers, attendants and slaves, and after remaining a few days descended the Nile to El Mekheyref, crossed the Desert to Sowakin, on the Red Sea, and sailed thence for Djidda, the port of Mecca. During her stay Lattif Pasha was exceedingly courteous to her, introducing her to his wives, bestowing upon her handsome presents, and furnishing her with boats and camels for her journey. Dr. Reitz availed himself of the occasion to make the people of Dar-Fūr better acquainted with Europeans. All the Frank residents assembled at his house, in Christian costume, and proceeded to the residence of the Lady Sowakin. They found her sitting in state, with two black slaves before her on their hands and knees, motionless as sphinxes. On each side stood her officers and interpreters. She was veiled, as well as her female attendants, and all exhibited the greatest surprise and curiosity at the appearance of the Franks. The gifts they laid before her—silks, fine soaps, cosmetics, bon-bons, &c.—she examined with childish delight, and when the Consul informed her that the only object of the Europeans in wishing to enter Dar-Fūr was to exchange such objects as these for gum and elephants' teeth, she promised to persuade Sultan Adah to open his kingdom to them.

The next day her principal officers visited the Consul's house, and spent a long time examining its various wonders. The pictures, books and furniture filled them with astonishment, and they went from one object to another, like children, uttering exclamations of surprise and delight. What most startled them was a box of lucifer matches, which was entirely beyond their comprehension. They regarded the match with superstitious awe, and seemed to consider that the fire was produced by some kind of magic. Their relation of what they saw so excited the curiosity of the Lady Sowakin, that she came on the following day, with her women. She was no less astonished than her attendants had been, but was most attracted by the Consul's large mirror. She and her women spent half an hour before it, making gestures, and unable to comprehend how they were mimicked by the reflected figures. As she was unacquainted with its properties, she threw back her veil to see whether the image would show her face. The Consul was standing behind her, and thus caught sight of her features; she was black, with a strongly marked but not unpleasant countenance, and about forty-five years of age. He had a breakfast prepared for the ladies, but on reaching the room the attendants all retired, and he was informed that the women of rank in Dar-Fūr never eat in the presence of the men. After they had finished the repast, he observed that they had not only partaken heartily of the various European dishes, but had taken with them what they could not eat, so that the table exhibited nothing but empty dishes. When they left, the Lady reiterated her promise, and added that if the Consul would visit Dar-Fūr, the Sultan would certainly present him with many camel-loads of elephants' teeth, in consideration of his courtesy to her.

To the westward of Dar-Fūr, and between that country and Bornou, lies the large kingdom of Waday, which has never been visited by a European. I learned from some Kordofan merchants, who had visited the frontiers of Dar-Fūr on their trading expeditions, that Sultan Adah had conquered a great part of Waday, and would probably soon become involved in war with the Sultan of Bornou. It is said that there is in the country of Waday a lake called Fittre, which is a hundred and fifty miles in length, and receives several rivers. At the south-western extremity of Dar-Fūr, in lat. 6° N. there is a small country, called Fertit. I often heard it mentioned by the Ethiopian traders, one of whom showed me a snuff-box, which he had bought of a native of the country. It was made from the hard shell of a fruit about the size of an orange, with a stopper roughly wrought of silver. Almost the entire region south of lat. 10° N. and lying between the White Nile and the Gulf of Guinea is unknown ground, and presents a rich field for future explorers.

The difficulties and dangers which have hitherto attended the path of African discovery, are rapidly diminishing, and the time is not far distant when every mystery, hidden in the heart of that wonderful Continent, will be made clear. Where a traveller has once penetrated, he smoothes the way for those who follow, and that superior intelligence which renders the brute creation unable to bear the gaze of a human eye, is the defence of the civilized man against the barbarian. Bruce, journeying from Abyssinia to Egypt, in the year 1772, was beset by continual dangers, and even Burckhardt, in 1814, though successfully disguised as a Mussulman shekh, or saint, was obliged to keep his journal by stealth. At present, however, a

Frank may travel in comparative safety, from Cairo to the borders of Dar-Fūr and Abyssinia, while the White Nile and its tributaries afford avenues to the very heart of the unexplored regions beyond. The climate is the greatest obstacle in the way of discovery, and the traveller whose temperament is best adapted for the heats of the inter-tropical zone, possesses the best chance of success.

CHAPTER XXIV.

EXCURSIONS AND PREPARATIONS

Excursions around Khartoum—A Race into the Desert—Euphorbia Forest—The Banks of the Blue Nile—A Saint's Grave—The Confluence of the Two Niles—Magnitude of the Nile—Comparative Size of the Rivers—Their Names—Desire to penetrate further into Africa—Attractions of the White Nile—Engage the Boat *John Ledyard*—Former Restrictions against exploring the River—Visit to the Pasha—Despotic Hospitality—Achmet's Misgivings—We set sail.

My morning rides with Dr. Reitz, around Khartoum, gradually extended themselves into the neighboring country, within the limits which a fast dromedary could reach in two hours' travel. In this way I became familiar with the scenery along the banks of both Niles, and the broad arid plains between them. As I rarely appeared in public except in the Consul's company, and attended with all the state which his household could command, I was looked upon by the inhabitants as a foreign prince of distinguished rank. The Pasha's soldiers duly presented arms, and the people whom I met in the streets stopped and saluted me profoundly, as I passed. The Consul had succeeded in making a strong impression of his own power and importance, and this was reflected upon his guest. One morning, as we were riding towards the palace, a man cried out: "May God prolong your days, O Consul! and the days of the strange lord,—for you make a grand show with your horses, every day!"

There was one of our rides which I never call to mind without a leap of the heart. The noble red stallion which I usually mounted had not forgotten the plains of Dar-Fūr, where he was bred, and whenever we came upon the boundless level extending southward from the town, his wild blood was aroused. He pricked up his ears, neighed as grandly as the war-horse of Job, champed furiously against the restraining bit, and ever and anon cast a glance of his large, brilliant eye backward at me, half in wonder, half in scorn, that I did not feel the same desire. The truth is, I was tingling from head to foot with equal excitement, but Dr. Reitz was a thorough Englishman in his passion for trotting, and was vexed whenever I rode at any other pace. Once, however, the sky was so blue, the morning air so cool and fresh, and the blood so lively in my veins, that I answered the fierce questioning of Sultan's eye with an involuntary shout, pressed my knees against his sides and gave him the rein. O Mercury, what a rush followed! We cut the air like the whizzing shaft from a Saracen crossbow; Sultan stretched out until his powerful neck was almost on a level with his back, and the glorious rhythm of his hoofs was accompanied by so little sense of effort, that it seemed but the throbbing of his heart, keeping time with my own. His course was as straight as a sunbeam, swerving not a hair's-breadth to the right or left, but forward, forward into the freedom of the Desert. Neck and neck with him careered the Consul's milk-white stallion, and I was so lost in the divine excitement of our speed, that an hour had passed before I was cool enough to notice where we were going. The Consul finally called out to me to stop, and I complied, sharing the savage resistance of Sultan, who neighed and plunged with greater ardor than at the start. The minarets of Khartoum had long since disappeared; we were in the centre of a desolate, sandy plain, broken here and there by clumps of stunted mimosas—a dreary landscape, but glorified by the sunshine and the delicious air. We rode several miles on the return track, before we met the pursuing attendants, who had urged their dromedaries into a gallop, and were sailing after us like a flock of ostriches.

A few days after my arrival, we had the dromedaries saddled and rode to Kereff, a village on the Blue Nile, about two leagues distant. The path was over a wide plain, covered with dry grass, and resembling an Illinois prairie after a long drought. In the rainy season it is green and luxuriant with grass and a multitude of flowers. The only trees were the savage white thorn of the Desert, until we approached the river, where we found forests of the large euphorbia, which I had first noticed as a shrub in Upper Egypt. It here became a tree, upwards of twenty feet in height. The branches bent over my head, as I rode through on the Consul's tallest dromedary. The trees were all in blossom, and gave out a subtle, sickening odor. The flowers appear in whorls around the stem, at the base of the leaves; the corolla is entire, but divided into five points, white in the centre, with a purple stain at the extremity. The juice of this plant is viscid and milky, and the Arabs informed me that if a single drop of it gets into the eye it will produce instant blindness.

Beyond these thickets extended patches of wheat and cotton to the banks of the Blue Nile, where the hump-backed oxen of Sennaar were lazily turning the creaking wheels of the *sakies.* The river had here a breadth of more than half a mile, and shone blue and brilliant in the morning sun. Before reaching Kereff, we visited five villages, all built of mats and clay. The inhabitants were warming themselves on the sunny side of the huts, where they still shivered in the cold north-wind. At Kereff, two men brought a large gourd, filled with sour milk, which was very cool and refreshing. The principal wealth of the people consists in their large flocks of sheep and goats. They cultivate barely sufficient wheat and dourra to supply them with a few cakes of coarse bread, and their favorite beverage of *om bilbil.*

On our return we passed the grave of a native saint, which was decorated with rows of pebbles and a multitude of white pennons, fluttering from the tops of poles stuck in the ground. Several women were seated at the head, apparently paying their devotions to the ghost of the holy man. The older ones were unveiled and ugly, but there was a damsel of about eighteen, who threw part of her cotton mantle over her face, yet allowed us to see that she was quite handsome. She had a pale yellow complexion, showing her Abyssinian descent, large, almond-shaped eyes, and straight black hair which diffused an odor of rancid butter. I found it most agreeable to admire her beauty from the windward side. An old beggar-woman, whose gray hair, skinny face and bleared eyes, flashing from the bottom of deep sockets, made her a fitting picture of a Lapland witch, came up and touched our hands, which she could barely reach as we sat on the dromedaries, which saved us the horror of having her kiss them. We gave her a back sheesh, which she took as if it had been her right. After invoking the name of Allah many times, she went to the grave and brought each of us a handful of dirt, which we carefully put into our pockets, but as carefully emptied out again after we had reached home.

The next morning I rode with the Consul to the junction of the two Niles, about a mile and a half to the west of Khartoum. The land all around is low, and the two rivers meet at right angles, but do not mingle their waters till they have rolled eight or ten miles in their common bed. The White Nile is a light-brown, muddy color, the Blue Nile a dark bluish-green. Both rivers are nearly of equal breadth at the point of confluence, but the current of the latter is much the stronger. There is a low green island, called Omdurman, in the White Nile, at its junction. The ferry-boat had just brought over a party of merchants from Kordofan, with their packages of gum A number of large vessels, belonging to the government, were hauled up on the bank, and several Arabs, under the direction of a Turkish ship-builder, were making repairs. We rode a short distance up the White Nile, over a beach which was deeply printed with the enormous foot-prints of a whole herd of hippopotami, and then home through the fields of blossoming beans.

The Nile was to me a source of greater interest than all the negro kingdoms between Khartoum and Timbuctoo. There, two thousand miles from his mouth, I found his current as broad, as strong, and as deep as at Cairo, and was no nearer the mystery of his origin. If I should ascend the western of his two branches, I might follow his windings twelve hundred miles further and still find a broad and powerful stream, of whose source even the tribes that dwell in those far regions are ignorant. I am confident that when the hidden fountains shall at last be reached, and the problem of twenty centuries solved, the entire length of the Nile will be found to be not less than *four thousand miles*, and he will then take his rank with the Mississippi and the Amazon—a sublime trinity of streams! There is, in some respects, a striking resemblance between the Nile and the former river. The Missouri is the true Mississippi, rolling the largest flood and giving his color to the mingled streams. So of the White Nile, which is broad and turbid, and pollutes the clear blue flood that has usurped his name and dignity. In spite of what geographers may say—and they are still far from being united on the subject—the Blue Nile is not the true Nile. There, at the point of junction his volume of water is greater,* but he is fresh from the mountains and constantly fed by large, unfailing affluents, while the White Nile has rolled for more than a thousand miles on nearly a dead level, through a porous, alluvial soil, in which he loses more water than he brings with him.

* Capt. Peel, who measured the volume of water in the two rivers, gives the following result: Breadth of the Blue Nile at Khartoum, 768 yards; average depth, 16.11 feet; average current, 1.564 knots; volume of water, 5,820,600 cubic feet per minute. Breadth of the White Nile immediately above the junction, 483 yards; average depth, 13.92 feet; average current, 1.47 knots; volume of water, 2,985,400 feet per minute. Breadth of the Nile below the junction, 1107 yards; average depth, 14.38 feet; average current, 2 knots; volume of water, 9,526,700 cubic feet per minute. This measurement was made in the latter part of October, 1851. It can hardly be considered conclusive, as during the preceding summer the rains had been unusually heavy in the mountains of Abyssinia, which may have occasioned a greater disproportion than usual, in the volume of the two rivers.

The Blue Nile, whose source the honest, long-slandered Bruce did actually discover, rises near lat. 11° N. in the mountains of Godjam, on the south-western frontier of Abyssinia. Thence it flows northward into the great lake of Dembea, or Tzana, near its southern extremity. The lake is shallow and muddy, and the river carries his clear flood through it without mixing. He then flows to the south and south-east, under the name of Tzana, along the borders of the kingdom of Shoa, to between lat. 9° and 10°, whence he curves again to the north and finds his way through the mountains of Fazogl to the plains of Sennaar. His entire length cannot be less than eight hundred miles. The stream is navigable as far as the mountains, about three hundred miles from Khartoum, where it is interrupted by rapids. The Arabic name *El-bahr el-Azrek*, means rather "black" than "blue," the term *azrek* being used with reference to objects of a dark, blue-black color; and besides, it is called *black*, in contradistinction to the *Bahr el-Abiad*, the *white* Nile. The boatmen here also frequently speak of the black river as *he*, and the white as *she*. When I asked the reason of this, they replied that it was because the former had a stronger current. It is remarkable that the name "Nile," which is never heard in Egypt, (where the river is simply called *el-bahr*, "the sea,") should be retained in Ethiopia. There the boatmen speak of "*el-bahr el-Nil*," which name they also sometimes apply to the Blue Nile. It is therefore easy to understand why the latter river should have been looked upon as the main current of the Nile.

After I had been eight or ten days in Khartoum, I began to think of penetrating further into the interior. My intention, on leaving Cairo, was to push on as far as my time and means would allow, and the White Nile was the great point of attraction. The long journey I had already made in order to reach Soudân only whetted my desire of seeing more of the wild, barbaric life of Central Africa, and, owing to the good luck which had saved me from any delay on the road, I could spare three or four weeks for further journeys, before setting out on my return to Egypt. Some of my friends in Khartoum counselled one plan and some another, but after distracting myself in a maze of uncertainties, I returned to my first love, and determined to make a voyage up the White Nile. There was little to be gained by visiting Kordofan, as I had already seen Central African life to better advantage in Khartoum. Sennaar is now only interesting as a station on the way to Abyssinia or the mountains of Fazogl, and in the wild regions along the Atbara it is impossible to travel without an armed escort. As it is exceedingly dangerous for a single boat to pass through the extensive negro kingdoms of the Shillooks and the Dinkas, I had hoped to accompany Dr. Knoblecher's expedition some distance up the river and then take my chance of returning. The boat belonging to the Catholic Mission, however, had not arrived from Cairo, and the season was so far advanced that the expedition had been postponed until the following November. At the time of my visit, nevertheless, a Maltese trader named Lattif Effendi, was fitting up two large vessels which were shortly to leave on a trading voyage which he intended pushing as far as the Bari country. I could have made arrangements to accompany him, but as he could not return before some time in June, I should have been obliged, in that case, to pass the sickly season in Soudân—a risk scarcely worth the profit, as, with the best possible good luck, I might barely have reached the point attained by Dr. Knoblecher. The Consul proposed my going with Lattif Effendi until I should meet the yearly expedition on its return, and then come down the river with it. This would have enabled me to penetrate to lat. 9°, or perhaps 8°, but after passing the islands of the Shillooks, one sees little except water, grass and mosquitoes, until he reaches the land of the Kyks, in lat. 7°. After weighing carefully all the arguments on both sides, I decided to take a small boat and ascend as far as the islands. Here the new and rich animal and vegetable world of the magnificent river begins to unfold, and in many respects it is the most impressive portion of his stream.

I was fortunate in finding a small vessel, of the kind called *sandal*—the only craft in port, except the Pasha's dahabiyeh, which would have answered my purpose. It belonged to a fat old Turk, named Abou-Balta, from whom I engaged it for three hundred and twenty-five piastres. The crew consisted of a raïs, five strong Dongolese sailors, and a black female slave, as cook. The raïs knew the river, but positively refused to take me further than the island of Aba, somewhere between lat. 12° and 13°, on account of the danger of venturing among the Shillooks, without an armed force. I named the boat the *John Ledyard*, in memory of the first American traveller in Africa. The name was none the less appropriate, since Ledyard was buried beside the Nile, at the outset of a journey undertaken for the purpose of discovering its sources. Dr. Reitz gave me two sheep as provision for the voyage, and the remainder of my outfit cost me about a hundred and twenty piastres in the bazaars of Khartoum.

I reached Khartoum at a favorable season for making the

voyage. Formerly, it had been very difficult for any European to obtain permission to sail on the White Nile, owing to the trade of the river having been completely monopolized by the Pasha of Soudân, in defiance of the Treaty of 1838, which made the river free to merchants of all nations. No later than the previous winter, Count Dandolo, an Italian traveller who visited Khartoum, encountered much opposition before he succeeded in obtaining a boat for the Islands of the Shillooks. Owing to the vigorous efforts of Dr. Reitz, the monopoly had at last been broken down, and the military guard formerly stationed at the confluence of the two rivers, no longer existed. I did not even inform the Pasha of my intention to make the voyage until after I had taken the boat and completed my preparations. I then paid him a visit of ceremony, in company with the Consul. He was very affable, and insisted on our remaining for dinner, although we had invited two friends to help us eat a roasted ram. We urged this in excuse, but he cut us off by exclaiming: "I am ruler here, and my commands dare not be disobeyed," and immediately sent a servant to order our guests, in his name, to eat the ram themselves. He then despatched messengers for Abd-el-Kader Bey, Governor of Kordofan, and Ruffaä Bey, who were brought to the palace in the same arbitrary manner. Having thus secured his company, he retired for the usual prayers before dinner, leaving us to enjoy the preparatory pipe. Among the manifold dishes served at dinner, were three or four kinds of fish from the White Nile, all of them of excellent flavor. The Pasha continued his discussion of Louis Napoleon's *coup d'état*, taking delight in recommending a sanguinary policy as the only course, and could not enough praise Sultan

Mahmoud I. for his execution of forty thousand Janissaries in one day.

Finally, on the morning of the 22d of January, my effects were all on board, and my raïs and sailors in readiness. Achmet and Ali preceded me to the boat with many misgivings, for we were now going into regions where the Pasha's name was scarcely known—where the Egyptian sway had never reached—a land of *kaffirs*, or infidels, who were supposed to be nearly related to the terrible "Nyàm-Nyàms," the anthropophagi of Central Africa. Achmet could not comprehend my exhilaration of spirits, and in reply to my repeated exclamations of satisfaction and delight, observed, with a shake of the head: "If it were not that we left Cairo on a lucky day, O my master! I should never expect to see Khartoum again." Fat Abou-Balta, who had promised to accompany me as far as the first village on the White Nile, did not make his appearance, and so we pushed off without him. Never was name more wrongly applied than that of Abou-Balta (the "father of hatchets"), for he weighed three hundred pounds, had a face like the full moon, and was the jolliest Turk I ever saw. Dr. Reitz, whose hospitality knew no bounds, sent his dromedaries up the river the day previous, and accompanied me with his favorite servants—two ebony boys, with shining countenances and white and scarlet dresses.

The White Nile.

CHAPTER XXV.

VOYAGE UP THE WHITE NILE.

Departure from Khartoum—We enter the White Nile—Mirage and Landscape—The Consul returns—Progress—Loss of the Flag—Scenery of the Shores—Territory of the Hassaniyehs—Curious Conjugal Custom—Multitudes of Water Fowls—Increased Richness of Vegetation—Apes—Sunset on the White Nile—We reach the Kingdom of the Shillook Negroes.

"At night he heard the lion roar
 And the hyena scream,
And the river-horse as he crushed the reeds
 Beside some hidden stream;
And it passed like a glorious roll of drums
 Through the triumph of his dream."—LONGFELLOW.

THE men pushed away from shore with some difficulty, as a violent north-wind drove the boat back, but the sail once unfurled, we shot like an arrow between the gardens of Khartoum and the green shores of the island of Tuti. Before reaching the confluence of the rivers, a jut of land obliged the sailors again to take to their poles and oars, but a short time sufficed to bring us to the turning-point. Here the colors of the different streams are strongly marked. They are actually blue and white, and meet in an even line, which can be seen extending far down the common tide. We tossed on the agitated line of their junction, but the wind carried us in a few minutes past the island of Omdurman, which lies opposite The first American flag that ever floated over the White Nile, fluttered gayly at the mast-head, pointing to the south—to those vast, mysterious regions out of which the mighty stream finds its way. A flock of the sacred ibis alighted on the sandy shore of the island, where the tall king-heron, with his crest of stately feathers, watched us as he walked up and down. In front, over the island of Moussa Bey, a broad mirage united its delusive waters with those of the true river and lifted the distant shores so high above the horizon that they seemed floating in the air. The stream, which is narrow at its junction with the Blue Nile, expanded to a breadth of two miles, and the shores ahead of us were so low that we appeared to be at the entrance of a great inland sea. Our course swerved to the eastward, so that we were in the rear of Khartoum, whose minaret was still visible when we were ten miles distant. The low mud dwellings of the town were raised to twice their real height, by the effect of the mirage. The shores on either side were sandy tracts, almost uncultivated, and covered with an abundant growth of thorns, mimosas and a small tree with thick green foliage. By twelve o'clock we reached the point where Dr. Reitz had sent his dromedaries, which were in readiness, kneeling on the beach. We could not approach the shore, on account of the mud, but the sailors carried us out on their shoulders. I rode with him to a small Arab hamlet, scattered among the thorny thickets. There were but two mud houses, the other dwellings being merely rude tents of grass matting; few of the inhabitants were at home, but those few were peaceable and friendly. As the Consul had a ride of four or five hours before him, he wished me good luck and set off northward, while the sailors, who were in waiting, carried me back to the boat.

All the afternoon I sped before a strong wind up the magnificent river. Its breadth varied from two to three miles, but its current was shallow and sluggish. The shores were sandy, and covered with groves of the gum-producing mimosa, which appeared for the first time in profusion. About four o'clock I passed a low, isolated hill on the eastern bank, which the sailors called *Djàr en-nebbee*, and near sunset, a long ridge on the right, two miles inland, broke the dead level of the plains of Kordofan. The sand-banks were covered with wild geese and ducks in myriads, and here and there we saw an enormous crocodile lounging on the edge of the water. The sun went down; the short twilight faded, and I was canopied by a superb starlit heaven. Taurus, Orion, Sirius and the Southern Cross sparkled in one long, unbroken galaxy of splendor. The breeze was mild and light, and the waves rippled with a pleasant sound against the prow. My sailors sat on the forward deck, singing doleful songs, to which the baying of dogs and the yells of hyenas made a fit accompaniment. The distant shores of the river were lighted with the fires of the Mohammediyeh Arabs, and we heard the men shouting to each other occasionally. About nine o'clock we passed their principal village, and approached the territories of the Hassaniyehs.

The wind fell about ten o'clock, and the boat came to anchor. I awoke an hour or two after midnight and found it blowing again fresh and strong; whereupon I roused the raïs and sailors, and made them hoist sail. We gained so much by this move, that by sunrise we had passed the village of Shekh Moussa, and were entering the territories of the Hassaniyeh Arabs; the last tribe which is subject to the Pasha of Soudân. Beyond them are the primitive Negro Kingdoms of Central Africa, in almost the same condition now as they have been for thousands of years past. About sunrise the raïs ordered the sails to be furled, and the vessel put about. The men were rowing some time before I discovered the cause. Whilst attempting to hoist my flag, one of them let it fall into the water, and instead of jumping in after it, as I should have done had I seen it, suffered the vessel to go some distance before he even announced the loss. We were then so far from the spot, that any attempt to recover it would have been useless, and so the glorious stars and stripes which had floated thus far triumphantly into Africa, met the fate of most travellers in those regions. They lay imbedded in the mud of the White Nile, and I sailed away from the spot with a pang, as if a friend had been drowned there. The flag of one's country is never dearer to him than when it is his companion and protector in foreign lands.

During the whole forenoon we sailed at the rate of six or seven miles an hour, in the centre of the river, whose breadth varied from two to three miles. The shores no longer presented the same dead level as on the first day. They were banks of sandy soil, ten or twelve feet in height, and covered with forests of the gum-bearing mimosa, under which grew thickets of a dense green shrub, mixed with cactus and euphorbia. The gum is a tree from twenty to thirty feet in height, with a thick trunk and spreading branches, and no Italian oak or chestnut presents a greater variety of picturesque forms to the painter's eye. The foliage is thin, allowing the manifold articulations of the boughs and twigs to be seen through it. It was most abundant on the Kordofan side, and the greater proportion of the gum annually exported to Egypt comes from that country. The broad tide of the river and the wild luxuriance of the continuous forests that girdled it, gave this part of its course an air of majesty, which recalled the Mississippi to my mind. There was not a single feature that resembled Egypt.

Towards noon we reached the more thickly populated districts of the Hassaniyeh. The town of Damas, on the east, and Tura, on the west, not very distant from each other, were the first I saw since leaving Khartoum. They were merely clusters of *tokuls*, or the straw huts of the natives, built in a circular form, with a conical roof of matting, the smoke escaping through an opening in the top. At both these places, as well as at other points along the river, the natives had ferries, and appeared to be busy in transporting men, camels and goods from one bank to the other. On account of the breadth of the river the passage was long, and the boatmen eased their labor by making a sail of their cotton mantles, which they fastened to two upright sticks. The shores were crowded with herds of sheep and goats, and I saw near Damas a large drove of camels which were waiting an opportunity to cross. The Hassaniyehs own no camels, and this was probably a caravan from Khartoum, bound for Kordofan. In some places the people brought donkeys laden with water-skins, which they filled from the river. I noticed, occasionally, a small patch of beans, but nothing that looked like a regular system of cultivation. The Hassaniyehs are yellow, with straight features, and resemble the Fellahs of Lower Egypt more than any other Central-African tribe. Those whom we saw at a distance from the villages retreated with signs of fear as my vessel approached the shore. Dr. Péney, the Medical Inspector of Soudân, described to me, while in Khartoum, some singular customs of these Arabs. The rights of women, it appears, are recognized among them more thoroughly than among any other savage people in the world. When a woman is married, her father states that one fourth of her life thenceforth is reserved for her own use, and the husband is obliged to respect this reservation. Every fourth day she is released from the marriage vow, and if she loves some one else better than her husband, he can dwell in her tent that day, obliging the husband himself to retire. Their hospitality is such, moreover, that if a stranger visits one of their settlements they furnish him, for four days, with a tent and a wife. They should add a family of children, and then their hospitality would be complete. No reproach whatever attaches to the woman, on account of this temporary connection. The Hassaniyeh, in other respects, are not more immoral than other tribes, and these customs appear to be connected with their religious faith.

After passing Tura (the terminus of a short caravan route of four days to Obeid, the capital of Kordofan), a mountain range, some distance from the river, appeared on the right bank. The peaks were broken and conical in form and their pale-violet hue showed with fine effect behind the dark line of the gum forests. With every hour of our progress, the vegetation grew more rank and luxuriant. On the eastern bank the gum gave place to the flowering mimosa, which rose in a dense rampart from the water's edge and filled the air with the fragrance of its blossoms. Myriads of wild geese, ducks, cranes, storks, herons and ibises sat on the narrow beaches of sand or circled in the air with hoarse clang and croaking. Among them I saw more than one specimen of that rare and curious water-bird, whose large, horny bill curves upward instead of downward, so that it appears to have been put on the wrong way. As he eats nothing but small fish, which he swallows with his head under water, this is not such a great inconvenience as one would suppose. The bars which occasionally made out into the current served as a resting-place for crocodiles, which now began to appear in companies of ten or fifteen, and the forests were filled with legions of apes, which leaped chattering down from the branches to look at us. A whole family of them sat on the bank for some time, watching us, and when we frightened them away by our shouts, it was amusing to see a mother pick up her infant ape, and scamper off with it under her arm. The wild fowl were astonishingly tame, and many of them so fat that they seemed scarcely able to fly. Here and there, along the shore, large broods of the young were making their first essays in swimming. The boatmen took great delight in menacing the old birds with pieces of wood, in order to make them dive under water. There were some superb white cranes, with a rosy tinge along the edges of their wings, and I saw two more of the crested king-herons

After passing the island of Tshebeshi, the river, which still retains its great breadth, is bordered by a swampy growth of reeds. It is filled with numerous low islands, covered with trees, mostly dead, and with waste, white branches which have drifted down during the inundation. In the forests along the shore many trees had also been killed by the high water of the previous summer. There are no habitations on this part of the river, but all is wild, and lonely, and magnificent. I had seen no sail since leaving Khartoum, and as the sun that evening threw his last red rays on the mighty flood, I felt for the first time that I was alone, far in the savage heart of Africa. We dashed along at a most exciting rate of speed, brushing the reeds of the low islands, or dipping into the gloom of the shadows thrown by the unpruned forests. The innumerable swarms of wild birds filled the air with their noise, as they flew to their coverts, or ranged themselves in compact files on the sand. Above all their din, I heard at intervals, from the unseen thickets inland, the prolonged snarling roar of some wild beast. It was too deep-toned and powerful for a leopard, and we all decided that it was a lion. As I was watching the snowy cranes and silvery herons that alighted on the boughs within pistol-shot, my men pointed out a huge hippopotamus, standing in the reeds, but a short distance from the vessel. He was between five and six feet high, but his head, body and legs were of enormous bulk. He looked at us, opened his great jaws, gave his swine-like head a toss in the air, and plunged hastily into the water. At the same instant an immense crocodile (perhaps twenty feet in length) left his basking-place on the sand and took refuge in the river. Soon afterwards two hippopotami rose in the centre of the stream, and, after snorting the water from their nostrils, entertained us with a peculiar grunting sound, like the lowest rumbling note of a double-bass. The concert was continued by others, and resumed from time to time through the night. This was Central Africa as I had dreamed it—a grand though savage picture, full of life and heat, and with a barbaric splendor even in the forms of Nature.

As the new moon and the evening star went down together behind the mimosa forests on the western bank, we reached the island of Hassaniyeh, having sailed upward of one hundred and forty miles since the evening before. I had every prospect of reaching my destination, the island of Aba, in the archipelago of the Shillooks, before noon the next day, or in two days from Khartoum—a distance of more than two hundred and fifty miles! Better sailing than this was never made on the Nile. Four more days of such wind would have taken me to the Bahr el-Ghazal, in lat. 9°—the land of lions, elephants and giraffes, where the Nile becomes a sea of grass. It became more difficult for me to return, the further I advanced. At nine o'clock we passed the island of Hassaniyeh, and saw the fires of the Shillook negroes burning brightly on the western bank. The wind blew more briskly than ever, and I dashed onward in the starlight with the painful knowledge that I was fast approaching the point beyond which I dared not go

CHAPTER XXVI.

ADVENTURES AMONG THE SHILLOOK NEGROES.

Morning—Magnificence of the Island Scenery—Birds and Hippopotami—Flight of the Natives—The Island of Aba—Signs of Population—A Band of Warriors—The Shekh and the Sultan—A Treaty of Peace—The Robe of Honor—Suspicions—We walk to the Village—Appearance of the Shillooks—The Village—The Sultan gives Audience—Women and Children—Ornaments of the Natives—My Watch—A Jar of Honey—Suspicion and Alarm—The Shillook and the Sultan's Black Wife—Character of the Shillooks—The Land of the Lotus—Population of the Shillook Kingdom—The Turning Point—A View from the Mast-Head.

We sailed nearly all night with a steady north-wind, which towards morning became so strong that the men were obliged to take in sail and let us scud under bare poles. When I rose, in the gray of early dawn, they were about hoisting the little stern-sheet, which alone sufficed to carry us along at the rate of four miles an hour. We had passed the frontier of Egyptian Soudân soon after sunset, and were then deep in the negro kingdom of the Shillooks. The scenery had changed considerably since the evening. The forests were taller and more dense, and the river more thickly studded with islands, the soil of which was entirely concealed by the luxuriant girdle of shrubs and water-plants, in which they lay imbedded. The *ambak*, a species of aquatic shrub, with leaves resembling the sensitive plant and winged, bean-like blossoms of a rich yellow hue, grew on the edge of the shore, with its roots in the water and its long arms floating on the surface. It formed impenetrable ramparts around the islands and shores, except where the hippopotamus and crocodile had trodden paths into the forests, or the lion and leopard had come down to the river's margin to drink. Behind this floating hem of foliage and blossoms appeared other and larger shrubs, completely matted together with climbing vines, which covered them like a mantle and hung from their branches dangling streamers of white and purple and yellow blossoms. They even stretched to the boughs of the large mimosa, or sont trees, which grew in the centre of the islands, thus binding all together in rounded masses. Some of the smaller islands resembled floating hills of vegetation, and their slopes and summits of impervious foliage, rolling in the wind, appeared to keep time with the rocking of the waves that upheld them. The profusion of vegetable life reminded me of the Chagres River. If not so rich and gorgeous, it was on a far grander scale. The river had still a breadth of a mile and a half, where his current was free, but where island crowded on island in a vast archipelago of leafy shores, he took a much wider sweep. The waves danced and glistened in the cool northern wind, as we glided around his majestic curves, and I stood on deck watching the wonderful panorama unfold on either side, with a feeling of exultation to which I gave free vent. In no other river have I seen landscapes of larger or more imposing character.

All the rich animal world of this region was awake and stirring before the sun. The wild fowls left their roosts; the *zikzaks* flew twittering over the waves, calling up their mates, the sleepy crocodiles; the herons stretched their wings against the wind; the monkeys leaped and chattered in the woods, and at last whole herds of hippopotami, sporting near the shore, came up spouting water from their nostrils, in a manner precisely similar to the grampus. I counted six together, soon after sunrise, near the end of an island. They floundered about in the shallows popping up their heads every few minutes to look at us, and at last walked out through the reeds and stood upon the shore. Soon afterwards five more appeared on the other side of the river, and thenceforth we saw them almost constantly, and sometimes within fifty yards. I noticed one which must have been four feet in breadth across the ears, and with a head nearly five feet long. He opened his mouth wide enough to show two round, blunt tusks, or rather grinders, one on each side. They exhibited a great deal of curiosity, and frequently turned about after we had passed, and followed for some time in our wake.

Soon after sunrise the raïs observed some Shillooks in the distance, who were sinking their canoes in the river, after which they hastily retreated into the woods. We ran along beside the embowering shores, till we reached the place. The canoes were carefully concealed and some pieces of drift-wood thrown over the spot, as if left there by the river. The raïs climbed to the mast-head and called to the people, assuring them that there was no danger, but, though we peered sharply into the thickets, we could find no signs of any human being. The river here turned to the south, disclosing other and richer groups of islands, stretching beyond one another far into the distance. Directly on our left was the northern point of the island of Aba, our destination. As the island is six or eight miles in length, I determined to make the most of my bargain, and so told the raïs that he must take me to its further end, and to the villages of the Shillooks, whom I had come to see. Abou-Hammed was small in body, but had a stout heart. The Consul and fat Abou-Balta had given him special instructions to keep me out of danger, yet he could not refuse my demands. We sailed two or three miles along the shore of Aba, looking into the depths of its ambak forests for traces of the Shillooks, who, according to the raïs, had a village on the island. On our right extended a chain of smaller islands—bowery masses of leaves and blossoms—and beyond them the wild forests of the western bank. Glorious above description was that world of waves and foliage—of wood, water and sky.

At last, on rounding one of the coves of Aba, we came upon a flock of sheep, feeding along the shore. A light thread of smoke arose from among some dead, fallen trees, a few paces in the forest, but no person was to be seen. The boat was run to the shore, and we landed and examined the spot. The natives had evidently just left, for the brands were burning, and we saw the prints of their long feet in the ashes. The raïs and sailors walked on tiptoe through the woods, looking for the hidden inhabitants. The mimosas, which here grow to the height of fifty feet, met above our heads and made a roof against the sun. Some large gray apes, startled by our visit, leaped with wonderful dexterity from tree to tree. I found several abandoned fire-places during my walk, and near the shore saw many footprints in the soft soil. The forest was quite clear of underwood, but the ground was cumbered with the trunks of dead trees. There were but few flowering plants and I was too much interested in the search for the Shillooks to examine them.

The raïs finally descried the huts of the village at a distance, near the extremity of the island. We returned to the vessel, and were about putting off in order to proceed thither, when a large body of men, armed with spears, appeared in the forest, coming towards us at a quick pace. The raïs, who had already had some intercourse with these people and knew something of their habits, advanced alone to meet them. I could see, through the trees, that a consultation was held, and shortly, though with some signs of doubt and hesitation, about a dozen of the savages advanced to within a short distance of the vessel, while the others sat down on the ground, still holding the spears in their hands. The raïs now returned to the water's edge, and said that the Shillooks had come with the intention of fighting, but he had informed them that this was a visit from the Sultan's son, who came to see them as a friend, and would then return to his father's country. Thereupon they consented to speak with me, and I might venture to go on shore. I landed again, with Achmet, and walked up with the raïs to the spot where the men were seated. The shekh of the island, a tall, handsome man, rose to greet me, by touching the palm of his right hand to mine and then raising it to his forehead. I made a like salutation, after which he sat down. The vizier (as he called himself), an old man excessively black in complexion, then advanced, and the other warriors in succession, till all had saluted me. The conversation was carried on in the Arabic jargon of Soudân, which the shekh and some of his men spoke tolerably well, so that I could understand the most of what was said. "Why don't you bring the Sultan's carpet that he may rest?" said the shekh to one of my sailors. The carpet and pillows were immediately brought, and I stretched myself out in front of the shekh and vizier, who sat upon a fallen tree, while the others squatted upon the ground. The shekh at first took no part in the conversation, but sat looking at me steadily, from under his heavy eyebrows. Our negotiations were conducted in genuine diplomatic style. Whenever His Majesty of the Shillooks had any thing to say, he mentioned it to his vizier, who addressed Achmet, my vizier, who communicated it to me, the Sultan. The spectators observed the most profound silence, and nothing could surpass the gravity and solemnity of the scene.

In the mean time the other warriors had come up and taken their seats around us, each one greeting me before he sat down, with "*ow-wow-wobba!*" (probably a corruption of the Arabic "*mar-habba?*" "how d'ye do?") The vizier, addressing me through Achmet, said: "Tell us what you want; if you come to fight, we are ready for you." I assured the shekh through him that I came as a friend, and had no intention of molesting them, but he was not satisfied, and repeated three or four times, drawing a mark between us on the ground: "if you are really friends, we will be friends with you; but if you are not, we are ready to fight you." Achmet at last swore by the Prophet Mohammed, and by the wisdom of Allah, that we had come in peace; that the Sultan wished to pay him a visit, and would then return home. At the request of the raïs we had come on shore unarmed, but it had not the anticipated effect. "Why have you no arms?" said the shekh; "are you afraid of us?" I told him that it was in order to show that I had no hostile intentions, but the people seemed to consider it as mark of either treachery or fear. I brought some tobacco with me, which I gave to the shekh, but he received it coldly, and said: "Where is the dress which the Sultan has brought for me?" This reminded me that I had entirely neglected to provide myself in Khartoum with muslin and calico, for presents. I remedied the deficiency, however, by going on board and taking one of my shirts and a silk handkerchief, as well as some beads and ear-rings for the wives of the two dignitaries. Achmet added a shirt and a pair of Turkish drawers, and brought a fresh supply of tobacco for the warriors. The shekh took the presents with evident gratification, and then came the work of clothing him. He was entirely at a loss how to put on the garments, but Achmet and the raïs unwound the cotton cloth from his loins, stuck his legs into the drawers, his arms into the shirt-sleeves, and tied the handkerchief about his head. Once clothed, he gave no more attention to his garments, but wore them with as much nonchalance as if he had never possessed a scantier costume. The vizier, who had shown manifest ill-humor at being passed by, was quieted by the present of a shirt, which was put upon his shoulders in like manner. He gave me his name as *Adjeb-Seedoo* ("He pleases his Master"), a most appropriate name for a vizier. The shekh's name, *Abd-en-noor* ("the Slave of Light"), was hardly so befitting, for he was remarkably dark. I was much amused at my servant Ali, who had shown great terror on the first appearance of the savages. He had already become so familiar, that when the shekh did not seem to understand the use of the beads and ear-rings, Ali pinched his ears very significantly, and took hold of his neck to show how they must be worn.

By this time coffee had been prepared and was brought to

them. But they had been so accustomed to inhumanity and deception on the part of the Turks, that they still mistrusted us and no one would drink, for fear that it contained poison. To quiet them, therefore, I drank a cup first, after which they took it readily, but many of them, who then tasted coffee for the first time, did not seem to relish it. A drove of sheep happening to pass by, the shekh ordered one of the rams to be caught and put on board the vessel, for the Sultan's dinner. The men soon began to demand tobacco, clothes, and various other things, and grew so importunate that Achmet became alarmed, and even the raïs, who was a man of some courage, seemed a little uneasy. I thought it time to give a change to affairs, and therefore rose and told the shekh I was ready to visit his village. We had intended returning on board and sailing to the place, which was at the southern extremity of the island, about a mile distant, but reflecting that this might occasion mistrust, and that the best way of avoiding danger is to appear unconscious of it, I called Achmet and the raïs to accompany me on foot. While these things were transpiring, a number of other Shillooks had arrived, so that there were now upwards of fifty. All were armed—the most of them with iron-pointed spears, some with clubs, and some with long poles, having knobs of hard wood on the end. They were all tall, strong, stately people, not more than two or three under six feet in height, while the most of them were three or four inches over that standard. Some had a piece of rough cotton cloth tied around the waist or thrown over the shoulders, but the most of them were entirely naked. Their figures were large and muscular, but not symmetrical, nor was there the least grace in their movements. Their faces resembled a cross between the Negro of Guinea and the North American Indian, having the high cheek bones, the narrow forehead and pointed head of the latter, with the flat nose and projecting lips of the former. Their teeth were so long as to appear like tusks, and in most of them one or two front teeth were wanting, which gave their faces a wolfish expression. Their eyes were small and had an inflamed look, which might have been occasioned by the damp exhalations of the soil on which they slept. Every one wore an armlet above the elbow, either a segment of an elephant's tusk, or a thick ring of plaited hippopotamus hide. The most of them had a string of glass beads around the neck, and the shekh wore a necklace of the large white variety, called "pigeon eggs" by the traders on the White Nile. They had no beards, and their hair was seared or plucked out on the forehead and temples, leaving only a circular crown of crisp wool on the top of the head. Some had rubbed their faces and heads with red ashes, which imparted a livid, ghastly effect to their black skins.

The shekh marched ahead, in his white garments and fluttering head-dress, followed by the warriors, each carrying his long spear erect in his hand. We walked in the midst of them, and I was so careful to avoid all appearance of fear that I never once looked behind, to see whether the vessel was following us. A violent dispute arose among some of the men in front, and from their frequent glances towards us, it was evident that we were in some way connected with the conversation. I did not feel quite at ease till the matter was referred to the shekh, who decided it in a way that silenced the men, if it did not satisfy them. As we approached the village, good-humor was restored, and their demeanor towards us was thenceforth more friendly. They looked at me with curiosity but without ill-will, and I could see that my dress interested them much more than my person. Finally we reached the village, which contained about one hundred tokuls of straw, built in a circular form, with conical roofs. They were arranged so as to inclose a space in the centre, which was evidently intended as a fold for their sheep, as it was further protected by a fence of thorns. Guards were stationed at intervals of about twenty yards, along the side fronting the river, each leaning back against his spear, with one of his legs drawn up, so that the foot rested against the opposite knee. At the principal entrance of the village, opposite which I counted twenty-seven canoes drawn up against the shore, we made halt, and the shekh ordered a seat to be brought. An *angareb*, the frame of which was covered with a net-work of hippopotamus thongs, was placed in the shade of a majestic mimosa tree, and the shekh and I took our seats. Another angareb was brought and placed behind us, for our respective viziers. The warriors all laid aside their spears and sat on the ground, forming a semicircle in front of us. A swarm of naked boys, from eight to twelve years of age, crept dodging behind the trees till they reached a convenient place in the rear, where they watched me curiously, but drew back in alarm whenever I turned my head. The village was entirely deserted of its inhabitants, every one having come to behold the strange Sultan. The females kept at a distance at first, but gradually a few were so far overcome by their curiosity that they approached near enough for me to observe them closely. They were nude, except a small piece of sheepskin around the loins, and in their forms were not very easy to distinguish from the men, having flat, masculine breasts and narrow hips. They were from five feet eight inches to six feet in height. The raïs informed me that the Shillooks frequently sell their women and children, and that a boy or girl can be bought for about twenty measures of dourra.

After undergoing their inspection half an hour, I began to get tired of sitting in state, and had my pipe brought from the boat. I saw by an occasional sidelong glance that the shekh watched me, but I smoked carelessly until the tobacco was finished. Some of the men were already regaling themselves with that which I had given them. They had pipes with immense globular bowls of clay, short, thick stems of reed, and mouth-pieces made of a variety of wild gourd, with a long, pointed neck. A handful of tobacco was placed in the bowl and two or three coals laid upon it, after which the orifice was closed with clay. The vizier, Adjeb-Seedoo, who had something of the Yankee in his angular features and the shrewd wrinkles about the corners of the eyes, chewed the tobacco and squirted out the saliva between his teeth in the true Down-East style. I bargained for his pipe at two piastres, and one of the ivory arm-rings at five, but as I had no small silver money (the only coin current among them), did not succeed in getting the former article. I obtained, however, two of the arm-rings of hippopotamus hide. While these things were going on, the shekh who had been observing me closely, saw the chain of my watch, which he seized. I took out the watch and held it to his ear. He started back in surprise, and told the men what he had heard, imitating its sound in a most amusing manner. They all crowded around to listen, and from their looks and signs seemed to think the case contained some bird or insect. I therefore opened it, and showed them the motion of the balance-wheel and of the hand on the smaller dial of the face. Their astonishment was now changed to awe and they looked at it silently, without daring to touch it.

I profited by this impression to make a move for starting, before their greed for presents should grow into a resolve to rob us by force. I had asked the shekh two or three times to have a cup of water brought for me, but he seemed to pay no attention to the request. Soon, however, one of the men brought a large earthen jar, stopped with clay, and placed it at my feet. Thereupon the shekh turned to me, saying: "There is plenty of water in the river, and here I give you honey to mix with it." The jar was taken on board, and contained, in fact, nearly a gallon of wild honey, which had a rich, aromatic taste, like the odor of the mimosa flowers. The trading-vessels on the White Nile purchase this honey, but as the natives, in their hatred of the Turks, frequently mix with it the juice of poisonous plants, they are obliged to taste it themselves before they can sell it. I did not require this proof at their hands, preferring to trust them unreservedly, at least in my demeanor. Trust always begets a kindred trust, and I am quite sure that my safety among those savages was owing to my having adopted this course of conduct.

I went on board to get the money for the arm-rings, and after Achmet had paid the men, directed him and the raïs to return. Several of the Shillooks followed, offering articles for sale, and the vizier, who had waded out, holding up his new shirt so that it might not be wet, climbed upon the gunwale of the boat and peered into the cabin. I changed my position so as to stand between him and the door, gave him two onions which he saw on deck and had an appetite for, and hurried him away. The shekh and all the warriors had come down to the shore, but without their spears, and were seated on the ground, holding a consultation. By this time, however, the raïs was at the helm, and the sailors had begun to shove the bow of my boat into the stream. I called out: "O Shekh Abd-en-noor!" in a familiar way, and waved my hand as a token of parting. He rose, returned the salute, made a gesture to his men, and they all went slowly back to the village. As we were leaving, the sailors informed me that one of the Shillooks, who had come down to the boat while I was seated with the shekh on shore, took a fancy to the fat black slave who cooks for them, and expressed his determination to take her. They told him she was one of the Sultan's wives, and that as His Majesty was now the shekh's friend, he dare not touch her. "Oh," said the Shillook, "if she is the Sultan's wife, that is enough;" and he immediately returned to the shore. I forgave the impertinence of the sailors in passing off such a hideous creature as *one* of my wives, in consideration of the adroitness with which they avoided what might have been a serious difficulty.

The Shillooks have not the appearance of men who are naturally malicious. The selfish impudence with which they demand presents, is common to all savage tribes. But the Turks and even the European merchants who take part in the annual trading expeditions up the river, have dealt with them in such a shameful manner that they are now mistrustful of all strangers, and hence it is unsafe to venture among them. I attribute the friendly character of my interview with them as much to good luck as to good management. The raïs afterwards informed me that if the shekh had not been satisfied with the dress I gave him, he would certainly have attempted to plunder the vessel. He stated that the Shillooks are in the habit of going down the river as far as the country of the Hassaniyehs, sinking their boats and concealing themselves in the woods in the day-time, while by night they venture into the villages and rob the people of their dourra, for which they have a great fondness. They cultivate nothing themselves, and their only employment is the chase of the elephant, hippopotamus and other wild beasts. All the region east of the river abounds with herds of elephants and giraffes, but I was not fortunate enough to get sight of them.

Here is the true land of the lotus, and the Shillooks, if not the *lotophagoi* of the Greeks, are, with the exception of the Chinese, the only modern eaters of the plant. I was too late to see it in blossom, and there were but few specimens of it among these islands; but not far beyond Aba it appears in great profusion, and both the seeds and roots are eaten by the natives. Dr. Knoblecher, who ate it frequently during his voyage, informed me that the root resembles the potato in consistence and taste, with a strong flavor of celery. These islands are inhabited only by the hunters and fishers of the tribe, who abandon them in summer, when they are completely covered by the inundation. At lat. 12°, or about thirty miles south of Aba, both banks of the river are cultivated, and thence, for upwards of two hundred miles, the villages are crowded so close to each other all along the shores, that they almost form two continuous towns, fronting each other. This part of the White Nile is the most thickly populated region in Africa, and perhaps in the world, China alone excepted. The number of the Shillooks is estimated at between two and three millions, or equal to the population of all Egypt.

As we weighed anchor, I found that the men had taken down both sails and shipped the oars for our return to Khartoum. We had reached the southern point of the island, in about lat. 12° 30′ north, and the north-wind was still blowing strongly. The rounded tops of the mimosa forests bent southward as they tossed; the flowery arms of the ambak-trees waved to the south, trailing against the current, and my heart sank within me at the thought of retracing my steps. We had sailed two hundred and fifty miles in forty-eight hours; the gateway to the unknown South was open, and it seemed a treason against Fortune to turn my face towards the Mediterranean. "Achmet!" said I, "tell the men to set the *trinkeet* again. We will sail to the Bahr el-Ghazàl." The Theban's face became ghastly at the bare idea. "O Master!" he exclaimed, "are you not satisfied with your good fortune? We are now nearly at the end of the earth, and if we go further, it will be impossible to return." Raïs Abou-Hammed declared that he had kept his word, and that he should now return, as it had been agreed, before we left Khartoum. I knew there was certain danger in going further, and that I had no right to violate my agreement and peril others as well as myself; but there lay the great river, holding in his lap, to tempt me on, isles of brighter bloom and spreading out shores of yet richer foliage. I was in the centre of the Continent. Beyond me all was strange and unknown, and the Gulf of Guinea was less distant than the Mediterranean, which I left not three months before. Why not push on and attempt to grasp the Central African secret? The fact that stronger, braver and bolder men had failed, was one lure the more. Happily for me, perhaps, my object on commencing the voyage had been rest and recreation, not exploration. Had I been provided with the necessary means and scientific appliances for making such an attempt useful, it would have been impossible to turn back at that point.

I climbed to the mast-head and looked to the south, where the forest archipelago, divided by glittering reaches of water, wove its labyrinth in the distance. I thought I saw—but it may have been fancy—beyond the leafy crown of the farthest isles, the faint blue horizon of that sea of water and grass, where the palm again appears and the lotus fringes the shores. A few hours of the strong north-wind, now blowing in our faces, would have taken me there, but I gave myself up to Fate and a pipe, which latter immediately suggested to me that though I was leaving the gorgeous heart of Africa, I was going back to Civilization and Home.

CHAPTER XXVII.

THE WHITE NILE.

Explorations of the White Nile—Dr. Knoblecher's Voyage in 1849-50—The Lands of the Shillooks and Dinkas—Intercourse with the Natives—Wild Elephants and Giraffes—The Sobat River—The Country of Marshes—The Gazelle Lake—The Nuehrs—Interview with the Chief of the Kyks—The Zhir Country—Land of the Baris—The Rapids Surmounted—Arrival at Logwek, in Lat. 4° 10′ North—Panorama from Mt. Logwek—Sources of the White Nile—Character of the Bari Nation—Return of the Expedition—Fascination of the Nile.

Let me here pause a moment, at the turning-point of my journey, and cast a glance up the grand and wonderful vista which the White Nile opened to my view. The exploration of this river within the last fifteen years constitutes the most interesting chapter in the annals of African Discovery. It has been ascended to lat. 4° north, eight degrees of latitude, or four hundred and eighty geographical miles—and at least eight hundred miles, following the course of the stream—beyond the island of Aba. Of the Europeans who at different times accompanied the exploring fleets of Mohammed Ali, or the annual trading expeditions, three kept journals and made scientific observations, and two—D'Arnaud and Werne—have published accounts of the voyage. Werne's book, however, is taken up with peevish comments on the conduct of D'Arnaud and Sabatier, and the report of the former, as I learned from Dr. Knoblecher himself, is incorrect in many particulars. The most satisfactory account is that of Dr. Knoblecher, who ascended about fifty miles beyond the point reached by previous expeditions. During my stay in Khartoum, I received from him full particulars of his adventures, and was allowed to inspect his journals and sketch-books. His reports are exceedingly curious and interesting, and I herewith present a brief outline of them.

Dr. Knoblecher was specially educated, in the Propaganda at Rome, as a missionary for Central Africa. After studying the Arabic language for a year in Syria, he proceeded to Khartoum, where a Catholic Mission had already been established. There, however, the Mission found its sphere of operations circumscribed by the jealousy of the government, as all attempts to make proselytes of Mussulmen are forbidden, and the highest ambition of the slaves who are brought from the interior is to be considered faithful followers of the Prophet. Dr. Knoblecher was therefore directed to accompany the annual trading expedition up the White Nile, for the purpose of ascertaining the practicability of establishing a missionary station among some of the native negro tribes near the Equator. He experienced much difficulty at the outset, on account of the jealousy of the Egyptian traders, who find the company of a European a restraint upon their violent and lawless practices, but through the influence of the Pasha, who was at last brought to give his consent, the missionaries secured a place in the expedition, and on the 13th of November, 1849, set sail from Khartoum There were seven vessels in the flotilla, and that of Dr. Knoblecher, though the smallest, proved to be the best sailer and usually kept the lead. He had on board a faithful and experienced Nubian pilot, named Suleyman Abou-Zeid.

After fourteen days' sailing, the expedition passed the islands of the Shillooks and reached that part of the river where the banks are covered with continuous villages. The number of these is estimated at seven thousand. It is worthy of notice that their circular tokuls of mud and reeds are precisely similar in form and construction to those of the tribes on the Niger and Senegal Rivers, with whom the Shillooks have no communication, and from whom they differ in language, appearance and character. While threading the mazes of the archipelago, a violent whirlwind passed over the river and completely dismasted one of the boats. Beyond the islands the river expands so that the marshy shores are barely visible in some places. The lotus grows abundantly in the shallows, and the appearance of the thousands of snowy blossoms as they flash open at sunrise, is described as a scene of vegetable pomp and splendor, which can be witnessed in no other part of the world. The forests of sont trees which cover the islands give place to doum-palms and immense tamarinds, and beyond lat. 10°, in the land of the Dinkas, the beautiful dhelleb-palm is first seen. It has a tall, graceful trunk, thick in the middle, but tapering towards the top and bottom, and a rich crown of large, fan-like leaves.

On the twenty-eighth of November the expedition succeeded, after some difficulty, in establishing an intercourse with the Dinkas and Shillooks, who inhabited the opposite banks of the river. The latter in consideration of some colored glass beads, fur nished a number of oxen for provisions. Dr. Knoblecher described their running, when they drove the cattle together, as resembling that of the gazelle; they leap high into the air, drawing up their long legs as they rise, and clear the ground at a most astonishing speed. The next day the vessels reached a large town called Vav, where the people received them without the least appearance of fear, and brought quantities of elephants' tusks to trade for beads. Herds of wild elephants and giraffes were now frequently seen on the banks of the river, and the former sometimes threw up their trunks and spirted water into the air when they saw the vessels. Numbers of white herons were perched composedly upon their backs and heads. The giraffes, as they gazed with wonder at the fleet, lifted their heads quite above the tops of the mimosa trees. On the second of December, the expedition passed the mouth of the Sobat River, the only tributary stream which comes to the White Nile from the east. Its source is supposed to be in the country of the Gallas, south of the kingdom of Shoa. Its breadth, at its entrance into the Nile, is six hundred and fifty feet. Werne, who ascended it about eighty miles, with D'Arnaud's expedition, states that its shores are higher than those of the Nile, and that the surface of the country became more elevated as he ascended, whence he infers that the White Nile, as far as it has been explored, flows in a depressed basin of the table-land of Central Africa.

From lat. 9° 26′ to 6° 50′ N. there is a complete change in the scenery. The magnificent forests disappear, and the shores become marshy and unhealthy, covered with tall grass, whose prickly stalks render landing difficult, and embarrass the navigation of the shallows. The air is heavy with noxious miasmas and filled with countless swarms of gnats and mosquitoes The water of the river is partially stagnant, and green with vegetable matter, occasioning serious disorders to those who drink it. Dr. Knoblecher clarified it by means of alum, and escaped with a sore mouth. In order to sleep, however, he was obliged to wear thick gloves and muffle up his face, almost to suffocation. The *Bahr el-Ghazàl*, or Gazelle Lake, lies in lat. 9° 16′ N. It is thus named from the Gazelle River, which flows into it on the western side, and which has never yet been explored. Its depth is about nine feet, but the reeds and water-plants with which it is filled reach to the surface, and render the navigation difficult. Its shores are inhabited by the Nuehr negroes, a stupid, imbruted race, many of whom are frequently carried off by the traders and sold as slaves. For this reason it is now very difficult to procure elephants' teeth from them.

After leaving the Gazelle Lake, the course of the White Nile becomes exceedingly tortuous, and its current sluggish. Innumerable estuaries, or blind channels, which lose themselves among the reeds, perplexed the pilots, and delayed the progress of the expedition. The land of the Kyks succeeded to that of the Nuehrs, which terminated about the eighth parallel of latitude. The former are a race of herdsmen, who have great numbers of cattle and sheep. Dr. Knoblecher found them exceedingly shy, on account of the threats of one of their *kogiurs*, or soothsayers, who had warned them against holding any intercourse with the traders. On the twenty-second of December they reached the village of Angwen, where the King of the Kyks resided. The monarch received them with great kindness, and paid distinguished homage to Padre

Angelo Vinco, Dr. Knoblecher's companion, whom, on account of his spectacles and gray beard, he took to be a magician He begged the Padre to grant him four favors, viz:—abundance of children; the death of the enemy who had slain his father; victory in all his fights, and a cure for the wound in his head. The latter gift was easily bestowed, by means of a plaster, but he was not satisfied until an image of the Virgin had been hung around his neck.

South of the Kÿks dwell the Elliàbs, who are less timid than the southern tribes, because they come less frequently into contact with the traders. In their country the White Nile divides into two branches, and here the expedition separated, each division taking a different channel. The water was so low that the vessels stuck fast in the mud, but were relieved by the friendly natives, who dragged them through the shallows by means of long tow-ropes. For this service they were paid in glass beads. The further the vessels went into regions where intercourse with the Egyptian traders is rare, and therefore fewer outrages are perpetrated, the more friendly, confiding and unconcerned was the behavior of the natives.

On the thirty-first of December the expedition reached the country of the Zhirs. The people came down to the water's edge to greet them, the women clapping their hands and singing a song of welcome. On the second of January, 1850, Dr. Knoblecher saw in the south-east the granite mountain of Nierkanyi, which lies in the Bari country, in about the fifth degree of north latitude. It was the first elevation he had seen since leaving Djebel Defafangh, in the country of the Dinkas, in lat. 10° 35′. All the intervening space is a vast savannah, interspersed with reedy swamps of stagnant water

The Zhirs own numerous flocks and herds, and cultivate large fields of sesamè and dourra. They are very superior to the Nuehrs and Kyks in stature, symmetry of form and their manners toward strangers. In all these tribes, the men go entirely naked, while the women wear a narrow girdle of sheepskin around the loins. Dr. Knoblecher, however, confirmed the statement of Werne as to the modesty of their demeanor and the evident morality of their domestic life.

After leaving the Zhirs the expedition entered the country of the Baris, and on the fourteenth of January reached the rapids of the White Nile, at the island of Tsanker, in 4° 49′ N. This was the farthest point reached by all previous expeditions, as they found it impossible to advance further with their vessels. The Nubian pilot, Suleyman Abou-Zeid, determined to make the attempt, and on the following day, aided by a strong north-wind, stemmed the rapid and reached the broad, lake-like expanse of river above it. Continuing his voyage, Dr. Knoblecher sailed sixteen miles further, to the Bari village of Tokiman. The country was exceedingly rich and beautiful, abounding in trees, and densely peopled. The current of the river was more rapid, its waters purer, and the air seemed to have entirely lost the depressing miasmatic exhalations of the regions further north. The inhabitants of Tokiman showed great astonishment at the sight of the vessels and their white occupants Nothing, however, affected them so much as the tones of a harmonica, played by Dr. Knoblecher. Many of the people shed tears of delight, and the chief offered the sovereignty of his tribe in exchange for the wonderful instrument.

On the sixteenth, the expedition reached the village of Logwek, which takes its name from a solitary granite peak about six hunared feet high, which stands on the left bank of the Nile. It is in lat. 4° 10′ N., and this is the most southern point which has yet been reached on the White Nile. Dr Knoblecher ascended the mountain, which commanded a view of almost the entire Bari country. Towards the south-west the river wound out of sight between the mountains Rego and Kidi, near which is the mountain of Kereg, containing rich iron mines which are worked by the natives. Towards the south, on the very verge of the horizon, rose a long range of hills, whose forms could not be observed with exactness, owing to the great distance. Beyond the Logwaya range, which appeared in the east, dwell the Berri tribes, whose language is distinct from the Baris, and who are neighbors of the Gallas—that warlike race, whose domain extends from Abyssinia to the wilds of Mozambique, along the great central plateau of Uniamesi. The natives of Logwek knew nothing whatever of the country to the south. The farthest mountain-range was probably under the parallel of lat. 3° N., so that the White Nile has now been traced nearly to the Equator. At Logwek, it was about six hundred and fifty feet wide, and from five to eight feet deep, at the time of Dr. Knoblecher's visit, which was during the dry season. Such an abundance of water allows us to estimate with tolerable certainty the distance to its unknown sources, which must undoubtedly lie beyond the Equator.

The great snow mountain of Kilimandjarò, discovered in 1850 by Dr. Krapf, the German missionary, on his journey inland from Mombas, on the coast of Zanzibar, has been located by geographers in lat. 3° S. It is therefore most probable that the source of the White Nile will be found in the range of mountains, of which Kilimandjarò is the crowning apex. The geographer Berghaus, in a long and labored article, endeavors to prove that the Gazelle River is the true Nile, and makes it rise in the great lake N'Yassi, in lat. 13° S. Dr Knoblecher, however, who examined the Bahr el-Ghazàl at its mouth, says it is an unimportant stream, with a scarcely perceptible current. He considers the White Nile as being, beyond all question, the true river. He also informed me, that, while at Logwek, some of the natives spoke of people white like himself, who lived far towards the south. I do not believe in the fable of a white civilized race in the interior of Africa, and consider this rather as referring to the Portuguese settlements on the coast of the Indian Ocean, reports of which would readily be carried inland, from one tribe to another. Dr. Knoblecher is of the opinion that no exploring expedition from Khartoum will be successful; that the traveller must first stop in the Bari country long enough to gain some knowledge of its people, and then, with a company of the natives as his attendants, make that his starting point.

The shortness of Dr. Knoblecher's stay among the Baris did not permit him to obtain much information concerning them. They appeared to be worshippers of trees, like the Dinkas and Shillooks, but to have a glimmering idea of the future existence of the soul. They are brave and fearless in their demeanor, yet cheerful, good-natured and affectionate towards each other. Werne frequently observed the men walking along the shore with their arms around each other's necks. They are even more colossal in their stature than the Shillooks, many of them reaching a height of seven feet. Their forms are well-knit, symmetrical, and indicate great strength and activity. In smelting and working up the iron ore of Mount Kereg they show a remarkable skill. Many of the spears in Dr. Knoblecher's possession are as elegantly formed and as admirably tempered as if they had come from the hands of a European blacksmith. They also have war-clubs of ebony, which are nearly as hard and heavy as iron. One end is of a sloping, oval form, and the other sharp, and they are said to throw them a distance of fifty or a hundred yards with such precision that the sharp point strikes first and the club passes through the body like a lance. I have in my possession some of these clubs, which were presented to me by Dr. Knoblecher.

On the seventeenth of January the expedition left Logwek on its return to Khartoum, the traders having procured all the ivory which the natives had collected since the previous year. The Missionaries were prevented from accomplishing their object by the jealousy of the traders, who persuaded the Bari chiefs that they were magicians, and that if they were allowed to remain, they would bewitch the country, prevent the rains from falling and destroy the crops of dourra. In consequence of these reports the chiefs and people, who had been on the most friendly terms with Dr. Knoblecher and Padre Angelo, suddenly became shy and suspicious, and refused to allow the latter to take up their residence among them. The design of the mission was thus frustrated, and the Vicar returned with the expedition to Khartoum. He designed leaving for the Bari country in November, 1852, but up to the present moment* no account has been received of the fulfilment of his plans.

The pictures which these recent explorations present to us

*July, 1854.

add to the stately and sublime associations with which the Nile is invested, and that miraculous flood will lose nothing of his interest when the mystery which veils his origin shall be finally dispelled. Although in standing upon the threshold of his vast central realms, I felt that I had realized a portion of my dream, I could not turn away from the vision of those untrodden solitudes, crowned by the flashing snows of Kilimandjarò, the monarch of African mountains, without a keen pang of regret. Since Columbus first looked upon San Salvador, the Earth has but one emotion of triumph left in her bestowal—and that she reserves for him who shall first drink from the fountains of the White Nile, under the snow-fields of Kilimandjarò.

CHAPTER XXVIII.

THE HASSANIYEH ARABS.

We leave the Islands of the Shillooks—Tropical Jungles—A Whim and its Consequences—Lairs of Wild Beasts—Arrival among the Hassaniyehs—A Village—The Woman and the Sultan—A Dance of Salutation—My Arab Sailor—A Swarthy Cleopatra—Salutation of the Saint—Miraculous Fishing—Night View of a Hassaniyeh Village—Wad Shèllayeh—A Shekh's Residence—An Ebony Cherub—The Cook Attempts Suicide—Evening Landscape—The Natives and their Cattle—A Boyish Governor—We reach Khartoum at Midnight.

After we parted from the Shillooks the men rowed lustily, and, taking to the western side of the river, soon put an island between us and the village. It was about two o'clock when we left, and the wind fell sufficiently before night to allow them to make considerable progress. We swept along, under the lee of the islands, brushing the starry showers of yellow blossoms that trailed in the water, and frightening the ibises and herons from their coverts among the reeds. The hippopotami snorted all around us, and we had always a convoy of them following in our wake. The sun sank, and a moon, four days old, lighted the solitude of the islands, but the men still rowed vigorously, until we had passed the spot where the Shillooks buried their canoes in the morning. They then deemed it safe to come to anchor in the middle of the stream, though the watch-fires of the savages were still blazing brightly in the distance. During the night the wind blew violently, and the river was rough and agitated. We all went to sleep, therefore, feeling certain that no predatory canoes would venture to follow us.

In the morning there was a strong head-wind, and the temperature was so cold that I was obliged to wear my thick capote of camel's hair while I sat on deck, looking regretfully at the beautiful islands I was leaving behind me. Achmet heated and strained the honey given me by the Shillooks, which yielded between three and four quarts of rich liquid. While the men made fast to the bank for breakfast, I went on shore to get a glimpse of the country behind the forests. Paths trodden by wild beasts led through the walls of tangled vines that elsewhere were impenetrable, and I crept along them, under the boughs of strange trees and through thickets of luxuriant shrubs. At length I reached an open patch of grass four or five feet in height, and so dry and yellow that it snapped like glass under my feet. It was dotted with clumps of high shrubs, knotted all over with wild, flowering vines, which formed admirable lairs for the lions and leopards. There was a strong smell of lions about the place, and I deemed it prudent not to venture far, since the rank animal odor peculiar to that beast grew more marked the further I went. The jungle in which I stood covered a tongue of land inclosed between two coves of the river, and through the openings in the thickets I saw that it led to other open tracts further inland. The wind was blowing towards the river, and as I stood in the midst, contemplating the wild, lawless grouping of the different trees and shrubs some imp of darkness whispered in my ear "What a magnificent conflagration this would make! and then, perhaps, you might have the satisfaction of burning out a brace of lions!" Without more ado, I whipped out a box of matches, and struck fire in one of the thickest tufts.

The effect was instantaneous, and so was my repentance There was a crack and a crash, like the explosion of powder, and a sheet of red flame leaped into the air. In a few seconds it had spread to a broad swath of fire, rolling rapidly before the wind, and leaving the earth behind it as bare as the palm of my hand. The rank grass roared and snapped as the terrible power I had so thoughtlessly awakened, licked it away; and not the grass alone. It seized on the vines and tore them down, swung itself by them into the boughs of the trees, and found richer aliment in their gums and juices. It spread on both sides and against the wind, and soon the long spires of scarlet flame, twisting in the air, rose high and hot above the dome-like tops of the mimosa forests. Before we left the place, the volumes of smoke reached nearly to the other side of the Nile. As I heard its relentless feet trampling down the thickets, I tormented myself with pictures of the evil which I had perhaps originated. I fancied it spreading from day to day, lapping the woods in coils of flame and flinging their burning boughs from island to island, till of all the glory of vegetation which had filled me with such rapture, there was nothing but a few charred trunks standing in beds of ashes. I saw the natives with their flocks and herds flying before it, the wild beasts leaping into the flood for refuge from its red fangs, and all that glorious region given up to terror and desolation. As we moved slowly away, against the wind, I watch ed its progress with a troubled conscience and an anxious heart. Now it paused and I flattered myself that there was the end, but the next moment the black clouds rolled up denser than ever. Thus it wavered for some time, but at last, thank God! it seemed to fade gradually away, and I gave myself the hope that it had not extended beyond the jut of land whereon it was kindled.

At noon we passed the locality marked on D'Arnaud's map as El-Ais, but there was no sign of habitation. The raïs said there had been a town some distance inland, but it is now deserted. The river here makes a curve to the west, and our small stern-sail was bound to the foremast, in order to use the side-wind. My sailors were unremitting in their labors, and rowed, poled and tracked the whole day. I sat in the sun all the while, looking on the incomparable shores. We saw multitudes of gazelles along the water's edge, on both sides. They were in companies of forty or fifty, and so little shy, that they often allowed us to approach within fifty yards. Wild fowl were as abundant as ever, and I greatly regretted having brought no rifle and fowling-piece. When we reached the northern extremity of Hassaniyeh, at sunset, I went ashore on the eastern bank, hoping to find a gazelle. The thickets were almost impenetrable, and I made my way with difficulty into a more open space, where the trees grew in clumps and the lion-paths had broken a way between them. Each of these clumps was woven into a single mass with vines, forming coverts of deepest shade, wherein a beast might crouch unobserved, even at mid-day. The ground was covered with dry bur-grass, whose heads pierced through my clothes. One of the sailors accompanied me with a club, but was in such deadly fear of lions that he obliged me to return to the shore. Certainly, this is the paradise of wild beasts. Such convenient lairs they can find in no other part of the world, and the thousands of gazelles and antelopes that range through the wilderness furnish them with a choice bill of fare. The trees and vines were nearly all new to me. I noticed in particular, a succulent vine, resembling the cactus and cereus families, but with square, fluted joints. It grew so thickly as frequently to conceal entirely the tree that supported it. I also saw a shrub with leaves like the ivy, but a large, purple, bell-shaped flower, and another with delicate, fern-like leaves of a dark-green color, and white, fragrant blossoms. There was a greater variety in the vegetable world than I had yet seen. What must be the splendor of the land during the rainy season! I found a peculiar fascination in tracing the wild paths through the thickets. It was a labyrinth to which there was no end, and the sense of danger gave a spice to its richness and novelty. Occasionally, I saw large holes in the ground, which my attendant said were those of serpents. No gazelle was to be seen, and when I reached the shore again, the wild geese had left. The wind fell at sunset, and the sailors rowed cheerily down stream, singing the while a barbaric chorus, which they had learned from the slaves brought from Fazogl.

The sun, next morning, showed us a very different landscape from that of the previous two days. The river was broader, but the shores were clothed with a more scanty vegetation, and the few islands in the stream were but beds of sand. When the men stopped for breakfast we were in the neighborhood of a village of Hassaniyehs, as I had previously conjectured, from the camels and donkeys grazing among the thorns.

Leaving the sailors to kill one of our sheep, I took Achmet and the raïs, and followed the paths inland through a wood of scattering mimosas. After a walk of ten minutes we came to the village, or rather encampment, since the dwellings were mere tents of sticks and reeds. They were barely large enough to cover the two or three angarebs, which served as a bed for the whole family. Although the sun was an hour high, not more than half the inhabitants were stirring. The others, men and women, thrust their heads from under their dirty cotton mantles and looked at us with astonishment not unmixed with fear. The women who had already risen sat on the ground kindling the fires, or spinning with a rude distaff the raw cotton which these people cultivate. We found two or three men, whom we saluted with the usual "Peace be with you!" and the raïs informed them that the Sultan's son, returning from a visit to the Shillooks, with whom he had made a treaty of peace, had come to see them. Thereupon one of them brought an angareb and set it in the shade for me, while another caught a she-goat that was browsing among the bushes, and soon returned with a gourd half full of warm milk, which he gave me. As sour milk is considered a great delicacy among these people, a gourd of it was also procured for me. The woman who brought it knelt and placed it at my feet, but as I could not drink it and did not wish to refuse their gift, I asked one of the men to take it to the boat. He hesitated, evidently afraid to trust himself with us, whereupon the woman said: "I am not afraid to go with the Sultan; I will take it." As we started to return, the man, whose sense of bravery, and perhaps his jealousy also, was touched by this remark, came likewise and accompanied us to the river. When we reached the vessel I sent the milk on board for the sailors' use, and gave the woman two piastres in copper money and a handful of tobacco. She immediately put her hand to her mouth and uttered a piercing, prolonged cry, which the raïs said was intended as an expression of great joy. After repeating this two or three times she dropped on her knees, and before I could divine her intention, kissed my red slipper.

In a short time I received word that the women of the village would come to perform a dance of welcome and salutation, if I would allow them. As the wind was blowing strongly against us and the sailors had not finished skinning the sheep, I had my carpet spread on the sand in the shade of a group of mimosas, and awaited their arrival. Presently we heard a sound of shrill singing and the clapping of hands in measured beat, and discerned the procession advancing slowly through the trees. They came two by two, nearly thirty in all, singing a shrill, piercing chorus, which sounded more like lamentation than greeting. When they had arrived in front of me, they ranged themselves into a semicircle with their faces towards me, and, still clapping their hands to mark the rhythm of the song, she who stood in the centre stepped forth, with her breast heaved almost to a level with her face, which was thrown back, and advanced with a slow, undulating motion till she had reached the edge of my carpet. Then, with a quick jerk, she reversed the curve of her body, throwing her head forward and downward, so that the multitude of her long twists of black hair, shining with butter, brushed my cap. This was intended as a salutation and sign of welcome. I bowed my head at the same time, and she went back to her place in the ranks. After a pause the chorus was resumed and another advanced, and so in succession, till all had saluted me, a ceremony which occupied an hour. They were nearly all young, between the ages of fourteen and twenty, and some were strikingly beautiful. They had the dark-olive Arab complexion, with regular features, teeth of pearly whiteness, and black, brilliant eyes. The coarse cotton robe thrown over one shoulder left free the arms, neck and breasts, which were exquisitely moulded. Their bare feet and ankles were as slender as those of the Venus of Cleomenes. Owing to the skirts worn by the American women I have no recollection of ever having seen an entire foot belonging to them, and therefore can make no comparison; but I doubt if one in a thousand stands on so light and beautiful a pedestal as those wild African girls. There were two or three old women in the company, but they contented themselves with singing and did not venture into the lists with the younger ones.

Several of the men, who had followed in the rear of the women, came and sat near us, on the sand. They were all evidently delighted with the occasion, and encouraged the more timid of the dancers by their words. One of them was an old man, with a long gray moustache and beard, carrying in his hand a spear, pointed with iron. My raïs and sailors were on the ground, and one of the latter, a splendid fellow, whose form was almost perfect in its manly strength, took his station among the women and acted as master of the ceremonies. He drew a line in the sand down the centre of the ring, and another along the edge of my carpet, and she who did not dance down the line until the final toss of her head threw her hair over the Sultan's cap, was obliged to perform her part over again. My sailor clapped his hands, joined in the song, and moved with such entire and absolute grace in the dance, that he almost drew away my attention from the women. He was of the Djaaleyn tribe, and therefore of pure Arabian blood. As the ceremony was prolonged, they accompanied the dance with a hard, guttural breathing, in time with the music, and some of the old women, in their anxiety to encourage the younger and more timid dancers, leaned forward with eager eyes, uttering short, quick screams at intervals. It was a most remarkable scene; the figures and the dancers were unlike any thing I ever witnessed. For the first time, in fact—perhaps because I had hitherto seen few women unveiled—I found undoubted beauty in the Arab female countenance.

The last dancer was the wife of the Shekh, who came towards the close, with two negro slaves behind her. She was a woman of twenty, and the most beautiful of the group. Making allowance for the difference in complexion, she had a strong resemblance to the Cleopatra of Guido. Her eyes were large, black and lustrous; her face the full, ripe oval of the South, with a broad, round forehead, perfect lips and a most queenly neck and chin. She wore a diadem of white beads, under which her thick hair—unfortunately plastered with butter—hung to her shoulders in at least fifty slender braids. She went through the monotonous movement of the dance with the stately ease of a swan gliding down a stream, and so delighted my sailors and the men who had come down from the village, that she was obliged to repeat her salutation several times. I bowed lower to her than to the others, but took care to keep her unctuous braids from touching my face. When all was concluded, I directed Achmet to distribute a few handfuls of copper money among them, whereupon they returned to the village, uttering sharp yells of joy as they went. After they had left, I asked the men whether what I had heard in Khartoum, concerning the peculiar conjugal customs of the tribe, was true, and they replied that it was.

As we were about leaving, one of the shekhs, or holy men of the tribe, came down to greet me. He was an old man in a blue cotton mantle, and had with him two attendants. After touching my hand twice and asking many times for my health, he commenced singing passages of the Koran, in a loud, resonant, and not unmusical tone, somewhat resembling the sunset cry of the muezzin from his minaret. The two others responded, and thus this religious entertainment was kept up for some time. But the raïs was at his post and the wind had fallen, so I acted my despotic character of Sultan, by leaving the holy man in the midst of his chanting and going on board. When we left he was still standing under the mimosas, singing of Mohammed, the Prophet of God.

We made but little headway during the afternoon, although the men worked faithfully. Djebel Deyoos, whose loose cluster of peaks is seen for a great distance over the plains of Kordofan, still kept us company, and did not pass out of our horizon until the next evening. The men towed for several hours, and as the shore was flat and the river very shallow they were obliged to walk in the water. While Achmet was preparing dinner, a fish about the size of a herring vaulted upon deck and fell at his feet. He immediately clapped it into the frying-pan and presented me with an acceptable dish. To his unbounded astonishment and my great satisfaction, the same thing happened three days in succession, at precisely the same hour. "Wallah, master!" he exclaimed: "it is wonderful! I never knew such a thing to happen in Egypt, and it must certainly be a sign of good fortune. If you were not a lucky man, the fish would never offer themselves for your dinner in this way."

By night the men could make no headway against the wind, which continued unabated nearly all the next day. They worked hard, stimulated by the promise of an abundant supply of mareesa at the next Hassaniyeh village. In the afternoon we passed Tura, which I recognized by the herds of camels on shore and the ferry-boats passing back and forth across the broad stream. I walked an hour or two while the men were towing, but was obliged to keep to the shore, on account of the burr-grass which covered all the country inland. This part of the river is thickly settled by the Hassaniyehs, whose principal wealth appears to consist in their sheep, goats and camels. They complained very much of the Shillooks, who come down the river on predatory incursions, carry off their sheep and dourra, and frequently kill the children who tend the herds.

By dint of unremitting exertions, we reached a small village which the raïs called Wad Shèllayeh, about two hours after sunset. The men carried me ashore through the shallows, and I went with them to the village to perform my promise regarding the mareesa. We extinguished the lantern for fear of alarming the inhabitants, and walked slowly through the wilderness of thorns. The village lay half a mile inland, between two low hills of sand. The dwellings were mere tokuls, like those of the Shillooks, and made of the long grass of the Desert. Each house was surrounded with a fence of thorns. The inhabitants were sitting at the doors in the moonlight, calling out to each other and exchanging jokes, while herds of the slender yellow dogs of Soudân barked on all sides. While the raïs and sailors were procuring their mareesa I entered one of the tokuls, which was superior to those I had already seen, inasmuch as it contained an inner chamber or tent, made of fine yellow grass, and serving as a canopy to the family angareb. The people had kindled a fire on the ground, and the dry mimosa branches were blazing in close proximity to the straw walls of their dwelling. They were greatly inferior to the Hassaniyehs of the first village, both in appearance and courtesy of manners. The mareesa, which the raïs at last brought, was weak, insipid stuff, and I returned to the boat, leaving the men to drain the jars.

In the morning we reached another large Hassaniyeh village, which was also called Wad Shèllayeh. It was the only village on the river worthy of notice, as it had four vessels moored to the shore, and boasted a few mud houses in addition to its array of tokuls. Several of the latter were built in tent form and covered with a striped cloth made of camel's hair. I entered the residence of the shekh, who, however, was absent with his wife to attend the funeral of a relative. The tent was thirty feet long, with an arched top, and contained two inner chambers. The sides were ornamented with gourds, skins and other articles, grouped with some taste, and large quantities of the *cowries*, or small white shells, which are used as currency in some parts of Central Africa, were sewed upon the cloth cover, in the form of crosses and stars. I looked into the principal chamber, which inclosed a broad and handsome angareb, made of plaited palm-leaves. The walls were entirely concealed by the articles hung upon them, and every thing exhibited a taste and neatness which is rare among the

Arab tribes. The tent was in charge of the shekh's niece, a handsome girl of about eighteen, and an old woman with three children, the youngest of which was suckled by a black slave. He was an ebony Cupid of a year old, rejoicing in the branches of white shells that hung from his neck, wrists and ankles. He exhibited a curiosity to touch me, and I took him in my arms and addressed him in Christian nursery tongue. The sound of my voice, however, was more horrible than the color of my skin. He set up a yell and kicked out his little black, satin-skinned legs till I was obliged to hand him over to the slave nurse.

From the bank on which the village is built, I could see beyond the trees of the opposite shore, a wide stretch of the plains of Kordofan—a level savanna of yellow grass, extending without a break to the horizon. During the afternoon, while the men were resting from their rowing, Bahr, the Dinka cook, got into a dispute with one of them, and finally worked herself into such a rage that she jumped overboard with the intention of drowning herself, and would have done so, had not one of the sailors plunged after her and hauled her ashore, in spite of her violent struggles and endeavors to thrust her head under water. When she found she could not indulge in this recreation, she sat down on the ground, burst into a paroxysm of angry tears, and in a quarter of an hour went back to grind her dourra, in the best possible humor. Her name, Bahr, signifies "the sea," but she was an Undine of the Black Sea, and the White Nile refused to receive her.

We went gloriously down stream that evening, with a light west wind filling the little sail and the men at their oars, singing shrill choruses in the Dongolese and Djaaleyn dialects.

The White Nile, which is here three miles broad, was as smooth as glass, and glimmered far and bright under the moon. The shores were still, in all their dead level expanse, and had it not been for the uneven line which their belts of thorn-trees drew along the horizon, I could have imagined that we were floating in mid-ocean. While the men halted for breakfast the next morning, I landed and walked ahead, hoping to shoot a wild duck with my pistol. Notwithstanding there were hundreds along the shore, I found it impossible to get within shooting distance, as they invariably made into the river on my approach. An attempt to gain something by running suddenly towards them, terminated in my sticking fast in the mud and losing my red slippers. I then crept through the scattering wood of mimosas to get a chance at a pigeon, but some spirit of mistrust had taken possession of the birds, and as long as I had a shot left there were none within reach. When my two barrels were spent they sat on every side in the most familiar proximity.

Notwithstanding there were very few villages on the river's bank, the country was thickly inhabited. The people prefer building their dwellings a mile inland, and going to the river for water. This custom probably originated in their fear of the Shillooks, which led them to place their dwellings in situations most easy of defence. At one of the fording-places I found a number of women and children filling the water-skins and lifting them upon the backs of donkeys. Many hundreds of the hump-backed cattle, peculiar to the country, were collected along the shore. They have straight backs behind the hump, (which is a projection above the shoulders, four to six inches high), clean flanks, large, powerful necks, and short, straight horns. They eyed me with an expression of great curiosity and some of the bulls evidently deliberated whether they should attack me. The people in this region were Hassaniyehs, and the men resembled those of the first village I visited. They were tall, with straight features and a feminine expression of countenance, which was probably caused by their wearing their hair parted in the middle, plaited into long braids and fastened at the back of the head.

About noon we came in sight of Djebel Tinneh, which stands over against the village of Shekh Moussa, and serves as a landmark to the place. At sunset we saw the boat of Reschid Kashif, the Governor of the tributary territories of the White Nile, anchored near the western bank. Two of my sailors had previously been employed by him, and as they had not received all their wages, they asked permission to cross the river and apply for the money. This Reschid Kashif was a boy of twelve or thirteen years of age, son of the former Governor, Suleyman Kashif, who was so much esteemed by the tribes on the river that after his death the Pasha invested his young child with the office. The latter was also quite popular with the natives, who attributed to him a sagacity marvellous for his years. He paid the men the money due them, sent his compliments to me, and inquired why I did not visit him. It was dusk by this time, and I did not wish to delay the boat; besides, as I was a stranger and a Sultan, courtesy required that he should pay the first visit.

We made the remainder of the voyage without further incident than that of slaughtering one of our sheep, near Djebel Aûllee. The wind was so light that our progress down the stream was rapid, and at sunset on Friday, January thirtieth,

I recognized the spot where Dr. Reitz took leave of me, on the upward voyage. The evening on the broad river was glorious; the half-moon, being just overhead, was unseen, yet filled the air with light, and my natal planet burned white and clear in the west. At ten o'clock we reached the island of Omdurman, and wheeled into the Blue Nile. The camp-fires of Kordofan merchants were gleaming on the western bank. The barking of the dogs in Khartoum and the creaking wheels of the sakias were welcome sounds to our ears, as we slowly glided past the gardens. Ere long, the minaret of the city glimmered faintly in the moonlight and we recognized the buildings of the Catholic Mission. "God is great!" said Achmet, devoutly; "since we have been so near the end of the world, Khartoum appears to me as beautiful as Cairo." It was nearly midnight when we came to anchor, having made a voyage of about five hundred miles in nine days. My friends were all abed, and I lay down for the night in the little cabin of my boat, exclaiming, like Achmet: "God is great!"

CHAPTER XXIX.

INCIDENTS OF LIFE IN KHARTOUM.

The Departure of Abd-el Kader Bey—An Illuminated Picture—The Breakfast on the Island—Horsemanship—The Pasha's Stories—Departure of Lattif Effendi's Expedition—A Night on the Sand—Abou-Sin, and his Shukoree Warriors—Change in the Climate—Intense Heat and its Effects—Preparations for Returning—A Money Transaction—Farewell Visits—A Dinner with Royal Guests—Jolly King Dyaab—A Shillook Dance—Reconciliation—Taking Leave of my Pets.

I AROSE at sunrise, and leaving Achmet to have my baggage removed, walked through the town to my head-quarters at the Consular residence. I found Dr. Reitz's horses saddled in the court, and himself walking in the garden. He was greatly surprised to see me, not having expected me for another week. After the first greetings were over, he informed me that Abd-el Kader Bey, the Governor of Kordofan, was about leaving for Obeid, and his friends intended to accompany him as far as the island of Moussa Bey, in the White Nile. During my absence, Mohammed Kheyr had presented Dr. Reitz with a fine Dongolese horse, which he offered to me, that I might participate in the festivities. While I was at the Catholic Mission, relating my adventures to Dr. Knoblecher, a messenger came to announce that Abd-el Kader's boat had left, and that he, with the other chiefs of Khartoum, were ready to set out on horseback for the White Nile. We rode at once to the house of Moussa Bey, who had quite recovered from his illness. The company was already mounted in the square before the house, and only awaited our arrival. We dashed through the lanes of the slave quarter, raising such a cloud of dust that little except red caps and horses' tails was visible, until we came out upon the open plain, where our cavalcade made a showy and picturesque appearance.

The company consisted of Abd-el Kader Bey, Moussa Bey, Musakar Bey, Ali Bey Khasib, Abou-Sin and Owd-el Kerim, the Shukoree chiefs, Ali Effendi, Mohammed Kheyr, Dr. Reitz, Dr. Péney and myself, besides a number of inferior officers and at least fifty attendants: in short, everybody of consequence in Khartoum except the Pasha, who was represented by one of his Secretaries. The Beys were mounted on fine Arabian stallions, Dr. Péney on a tall dromedary, and the Arab chiefs on mules and donkeys, while the grooms and pipe-bearers ran behind on foot. I shall long remember the brilliant picture of that morning. The sky was clear and hot, and the palms rustled their shining leaves in a light wind. The fields of beans lay spread out between us and the river, their purple blossoms rolling in long drifts and flakes of color, and warm, voluptuous perfume. The red caps, the green and scarlet housings of the horses, the rich blue, brown, purple and violet dresses of the Beys, and the snowy robes of the Arabs, with their crimson borders thrown over the shoulder, projected against the tawny hue of the distant plains, and the warm blue of the sky, formed a feast of color which, in its entire richness and harmony, so charmed my eye that the sight of it became a luxury to the sense, as palpable as that of an exquisite flavor to the palate. Away we went at full gallop, the glittering array of colors dancing and interchanging to the rapid music, as our horses' hoofs tore the bean-vines and flung their trailing blossoms into the air, until we reached the bank of the White Nile, where the Bey's vessel was just coming to land. Here the Arab shekhs and the greater part of the inferior officers embraced Abd-el Kader and returned to Khartoum.

The rest of us crossed to the island of Moussa Bey and walked over the thick green turf to a large mimosa tree, of the variety called *'araz*, where the carpets were spread on the ground for us and the slaves were ready with our pipes. We lay there two or three hours, in the pleasant shade, talking, smoking, and lazily watching the motions of the attendants, who were scattered all over the island. An Albanian in a scarlet dress shot a wild goose, and Dr. Reitz tried to bring down an ibis, but failed. Finally the *showrmeh*—an entire sheep, stuffed with rice—appeared, garnished with bread, onions, radishes and grapes. We bared our right arms and buried our hands in the smoking flesh with such good will, that in half an hour the dish contained nothing but a beautiful skeleton. Abd-el Kader Bey honored me by tearing off a few choice morsels with his own fingers and presenting them to me. A bowl of rice cooked in milk and sweetened, completed the repast. At noon we went on board the *sandal*, and after being shipped to the other side, took leave of Abd-el Kader with an embrace and "God grant you a prosperous journey!"—to which he replied: "God grant it!" He sailed off, up the White Nile, for Tura, with a fine breeze, and we turned homewards. The wind which blew across the plain in our faces, was as hot and dry as the blast of a furnace, and my head reeled under the terrible intensity of the sunshine. The Beys took every opportunity of displaying their horsemanship, dashing over the bean-fields in wild zigzags, reining up in mid-career, throwing their crooked canes into the air after the manner of a jereed, and describing circles and ellipses at full gallop. The finest of all was my handsome Albanian friend, Musakar Bey.

I called upon the Pasha the same afternoon, to give him an account of my voyage up the White Nile, and was obliged to remain and dine with him. He was very much interested in my adventures with the Shillooks, but gave me to understand that the negroes had great fear of his power, and that if they had not known I was under his protection they would certainly have killed me. When I spoke of the giant stature of the Shillooks he confirmed what I had already heard, that the Kyks and Baris are full seven feet in height. He also stated that his predecessor, Achmet Pasha Menekleh, had captured in the regions beyond Fazogl thirty blacks, who were nine feet high and terrible to behold. They were brought to Khartoum in chains, he said, but refused to eat, howled like wild beasts, and died in paroxysms of savage fury. When I remembered that the Pasha had already told me that there was a subterraneous passage from Alexandria to the Fyoom (a distance of two hundred miles), made by Alexander the Great, and that the Sultan at Constantinople had an ape which grew to be twenty feet in height, I received this last communication with a grain of allowance. He fully believed in the existence of the N'yàm-N'yàms (a horribly suggestive name), or cannibals, who I have no doubt, are a fabulous race. Dr. Barth heard of them in Adamowa, south of Lake Tsad, and Dr

Knoblecher in the Bari country, but no one has ever yet seen them.

The expedition of Lattif Effendi had met with many delays, but on Monday, the second of February, every thing was ready for its departure. It consisted of two large *nekkers* or trading-vessels, each armed with a cannon, and carrying six soldiers in addition to the crew. It was also provided with interpreters, who spoke the languages of the different tribes. Fat Abou-Balta, who was the owner of one of the vessels, Dr. Péney, Dr. Reitz and myself, made up a party to accompany Lattif Effendi the first stage of his voyage. We took the same little *sandal* in which I had sailed, and pushed away from Khartoum at sunset, followed by the nekkers. The relatives of the sailors were crowded on the bank to bid them good-bye, and as the vessels weighed anchor, the women set up the shrill "*lu-lu-lu-lu-lu*," which they use to express all emotions, from rapture down to despair. We had a light, but favoring wind, and at nine o'clock reached a long, sandy beach about five miles above the mouth of the White Nile, where we came to a halt. The vessels were moored to the shore, fires kindled, pipes lighted and coffee made, and we gathered into groups on the sand, in the light of the full moon. At midnight the customary sheep made its appearance, accompanied by two bottles of claret, whereat Abou-Balta affected to be scandalized, so long as any Moslem attendants were in the neighborhood. When the coast was clear, he sprawled out like another Falstaff, his jolly face beaming in the moonlight, and took a sly taste of the forbidden beverage, which he liked so well that he no longer resented the wicked nickname of "*gamoos el-bahr*" (hippopotamus), which we bestowed upon him. We tried to sleep a little, but although the sand was soft, the night air was chilly, and I believe nobody succeeded but Abou-Balta, whose enormous belly shook with the force of his snoring, as he lay stretched out on his back. By three in the morning everybody was tired; the fires had burned out, the meats of the banquet had grown cold, and the wind blew more freshly from the north. Lattif Effendi called his sailors on board and we took leave of him. The two nekkers spread their huge wings and sailed off in the moonlight for the land of the Baris, while we made our slow way back to Khartoum, where we arrived at daybreak.

During my absence there had been three distinguished arrivals—Abou-Sin, the great shekh of the Shukorees (the father of Owd-el Kerim), Melek Dyaab, the king of Dar El-Màhass, and Ali, shekh of the Ababdehs—all of whom had been summoned by the Pasha, for the purpose of consulting with them on the condition of their territories. Abou-Sin was one of the stateliest and most dignified personages I had ever seen. He was about seventy-five years of age, six feet six inches in height, straight as a lance, with a keen, fiery eye, and a gray beard which flowed to his waist. Dr. Péney, who had visited the old shekh in Takka, informed me that he could bring into the field four thousand warriors, each mounted on his own dromedary. The Shukorees wear shirts of chain-mail and helmets with chain-pieces falling on each side of the face, like their Saracen ancestors. Their weapons are still the sabre and lance, with which they have maintained their independence against all enemies, except the cannon of Mohammed Ali. Dr. Reitz took me to visit the Shekh, who was living in an humble mud building, not far from the Pasha's palace. We found him giving audience to a number of inferior shekhs, who were seated upon the earthen floor, below his divan. His son, Owd-el Kerim, was among them. The Consul took his seat at the shekh's side, and I did the same, but, although nothing was said, I saw that those present mentally resented our presumption, and felt that I had been guilty of a breach of decorum. The object of our visit was to invite the shekh to dine with us. and he graciously complied. Owd-el Kerim was included in the invitation, but he excused himself on the ground that he did not dare to eat at the same table with his father. I was delighted with this trait, which recalled the patriarchal days of the Old Testament, and justified the claim of the Arabs to the blood of Abraham.

After my return the weather had suddenly changed, and every thing denoted the approach of the hot and sickly season. The thermometer stood at 105° in the shade, at noon, and there was an intensely hot wind from the south. On account of the languor and depression consequent upon such a heat, it required an extraordinary effort to make the necessary entries in my journal. I barely succeeded in moving about sufficiently to shake off the feverish humors which in that climate so rapidly collect in the system. I always placed a cool earthen jug of water at my bedside, and when I awoke in the middle of the night with a heavy head and parched throat, would take a full draught, which immediately threw me into a profuse sweat, after which I slept soundly and healthily until morning. He who lives in Khartoum in the hot season must either sweat or die. M. Drovetti, of Alexandria (son of the French Consul Drovetti, with whom Belzoni had so many quarrels), arrived about this time and was immediately prostrated with fever.

Many of the Franks and Egyptians were also affected, and Achmet, who felt plethoric symptoms, must needs go to a barber and be bled in the head. He besought me to return to Egypt, and as I had already accomplished much more than I anticipated, I began at once to prepare for the homeward journey.

The route which I fixed upon was that across the Beyooda Desert to Napata, the ancient capital of Ethiopia, thence to Dongola, and through the Nubian kingdoms to the Second Cataract of the Nile, at Wadi Halfa. The first part of the journey, through the countries of the Kababish and the Howoweet, was considered rather dangerous, and as a precautionary measure I engaged three of the former tribe, as guide and camel-drivers. I purchased two large Shukoree dromedaries for myself and Achmet, at three hundred and two hundred and fifty piastres respectively, and hired three others from the Kababish, at fifty piastres for the journey to Eddabe, on the Dongolese frontier, by way of Napata. The contract was formally made in the presence of the shekh of Khartoum and Dr. Reitz, both of whom threatened the Arabs with destruction in case they should not convey me safely through the Desert. The Consul also did me good service in the negotiation of my draft on Fathalla Musallee, a Coptic merchant, who demanded twenty per cent. for the exchange. This, as my funds were getting low, would have been a serious loss, but by some arithmetical legerdemain, which I could not understand, the Consul so bewildered poor Fathalla's brain, that he was finally made to believe that a discount of five per cent. would somehow profit him more in the end than one of twenty per cent. Fathalla paid the money with a melancholy confusion of ideas, and I doubt whether he has to this day discovered in what way he increased his profits by the operation.

My provision-chests were replenished with coffee, sugar rice, dates and *mishmish* (dried apricots), from the bazaar and Achmet worked so cheerily with the prospect of leaving Soudân, that every thing was in readiness at a day's notice. Rather than wait until the following Monday, for luck's sake, I fixed upon Thursday, the fifth of February, for our departure. Many of the subordinate Egyptian officers prepared letters to their families, which they intrusted to Achmet's care, and poor old Rufaā Bey, more than ever disgusted with his exile, charged me with a letter to his wife and another to Mr. Murray, through whose aid he hoped to get permission to return to Egypt. I paid a farewell visit to the Pasha, who received me with great courtesy, informing me (what I already knew), that he was about to be superseded by Rustum Pasha, who, he predicted, would not find the government of Soudân an easy one.

I was sorry to part with Vicar Knoblecher and his brethren. Those self-sacrificing men have willingly devoted themselves to a life—if life it can be called, which is little better than death—in the remote heart of Africa, for the sake of introducing a purer religion among its pagan inhabitants, and I trust they will be spared to see their benevolent plans realized. They are men of the purest character and animated by the best desires. Aboona Suleyman, as Dr. Knoblecher is called, is already widely known and esteemed throughout Soudân, and although he can do but little at present in the way of religious teaching, he has instituted a school for the children of the Copts, which may in time reform the (so-called) Christian so ciety of Khartoum. If he should succeed in establishing a mission in the country of the Baris, the result will be not less important to Science than to Christianity, and the experiment is one which should interest the world.

On the evening before my departure the shekhs Abou-Sin, Ali, the Ababdeh, and Melek Dyaab came to dine with Dr. Reitz. Abou-Sin was grave and stately as ever, and I never looked at him without thinking of his four thousand mailed warriors on their dromedaries, sweeping over the plains of Takka. Shekh Ali was of medium size, with a kind, amiable face, and a touch of native refinement in his manner. King Dyaab, however, who wore a capacious white turban and a robe of dark-blue cloth, was the "merry monarch" of Central Africa. His large eyes twinkled with good humor and his round face beamed with the radiance of a satisfied spirit. He brought a black Dongolese horse as a present for Dr. Reitz, and requested me to put him through his paces, on the plain before the house, as it would have been contrary to African etiquette for the Doctor himself to test the character of the gift. I complied, but the saddle was adapted only for the short legs of the fat king, and after running a circular course with my knees drawn up nearly to my chin, the resemblance of the scene to the monkey-riding of the circus struck me so forcibly, that I jumped off and refused to mount again, greatly to the monarch's disappointment.

Shekhs Abou-Sin and Ali took their departure shortly after the disposal of the roast sheep and salad which constituted the dinner, but King Dyaab and Dr. Péney remained until a late hour, smoking a parting pipe with me, and partaking of a mixture of claret, lemons, pomegranate juice and spices, which the Consul compounded into a sherbet of the most deli cious flavor. King Dyaab drank my health with a profusion of good wishes, begging me to remain another week and ac company his caravan. His palace in Dar El-Màhass, he said was entirely at my disposal and I must remain several weeks with him. But there is nothing so unpleasant to me as to postpone a journey after all the preparations are made, and I was reluctantly obliged to decline his invitation. I take pleasure, however, in testifying to the King's good qualities, which fully entitle him to the throne of Dar El Màhass, and were I installed in his capital of Kuke, as court-poet, I should certainly write a national ballad for the Mahassees, commencing in this wise:

> "El Melek Dyaab is a jolly old King,
> And a jolly old King is he," etc.

After the Melek had bestowed a parting embrace by throwing his arms around my waist and dropping his round head on my shoulder like a sixty-eight pound shot, he was sent home in state on the back of Sultan, the Dar-Fūr stallion. The moonlight was so beautiful that the Consul and I accompanied Dr. Péney to his residence. The latter suggested another pipe in the open air of his court-yard, and awoke his Shillook slaves, who were lying asleep near the house, to perform a dance for our amusement. There were three—two males and a female—and their midnight dance was the most uncouth and barbaric thing I saw in Khartoum. They brandished their clubs, leaped into the air, alighting sometimes on one foot and sometimes on both, and accompanied their motions with a series of short, quick howls, not unlike the laughter of a hyena. After the dance, Dr. Reitz effected a reconciliation between one of the men and the woman, who had been married, but were about to separate. They knelt before him, side by side, and recounted their complaints of each other, which were sufficiently ludicrous, but a present of three piastres (fifteen cents!), purchased forgetfulness of the past and renewed vows for the future.

I felt a shadow of regret when I reflected that it was my last night in Khartoum. After we walked home I roused the old lioness in her corner, gave her a farewell hug and sat down on her passive back until she stretched out her paws and went to sleep again. I then visited the leopard in the garden, made him jump upon my shoulders and play his antics over once more. The hyenas danced and laughed fiendishly, as usual when they saw me, but the tall Kordofan antelope came up softly and rubbed his nose against my leg, asking for the dourra which I was accustomed to give him. I gave him, and the gazelles, and the leopard, each an affectionate kiss, but poked the surly hyenas until they howled, on my way to bed.

CHAPTER XXX.

THE COMMERCE OF SOUDAN.

The Commerce of Soudân—Avenues of Trade—The Merchants—Character of the imports—Speculation—The Gum Trade of Kordofan—The Ivory Trade—Abuses of the Government—The Traffic in Slaves—Prices of Slaves—Their Treatment.

Before taking a final leave of Soudân, it may be well to say a few words concerning the trade of the country. As the Nile is the principal avenue of communication between the Mediterranean and the eastern half of Central Africa, Soudân is thus made a centre of commerce, the character of which may be taken as an index to all the interior traffic of the continent.

European goods reach Soudân through two principal channels; by the port of Sowakin, on the Red Sea, and the caravan route up the Nile and across the Great Nubian Desert. Of late years the latter has become the principal thoroughfare, as winter is the commercial season, and the storms on the Red Sea are very destructive to the small Arab craft. The merchants leave Cairo through the autumn, principally between the first of October and the first of December, as they travel slowly and rarely make the journey in less than two months and a half. The great proportion of them take the same route

I followed, from Korosko to Berber, where they ship again for Khartoum Those who buy their own camels at Assouan, make the whole trip by land; but it is more usual for them to buy camels in Soudân for the return journey, as they can sell them in Upper Egypt at advanced prices. In fact, the trade in camels alone is not inconsiderable. On my way to Khartoum I met many thousands, in droves of from one to five hundred, on their way to Egypt.

The merchants who make this yearly trip to Soudân are mostly Egyptians and Nubians. There are a number of Syrians established in the country, but they are for the most part connected with houses in Cairo, and their caravans between the two places are in charge of agents, natives, whose character has been proved by long service. There were also three or four French and Italian merchants, and one Englishman (Mr. Peterick, in Kordofan), who carried on their business in the same manner. It is no unusual thing for Nubians who have amassed two or three thousand piastres by household service in Cairo, to form partnerships, invest their money in cotton goods, and after a year or two on the journey (for time is any thing but money to them), return to Egypt with a few hundred weight of gum or half a dozen camels. They earn a few piastres, perhaps, in return for the long toils and privations they have endured; but their pride is gratified by the title of *Djellabiàt*—merchants. It is reckoned a good school, and not without reason, for young Egyptians who devote themselves to commerce. I met even the sons of Beys among this class. Those who are prudent, and have a fair capital to start upon, can generally gain enough in two or three years to establish themselves respectably in Egypt.

The goods brought into Central Africa consist principally of English muslins and calicoes, the light red woollen stuffs of Barbary, cutlery, beads and trinkets. Cloths, silks, powder, tobacco, and arakee, are also brought in considerable quantities, while in the large towns there is always a good sale for sugar, rice, coffee and spices. The Turkish officials and the Franks are very fond of the aniseed cordial of Scio, maraschino, rosoglio, and the other Levantine liquors; and even the heavy, resinous wines of Smyrna and Cyprus find their way here. The natives prefer for clothing the coarse, unbleached cotton stuffs of their own manufacture, one mantle of which is sufficient for years. As may readily be supposed, the market is frequently glutted with goods of this description, whence the large houses often send money from Cairo for the purchase of gum and ivory, in preference to running any risk. At the time of my visit, all sorts of muslins and calicoes might be had in Khartoum at a very slight advance on Cairo prices, and the merchants who were daily arriving with additional bales, complained that the sale would not pay the expenses of their journey. The remarkable success of the caravans of the previous year had brought a crowd of adventurers into the lists, very few of whom realized their expectations. It was the California experience in another form. No passion is half so blind as the greed for gain.

Khartoum is the great metropolis of all this region. Some few caravans strike directly through the Beyooda Desert, from Dongola to Kordofan, but the great part come directly to the former place, where they dispose of their goods, and then proceed to Kordofan for gum, or wait the return of the yearly expedition up the White Nile, to stock themselves with ivory

On both these articles there is generally a good, sometimes a great, profit. The gum comes almost entirely from Kordofan, where the quantity annually gathered amounts to thirty thousand *contar*, or cwt. It is collected by the natives from that variety of the mimosa called the *ashaba*, and sold by them at from fifty-five to sixty piastres the contar. Lattif Pasha at one time issued a decree prohibiting any person from selling it at less than sixty piastres, but Dr. Reitz, by an energetic protest, obtained the revocation of this arbitrary edict. The cost of carrying it to Cairo is very nearly fifty piastres the contar, exclusive of a government tax of twelve and a half per cent.; and as the price of gum in Cairo fluctuates according to the demand from one hundred and fifty to two hundred and fifty piastres, the merchant's gain may be as low as ten or as high as one hundred per cent. The gum brought from Yemen and the shores of the Red Sea is considered superior in quality but is not produced in such abundance.

The ivory is mostly obtained from the negro tribes on the White Nile. Small quantities are occasionally brought from Dar-Für and the unknown regions towards Bornou, by Arab caravans. The trading expeditions up the White Nile, until the winter of 1851–2, were entirely under the control of the Pasha of Soudân, in spite of the treaty of 1838, making it free to all nations. The expedition of that winter, which sailed from Khartoum about two months before my arrival, consisted of seven vessels, accompanied by an armed force. The parties interested in it consisted of the Pasha, the Egyptian merchants, and the *rayahs*, or European merchants. The gains were to be divided into twenty-four parts, eight of which went to the Pasha, nine to the Turks and seven to the Franks. Dr.

Reitz undertook to enforce the treaty, and actually ran two vessels belonging to Austrian *protégés* past the guard established at the junction of the Niles. The Pasha thereupon had all the sailors belonging to these vessels arrested, but after two days of violent manœuvres and counter-manœuvres, allowed the vessels to proceed. The unjust monopoly was therefore virtually annulled—an important fact to Europeans who may wish to engage in the trade. The vessels take with them great quantities of glass beads, ear, arm and nose rings, and the like, for which the natives readily barter their elephants' teeth. These are not found in abundance before reaching the land of the Nuèhrs and the Kyks, about lat. 7°, and the best specimens come from regions still further south. They are sold in Khartoum at the rate of twelve hundred piastres the cwt., and in Cairo at twenty-two hundred, burdened with a tax of twelve and a half per cent.

The Government has done its best to cramp and injure Trade, the only life of that stagnant land. In addition to the custom-house at Assouan, where every thing going into Egypt must pay duty, the Pasha and his satellites had established an illegal custom-house at Dongola, and obliged merchants to pay another toll, midway on their journey. This was afterwards abolished, on account of the remonstrances which were forwarded to Cairo. I found the Pasha so uniformly courteous and affable, that at first I rejected many of the stories told me of his oppression and cruelty, but I was afterwards informed of circumstances which exhibited his character in a still more hideous light. Nevertheless, I believe he was in most respects superior to his predecessors in the office, and certainly to his successor.

The traffic in slaves has decreased very much of late. The wealthy Egyptians still purchase slaves, and will continue to do so, till the "institution" is wholly abolished, but the despotic rule exercised by the Pasha in Nubia has had the effect of greatly lessening the demand. Vast numbers of Nubians go into Egypt, where they are engaged as domestic servants, and their paid labor, cheap as it is, is found more profitable than the unpaid service of negro slaves. Besides, the tax on the latter has been greatly increased, so that merchants find the commodity less profitable than gum or ivory. Ten years ago, the duty paid at Assouan was thirty piastres for a negro and fifty for an Abyssinian: at present it is three hundred and fifty for the former and five hundred and fifty for the latter, while the tax can be wholly avoided by making the slave free. Prices have risen in consequence, and the traffic is proportionately diminished. The Government probably derives as large a revenue as ever from it, on account of the increased tax, so that it has seemed to satisfy the demands of some of the European powers by restricting the trade, while it actually loses nothing thereby. The Government slave-hunts in the interior, however, are no longer carried on. The greater part of the slaves brought to Khartoum, are purchased from the Galla and Shangalla tribes on the borders of Abyssinia, or from the Shillooks and Dinkas, on the White Nile. The captives taken in the wars between the various tribes are invariably sold. The Abyssinian girls, who are in great demand among the Egyptians, for wives, are frequently sold by their own parents. They are treated with great respect, and their lot is probably no worse than that of any Arab or Turkish female. The more beautiful of them often bring from two hundred to five hundred dollars. Ordinary household servants may be had from one to two thousand piastres. My dragoman, Achmet, purchased a small girl for twelve hundred piastres, as a present for his wife. He intended making her free, which he declared to be a good thing, according to his religion; but the true reason, I suspect, was the tax at Assouan.

The Egyptians rarely maltreat their slaves, and instances of cruelty are much less frequent among them than among the Europeans settled here. The latter became so notorious for their violence that the Government was obliged to establish a law forbidding any Frank to strike his slave; but in case of disobedience to send him before the Cadi, or Judge, who could decide on the proper punishment. Slavery prevails throughout all the native kingdoms of Central Africa, in more or less aggravated forms.

The Egyptian merchants who are located in Khartoum as agents for houses in Cairo, consider themselves as worse than exiles, and indemnify themselves by sensual indulgence for being obliged to remain in a country which they detest. They live in large houses, keep their harems of inky slaves, eat, drink and smoke away their languid and wearisome days. All the material which they need for such a life is so cheap that their love of gain does not suffer thereby. One of the richest merchants in the place gave me an account of his housekeeping. He had a large mud palace, a garden, and twenty servants and slaves, to maintain which cost him eight thousand piastres (four hundred dollars) a year. He paid his servants twenty piastres a month, and his slaves also—at least so he told me, but I did not believe it.

As for the native Fellahs of Soudân, they are so crushed and imposed upon, that it is difficult to judge what their natural capacities really are. Foreigners, Frank as well as Egyptian, universally complain of their stupidity, and I heard the Pasha himself say, that if he could have done any thing with them Abbas Pasha might whistle to get Soudân from him. That they are very stupid, is true, but that they have every encouragement to be so, is equally true. Dr. Knoblecher, who, of all the men I saw in Khartoum, was best qualified to judge correctly, assured me that they needed only a just and paternal government, to make rapid progress in the arts of civilization.

CHAPTER XXXI.

FROM KHARTOUM TO EL METEMMA.

Farewell Breakfast—Departure from Khartoum—Parting with Dr. Reitz—A Prediction and its Fulfilment—Dreary Appearance of the Country—Lions—Burying-Grounds—The Natives—My Kababish Guide, Mohammed—Character of the Arabs—Habits of Deception—My Dromedary—Mutton and Mareesa—A Soudân Ditty—The Rowyân—Akaba Gerri—Heat and Scenery—An Altercation with the Guide—A Mishap—A Landscape—Tedious Approach to El Metemma—Appearance of the Town—Preparations for the Desert—Meeting Old Acquaintances.

The wind blew so violently on the morning of my departure from Khartoum, that the ferry-boat which had been engaged to convey my equipage to the Kordofan shore, could not round the point at the junction of the Niles. My camels, with the Kababish guide and drivers, had been ferried over the evening previous, and were in readiness to start. In this dilemma Dr. Péney, with whom I had engaged to take a parting breakfast, kindly gave me the use of his *nekker* and its crew. Our breakfast was a *fête champêtre* under the beautiful nebbuk tree in the Doctor's court-yard, and consisted of a highly-spiced *salmi* of his own compounding, a salad of lettuce and tomatoes, and a bottle of Cyprus wine. The coolness and force of the north-wind gave us a keen appetite, and our kind host could not say that we slighted his culinary skill, for verily there was nothing but empty plates to be seen, when we arose from the table. Dr. Reitz and I hastened on board the nekker, which immediately put off. I left Khartoum, regretting to leave a few friends behind me in that furnace of Soudân, yet glad to escape therefrom myself. A type of the character of the place was furnished us while making our way to Omdurman. We passed the body of a woman, who had been strangled and thrown into the water; a sight which the natives regarded without the least surprise. The Consul immediately dispatched one of his servants to the Governor of the city, asking him to have the body taken away and properly interred. It was full two hours before we reached the western bank of the Nile, opposite Omdurman. Achmet, who had preceded me, had drummed up the Kababish, and they were in readiness with my camels. The work of apportioning and loading the baggage was finished by noon, and the caravan started, preceded by the guide, Mohammed, who shook his long spear in a general defiance of all enemies.

Dr. Reitz and I, with our attendants, set off in advance on a quick trot. Our path led over a bleak, barren plain, covered with thorns, through which the wind whistled with a wintry sound. The air was filled with clouds of sand, which gave a pale and sickly cast to the sunshine. My friend was unwell and desponding, and after we had ridden eight miles, he halted to rest in a deep, rocky gully, where we were sheltered from the wind. Here we lay down upon the sand until the caravan came along, when we parted from each other. "You are going back to Europe and Civilization;" said he mournfully "you have an encouraging future before you—while I can only look forward to the prospect of leaving my bones in this accursed land." He then embraced me, mounted his dromedary, and was soon lost to my sight among the sand and thorns. Little did I then imagine that his last words were the unhappy prediction which another year would see verified! *

We halted for the night near the village of Gerrari. I slept but indifferently, with the heavy head and gloomy spirits I had brought from Khartoum; but the free life of my tent did not fail of its usual effect, and I rose the next morning fresh, strong, and courageous. We were obliged to travel slowly, on account of the nature of the road, which, for the greater part of the distance to El Metemma, lay in the Desert, just beyond the edge of the cultivated land. For the first day

* Dr. Constantine Reitz died about a year after my departure from Soudân, from the effects of the climate. He had been ill for some months, and while making a journey to Kordofan, felt himself growing worse so rapidly that he returned to Khartoum, where he expired in a few days. He was about thirty-three years of age, and his many acquirements, joined to a character of singular energy and persistence, had led his friends to hope for important results from his residence in Central Africa. With manners of great brusqueness and eccentricity, his generosity was unbounded, and this, combined with his intrepidity and his skill as a horseman and a hunter, made him a general favorite with the Arab chieftains of Ethiopia, whose cause he was always ready to advocate, against the oppressive measures of the Egyptian Government. It will always be a source of satisfaction to the author, that, in passing through Germany in September, 1852, he visited the parents of Dr. Reitz, whose father is a *Forstmeister*, or Inspector of Forests, near Darmstadt. The joy which they exhibited on hearing from their son through one who had so recently seen him, was mixed with sadness as they expressed the fear that *they* would never see him again—a fear, alas! too soon realized.

or two, we rode over dry, stony plains, covered with thickets of the small thorny mimosa and patches of long yellow grass. The country is crossed by deep gullies, through which the streams formed by the summer rains flow to the Nile. Their banks are lined with a thick growth of sont, nebbuk, and other trees peculiar to Central Africa, in which many lions make their lairs and prey upon the flocks of the Arabs. One bold, fierce fellow had established himself on the island of Musakar Bey, just below the junction of the Nile, and carried off nightly a sheep or calf, defying the attempts of the natives to take him. Our view was confined to the thorns, on whose branches we left many shreds of clothing as mementoes of the journey, and to the barren range of Djebel Gerrari, stretching westward into the Desert. Occasionally, however, in crossing the low spurs which ran out from this chain, the valley of the Nile—the one united Nile again—lay before us, far to the east and north-east, the river glistening in the sun as he spread his arms round island after island, till his lap could hold no more. The soil is a poor, coarse gravel, and the inhabitants support themselves by their herds of sheep and goats, which browse on the thorns. In places there are large thickets of the *usher*, or euphorbia, twenty feet high. It grows about the huts of the natives, who make no attempt to exterminate it, notwithstanding the poisonous nature of its juice. Every mile or two we passed a large Arab burying-ground, crowded with rough head and foot-stones, except where white pennons, fluttering on poles, denoted a more than ordinary sanctity in the deceased. The tomb of the Shekh, or holy man of Merreh, was a conical structure of stones and clay, about fifteen feet in breadth at the base, and twenty feet high. The graves are so numerous and the dwellings so few, that one nas the impression of travelling in a country depopulated by the pestilence; yet we met many persons on the road—partly Kababish, and partly natives of Dongola and Màhass. The men touched their lips and foreheads on passing me, and the women greeted me with that peculiar "*hab-bab-ba!*" which seems to be the universal expression of salutation among the various tribes of Central Africa.

My guide, Mohammed, was a Kababish, and the vainest and silliest Arab I ever knew. He wore his hair in long braids, extending from the forehead and temples to the nape of the neck, and kept in their places by a layer of mutton-fat, half an inch thick, which filled up the intervening spaces. His hollow cheeks, deep-sunken eyes, thin and wiry beard, and the long spear he carried in his hand made him a fair representative of Don Quixote, and the resemblance was not diminished by the gaunt and ungainly camel on which he jogged along at the head of my caravan. He was very devout, praying for quite an unreasonable length of time before and after meals, and always had a large patch of sand on his forehead, from striking it on the ground, as he knelt towards Mecca. Both his arms, above the elbows, were covered with rings of hippopotamus hide, to which were attached square leathern cases, containing sentences of the Koran, as charms to keep away sickness and evil spirits. The other man, Saïd, was a Shygheean, willing and good-natured enough, but slow and regardless of truth, as all Arabs are. Indeed, the best definition of an Arab which I can give, is—a philosophizing sinner. His fatalism gives him a calm and equable temperament under all circumstances, and "God wills it!" or "God is merciful!"

is the solace for every misfortune. But this same careless ness to the usual accidents of life extends also to his speech and his dealings with other men. I will not say that an Arab never speaks truth: on the contrary, he always does, if he happens to remember it, and there is no object to be gained by suppressing it; but rather than trouble himself to answer correctly a question which requires some thought, he tells you whatever comes uppermost in his mind, though certain to be detected the next minute. He is like a salesman, who, if he does not happen to have the article you want, offers you something else, rather than let you go away empty-handed. In regard to his dealings, what Sir Gardner Wilkinson says of Egypt, that "nobody parts with money without an effort to defraud," is equally true of Nubia and Soudân. The people do not steal outright; but they have a thousand ways of doing it in an indirect and civilized manner, and they are perfect masters of all those petty arts of fraud which thrive so greenly in the great commercial cities of Christendom. With these slight drawbacks, there is much to like in the Arabs, and they are certainly the most patient, assiduous and good-humored people in the world. If they fail in cheating you, they respect you the more, and they are so attentive to you, so ready to take their mood from yours—to laugh when you are cheerful, and be silent when you are grave—so light-hearted in the performance of severe duties, that if you commence your acquaintance by despising, you finish by cordially liking them.

On a journey like that which I was then commencing, it is absolutely necessary to preserve a good understanding with your men and beasts; otherwise travel will be a task, and a severe one, instead of a recreation. After my men had vainly tried a number of expedients, to get the upper hand of me, I drilled them into absolute obedience, and found their character much improved thereby. With my dromedary, whom I called Abou-Sin, (the Father of Teeth), from the great shekh of the Shukoree Arabs, to whom he originally belonged, I was soon on good terms. He was a beast of excellent temper, with a spice of humor in his composition, and a fondness for playing practical jokes. But as I always paid them back, neither party could complain, though Abou-Sin sometimes gurgled out of his long throat a string of Arabic gutturals, in remonstrance. He came up to my tent and knelt at precisely the same hour every evening, to get his feed of dourra, and when I was at breakfast always held his lips pursed up, ready to take the pieces of bread I gave him. My men, whom I agreed to provide with food during the journey, were regaled every day with mutton and mareesa, the two only really good things to be found in Soudân. A fat sheep cost 8 piastres (40 cents), and we killed one every three days. The meat was of excellent flavor. Mareesa is made of the coarse grain called dourra, which is pounded into flour by hand, mixed with water, and heated over a fire in order to produce speedy fermentation. It is always drunk the day after being made, as it turns sour on the third day. It is a little stronger than small beer, and has a taste similar to wheat bran, unpleasant on the first trial and highly palatable on the second. A jar holding two gallons costs one piastre, and as few families, however poor, are without it, we always found plenty of it for sale in the villages. It is nutritious, promotive of digestion, and my experience went to prove that it was not only a harmless but most wholesome drink in that stifling climate. *Om bilbil*, the mother of nightingales, which is made from wheat, is stronger, and has a pungent flavor. The people in general are remarkably temperate, but sailors and camel-men are often not content without arakee, a sort of weak brandy made from dates. I have heard this song sung so often that I cannot choose but recollect the words. It is in the Arabic jargon of Soudân:

"El-toombak sheràboo dowaïa,
Oo el karafeen ed dowa il 'es-sufaïa,
Oo el àrakee legheetoo monnaïa,
Om bilbil bukkoosoo burraïa."

[Tobacco I smoke in the pipe; and mareesa is a medicine to the *sufaïa*; (*i. e.* the bag of palm fibres through which it is strained), but arakee makes me perfectly contented, and then I will not even look at bilbil].

The third day after leaving Khartoum, I reached the mountains of Gerri, through which the Nile breaks his way in a narrow pass. Here I hailed as an old acquaintance the island-hill of Rowyàn (the watered, or unthirsty). This is truly a magnificent peak, notwithstanding its height is not more than seven hundred feet. Neither is Soracte high, yet it produces a striking effect, even with the loftier Apennines behind it. The Rowyàn is somewhat similar to Soracte in form. There are a few trees on the top, which shows that there must be a deposit of soil above its barren ramparts, and were I a merchant of Khartoum I should build a summer residence there, and by means of hydraulics create a grove and garden around it. The *akaba*, or desert pass, which we were obliged to take in order to reach the river again, is six hours in length, through a wild, stony tract, covered with immense boulders of granite, hurled and heaped together in the same chaotic manner as is exhibited in the rocks between Assouan and Philæ. After passing the range, a wide plain again opened before us, the course of the Nile marked in its centre by the darker hue of the nebbuks and sycamores, rising above the long gray belts of thorn-trees. The mountains which inclose the fallen temples of Mesowuràt and Naga appeared far to the east. The banks of the river here are better cultivated than further up the stream. The wheat, which was just sprouting, during my upward journey, was now two feet high, and rolled before the wind in waves of dark, intense, burning green. The brilliancy of color in these mid-African landscapes is truly astonishing.

The north-wind, which blew the sand furiously in our faces during the first three days of the journey, ceased at this point and the weather became once more intensely hot. The first two or three hours of the morning were, nevertheless, delicious. The temperature was mild, and there was a June-like breeze which bore far and wide the delicate odor of the mimosa blossoms. The trees were large and thick, as on the White Nile, forming long, orchard-like belts between the grain-fields and the thorny clumps of the Desert. The flocks of black goats which the natives breed, were scattered among these trees, and numbers of the animals stood perfectly upright on their hind legs, as they nibbled off the ends of the higher branches.

On the morning after leaving Akaba Gerri, I had two altercations with my men. Mohammed had left Khartoum without a camel, evidently for the purpose of saving money. In a day or two, however, he limped so much that I put him upon Achmet's dromedary for a few hours. This was an imposition, for every guide is obliged to furnish his own camel, and I told the old man that he should ride no more. He thereupon prevailed upon Saïd to declare that their contract was to take me to Ambukol, instead of Merawe. This, considering that the route had been distinctly stated to them by Dr. Reitz, in my presence, and put in writing by the *moodir*, Abdallah Effendi, and that the name of Ambukol was not once mentioned, was a falsehood of the most brazen character. I told the men they were liars, and that sooner than yield to them I would return to Khartoum and have them punished, whereupon they saw they had gone too far, and made a seeming compromise by declaring that they would willingly take me to Merawe, if I wished it.

Towards noon we reached the village of Derreira, nearly opposite the picturesque rapids of the Nile. I gave Mohammed half a piastre and sent him after mareesa, two gallons of which he speedily procured. A large gourd was filled for me, and I drank about a quart without taking breath. Before it had left my lips, I experienced a feeling of vigor and elasticity throughout my whole frame, which refreshed me for the remainder of the day. Mohammed stated that the tents of some of his tribe were only about four hours distant, and asked leave to go and procure a camel, promising to rejoin us at El Metemma the next day. As Saïd knew the way, and could have piloted me in case the old sinner should not return, I gave him leave to go.

Achmet and I rode for nearly two hours over a stony, thorny plain, before we overtook the baggage camels. When at last we came in sight of them, the brown camel was running loose without his load and Saïd trying to catch him. My provision-chests were tumbled upon the ground, the cafass broken to pieces and the chickens enjoying the liberty of the Desert. Saïd, it seemed, had stopped to talk with some women, leaving the camel, which was none too gentle, to take care of himself. Achmet was so incensed that he struck the culprit in the face, whereupon he cried out, with a rueful voice: "*ya khosara!*" (oh, what a misfortune!). After half an hour's labor the boxes were repacked, minus their broken crockery, the chickens caught and the camel loaded. The inhabitants of this region were mostly Shygheeans, who had emigrated thither. They are smaller and darker than the people of Màhass, but resemble them in character. In one of the villages which we passed, the *soog*, or market, was being held. I rode through the crowd to see what they had to sell, but found only the simplest articles: camels, donkeys, sheep, goats; mats, onions, butter, with some baskets of raw cotton and pieces of stuff spun and woven by the natives. The sales must be principally by barter, as there is little money in the country.

In the afternoon we passed another akaba, even more difficult for camels than that of Gerri. The tracks were rough and stony, crossed by frequent strata of granite and porphyry. From the top of one of the ridges I had a fine view of a little valley of mimosas which lay embayed in the hills and washed by the Nile, which here curved grandly round from west to south, his current glittering blue and broad in the sun. The opposite bank was flat and belted with wheat fields, beyond which stretched a gray forest of thorns and then the yellow savannas of Shendy, walled in the distance by long, blue, broken ranges of mountains. The summit of a hill near our road was surrounded with a thick wall, formed of natural blocks of black porphyry. It had square, projecting bastions at regular intervals, and an entrance on the western side. From its appearance, form and position, it had undoubtedly been a stronghold of some one of the Arab tribes, and can claim no great antiquity. I travelled on until after sunset, when, as no village appeared, I camped in a grove of large mimosas, not far from the Nile. A few Shygheean herdsmen were living in brush huts near at hand, and dogs and jackals howled incessantly through the night.

On the fifth day I reached the large town of El Metemma, nearly opposite Shendy, and the capital of a negro kingdom, before the Egyptian usurpation. The road, on approaching it, leads over a narrow plain, covered with a shrub resembling heather, bordered on one side by the river, and on the other by a long range of bare red sand-hills. We journeyed for more than three hours, passing point after point of the hills, only to find other spurs stretching out ahead of us. From the intense heat I was very anxious to reach El Metemma, and was not a little rejoiced when I discerned a grove of date-trees, which had been pointed out to me from Shendy, a month before, as the landmark of the place. Soon a cluster of buildings appeared on the sandy slopes, but as we approached, I saw they were ruins. We turned another point, and reached another group of tokuls and clay houses—ruins also. Another point, and more ruins, and so for more than a mile before we reached the town, which commences at the last spur of the hills, and extends along the plain for a mile and a half.

It is a long mass of one-story mud buildings, and the most miserable place of its size that I have seen in Central Africa

There is no bazaar, but an open market-place, where the people sit on the ground and sell their produce, consisting of dourra, butter, dates, onions, tobacco and a few grass mats. There may be a mosque in the place, but in the course of my ramble through the streets, I saw nothing that looked like one. Half the houses appeared to be uninhabited, and the natives were a hideous mixture of the red tribes of Màhass and Shygheea and the negro races of Soudân. A few people were moving lazily through the dusty and filthy lanes, but the greater portion were sitting in the earth, on the shady side of the houses. In one of the streets I was taken for the Medical Inspector of the town, a part of whose business it is to see that it is kept free from filth. Two women came hastily out of the houses and began sweeping vigorously, saying to me as I came up: "You see, we are sweeping very clean." It would have been much more agreeable to me, had the true Inspector gone his rounds the day before. El Metemma and Shendy are probably the most immoral towns in all Central Africa. The people informed me that it was a regular business for persons to buy female slaves, and hire them for the purpose of prostitution, all the money received in this vile way going into the owner's pocket.

I was occupied the rest of the day and the next morning in procuring and filling additional water-skins, and preparing to cross the Beyooda. Achmet had a quantity of bread baked, for the journey would occupy seven or eight days, and there was no possibility of procuring provisions on the road. Mohammed did not make his appearance at the appointed time, and I determined to start without him, my caravan being increased by a Dongolese merchant, and a poor Shygheean whose only property was a club and a wooden bowl, and who asked leave to help tend the camels for the sake of food and water on the way. All of the Beyooda, which term is applied to the broad desert region west of the Nile and extending southward from Nubia to Kordofan and Dar-Fūr, is infested with marauding tribes of Arabs, and though at present their depredations are less frequent than formerly, still, from the total absence of all protection, the traveller is exposed to considerable risk. For this reason, it is not usual to find small parties traversing this route, as in the Nubian Desert.

I added to my supplies a fat sheep, a water-skin filled with mareesa, a sheaf of raw onions (which are a great luxury in the Desert), and as many fowls as could be procured in El Metemma. Just as we were loading the camels, who should come up but Beshir and two or three more of the Mahassee sailors, who had formed part of my crew from Berber to Khartoum. They came up and kissed my hand, exclaiming: ' May God prosper you, O Effendi!" They immediately set about helping to load the camels, giving us, meanwhile, news of every thing that had happened. Beshir's countenance fell when I asked him about his Metemma sweetheart, Gammerò-Betahadjerò; she had proved faithless to him. The *America* was again on her way from Berber to Khartoum, with a company of merchants. The old slave, Bakhita, unable to bear the imputation of being a hundred and fifty years old, had run away from the vessel. When the camels were loaded and we were ready to mount, I gave the sailors a few piastres to buy mareesa and sent them away rejoicing.

CHAPTER XXXII.

THE BEYOODA DESERT.

Entering the Desert—Character of the Scenery—Wells—Fear of the Arabs—The Laloom Tree—Effect of the Hot Wind—Mohammed overtakes us—Arab Endurance—An unpleasant Bedfellow—Comedy of the Crows—Gazelles—We encounter a Sand-storm—The Mountain of Thirst—The Wells of Djeekdud—A Mountain Pass—Desert Intoxication—Scenery of the Table-land—Bir Khannik—The Kababish Arabs—Gazelles again—Ruins of an Ancient Coptic Monastery—Distant View of the Nile Valley—Djebel Berkel—We come into Port.

"He sees the red sirocco wheeling
Its sandy columns o'er the waste,
And streams through palmy valleys stealing,
Where the plumed ostrich speeds in haste."—FREILIGRATH.

WE left El Metemma at noon, on the tenth of February. Crossing the low ridge of red sand, at the foot of which the town is built, the wind came fresh to meet us, across the long, level savanna of yellow grass and shrubs which stretched away to the west and north, without a bound. The prospect was exhilarating, after the continual hem of thorns, which had lined our road from Khartoum. It was a great relief to turn the eye from the bare, scorching mud walls of the town, to the freshness and freedom of the Desert. I took a last look at the wheat-fields of the Nile, and then turned my face northward, towards the point where I expected to meet his current again. The plain was very level, and the road excellent for our camels. In places where there was a slight depression of the soil, a long, slender species of grass grew in thick tufts, affording nourishment to the herds of the wandering Arab tribes. There were also narrow belts of white thorn and a curious shrub, with leaves resembling the jasmine. In two hours we reached a well, where some Kababish were drawing water for their goats and asses. It was about twenty feet deep, and the water was drawn in skins let down with ropes. We kept on until sunset, when we encamped in an open, gravelly space, surrounded with patches of grass, on which the camels browsed. The hot weather of the past two or three days had called into life a multitude of winged and creeping insects, and they assailed me on all sides.

The next morning, after travelling more than two hours over the plain, we reached a series of low hills, or rather swells of the Desert, covered with black gravel and fragments of porphyritic rock. They appeared to be outlying spurs of a mountain range which we saw to the northwest. From the highest of them we saw before us a long, shallow valley, opening far to the north-east. It was thickly covered with tufts of yellowish-green grass, sprinkled with trees of various kinds. The merchant pointed out a grove in the distance as the location of Bir Abou-leer, the first well on the road. His sharp eye discerned a company of Arabs, who were encamped near it, and who, seeing Achmet and myself in our Turkish dresses, were preparing to fly. He urged his dromedary into a fast trot and rode ahead to reassure them. They were a tall, wild-looking people, very scantily dressed; the men had long black hair, moustaches and beards, and carried spears in their hands They looked at us with suspicion, but did not refuse the customary "hab-bab-ba!" The wells were merely pits, not more than four or five feet deep, dug in the clayey soil, and containing at the bottom a constant supply of cool, sweet water. We watered our camels in basins scooped for that purpose in the earth, and then took breakfast under the thorns. Among the trees in the wady was one resembling the nebbuk in foliage, and with a fruit similar in appearance, but larger and of different flavor. The Arabs called it *laloom*, and gathered some of the fruit for me to taste. It has a thin, brittle outer rind, containing a hard stone, covered with a layer of gummy paste, most intensely sweet and bitter in the mouth. It has precisely the flavor of the medicine known to children as Hive Syrup.

We resumed our course along the wady, nearly to its termination at the foot of the mountains, when the road turned to the right over another succession of hard, gravelly ridges, flanked on the west by hills of coal-black porphyry. During the afternoon the wind was sometimes as hot as a furnace-blast, and I felt my very blood drying up in its intensity. I had no means of ascertaining the temperature, but it could not have been less than 105°. Nevertheless, the sky was so clear and blue, the sunshine so perfect, and the Desert so inspiring that I was in the most exulting mood. In fact, the powerful dry heat of the air produced upon me a bracing effect, similar to that of sharp cold. It gave me a sensation of fierce, savage vigor, and I longed for an Arab lance and the fleet hoofs of the red stallion I had left in Khartoum. At times the burning blasts were flavored with a strong aromatic odor, like that of dried lavender, which was as stimulating to the lungs as herb-tea to the stomach. Our provisions soon felt the effects of this continual dry heat. Dates became as pebbles of jasper, and when I asked my servant for bread, he gave me a stone.

As we were journeying along over the plain, we spied a man on a camel trotting behind us, and in half an hour, lo! Mohammed the guide. The old scamp came up with a younger brother behind him, whom he had brought without asking permission, and without bringing food for him. This made eight persons I was obliged to feed, and as our bread and meat were only calculated for six, I put them on allowance. Mohammed had his hair newly plaited and covered with a layer of mutton-fat, a quarter of an inch thick. I saw very little of the vaunted temperance of the Arabs. True, they will live on dates—when they can get nothing else; and they will go without water for a day—when they have none. I found a quart of water daily amply sufficient for my own needs, notwithstanding the great heat we endured; but I do not think one of the men drank less than a gallon in the same time, and as for their eating, Achmet frequently declared that they would finish a whole sheep before getting to "el hamdu lillah!"—the usual Arabic grace after meat.

Towards sunset we reached an open space of ground which had not been touched since the rains of the previous summer. The soil had been washed smooth and then dried away in the sun, leaving a thin, cracked crust, like that which frequently forms after a light snow-fall. Our camel's feet broke through at every step, making the only trails which crossed it, except those of gazelles and vultures. Achmet was about to pitch my tent near some snaky-looking holes, but I had it moved to a clearer spot. I slept without interruption, but in the morning, as he was about to roll up my mattrass, he suddenly let it drop and rushed out of the tent, exclaiming: "Oh master, come out! come out! There is a great snake in your bed!" I looked, and truly enough, there was an ugly spotted reptile coiled up on the straw matting. The men heard the alarm, and my servant Ali immediately came running up with a club. As he was afraid to enter the tent, he threw it to me, and with one blow I put the snake beyond the power of doing harm. It was not more than two feet long, but thick and club-shaped, and with a back covered with green, brown and yellow scales, very hard and bright. The Arabs, who by this time had come to the rescue, said it was a most venomous creature, its bite causing instant death. "*Allah kereem!*" (God is merciful!) I exclaimed, and they all heartily responded: "God be praised!" They said that the occurrence denoted long life to me. Although no birds were to be seen at the time, not ten minutes had elapsed before two large crows appeared in the air. After wheeling over us once or twice, they alighted near the snake. At first, they walked around it at a distance, occasionally exchanging glances, and turning up their heads in a shrewd manner, which plainly said: "No you don't, old fellow! want to make us believe you're dead, do you?" They bantered each other to take hold of it first, and at last the boldest seized it suddenly by the tail, jumped backward two or three feet and then let it fall. He looked at the other, as much as to say: "If he's not dead, it's a capital sham!" The other made a similar essay, after which they alternately dragged and shook it, and consulted some time, before they agreed that it was actually dead. One of them then took it by the tail and sailed off through the air, its scales glittering in the sun as it dangled downward.

On the third day we left the plain and entered on a region of black, stony ridges, with grass and thorns in the long hollows between them. The sky was so clear that the moon (in her last quarter) was visible until nearly noon. About ten o'clock, from one of the porphyry hills, I caught sight of Djebel Attshan, or the Mountain of Thirst, which crosses the middle of the Beyooda. It was in the north and north-west, apparently about thirty miles distant. During the morning I saw four beautiful gazelles, not more than a stone's throw distant. One of them was lame, which induced me to believe that I could catch it. I got down from my camel and crept stealthily to the crest of the ridge, but when I looked down the other side, no gazelle was to be seen. Half a dozen narrow gullies branched away among the loose mounds of stones, and further search would have been useless.

At noon we reached another and different region. The grass and thorns disappeared, and the swells of black gravel gave place to long drifts of bright yellow sand which extended on all sides as far as the eye could reach. We toiled on, over drift after drift, but there was still the same dreary yellow waste, whitening in the distance under the glare of the sun. At first, the air was so tremulous with the radiated heat, that the whole landscape glittered and wavered like the sea, and the brain became giddy from gazing on its unsteady lines. But as the wind began to blow more violently, this disappeared. The sky then became obscured nearly to the zenith, with a dull purple haze, arising from the myriads of fine grains of sand with which the air was filled. The sun became invisible, although there were no clouds in the sky, and we seemed to be journeying under a firmament of rusty copper. The drifts were constantly forming and changing shape, and the sand vibrated along their edges or scudded in swift ripples over the plain, with that dry, sharp sound one hears in winter, when the " North-wind's masonry" is going on. The air was withering in its fierce heat and occasioned intense thirst, which, fortunately, we were able to relieve. The storm grew more violent and the burning labyrinths of sand more intricate, as we advanced. The path was hidden under drifts five or six feet in height, and the tall yellow walls were creeping every minute nearer, to cover it completely. The piles of stones, however, which the Arabs have made on the tops of the ridges and replace as often as they are thrown down, guided us, and after three hours and a half in a spot which might serve as the fourth circle of Dante's Hell, we emerged on the open plain and saw again the Mountain of Thirst, which had been hidden all this time. The camels, which were restless and uneasy in the sand, now walked more cheerily. The sun came out again, but the sky still retained its lurid purple hue. We all drank deeply of the brown leathery contents of our water-skins and pushed steadily onward till camping-time, at sunset. While the storm lasted, the Arabs crouched close under the flanks of the camels and sheltered themselves from the sand. Achmet and the Dongolese merchant unrolled their turbans and muffled them around their faces, but on following their example I experienced such a stifling sensation of heat that I at once desisted, and rode with my head exposed as usual.

We halted in a meadow-like hollow, full of abundant grass, in which the weary camels made amends for their hardships. The wind howled so fiercely around my tent that I went to sleep expecting to have it blown about my ears before morning. Djebel Attshan was dimly visible in the starlight, and we saw the light of fires kindled by the Arabs who live at the wells of Djeekdud. Saïd was anxious to go on to the wells and have a carouse with the natives, and when I refused threatened to leave me and go on alone to Merawe. "Go!" said I, "just as soon as you like"—but this was the very thing he did not want. The heat which I had absorbed through the day began to ooze out again as the temperature of the air fell, and my body glowed until midnight like a mass of molten metal. On lifting up my blanket, that night, a large scorpion tumbled out, but scampered away so quickly that we could not kill him.

We were up betimes the next morning, and off for Bir Djeekdud. At ten o'clock we entered a wide valley extending to the southern base of the mountains. It was quite overgrown with bushy tufts of grass and scattering clumps of trees. Herds of goats and sheep, with a few camels and donkeys, were browsing over its surface, and I saw the Arab herdsmen at a distance. The wells lie in a narrow wady, shut in by the mountains, about two miles east of the caravan track. We therefore halted in the shade of a spreading mimosa, and sent Saïd and the guide's brother with the water-skins. I took my breakfast leisurely, and was lying on my back, half lulled to sleep by the singing of the wind, when the Dongolese arrived. He gave us to drink from his fresh supply of water, and informed us that the wells in the valley were not good, but that there was a deposit in the rocks above, which was pure and sweet. I therefore sent Ali off in all haste on one of my dromedaries, to have my skins filled from the latter place, which occasioned a further delay of two hours. An Arab family of the small Saürat tribe, which inhabits that region, was encamped at a little distance, but did not venture to approach.

Ali described the well as a vast natural hollow in the porphyry rock, in the centre of a basin, or valley, near the top of the mountain. The water is held as in a tank; it is from twenty to thirty feet deep, and as clear as crystal. The taste is deliciously pure and fresh. If I had known this in time, I should have visited the place. The valley of Djeekdud is about two miles broad, inclosed on the north by the dark-red porphyry rocks of the Mountain of Thirst, and on the south by a smaller group of similar formation. It is crossed in two places by broad strata of red granite. As water can readily be obtained in any part of it by digging, the whole of it is capable of cultivation.

Leaving our halting place, we journeyed westward through a gate of the mountains into a broader valley, where numerous herds of sheep were feeding. I saw but few Arabs, and those were mostly children, who had charge of the herds. The tribe resides principally in the mountains, on account of greater security against the attacks of enemies. The afternoon was hot like all preceding ones, and my Arabs drank immense quantities of water. We kept on our course until five o'clock, when we encamped opposite a broad valley, which broke into the mountains at right angles to their course. It was a wild spot, and the landscape, barren as it was, possessed much natural beauty. During the afternoon we left the high road to Ambukol, and took a branch track leading to Merawe, which lay more to the northward.

The next morning, after skirting the porphyry range for

several hours, we entered a narrow valley leading into its depths. The way was stony and rough, and we travelled for three hours, constantly ascending, up the dry bed of a summer stream. The mountains rose a thousand feet above us in some places. Near the entrance of the valley, we passed an Arab watering a large flock of sheep at a pool of green water which lay in a hollow of the rocks. After ascending the pass for nearly four hours, we crossed the summit ridge and entered on a high table-land, eight or ten miles in length and entirely surrounded by branches of the mountain chain. The plain was thinly covered with grass, mimosas and nebbuk, among which a single camel was browsing. At night we reached the opposite side, and encamped at the foot of a lofty black spur of the mountains, not far from a well which Mohammed called Bir Abou-Seray.

During the night I was troubled with a heavy feeling in the head, and found it almost impossible to sleep. I arose with a sensation of giddiness, which continued all day. At times I found it very difficult to maintain my seat on the dromedary. It required a great effort to keep my eyes open, as the sunshine increased the symptoms. This condition affected my mind in a singular manner. Past scenes in my life revived, with so strong an impression of reality, that I no longer knew where I was. The hot, yellow landscape around me, was a dream; the cries of my camel-drivers were fantastic sounds which my imagination had conjured up. After a most bewildering and fatiguing day, I drank several cups of strong tea, rolled myself in a thick cotton quilt, and sweat to distraction until morning. The moisture I lost relieved my head, as a shower clears a sultry sky, and the symptoms gradually left me Whether they were caused by breathing a more rarefied atmosphere,—for the plain was nearly fifteen hundred feet above the Nile level—in a heat more than usually intense, or by an attack of that malady which Richardson aptly calls the "intoxication of the Desert," I cannot decide.

After leaving Bir Abou-Seray, we continued our slow descent of the northern side of the mountain range, by a winding valley, following the dry bed of a summer river. The mountains were a thousand feet high and linked in regular ranges, which had a general north-east and south-west direction. The landscapes of the day were all exceedingly wild and picturesque. The vegetation was abundant along the banks of the river-bed, the doum-palm appearing occasionally among the groves of thorn and nebbuk. In some places the river had washed the bases of the mountains and laid bare their huge strata of rock, whose round black masses glittered in the sunshine, showing the gradual polish of the waves. Towards noon the pass enlarged into a broad plain, six miles in diameter, and entirely bounded by mountains. To the north-east it opened into another and larger plain, across whose blue surface rose the pyramidal peaks of a higher mountain chain than I had yet seen. Some of them were upwards of two thousand feet in height. The scenery here was truly grand and imposing. Beyond the plain we passed into a broader valley, girdled by lower hills. The river-bed, which we crossed from time to time, increased in breadth and showed a more dense vegetation on its banks. We expected to have reached another well, but there was no sign of it at sunset, and as I had already found that my guide, Mohammed, knew nothing of the road, I encamped at once.

We arose by daybreak, hoping to reach the Nile. After somewhat more than two hours' journey, we met a caravan of about three hundred camels, laden with bales of cotton drillings, for the clothing of the new regiments of soldiers then being raised in Soudân. The foremost camels were a mile from Bir Khannik, while the hindmost were still drinking at the well. The caravan had Kababish drivers and guides—wild, long-haired, half-naked Arabs, with spears in their hands and shields of hippopotamus hide on their shoulders. They told us we were still a day and a half from Merawe. We rode on to the well, which was an immense pit, dug in the open plain. It was about fifty feet deep, and the Arabs were obliged to draw the water in skins let down with ropes. The top curved into the well like a shallow bowl, from the earth continually crumbling down, and the mouth of the shaft was protected by trunks of trees, on which the men stood while they drew the water. Around the top were shallow basins lined with clay, out of which the camels drank. The fierce Kababish were shouting and gesticulating on all sides as we rode up—some leading the camels to kneel and drink, some holding the water-skins, and others brandishing their spears and swords in angry contention. Under the hot sun, on the sandy plain, it was a picture truly mid-African in all its features. The water had an insipid, brackish taste, and I was very glad that I had prevented my Arabs from drinking all we had brought from the porphyry fountain of Djeekdud We watered our camels, however, which detained us long enough to see a fight between two of the Kababish guides. There were so many persons to interfere that neither could injure the other, but the whole group of actors and sympathizers, struggling on the brink of the well, came near being precipitated to the bottom.

Our road now turned to the north, through a gap in the low hills and over a tract of burnt, barren, rolling wastes of white sand and gravel. Towards evening we came again to the river-bed, here broad and shallow. This part of the Desert is inhabited by the Saürat and Huni tribes, and we saw large herds of sheep and goats wherever the halfeh grass abounded. At sunset there were no signs of the Nile, so I had the tent pitched in the middle of the dry river-channel. In front of us, on a low mound, the red walls of a ruined building shone in the last rays of the sun.

The next day—the eighth since leaving El Metemma—was intensely hot and sultry, without a breath of air stirring. While walking towards the ruins, I came upon two herds of gazelles, so tame that I approached within thirty yards, and could plainly see the expression of surprise and curiosity in their dark eyes. When I came too near, they would bleat like lambs, bound away a little distance and then stop again. The building, which stood on the stony slope of a hill, was surrounded with loose walls, in a dilapidated condition. The foundation, rising about six feet above the earth, is stone, above which the walls are of brick, covered with a thin coating of cement. The building is about eighty feet in length by forty in breadth, but the walls which remain are not more than twenty feet high. It is believed to have been an ancient Coptic monastery, and probably dates from the earlier ages of Christianity. The ruins of other houses, built of loose stones, surround the principal edifice, which was undoubtedly a church, and the ground around is strewn with fragments of burnt brick and pottery. There is a churchyard near at hand, with tombstones which contain inscriptions both in Greek and Coptic.

We rode slowly down the broad river-bed, which gradually widened, and after two or three hours saw far in advance a line of red, glowing sand-hills, which I knew could not be on the southern side of the Nile. Still we went on, under the clear, hot sky, the valley widening into a plain the while, and I sought anxiously for some sign that the weary Desert was crossed. Finally, I saw, above the endless clusters of thorns, a line of darker, richer green, far away in the burning distance, and knew it to be a grove of date-palms—the glorious signal of the Nile. This put new life into me, and thenceforth I felt the scorching heat no longer. To the north, beyond the palms, appeared an isolated mountain of singular form—the summit being flat and the sides almost perpendicular. It must be Djebel Berkel, I thought, and I told Mohammed so, but he said it was not. Just then, I saw an Arab herdsman among the thorns and called out to him to know the name of the mountain. "Djebel Berkel," said he. He then accosted Mohammed: "Where are you going?" "To Merawe." "Are you the guide?" he again inquired, bursting into a loud laugh. "You are a fine guide; there is Merawe!" pointing in a direction very different from that we were going. This completed the old fellow's discomfiture. We were still five or six miles distant from the river and took a random path over the plain, in the direction indicated by the herdsman. The palms rose higher and showed a richer foliage; mud walls appeared in their shade, and a tall minaret on the opposite bank of the river pointed out the location of the town. I rode down out of the drear, hot sand—the sea where I had been drifting for seven wearisome days—to the little village of Abdòm, embow ered in a paradise of green; palms above, dazzling wheat-fields dark cotton-fields and blossoming beans below. A blessed resting-place!

Shekh Abd e'-Djebàl.

CHAPTER XXXIII.

THREE DAYS AT NAPATA.

Our whereabouts—Shekh Mohammed Abd e'-Djebàl—My residence at Abdôm—Crossing the River—A Superb Landscape—The Town of Merawe—Ride to Djebel Berkel—The Temples of Napata—Ascent of the Mountain—Ethiopian Panorama—Lost and Found—The Pyramids—The Governor of Merawe—A Scene in the Divan—The Shekh and I—The Governor Dines with me—Ruins of the City of Napata—A Talk about Religions—Engaging Camels for Wadi-Halfa—The Shekh's Parting Blessing.

"Under the palm-trees by the river's side."—Keats.

Abdôm, the friendly haven into which I had drifted after an eight days' voyage in the fiery sea of the Desert, is a village on the eastern bank of the Nile, which, after passing Abou-Hammed, flows to the south-west and south untill it reaches the frontier of Dongola. On the opposite bank is Merawe, the former capital of Dar Shygheea, which must not be confounded with the ancient Meroë, the ruins of which, near Shendy, I have already described. True, the identity of the names at first deceived antiquarians, who supposed the temples and pyramids in this neighborhood to have belonged to the capital of the old Hierarchy of Meroë; but it is now satisfactorily established that they mark the site of Napata, the capital of Ethiopia up to the time of the Cæsars. It was the limit of the celebrated expedition of the Roman soldiers, under Petronius. Djebel Berkel, at whose base the principal remains are found, is in lat. 18° 35′, or thereabouts.

I was welcomed to Abdôm by the Shekh or holy man of the place, who met me on the verge of the Desert, and conducted me to the best of his two houses. Shekh Mohammed, Abd e'-Djebàl (Mohammed, the Slave of the Mountains), was a dignified old man of sixty, with a gray beard and brown complexion, and was the owner of a water-mill, several fields of wheat and cotton, and an abundance of palm-trees. He had two wives, each of whom, with her family, occupied a separate house—a great mark of discretion on the part of Mohammed. Domestic quiet was thus secured to him, while he possessed that in which the Arab most glories and rejoices—a numerous family of children. His youngest wife, a woman of thirty, immediately vacated the house on my arrival, and took up her temporary residence in a tent of palm-matting, with her four children. The dwelling into which I was ushered was a square structure of clay, one story high, with one door and no windows. It had a flat roof of palm logs, covered with thatch, and the inside walls were hung with large mats, plaited with brilliantly-colored palm blades. Fancy vessels of baked clay, baskets, ostrich eggs, and other ornaments were suspended from the roof in slings of palm fibre, and a very large white mat covered half the floor. Here my bed was laid, and my camp-stool, placed in front of it, formed a table. The Shekh, who was with me nearly all the time of my stay, sat on the floor in front of me, and never entered or departed from the house, without saying *"Bismillàhi"* ("in the name of God"), as he crossed the threshold. Outside of the door was a broad divan, running along the north side of the house. It therefore pointed towards Mecca and was a most agreeable praying-place for the holy man. On my arrival, after first having taken a bath in the Nile, I sat there the rest of the day, tasting the luxury of coolness and shade, and steeping my eyes in the balm of refreshing colors. A clump of some twenty date-trees grew in front of the door, throwing over us a gorgeous canopy of leaves. Fields of wheat in head, waist-deep, surrounded the house, insulating it in a sea of greenness, over which I saw the hills of the Desert, no longer terrible, but soft and fair and far as clouds smouldering in the roseate fires of an Eastern sunrise.

Very early the next morning the Shekh and his sons and their asses were in readiness to accompany me to Djebel Berkel. We walked down between the Shekh's gardens to the Nile, where the ferry-boat was waiting to convey us across. I was enchanted with the picture which the shores presented. The air was filled with a light, silvery vapor (a characteristic of sultry weather in Africa), softening the deep, rich color of the landscape. The eastern bank was one bower of palms, standing motionless, in perfect groups, above the long, sloping banks of beans in blossom. Such grace and glory, such silence and repose, I thought I had never before seen in the vegetable world. Opposite, the ruined palaces of the old Shygheean Kings and the mud and stone hovels of modern Merawe rose in picturesque piles above the river bank and below the red sandstone bluffs of the Nubian Desert, which overhung them and poured the sand through deep rents and fissures upon their very roofs. The mosque, with a tall, circular minaret, stood embowered in a garden of date-palms, under one of the highest bluffs. Up the river, which stretched glittering into the distance, the forest of trees shut out the view of the Desert, except Djebel Berkel, which stood high and grand above them, the morning painting its surface with red lights and purple shadows. Over the misty horizon of the river rose a single conical peak, far away. The sky was a pale, sleepy blue, and all that I saw seemed beautiful dream-pictures—every where grace, beauty, splendor of coloring, steeped in Elysian repose. It is impossible to describe the glory of that passage across the river. It paid me for all the hardships of the Desert.

When we touched the other shore and mounted the little donkeys we had taken across with us, the ideal character of the scene disappeared, but left a reality picturesque and poetic enough. The beasts were without bridles, and were only furnished with small wooden saddles, without girths or stirrups. One was obliged to keep his poise, and leave the rest to the donkey, who, however, suffered himself to be guided by striking the side of his neck. We rode under a cluster of ruined stone buildings, one of which occupied considerable space, rising pylon-like, to the height of thirty feet. The Shekh informed me that it had been the palace of a Shygheean king, be fore the Turks got possession of the country. It was wholly dilapidated, but a few Arab families were living in the stone dwellings which surround it. These clusters of shattered buildings extend for more than a mile along the river, and are all now known as Merawe. Our road led between fields of ripening wheat, rolling in green billows before the breeze, on one side, and on the other, not more than three yards distant, the naked sandstone walls of the Desert, where a blade of grass never grew. Over the wheat, along the bank of the Nile, rose a long forest of palms, so thickly ranged that the eye could scarcely penetrate their dense, cool shade; while on the other hand the glaring sand-hills showed their burning shoulders above the bluffs. It was a most violent contrast, and yet, withal, there was a certain harmony in these opposite features. A remarkably fat man, riding on a donkey, met us. The Shekh compared him to a hippopotamus, and said that his fat came from eating mutton and drinking *om bilbil* day and night. At the end of the town we came to a sort of guard-house, shaded by two sycamores. A single soldier was in attendance, and apparently tired of having nothing to do, as he immediately caught his donkey and rode with us to Djebel Berkel.

We now approached the mountain, which is between three and four miles from the town. It rises from out the sands of the Nubian Desert, to the height of five hundred feet, presenting a front completely perpendicular towards the river. It is inaccessible on all sides except the north, which in one place has an inclination of 45°. Its scarred and shattered walls of naked standstone stand up stern and sublime in the midst of the hot and languid landscape. As we approached, a group of pyramids appeared on the brow of a sand-hill to the left, and I discerned at the base of the mountain several isolated pillars the stone-piles of ruined pylons, and other remains of temples. The first we reached was at the south-eastern corner of the mountain. Amid heaps of sandstone blocks and disjointed segments of pillars, five columns of an exceedingly old form still point out the court of a temple, whose adyta are hewn within in the mountain. They are not more than ten feet high and three in diameter, circular, and without capital or abacus, unless a larger block, rudely sculptured with the outlines of a Typhon-head, may be considered as such. The doorway is hurled down and defaced, but the cartouches of kings may still be traced on the fragments. There are three chambers in the rock, the walls of which are covered with sculptures, for the most part representing the Egyptian divinities. The temple was probably dedicated to Typhon, or the Evil Principle, as one of the columns is still faced with a caryatid of the short, plump, big-mouthed and bat-eared figure, which elsewhere represents him. Over the entrance is the sacred winged globe, and the ceiling shows the marks of brilliant coloring. The temple is not remarkable for its architecture, and can only be interesting in an antiquarian point of view. It bears some resemblance in its general style to the Temple-palace of Goorneh, at Thebes.

The eastern base of the mountain, which fronts the Nile, is strewn with hewn blocks, fragments of capitals, immense masses of dark bluish-gray granite, and other remains, which prove that a large and magnificent temple once stood there The excavations made by Lepsius and others have uncovered the substructions sufficiently to show the general plan of two buildings. The main temple was at the north-eastern corner of the mountain, under the highest point of its perpendicular crags. The remains of its small propylons stand in advance, about two hundred yards from the rock, going towards which, you climb the mound formed by the ruins of a large pylon, at the foot of which are two colossal ram-headed sphinxes of blue granite, buried to their necks in the sand. Beyond this is a portico and pillared court, followed by other courts and labyrinths of chambers. Several large blocks of granite, all more or less broken and defaced, lie on the surface or half quarried from the rubbish. They are very finely polished and contain figures of kings, evidently arranged in genealogical order, each accompanied with his name. The shekh had a great deal to tell me of the Franks, who dug up all the place, and set the people to work at hauling away the lions and rams, which they carried off in ships. I looked in vain for the celebrated pedestal; it has probably become the spoil of Lepsius.

While taking a sketch of the mountain from the eastern side, I found the heat almost insupportable. The shekh looked over my shoulder all the time, and at the end pronounced it *temam*—"perfect." I then proposed climbing the mountain, as he had said one could see the whole world from the top. He was bound to go with me wherever I went, but shrank from climbing El Berkel. It would require two hours, he said, to go up. After eating a slice of watermelon in the shade of one of the pillars, I took off my jacket and started alone, and very soon he was at my side, panting and sweating with the exertion. We began at the point most easy of ascent yet found it toilsome enough. After passing the loose fragments which lie scattered around the base, we came upon a steep slope of sliding sand and stones, blown from the desert.

We sank in this nearly to the knees, and slid backward at each step at least half as far as we had stepped forward. We were obliged to rest every three or four steps, and take breath, moistening the sand meanwhile with a rain of sweat-drops. "Surely there is no other mountain in the world so high as this," said the shekh, and I was ready to agree with him. At last we reached the top, a nearly level space of about ten acres. There was a pleasant breeze here, but the Ethiopian world below was dozing in an atmosphere of blue heat. There was too much vapor in the air to see the farthest objects distinctly, and the pyramids of Noori, further up the river, on its eastern bank, were not visible. The Nile lay curved in the middle of the picture like a flood of molten glass, on either side its palmy "knots of paradise," then the wheat fields, lying like slabs of emerald against the tawny sands, that rolled in hot drifts and waves and long ridgy swells to the horizon north and south, broken here and there by the jagged porphyry peaks. Before me, to the south-east, were the rugged hills of the Beyooda; behind me, to the north and west, the burning wilderness of the Great Nubian Desert.

As I sought for my glass, to see the view more distinctly, I became aware that I had lost my pocket-book on the way up. As it contained some money and all my keys, I was not a little troubled, and mentioned my loss to Shekh Mohammed. We immediately returned in search of it, sliding down the sand and feeling with our hands and feet therein. We had made more than half the descent, and I began to consider the search hopeless, when the shekh, who was a little in advance, cried out: "O Sidi! God be praised! God be praised!" He saw the corner sticking out of the sand, took it up, kissed it, and laid it on one eye, while he knelt with his old head turned up, that I might take it off. I tied it securely in a corner of my shawl and we slid to the bottom, where we found Achmet and the young shekhs in the shade of a huge projecting cliff, with breakfast spread out on the sand.

It was now noon, and only the pyramids remained to be seen on that side of the river. The main group is about a third of a mile from the mountain, on the ridge of a sand-hill. There are six pyramids, nearly entire, and the foundations of others. They are almost precisely similar to those of the real Meroë, each having a small exterior chamber on the eastern side. Like the latter, they are built of sandstone blocks, only filled at the corners, which are covered with a hem or moulding; the sides of two of them are convex. On all of them the last eight or ten courses next the top have been smoothed to follow the slope of the side. It was no doubt intended to finish them all in this manner. One of them has also the corner moulding rounded, so as to form a scroll, like that on the cornice of many of the Egyptian temples. They are not more than fifty feet in height, with very narrow bases. One of them, indeed, seems to be the connecting link between the pyramid and the obelisk. Nearer the river is an older pyramid, though no regular courses of stone are to be seen any longer. These sepulchral remains, however, are much inferior to those of Meroë.

The oldest names found at Napata are those of Amenoph III. and Remeses II. (1630 B. C. and 1400 B. C.) both of whom subjected Nubia to their rule. The remains of Ethiopian art, however, go no further than King Tirkaka, 730 B. C.—the Ethiopian monarch, who, in the time of Hezekiah, marched into Palestine to meet Sennacherib, King of Assyria. Napata, therefore, occupies an intermediate place in history between Thebes and Meroë, showing the gradual southward progress of Egyptian art and civilization. It is a curious fact that the old religion of Egypt should have been here met face to face, and overthrown, by Christianity, which, starting in the mountains of Abyssinia, followed the course of the Nile northward. In the sixth century of our era, Ethiopia and Nubia were converted to Christianity and remained thus until the fourteenth century, when they fell beneath the sword of Islam.

We rode back to the town on our uneasy donkey saddles. As I wanted small money, the shekh proposed my calling on Achmedar Kashif, the Governor of Merawe and Ambukol, and asking him to change me some *medjids*. We accordingly rode under the imposing stone piles of the old kings to the residence of the Kashif, a two-story mud house with a portico in front, covered with matting. It was the day for the people of the neighborhood to pay their *tulbeh*, or tax, and some of his officers were seated on the ground in the shade, settling this business with a crowd of Arabs. I went up stairs to the divan, and found the Kashif rolling himself in his shawl for dinner, which his slaves had just brought up. He received me cordially, and I took my seat beside him on the floor and dipped my fingers into the various dishes. There was a pan of baked fish, which was excellent, after which came a tray of scarlet watermelon slices, coffee, pipes, and lastly a cup of hot sugar syrup. He readily promised to change me the money, and afterwards accepted my invitation to dinner.

I stayed an hour longer, and had an opportunity of witnessing some remarkable scenes. A woman came in to complain of her husband, who had married another woman, leaving her with one child. She had a cow of her own, which he had forcibly taken and given to his new wife. The Kashif listened to her story, and then detaching his seal from his button-hole, gave it to an attendant, as a summons which the delinquent dare not disobey. A company of men afterwards came to adjust some dispute about a water-mill. They spoke so fast and in such a violent and excited manner, that I could not comprehend the nature of the quarrel; but the group they made was most remarkable. They leaned forward with flashing teeth and eyes, holding the folds of their long mantles with one hand, while they dashed and hurled the other in the air, in the violence of their contention. One would suppose that they must all perish the next instant by spontaneous combustion. The Kashif was calmness itself all the while, and after getting the particulars—a feat which I considered marvellous—quietly gave his decision. Some of the party protested against it, whereupon he listened attentively, but, finding no reason to change his judgment, repeated it. Still the Arabs screamed and gesticulated. He ejaculated *imshee!* ("get away!") in a thundering tone, dealt the nearest ones a vigorous blow with his fist, and speedily cleared the divan. The Kashif offered to engage camels and a guide for New Dongola, in case I chose to go by the Nubian Desert—a journey of three or four days, through a terrible waste of sand and rocks, without grass or water. The route being new, had some attractions, but I afterwards decided to adhere to my original plan of following the course of the river to Ambukol and Old Dongola.

I made preparations for giving the Kashif a handsome dinner. I had mutton and fowls, and Achmet procured eggs, milk and vegetables, and set his whole available force to work Meanwhile the shekh and I sat on the divan outside the door and exchanged compliments. He sold me a sword from Bornou, which he had purchased from an Arab merchant who had worn it to Mecca. He told me he considered me as his two eyes, and would give me one of his sons, if I desired. Then he rendered me an account of his family, occasionally pointing out the members thereof, as they passed to and fro among the palms. He asked me how many children I had, and I was obliged to confess myself wholly his inferior in this respect. "God grant," said he, "that when you go back to your own country, you may have many sons, just like that one," pointing to a naked Cupidon of four years old, of a rich chocolate-brown color. "God grant it," I was obliged to reply, conformably to the rules of Arab politeness, but I mentally gave the words the significance of "God forbid it!" The shekh, who was actually quite familiar with the ruins in Ethiopia, and an excellent guide to them, informed me that they were four thousand years old; that the country was at that time in possession of the English, but afterwards the Arabs drove them out. This corresponds with an idea very prevalent in Egypt, that the temples were built by the forefathers of the Frank travellers, who once lived there, and that is the reason why the Franks make a *hadj*, or pilgrimage to see them. I related to the shekh the history of the warlike Queen Candace, who once lived there, in her capital of Napata, and he was so much interested in the story that he wrote it down, transforming her name into *Kandasiyeh*. Some later traveller will be surprised to find a tradition of the aforesaid queen, no doubt with many grotesque embellishments, told him on the site of her capital.

Dinner was ready at sunset, the appointed time, but the Kashif did not come. I waited one hour, two hours; still he came not. Thereupon I invited Achmet and the shekh, and we made an excellent dinner in Turkish style. It was just over, and I was stretched out without jacket or tarboosh, enjoying my pipe, when we heard the ferrymen singing on the river below, and soon afterwards the Kashif appeared at the door. He apologized, saying he had been occupied in his divan. I had dinner served again, and tasted the dishes to encourage him, but it appeared that he had not been able to keep his appetite so long, and had dined also. Still, he ate enough to satisfy me that he relished my dishes, and afterwards drank a sherbet of sugar and vinegar with great gusto. He had three or four attendants, and with him came a Berber merchant, who had lately been in Khartoum. I produced my sketch-book and maps, and astonished the company for three hours. I happened to have a book of Shaksperean views, which I had purchased in Stratford-on-Avon. The picture of Shakspere gave the Kashif and shekh great delight, and the former considered the hovel in which the poet was born, "very grand." The church in Stratford they thought a marvellous building, and the merchant confessed that it was greater than Lattif Pasha's palace in Khartoum, which he had supposed to be the finest building in the world.

The next morning the shekh proposed going with me to the remains of a temple, half an hour distant, on the eastern bank of the river; the place, he said, where the people found the little images, agates and scarabei, which they brought to me in great quantities. After walking a mile and a half over the sands, which have here crowded the vegetation to the very water's edge, we came to a broad mound of stones, broken bricks and pottery, with a foundation wall of heavy limestone blocks, along the western side. There were traces of doors and niches, and on the summit of the mound the pedestals of columns similar to those of El Berkel. From this place commenced a waste of ruins, extending for nearly two miles towards the north-west, while the breadth, from east to west, was about equal. For the most part, the buildings were entirely concealed by the sand, which was filled with fragments of pottery and glass, and with shining pebbles of jasper, agate and chalcedony. Half a mile further, we struck on another mound, of greater extent, though the buildings were entirely level with the earth. The foundations of pillars were abundant, and fragments of circular limestone blocks lay crumbling to pieces in the rubbish. The most interesting object was a mutilated figure of blue granite, of which only a huge pair of wings could be recognized. The shekh said that all the Frank travellers who came there broke off a piece and carried it away with them. I did not follow their example. Towards the river were many remains of crude brick walls, and the ground was strewn with pieces of excellent hard-burnt bricks. The sand evidently conceals many interesting objects. I saw in one place, where it had fallen in, the entrance to a chamber, wholly below the surface. The Arabs were at work in various parts of the plain, digging up the sand, which they filled in baskets and carried away on donkeys. The shekh said it contained salt, and was very good to make wheat grow, whence I inferred that the earth is nitrous. We walked for an hour or two over the ruins, finding everywhere the evidence that a large capital had once stood on the spot. The bits of water-jars which we picked up were frequently painted and glazed with much skill. The soil was in many places wholly composed of the debris of the former dwellings. This was, without doubt, the ancient Napata, of which Djebel Berkel was only the necropolis. Napata must have been one of the greatest cities of Ancient Africa, after Thebes, Memphis and Carthage. I felt a peculiar interest in wandering over the site of that half-forgotten capital, whereof the ancient historians knew little more than we. That so little is said by them in relation to it is somewhat surprising, notwithstanding its distance from the Roman frontier.

In the afternoon, Achmet, with great exertion, backed by all the influence of the Kashif, succeeded in obtaining ten piastres worth of bread. The latter sent me the shekh of the camels, who furnished me with three animals and three men, to Wadi Halfa, at ninety-five piastres apiece. They were to accompany my caravan to Ambukol, on the Dongolese frontier where the camels from Khartoum were to be discharged. I spent the rest of the day talking with the shekh on religious matters. He gave me the history of Christ, in return for which I related to him that of the Soul of Mahomet, from one hundred and ten thousand years before the Creation of the World, until his birth, according to the Arab Chronicles. This quite overcame him. He seized my hand and kissed it with fervor, acknowledging me as the more holy man of the two. He said he had read the Books of Moses, the Psalms of David and the Gospel of Christ, but liked David best, whose words flowed like the sound of the *zumarra*, or Arab flute. To illustrate it, he chanted one of the Psalms in a series of not unmusical cadences. He then undertook to repeat the ninety-

attributes of God, and thought he succeeded, but I noticed that several of the epithets were repeated more than once.

The north wind increased during the afternoon, and towards night blew a very gale. The sand came in through the door in such quantities that I was obliged to move my bed to a more sheltered part of my house. Numbers of huge black beetles, as hard and heavy as grape-shot, were dislodged from their holes and dropped around me with such loud raps that I was scarcely able to sleep. The sky was dull and dark, hardly a star to be seen, and the wind roared in the palms like a November gale let loose among the boughs of a Northern forest. It was a grand roar, drowning the sharp rustle of the leaves when lightly stirred, and rocked my fancies as gloriously as the pine. In another country than Africa, I should have predicted rain, hail, equinoctial storms, or something of the kind, but there I went to sleep with a positive certainty of sunshine on the morrow.

I was up at dawn, and had breakfast by sunrise; nevertheless, we were obliged to wait a long while for the camels, or rather the pestiferous Kababish who went after them. The new men and camels were in readiness, as the camel-shekh came over the river to see that all was right. The Kashif sent me a fine black ram, as provision for the journey. Finally, towards eight o'clock, every thing was in order and my caravan began to move. I felt real regret at leaving the pleasant spot, especially the beautiful bower of palms at the door of my house. When my effects had been taken out, the shekh called his eldest son Saad, his wife Fatima, and their two young sons, to make their salaams. They all kissed my hand, and I then gave the old man and Saad my backsheesh for their services.

The shekh took the two gold medjids readily, without any hypocritical show of reluctance, and lifted my hand to his lips and forehead. When all was ready, he repeated the *Fatha*, or opening paragraph of the Koran, as each camel rose from its knees, in order to secure the blessing of Allah upon our journey. He then took me in his arms, kissed both my cheeks, and with tears in his eyes, stood showering pious phrases after me, till I was out of hearing. With no more vanity or selfishness than is natural to an Arab, Shekh Mohammed Abd e'-Djebàl had many excellent qualities, and there are few of my Central African acquaintances whom I would rather see again.

CHAPTER XXXIV.

OLD DONGOLA AND NEW DONGOLA.

Appearance of the Country—Korti—The Town of Ambukol—The Caravan reorganized—A Fiery Ride—We reach Edabbe—An Illuminated Landscape—A Torment—Nubian Agriculture—Old Dongola—The Palace-Mosque of the Nubian Kings—A Panorama of Desolation—The Old City—Nubian Gratitude—Another Sand-Storm—A Dreary Journey—The Approach to Handak—A House of Doubtful Character—The Inmates—Journey to El Ordee (New Dongola)—Khoorshid Bey—Appearance of the Town.

I LEFT Abdôm on the morning of February twentieth. Our road lay southward, along the edge of the wheat-fields, over whose waves we saw the island-like groups of palms at a little distance. For several miles the bank of the river was covered with a continuous string of villages. After skirting this glorious garden land for two hours, we crossed a sandy tract, overgrown with the poisonous euphorbia, to avoid a curve in the river. During the whole of the afternoon, we travelled along the edge of the cultivated land, and sometimes in the midst of it, obliging my camels to stumble clumsily over the raised trenches which carried water from the river to the distant parts of the fields. Large, ruined forts of unburnt brick, exceedingly picturesque at a distance, stood at intervals between the desert and the harvest-land.

The next morning was hot and sultry, with not a breath of air stirring. I rose at dawn and walked ahead for two hours, through thickets of euphorbia higher than my head, and over patches of strong, dark-green grass. The *sakias* were groaning all along the shore, and the people every where at work in the fields. The wheat was in various stages of growth, from the first thick green of the young blades to the full head. Barley was turning a pale yellow, and the dookhn, the heads of which had already been gathered, stood brown and dry. Djebel Deeka, on my right, rose bold and fair above the lines of palms, and showed a picturesque glen winding in between its black-purple peaks. It was a fine feature of the landscape, which would have been almost too soft and lovely without it.

Before nine o'clock we passed the large town of Korti, which, however, is rather a cluster of small towns, scattered along between the wheat-fields and the river. Some of the houses were large and massive, and with their blank walls and block-like groups, over which the doum-tree spread its arch and the date-palm hung its feathery crown, made fine African pictures—admirable types of the scenery along the Nubian Nile. Beyond the town we came upon a hot, dusty plain, sprinkled with stunted euphorbia, over which I could see the point where the Nile turns westward. Towards noon we reached the town of Ambukol, which I found to be a large agglomeration of mud and human beings, on the sand-hills, a quarter of a mile from the river. An extensive pile of mud in the centre denoted a fortress or government station of some sort There were a few lazy Arabs sitting on the ground, on the shady side of the walls, and some women going back and forth with water-jars, but otherwise, for all the life it presented, the place might have been deserted. The people we me' saluted me with much respect, and those who were seated rose and remained standing until I had passed. I did not enter the town, but made direct for a great acacia tree near its western end. The nine camels and nine men of my caravan all rested under the shade, and there was room for as many more. A number of Arabs looked on from a distance, or hailed my camel-men, to satisfy their curiosity regarding me, but no one came near or annoyed us in any way. I took breakfast leisurely on my carpet, drank half a gourd of mareesa, and had still an hour to wait, before the new camels were laden. The Kababish, who had accompanied me from Khartoum, wanted a certificate, so I certified that Saïd was a good camel-man and Mohammed worthless as a guide. They then drank a parting jar of mareesa, and we went from under the cool acacia into the glare of the fierce sun. Our road all the afternoon was in the Desert, and we were obliged to endure a most intense and sultry heat.

The next day I travelled westward over long *akabas*, or reaches of the Desert, covered with clumps of thorns, nebbuk and the jasmine tree. The long mountain on the opposite bank was painted in rosy light against the sky, as if touched with the beams of a perpetual sunrise. My eyes always turned to it with a sense of refreshment, after the weary glare of the sand. In the morning there was a brisk wind from the north-east, but towards noon it veered to the south-west, and then to the south, continuing to blow all day with great force. As I rode westward through the hot hours of the afternoon, it played against my face like a sheet of flame. The sky became obscured with a dull, bluish haze, and the sands of the Beyooda, on my left, glimmered white and dim, as if swept by the blast of a furnace. There were occasional gusts that made the flesh shrink as if touched with a hot iron, and I found it impossible to bear the wind full on my face. One who has never felt it, cannot conceive the withering effect of such a heat. The earth seems swept with the first fires of that conflagration beneath which the heavens will shrivel up as a scroll, and you instinctively wonder to see the palms standing green and unsinged. My camel-men crept behind the camels to get away from it, and Achmet and Ali muffled up their faces completely. I could not endure the sultry heat occasioned by such a preparation, and so rode all day with my head in the fire.

About three o'clock in the afternoon we approached the Nile again. There was a grove of sont and doum-trees on the bank, surrounding a large quadrangular structure of clay, with square towers at the corners. Grave-yards stretched for nearly a mile along the edge of the Desert, and six large, dome-like heaps of clay denoted the tombs of as many holy men. We next came upon the ruins of a large village, with a fort and a heavy palace-like building of mud. Before reaching Edabbe, the terminus of the caravan route from Kordofan, the same evening, I rode completely around the bend of the Nile, so that my dromedary's head was at last turned towards Wadi Halfa. I was hot, tired, and out of temper, but a gourd of cool water, at the first house we reached, made all right again. There were seven vessels in the river, waiting for the caravans. One had just arrived from Kordofan, and the packages of gum were piled up along the shore. We were immediately followed by the sailors, who were anxious that I should hire their vessels. I rode past the town, which does not contain more than thirty houses in all, and had my tent pitched on the river bank.

The Nile is here half a mile broad, and a long reach of his current is visible to the north and south. The opposite bank was high and steep, lined at the water's edge with a belt of beans and lupins, behind which rose a line of palms, and still higher the hills of pale, golden-hued sand, spotted like a leopard's hide, with clumps of a small mimosa. The ground was a clear, tawny yellow, but the spots were deep emerald. Below the gorgeous drapery of these hills, the river glittered in a dark, purple-blue sheet. The coloring of the mid-African landscapes is truly unparalleled. To me, it became more than a simple sense; it grew to be an appetite. When, after a journey in the Desert, I again beheld the dazzling green palms and wheat-fields of the Nile, I imagined that there was a positive sensation on the retina. I felt, or seemed to feel, physically, the colored rays—beams of pure emerald, topaz and amethystine lustre—as they struck the eye.

At Edabbe I first made acquaintance with a terrible pest, which for many days afterwards occasioned me much torment—a small black fly, as venomous as the musquito, and much more difficult to drive away. I sat during the evening with my head, neck and ears closely bound up, notwithstanding the heat. After the flies left, a multitude of beetles, moths, winged ants and other nameless creatures came in their place. I sat and sweltered, murmuring for the waters of Abana and Pharpar, rivers of Damascus, and longing for a glass of sherbet cooled with the snows of Lebanon.

We were up with the first glimmering of dawn. The sky

was dull and hazy, and the sun came up like a shield of rusty copper, as we started. Our path lay through the midst of the cultivated land, sometimes skirting the banks of the Nile, and sometimes swerving off to the belts of sont and euphorbia which shut out the sand. The sakias, turned by a yoke of oxen each, were in motion on the river, and the men were wading through the squares of wheat, cotton and barley, turning the water into them. All farming processes, from sowing to reaping, were going on at the same time. The cultivated land was frequently more than a mile in breadth, and all watered from the river. The sakias are taxed four hundred and seventy-five piastres each, notwithstanding the sum fixed by Government is only three hundred. The remainder goes into the private treasuries of the Governors. For this reason, many persons, unable to pay the tax, emigrate into Kordofan and elsewhere. This may account for the frequent tracts of the finest soil which are abandoned. I passed many fine fields, given up to the halfeh grass, which grew most rank and abundant. My dromedary had a rare time of it, cropping the juicy bunches as he went along. The country is thickly settled, and our road was animated with natives, passing back and forth.

About noon, we saw in advance, on the eastern bank of the Nile, a bold, bluff ridge, crowned with a large square building. This the people pointed out to us as the location of Old Dongola. As we approached nearer, a long line of mud buildings appeared along the brow of the hill, whose northern slope was cumbered with ruins. We left the caravan track and rode down to the ferry place at the river, over a long stretch of abandoned fields, where the cotton was almost choked out with grass, and the beans and lentils were growing wild in bunches. After my tent had been pitched in a cotton-patch, I took a grateful bath in the river, and then crossed in the ferry-boat to the old town. The hill upon which it is built terminates abruptly in a precipice of red sandstone rock, about a hundred feet in height. Four enormous fragments have been broken off, and lie as they fell, on the edge of the water. A steep path through drifts of sliding yellow sand leads around the cliffs, up to the dwellings. I found the ascent laborious, as the wind, which had veered to the west, was as hot as on the previous day; but a boatman and one of my camel-men seized a hand each and hauled me up most conveniently. At the summit, all was ruin; interminable lines of walls broken down, and streets filled up with sand. I went first to the Kasr, or Palace, which stands on the highest part of the hill. It is about forty feet in height, having two stories and a broad foundation wall, and is built mostly of burnt brick and sandstone. It is the palace of the former Dongolese Kings, and a more imposing building than one would expect to find in such a place. Near the entrance is an arched passage, leading down to some subterranean chambers, which I did not explore. It needed something more than the assurance of an old Nubian, however, to convince me that there was an underground passage from this place to Djebel Berkel. A broad flight of stone steps ascended to the second story, in which are many chambers and passages. The walls are covered with Arabic inscriptions, written in the plaster while it was yet moist. The hall of audience had once a pavement of marble, several blocks of which still remain, and the ceiling is supported in the centre by three shafts of granite, taken from some old Egyptian ruin. The floors are covered with tiles of burnt brick, but the palm-logs which support them have given away in many places, rendering one's footing insecure. Behind the hall of audience is a passage, with a niche, in each side of which is also an ancient pillar of granite. From the tenor of one of the Arabic inscriptions, it appears that the building was originally designed for a mosque, and that it was erected in the year 1317, by Saf-ed-deen Abdallah, after a victory over the infidels.

I ascended to the roof of the palace, which is flat and paved with stones. The view was most remarkable. The height on which Old Dongola is built, falls off on all sides, inland as well as towards the river, so that to the east one overlooks a wide extent of desert—low hills of red sand, stretching away to a dim, hot horizon. To the north, the hill slopes gradually to the Nile, covered with the ruins of old buildings. North-east, hardly visible through the sandy haze, rose a high, isolated peak, with something like a tower on its summit. To the south and east the dilapidated city covered the top of the hill—a mass of ashy-gray walls of mud and stone, for the most part roofless and broken down, while the doors, courts and alleys between them were half choked up with the loose sand blown in from the Desert. The graveyards of the former inhabitants extended for more than a mile through the sand, over the dreary hills behind the town. Among them were a great number of conical, pointed structures of clay and stones, from twenty to thirty feet in height. The camel-men said they were the tombs of *rossool*—prophets, or holy men. I counted twenty-five in that portion of the cemetery which was visible. The whole view was one of entire and absolute deso lation, heightened the more by the clouds of sand which filled the air, and which, in their withering heat, seemed to be raining ruin upon the land.

I afterwards walked through the city, and was surprised to find many large, strong houses of stone and burnt brick, with spacious rooms, the walls of which were plastered and whitewashed. The lintels of the doors and windows were stone, the roofs in many places, where they still remained, covered with tiles, and every thing gave evidence of a rich and powerful city. Now, probably not more than one-fifth of the houses are inhabited. Here and there the people have spread a roofing of mats over the open walls, and nestled themselves in the sand. I saw several such places, the doors, or rather entrances to which, were at the bottom of loose sand-hills that constantly slid down and filled the dingy dwellings. In my walk I met but one or two persons, but as we returned again to the river, I saw a group of Dongolese women on the highest part of the cliff. They were calling in shrill tones and waving their hands to some persons in the ferry-boat on the river below, and needed no fancy to represent the daughters of Old Dongola lamenting over its fall.

Some Dongolese *djellabiát*, or merchants, just returned from Kordofan, were in the ferry-boat. One of them showed me a snuff-box which he had bought from a native of Fertit, beyond Dar-Für. It was formed of the shell of some fruit, with a silver neck attached. By striking the head of the box on the thumb-nail, exactly one pinch was produced. The raïs took off his mantle, tied one end of it to the ring in the bow and stood thereon, holding the other end with both hands stretched above his head. He made a fine bronze figure-head for the boat, and it was easy to divine her name: *The Nubian.* We had on board a number of copper-hued women, whose eyelids were stained with *kohl*, which gave them a ghastly appearance.

Soon after my tent had been pitched, in the afternoon, a man came riding up from the river on a donkey, leading a horse behind him. He had just crossed one of the water-courses on his donkey, and was riding on, holding the horse's rope in his hand, when the animal started back at the water-course, jerking the man over the donkey's tail and throwing him violently on the ground. He lay as if dead for a quarter of an hour, but Achmet finally brought him to consciousness by pouring the contents of a leathern water-flask over his head, and raising him to a sitting posture. His brother, who had charge of a sakia on the bank, brought me an angareb in the evening, in acknowledgment of this good office. It is a good trait in the people, that they are always grateful for kindness. The angareb, however, did not prove of much service, for I was so beset by the black gnats that it was impossible to sleep. They assailed my nose, mouth, ears and eyes in such numbers that I was almost driven mad. I rubbed my face with strong vinegar, but it only seemed to attract them the more. I unwound my turban, and rolled it around my neck and ears, but they crept under the folds and buzzed and bit until I was forced to give up the attempt.

Our road, the next morning, lay near the river, through tracks of thick halfeh, four or five feet high. We constantly passed the ruins of villages and the naked frames of abandoned sakias. The soil was exceedingly rich, as the exuberant growth of halfeh proved, but for miles and miles there was no sign of life. The tyranny of the Turks has depopulated one of the fairest districts of Nubia. The wind blew violently from the north, and the sandy haze and gray vapor in the air became so dense that I could scarcely distinguish the opposite bank of the Nile. The river was covered with white caps, and broke on the beach below with a wintry roar. As we journeyed along through the wild green grass and orchards of sont, passing broken walls and the traces of old water-courses, I could have believed myself travelling through some deserted landscape of the North. I was chilled with the strong wind, which roared in the sont and made my beard whistle under my nose like a wisp of dry grass. Several ships passed us, scudding up stream under bare poles, and one, which had a single reef shaken out of her large sail, dashed by like a high-pressure steamer.

After two or three hours we passed out of this region. The Desert extended almost to the water's edge, and we had nothing but sand and thorns. The wind by this time was more furious than ever, and the air was so full of sand that we could not see more than a hundred yards on either hand. The sun gave out a white, ghastly light, which increased the dreariness of the day. All trace of the road was obliterated, and we could only travel at random among the thorns, following the course of the Nile, which we were careful to keep in view. My eyes, ears, and nostrils were soon filled with sand, and I was obliged to bind my turban so as nearly to cover my face, leaving only space enough to take a blind view of the way we were going. At breakfast time, after two hours of this martyrdom, I found a clump of thorns so thick as to shut off the wind, but no sooner had I dismounted and crept under its shelter than I experienced a scorching heat from the sun, and was attacked by myriads of the black gnats. I managed to eat something in a mad sort of way, beating my face and ears continually, and was glad to thrust my head again into the sand-storm, which drove off the worse pests. So for hours we pursued our journey. I could not look in the face of the wind, which never once fell. The others suffered equally, and two of the camel-men lagged so, that we lost sight of them entirely. It was truly a good fortune that I did not take the short road, east of the Nile, from Merawe to New Dongola. In the terrible wastes of the Nubian Desert, we could scarcely have survived such a storm.

Nearly all the afternoon we passed over deserted tracts, which were once covered with flourishing fields. The water-courses extend for nearly two miles from the river, and cross the road at intervals of fifty yards. But now the villages are level with the earth, and the sand whistles over the traces of fields and gardens, which it has not yet effaced. Two hours before sunset the sun disappeared, and I began to long for the town of Handak, our destination. Achmet and I were ahead, and the other camels were not to be seen any longer, so as sunset came on I grew restless and uneasy. The palms by this time had appeared again on the river's brink, and there was a village on our left, in the sand. We asked again for Handak. "Just at the corner of yon palms," said the people. They spoke with a *near* emphasis, which encouraged me. The Arabic dialect of Central Africa has one curious characteristic, which evidently springs from the want of a copious vocabulary. Degree, or intensity of meaning is usually indicated by accent alone. Thus, when they point to an object near at hand they say: *henăk*, "there;" if it is a moderate distance off, they lengthen the sound into "*hen-a-a-ak*;" while, if it is so far as to be barely visible, the last syllable is sustained with a full breath—"*hen-a-a-a-a-a-ăk!*" In the same way, *saă* signifies "an hour;" *sa-a-a-ă*, "two hours," &c. This habit of speech gives the language a very singular and eccentric character.

We pushed on till the spot was reached, but as far ahead as the sand would permit us to see, could discern no house. We asked again; the town commenced at the next corner of the palms ahead of us. I think this thing must have happened to us five or six times, till at last I got into that peculiarly amiable mood which sees nothing good in Heaven or Earth. If my best friend had come to meet me, I should have given him but a sour greeting. My eyes were blinded, my head dull and stupid, and my bones sore from twelve hours in the saddle. As it grew dark, we were overtaken by four riders mounted on fine dromedaries. They were going at a sweeping trot, and our beasts were ambitious enough to keep pace with them for some time. One of them was a stately shekh, with a white robe and broad gold border and fringe. From what the people said of him, I took him to be the Melek, or King of Dongola.

Meanwhile, it was growing dark. We could see nothing of the town, though a woman who had been walking beside us, said we were there already. She said she had a fine house, which we could have for the night, since it was almost impossible for a tent to stand in such a wind. As I had already dipped into the night, I determined to reach Handak at all hazards, and after yet another hour, succeeded. Achmet and I dismounted in a ruined court-yard, and while I sat on a broken wall, holding the camels, he went to look for our men. It was a dismal place, in the gathering darkness, with the wind howling and the sand drifting on all sides, and I wondered what fiend had ever tempted me to travel in Africa. Before long the woman appeared and guided us to a collection of miserable huts on the top of the hill. Her fine house proved to be a narrow, mud-walled room, with a roof of smoked dourra-stalks. It shut off the wind, however, and when I entered and found the occupants (two other women), talking to each other by the light of a pile of blazing corn-stalks, it looked absolutely cheerful. I stretched myself out on one of the angarebs, and soon relapsed into a better humor. But I am afraid we were not lodged in the most respectable house of Handak, for the women showed no disposition to leave, when we made preparations for sleeping. They paid no attention to my requests, except by some words of endearment, which, from such creatures, were sufficiently disgusting, and I was obliged to threaten them with forcible ejection, before they vacated the house. The camel-men informed me that the place is notorious for its harlotry.

As we had made a forced march of forty miles in one day, I gave the caravan a rest until noon, and treated the men to mutton and mareesa. Prices had already increased, since leaving Soudân, and I could not procure a sheep for less than seventeen piastres. The women, who had returned at sunrise begged me to give them the entrails, which they cut into pieces and ate raw, with the addition of some onions and salt. The old woman told me a piteous tale of the death of her son, and her own distress, and how King Dyaab (who had passed through Handak the day previous, on his way to Dar El-Màhass) had given her two piastres, and she hoped I would also give her something, that she might buy a new dress. I gave her the same as King Dyaab, which she at once asked me to take back again, as she expected at least nine piastres. Seeing I was about to take her at her word, she made haste to secure the money. Her youngest daughter, a bold, masculine thing, with hair cut close to her head, now came to me for backsheesh. "Oh!" said I, "you are going to do as the old woman did, are you?" "No," she exclaimed; "if you will give me two piastres, I will ask for no more. The old woman is a miserable wretch!" and she spat upon the ground to show her disgust. "Go!" I said; "I shall give nothing to a girl who insults her mother."

From Handak to El Ordee is two days' journey. The country presents the same aspect of desertion and ruin as that in the neighborhood of Old Dongola. Untenanted villages line the road during nearly the whole distance. The face of the country is level, and there is no mountain to be seen on either bank of the Nile. It is a melancholy, deserted region, showing only palms growing wildly and rankly along the river, fields covered with halfeh, water-courses broken down, sakias dismantled, and everywhere dwellings in ruin. Here and there a few inhabitants still lingered, tending their fields of stunted cotton, or watering some patches of green wheat. The general aspect of desolation was heightened by the strong north-wind, which filled the air with clouds of sand, making the sunshine so cold and white, that all the color faded out of the landscape. The palms were dull and dark, and the sand-hills beyond the Nile a dead, lifeless yellow. All this district swarms with black gnats, which seemed to have been sent as a curse upon its desertion, for they never appeared where the country was thickly inhabited and all the soil cultivated.

On the first day after leaving Handak, we passed the villages of Kiar, Sori and Urub, and stopped at a place called Tetti. The wind blew so violently during the night that everything in my tent, my head included, was thickly covered with dust. The next day we passed a large town called Hannak. The greater part of it was levelled to the earth, and evidently by violence, for the walls were of stone. It stood on a rocky rise, near the river, and had on its highest part the remains of some defences, and a small palace, in tolerable preservation. The hills behind were covered for half a mile with the graves of the former inhabitants, among which I noticed the cones and pyramids of several holy men. As we approached El Ordee (by which name New Dongola is usually called), the appearance of the country improved, although there was still as much deserted as cultivated land. The people we met were partly Dongolese and partly Arabs from the Desert, the latter with bushy hair, shining with grease, and spears in their hands. They cheered us with the news that El Ordee was not distant, and we would arrive there at *asser*—the time of afternoon prayer, two hours before sunset. My camel-men rejoiced at the prospect of again having mareesa to drink, and I asked old Mohammed if he supposed the saints drank mareesa in Paradise. "Why!" he joyfully exclaimed; "do you know about Paradise?" "Certainly;" said I, "if you lead a good life, you will go straight there, but if you are wicked, Eblis will carry you down into the flames." "Wallah!" said the old fellow, aside to Achmet; "but this is a good Frank. He certainly has Islam in his heart."

About two o'clock, we descried the minaret of El Ordee, its sugar-loaf top glittering white in the sun. The place was three or four miles distant, and we did not reach it until after more than an hour's travel. As we approached, it presented the usual appearance of the Nubian towns—a long line of blank mud walls, above which rise, perhaps, the second stories of a few more ambitious mud houses; here a sycamore, there a palm or two, denoting a garden within; a wide waste of sand round about, some filthy people basking in the sun, and a multitude of the vilest kind of dogs. Near the river there are some fine large gardens, as in Khartoum. I had already decided to stop two days, to rest my caravan, before commencing the long and toilsome march to Wadi-Halfa, but instead of hiring a house I went around the town and pitched my tent on the northern side, on a sandy plain, where I secured pure air and freedom from molestation by the inhabitants.

The morning after my arrival, the Governor, Khoorshid Bey, called at my tent, and I returned the visit in the afternoon. He was a stout, fair-skinned and brown-bearded man of thirty-eight, and looked more like an American than a Turk. I found him in the shop of a Turkish merchant, opposite the door of the mosque, which is built in the centre of the bazaar. Two soldiers were in attendance, and brought me coffee and sherbet. The Bey was particularly anxious to know whether the railroad from Alexandria to Cairo would be built, and how much it would cost. While I was sitting with him, the *mollahs* were chanting in the mosque opposite, as it was the Moslem Sunday, and groups of natives were flocking thither to say their prayers. Presently the voice of the muezzin was heard from the top of the minaret, chanting in a loud, melo dious, melancholy cadence the call to prayer—a singular cry, the effect of which, especially at sunset, is really poetic and suggestive. I took my leave, as the Bey was expected to perform his devotions with the other worshippers.

The town may be seen in an hour. It contains no sights, except the bazaar, which has about twenty tolerable shops, principally stocked with cottons and calicoes, and a great quantity of white shawls with crimson borders, which the people here are fond of wearing over their shoulders. Outside the bazaar, which has a roof of palm-logs covered with matting, are a few shops, containing spices, tobacco, beads, trinkets and the like small articles. Beyond this was the *soog*, where the people came with their coarse tobacco, baskets of raw cotton, onions, palm-mats, gourds, dates, faggots of fire-wood, sheep and fowls. In this market-place, which ascended and descended with the dirt-heaps left from ruined houses, there were four ostriches, which walked about, completely naturalized to the place. One of them was more than eight feet high—a most powerful and graceful creature. They were not out of place, among the groups of wild-haired Kababish and Bishàree, who frequented the market.

Below the river-bank, which is high, upwards of twenty small trading craft were lying. One had just arrived with a load of lime, which the naked sailors were carrying up the bank in baskets, on their heads. The channel of the Nile here is mainly taken up with the large, sandy island of Tor, and the stream is very narrow. The shore was crowded with women, washing clothes or filling their water-jars, men hoisting full water-skins on the backs of donkeys, and boys of all shades from whity-yellow to perfect black, bathing and playing on the brink. The northern part of the town appeared to be deserted, and several spacious two-story buildings were falling into ruins. I noticed not more than half a dozen houses which would be considered handsome in Berber or Khartoum. El Ordee ranks next after those places, in all the Egyptian territory beyond Assouan, but has the disadvantage of being more filthy than they.

CHAPTER XXXV.

JOURNEY THROUGH DAR EL-MÀHASS AND SUKKÔT.

We start for Wadi-Halfa—The Plague of Black Gnats—Mohammed's Coffin—The Island of Argo—Market-Day—Scenery of the Nile—Entering Dar El-Màhass—Ruined Fortresses—The Camel-Men—A Rocky Chaos—Fakir Bender—The Akaba of Màhass—Camp in the Wilderness—The Charm of Desolation—The Nile again—Pilgrims from Dar-Fūr—The Struggle of the Nile—An Arcadian Landscape—The Temple of Soleb—Dar Sukkôt—The Land of Dates—The Island of Sai—A Sea of Sand—Camp by the River—A Hyena Barbecue.

WE left El Ordee or New Dongola, before sunrise on the twenty-ninth of February. A boy of about fourteen years old came out from the town, helped load the camels, and insisted on accompanying me to Cairo. As my funds were diminishing, and I had no need of additional service, I refused to take him, and he went home greatly disappointed. We were all in fine health and spirits, from the two days' rest, and our ships of the Desert sailed briskly along the sands, with the palmy coasts green and fair on our right. For some miles from the town the land is tolerably well cultivated, but the grain was all much younger than in the neighborhood of Old Dongola. Beyond this, the country was again deserted and melancholy everywhere villages in ruin, fields given up to sand and thorns, and groves of date trees wasting their vigor in rank, unpruned shoots. The edge of the Desert was covered with grave-yards to a considerable extent, each one boasting its cluster of pyramids and cones, raised over the remains of holy shekhs. Towards noon I dismounted for breakfast in a grove of sont trees, but had no sooner seated myself on my carpet, than the small black flies came in such crowds that I was scarcely able to eat. They assailed my temples, ears, eyes and nostrils, and it was utterly impossible to drive them away. I was half crazy with the infliction, and at night my neck and temples were swollen and covered with blotches worse than those made by mosquito stings In fact, mosquitoes are mild and merciful in comparison. Had not my road been mostly in the Desert, away from the trees, I could scarcely have endured the journey. The few inhabitants along the river kindled fires of green wood and sat in the smoke.

In the afternoon the monotony of the Desert on the western bank was broken by a solitary mountain of a remarkable form It precisely resembled an immense coffin, the ends being apparently cut square off, and as the effect of a powerful mirage lifted it above the horizon, it seemed like the sarcophagus of the Prophet, in the Kaaba, to be suspended between heaven and earth. The long island of Argo, which I saw occasionally across an arm of the Nile, appeared rich and well cultivated. It belongs mostly to Melek Hammed, King of Dongola, who was expected at home the day I passed, on his return from Cairo, where he had been three months or more, for the purpose of representing to Abbas Pasha the distressed condition of the country, and obtaining some melioration of the system of misrule inflicted upon it. Near the town of Argo, on the opposite side of the island my map indicated a ruined temple, and I made a strong effort to see it; but at Binni, which was the nearest point, there was no ferry, and the people knew nothing of the temple nor of any thing else. I left the main road and followed the bank, but the terrible flies drove me away, and so, maddened and disgusted, I came at last to a *sakia*, where the people informed me that the ferry was still ahead and the ruins already some distance behind me. They said this deliberately and carelessly, sitting like black spectres in the midst of thick smoke, while I was crazily beating my ears. "Tell the caravan to go ahead," I said to Achmet, at length, "and don't talk to me of temples until we have got away from these flies."

The next morning Achmet had some difficulty in awaking me, so wrapt was I in dreams of home. I sat shivering in the cool air, trying to discover who and where I was, but the yellow glimmer of my tent-lining in the dim light of dawn soon informed me. During the day we passed through a more thickly settled country, and owing to the partial cultivation of the soil, were less troubled by that Nubian plague, which is always worse about the ruined villages and the fields given up to halfeh grass. It was market-day at the village of Hafier, and we met and passed many natives, some with baskets of raw cotton and some with grain. I noticed one man riding a donkey and carrying before him a large squash, for which he would possibly get twenty paràs (2½ cents). My camel-men, who had neglected to buy dourra in El Ordee, wanted to stop until noon in order to get it, and as I would not wait, remained behind.

The scenery had a wild and picturesque air, from the iso

lated mountain peaks, which now appeared on both sides of the river Djebel Arambo, with its high, precipitous sides and notched summit, stood steeped in soft purple vapor—a beautiful object above the long lines of palms and the green level of the islands in the river. The fields on the western bank were mostly taken up with young wheat, though I saw a single one of ripe barley, which a black Barabra was reaping, cutting off the stalks about one-third of the way below the heads, and depositing them in heaps. By noon, I knew from the land-marks that we must be opposite the island of Tombos, where there are some ruins. I made inquiries for it, but the bank was almost deserted, and the few inhabitants I found gathered in straw huts here and there among the rank palm-groves, could tell me nothing about it. All agreed, however, that there was no ferry at this part of the Nile, and to swim across was out of the question. The crocodiles swarm here, and are quite delicate in their tastes, much preferring white flesh to black. So my hope of Tombos vanished like that of Argo.

Beyond the island is a little ruined village, called Hannek, and here I took leave of Dar Dongola, in which I had been travelling ten days, and entered Dar El-Màhass, the kingdom of my friend Melek Dyaab. The character of the country changed on the very border. Long ridges of loose blocks of sandstone and granite, as at Assouan and Akaba Gerri, in Soudân, appeared in front, at first on the western bank, but soon throwing their lines across the stream and forming weirs and rapids in its current. The river is quite narrow, in some places not a hundred yards broad, and leads a very tortuous course, bearing away towards the north-west, until it meets the majestic barrier of Djebel Foga, when it turns to the north east. About two hours after passing Djebel Arambo, which stands opposite the northern extremity of Tombos, we reached the large and hilly island of Mosul, where the river divides its waters and flows for several miles through deep, crooked, rocky channels, before they meet again. Here there is no cultivation, the stony ridges running to the water's edge. The river-bed is so crowded and jammed with granite rocks, that from the shore it appears in some places to be entirely cut off. At this point there are three castellated mud ruins in sight, which at a distance resemble the old feudal fortresses of Europe. The one nearest which we passed was quadrangular, with corner bastions, three round and one square, all tapering inward towards the top. The lower part of the wall was stone and the upper part mud, while the towers were nearly fifty feet high. That on an island in the river, strongly resembled an Egyptian temple, with its pylons, porticoes, and walls of circuit. They were evidently built before the Turkish invasion, and were probably frontier forts of the Kings of El-Màhass, to prevent incursions from the side of Dongola.

We reached the eastern base of Djebel Foga about four o'clock, and I thought it best to encamp, on account of the camel-men, who had a walk of twenty-three miles with bags of dourra on their shoulders, before they could reach us. I had no sooner selected a place for my tent, on the top of a high bank overlooking the river, than they appeared, much fatigued and greatly vexed at me for leaving them in the lurch. I ordered my pipe to be filled, and smoked quietly, making no reply to their loud complaints, and in a short time the most complete harmony prevailed in our camp. The Nile at this place flowed in the bottom of a deep gorge, filled with rocks.

The banks were almost perpendicular, but covered with a rich growth of halfeh, which our camels greedily cropped, at the hazard of losing their balance and tumbling down into the river. I fancied there was already a taste of Egypt in the mountain air, and flattered myself that I had breathed the last of the languid atmosphere of Soudân.

The next morning led us deeper into the rocky chaos. The bed of the Nile was properly a gorge, so deep was it sunk among the stony hills, and confined within such narrow limits. The ridges of loose blocks of granite and porphyry roll after each other like waves, and their crests assume the most fantastic variety of forms. They are piled in heaps and balanced on each other, topped with round boulders or thrown together in twos and threes, as if some brood of Titan children had been at play in those regions and were frightened away in the midst of their employment. It is impossible to lose the impression that some freak of human or superhuman fancy gave the stones their quaint grouping. Between the ridges are shallow hollows, terminating towards the west in deep, rocky clefts, and opening on the river in crescent-like coves, between the jaggy headlands which tumble their boulders into its bed. High peaks, or rather conical piles of porphyry rock, rise here and there out of this sterile chaos. Toward the east, where the Nile winds away in a long chain of mazy curves, they form ranges and show compact walls and pinnacles. The few palms and the little eddies of wheat sprinkled along both banks of the river, are of a glorious depth and richness of hue, by contrast with the gray and purple wastes of the hills. In the sweet, clear air of the morning, the scenery was truly inspiring, and I rode over the high ridges in a mood the very opposite of that I had felt the day previous.

The Nile makes a great curve through the land of Màhass, to avoid which the road passes through an *akaba*, about forty miles in length. At the corner, where the river curves at a right angle from west to south, is a small ruined place called Fakir Bender. The high bank is a little less steep here than at other places, and its sides are planted with lupins. At the end of the village is an immense sont tree, apparently very old. A large earthen water-jar, with a gourd beside it, stood in the shade. The *fàkeer*, or holy man, from whom the place is named, was soon in attendance, and as our camels knelt under the tree, presented me with a gourd of cool water, "in the name of God." I gave him ten paras before we left, but he did not appear to be satisfied, for these holy men have great expectations. I ordered two water-skins filled, and after an hour's delay, we entered on the akaba.

Over rough and stony ridges, which made hard travelling for the camels, we came upon a rolling plain, bounded in the distance by a chain of hills, which we reached by the middle of the afternoon. The path, instead of seeking a pass or gorge, led directly up the side, which, though not very high, was exceedingly steep and covered with loose sand, up which the camels could scarcely climb. The top was a stratum of red porphyry, cropping out of the sand in immense masses. Behind us the dreary Desert extended to Djebel Foga and the mountains about the cataract: the palms of the Nile were just visible in the distance. Crossing the summit ridge, we entered a narrow plateau, surrounded by naked black peaks—a most savage and infernal landscape. The northern slope was completely covered with immense porphyry boulders, among which our path wound. Nearly every rock had a pile of small stones heaped upon it, as a guide to caravans, and merely for descending this ridge there were at least two hundred of them. The plain now extended away to the north and east, bounded by a confusion of black, barren mountains, out of which rose two lofty peaks. Towards evening we met a Nubian family, with their donkeys, on their way southward. They begged for water, which we gave them, as their supply was entirely exhausted. I found a bed of hard gravel large enough for my tent, but we had great difficulty in driving the pegs. The camel-men selected the softest places among the rocks for their beds, but the camels stretched their long necks on all sides in the vain search for vegetation. I sat at my tent door, and watched the short twilight of the South gather over the stony wilderness, with that strange feeling of happiness which the contemplation of waste and desolate landscapes always inspires. There was not a blade of grass to be seen; the rocks, which assumed weird and grotesque forms in the twilight, were as black as ink; beyond my camp there was no life in the Desert except the ostrich and the hyena—yet I would not have exchanged the charm of that scene for a bower in the gardens of the Hesperides.

The dawn was glimmering gray and cold when I arose, and the black summits of the mountains showed dimly through a watery vapor. The air, however, was dry, though cool and invigorating, and I walked ahead for two hours, singing and shouting from the overflow of spirits. I hoped to catch a glimpse of the Nile before mounting my dromedary, but one long black ridge of stones rose after another, and there was no sudden flash of green across the darkness of the Desert. At last, towards noon, through a notch in the drear and stony chaos, the double line of palms appeared in the north-east. The river came from the east, out of the black mountain wilderness. The valley is very narrow, and cultivation is only possible in the coves of soil embayed among the hills. I came down on one of them—a meadow of halfeh, back of the little village of Koyee—and stopped an hour to rest the camels. A caravan of merchants, bound for Kordofan and Dar-Für, had just encamped there, to rest during the hot hours, according to their custom. Among them were some *hadji*, or pilgrims from Dar-Für, on their way home from Mecca, and a negro from Fazogl, who had belonged to a European, and had lived in Naples. He was now free and going home, wearing a shabby Frank dress, but without money, as he came at once to beg of me. A Nubian woman came from the huts near at hand, bringing me a large gourd of buttermilk, which I shared with the camel-drivers.

I set the camels in motion again, and we entered a short akaba, in order to cross a broad stony ridge, which advanced quite to the river's edge. The path was up and down the sides of steep hollows, over a terrible waste of stones. Down these hollows, which shelved towards the river, we saw the palms of the opposite bank—a single dark-green line, backed by another wilderness, equally savage. Through all this country of Màhass the Desert makes a desperate effort to cut off the glorious old River. It flings rocks into its bed, squeezes him between iron mountains, compels him to turn and twist through a hundred labyrinths to find a passage, but he pushes and winds his way through all, and carries his bright waters in triumph down to his beloved Egypt. There was, to me something exceedingly touching in watching his course through that fragment of the pre-Adamite chaos—in seeing the type of Beauty and Life stealing quietly through the heart of a region of Desolation and Death. From the stony slopes of the hills I looked down on his everlasting palms with the same old joy new-created in my heart.

After passing the akaba, I came to a village which I took to be Soleb, but on inquiring, the people pointed ahead. I rode on, around a slight curve of the trees, and was startled by a landscape of most unexpected interest and beauty. Before me, over the crest of a black, rocky ridge, a cluster of shattered pillars stood around the falling doorway of a temple, the whole forming a picturesque group, cut clear against the sky. Its tint of soft yellow-gray, was finely relieved by the dark green of the palms and the pure violet of some distant jagged peaks on the eastern bank. Beyond it, to the west, three peaks of white and purple limestone rock trembled in the fiery glare from the desert sands. The whole picture, the Desert excepted, was more Grecian than Egyptian, and was perfect in its forms and groupings. I know of no other name for the ruin than the Temple of Soleb. It was erected by Amunoph III. or Memnon, and the Arcadian character of the landscape of which it is the central feature, harmonized thoroughly with my fancy, that Amunoph was a poet.

The temple stands on the west bank, near the river, and from whatever point it is viewed, has a striking effect. The remains consist of a portico, on a raised platform, leading to a court once surrounded by pillars. Then follows a second and more spacious portico, with a double row of three pillars on each side. This opens upon a second pillared court, at the opposite end of which is a massive doorway, leading to the adyta of the temple, now completely levelled to the earth. The entire length of the ruin is about two hundred feet. There are nine pillars, with a single block of their architrave, and portions of two of the porticoes still standing: the remainder of the temple is a mass of ruins. The greatest pains have been taken to destroy it completely, and all the mound on which it stands is covered with huge blocks, thrown one over the other in the wildest confusion. In one place, only, I noticed the disjointed segments of a column, still lying as they fell. The pedestals remain in many places, so that one can partially restore the original order. When complete, it must have been a majestic and imposing edifice. The material is the white limestone of the adjacent mountains, veined with purple streaks, and now much decomposed from the sun and rain. From the effect of this decomposition, the columns which remain standing are cracked and split in many places, and in the fissures thus made, numbers of little swallows and starlings have built their nests, where they sit peeping out through the sculptures of gods. The columns and doorways are covered with figures, now greatly blurred, though still legible. I noticed a new style of joining the portrait of a monarch with his cartouche, the latter representing his body, out of which his head and arms issued, like the crest of a coat of arms. The columns represent the stalks of eight water-plants bound together, with a capital, or rather prolonged abacus, like the Osiride column. They are thirty feet in height, without the pedestal, and five feet in diameter. This is the sum of my observations: the rest belongs to the antiquarian.

Before night, we passed a third akaba, to get around the limestone ridge, which here builds a buttress of naked rock over the Nile, and at sunset again saw the palms—but this time the renowned palms of Dar Sukkôt, for we had crossed the border of Dar El-Màhass. They lined the river in a thick grove of stems, with crowns of leafy luxuriance. The village of Noolwee, scattered for half a mile in their shade, was better built than any I saw in Dongola. Many of the houses were inclosed in square courts, and had a second story, the massive mud walls sloping towards each other like a truncated pyramid. Achmet, Ali and myself bought about fifty piastres worth of the celebrated dates of Sukkôt. They were the largest and best flavored I ever saw, and are said to preserve their quality for years. They are sold at a piastre for an earthen measure containing about two hundred. When gathered, they are first slightly dried in the large magazines, and then buried in the earth. The population of Sukkôt subsists apparently on the profits of selling them, for little else is cultivated along the river. Even here, nevertheless, where the people are better able to bear the grinding rule of Egypt, one meets with deserted fields and ruined dwellings. The King of El-Màhass informed me, when in Khartoum, that his people were obliged to pay six hundred piastres (thirty dollars) tax on each water-mill, being just double the lawful amount, (which, alone, is very oppressive), and that his country was fast becoming depopulated, in consequence.

On the following day I passed the large island of Sai. The country here is more open and the Nile has a less vexed course. The mountains, especially the lofty blue mass of Djebel Abyr, have not the forced and violent forms common to the porphyry formation. Their outlines are long, sloping, and with that slight but exquisite undulation which so charmed me in the hills of Arcadia, in Greece, and in Monte Albano near Rome. Their soft, clear, pale-violet hue showed with the loveliest effect behind the velvety green of the thick palm clusters, which were parted here and there by gleams of the bright blue river. From the northern end of Sai, the river gradually curves to the east. The western shore is completely invaded by the sands, and the road takes a wide sweep inland to avoid the loose, sliding drifts piled up along the bank. We had not gone far before we found a drift of brilliant yellow sand thirty feet high and two hundred yards in length, lying exactly across our road. It had evidently been formed within a few days. It was almost precisely crescent-shaped, and I could not account for the action of the wind in building such a mound on an open plain, which elsewhere was entirely free from sand. We rounded it and soon afterwards entered on a region of sand, where to the west and north the rolling yellow waves extended to the horizon, unbroken by a speck of any other color. It was a boundless, fathomless sea of sand to the eye, which could scarcely bear the radiated light playing over its hot surface. The day (for a wonder) was somewhat overcast, and as the shadows of small clouds followed one another rapidly over the glaring billows, they seemed to heave and roll like those of the sea. I was forced to turn away my head, faint and giddy with the sight. My camels tugged painfully through this region, and after two hours we reached a single sont tree, standing beside a well, and called *sugger el-abd* (the Tree of the Slave). It was pointed out by the camel-men as being half-way between El Ordee and Wadi Halfa.

We journeyed on all the afternoon through a waste of sandy and stony ridges, and as night drew near, I became anxious tc reach the river, no trace of which could be seen. I rode up one of the highest ridges, and lo! there were the tops of the date-groves in a hollow, not a quarter of a mile distant, on my right. The camels' heads were soon turned in that direction, and I encamped at once on the bank, where my beasts found sufficient grass and thorns for the first time in three days. The river here flows in a deep channel, buried among the hills, and there is neither cultivation nor population on the western bank. On the opposite side there was a narrow strip of soil, thickly planted with date-trees.

My camel-men kindled a fire in the splendid moonlight, and regaled themselves with the hind-quarters of a hyena, which they roasted in the coals and devoured with much relish. I had curiosity enough to eat a small piece, which was well-flavored though tough. The Nile roared grandly below our camp all night, in the pauses of the wind.

Abou-Sin, my Dromedary.

CHAPTER XXXVI.

THE BATN EL-HADJAR.

The Batn El-Hadjar, or Belly of Stone—Ancient Granite Quarries—The Village of Dal—A Ruined Fortress—A Wilderness of Stones—The Hot Springs of Ukmé—A Windy Night—A Dreary Day in the Desert—The Shekh's Camel Fails—Descent to Samneh—The Temple and Cataract—Meersheh—The Sale of Abou-Sin—We Emerge from the Belly of Stone—A Kababish Caravan—The Rock of Abou-Seer—View of the Second Cataract—We reach Wadi-Halfa—Selling my Dromedaries—Farewell to Abou-Sin—Thanksgiving on the Ferry-boat—Parting with the Camel men.

On the sixth day after leaving Dongola I passed through Sukkôt, and reached the commencement of Batn El-Hadjar—The Belly of Stone—as the savage mountain country for a hundred miles south of the Second Cataract is termed. With each day the road became more rough and toilsome, and my camels moved more languidly. In spite of the fatigue which we all endured, I felt so much strengthened by our free life and so much interested in the remarkable country through which we were passing, that I felt something like regret on approaching the southern limit of travel on the Nile. Not so my dragoman and servant, who could not enough thank God and the Prophet for having taken them in safety through countries which they deemed the verge of the world. Achmet positively declared he would never make the trip again, for no second journey could be equally fortunate. My camel-men, I found, had never before travelled to Wadi Halfa by the western bank, but by a wonderful Arab instinct, they never went astray from the road.

The Batn El-Hadjar marks its commencement by a range of granite hills, which break the river into a foaming cataract. After leaving camp, our road lay along the Nile, behind some high sand-hills. In front of us appeared Djebel Ufeer, a peak about fifteen hundred feet in height, its naked sides tinted of a deep, rich purple hue by the glowing air. The Nile flows directly towards its base, making a slight curve, as if to pass it on the eastern side, but finding the granite rocks heaped together too thickly, changes its course and washes the western foot of the mountain. The granite lies scattered about in vast masses, taking all sorts of quaint and fanciful shapes. The hills themselves are merely collections of boulders of all sizes, from three to twenty feet in diameter, piled on an enormous bed or stratum of the same. Intermixed with this are beds of a rich yellowish-red granite, which crops out under the piles of gray, and has been worked, wherever it appears in large masses. The traces of the ancient quarrymen still remain, in the blocks bearing marks of the wooden wedges by which they were split. In one place I noticed two fragments of a column, similar to those in the palace at Old Dongola. The granite is equal in quality and still more abundant than that at Assouan, but was only quarried to a limited extent. The aspect of the country is rugged in the highest degree, and how the Nile gets through it became more and more a wonder to me. His bed is deep-sunken between enormous stone-piles, back of which are high stone mountains, and wherever there is a hollow between them, it is filled with sand. The only vegetation was a few bunches of miserable grass, and some of those desert shrubs which grow at the very doors of Tartarus, so tenacious of life are they. A narrow shelf, on the opposite bank, high above the river, bore the renowned palm of Sukkôt, and frequently in the little coves I saw the living green of the young wheat. The steep banks were planted with lupins, as the people there had nothing to fear from the hippopotami.

While I was breakfasting off a great granite table, a man who rode by on a donkey cheered me with the news that the village of Dal was but a short distance ahead. I had fixed upon this as our resting-place for the night, but on finding it so near, resolved to push on to some natural hot springs and ruins of ancient baths, which the camel-men had informed me were about four hours further, to the right of the caravan track. At Dal, however, a difficult *akaba* commences, and my camels already marched so slowly and wearily that I judged it best to stop and give them a little rest. About the village there are some scattering doum and date-palms, which lead a hard existence, half buried in sand and choked with the old leaves, which the natives are too idle to prune. The people were in the fields, cutting some wheat which was just ripe, and two sakias, shaded by clusters of palms, watered a few patches of cotton. I made inquiries, but had much difficulty in finding the location of the hot springs. Finally, one of the men consented to become my guide in the morning, and conducted us to a camping-ground, where there was a little grass for the camels. Lured by the promise of backsheesh, he brought me the leanest of young sheep, which I purchased for eight piastres. The night was calm, cool and delicious, and steeped my whole frame in balm, after the burning day. The moon, nearly full, shone with a gray and hazy lustre, and some insect that shrilled like a tree-toad, reminded me of home.

Our Dallee guide, Hadji Mohammed, as he was called, from having made two pilgrimages to Mecca, was on hand before sunrise. Starting in advance of the caravan, I walked along the river-bank, towards a castellated building on an eminence which I had noticed the previous evening, while sketching the landscape. My path was over huge beds of gray granite, from which the old Egyptians might have cut obelisks of a single block, not only one hundred, but five hundred feet in length. The enormous masses which had been separated from these beds and rolled into rounded masses by the chafing of primeval floods, lay scattered on the surface, singly, or piled in fantastic groups. The building was a large fortress of stones and clay, with massive walls, on the summit of an island-like peak overhanging the river, and separated from the bank by a deep chasm, which is filled with water during the inundations, but was then dry, and its sides green with wheat and beans. Wild doum-palms, hanging heavy with green fruit, grew in the patches of soil among the rocks and overhung the ravine. The fortress was a very picturesque object, with its three square towers, backed by the roaring flood and the dark violet-blue crags of Djebel Mémé behind. The forms of the landscape—except the palms—were all of the far North, but the coloring was that of the ripe and glowing South. I was so absorbed in the scene, that the caravan passed unnoticed, having taken a path further from the river. After wandering about for some time, I climbed one of the granite piles and scanned the country in all directions, but could see nothing. Finally I descried a distant trail, and on reaching it, recognized the tracks of my camels. I hurried on, and in half an hour met Hadji Mohammed and one of my camel-men, coming back in great tribulation, fearful that I was lost.

Near the Cataract of Dal, an akaba commences, which extends to the village of Ukmé, in the Batn el-Hadjar, a distance of about fifteen miles. We passed behind some peaks of black porphyry, whose shoulders were covered with steep, sliding drifts of yellow sand, and travelled on through a wilderness of stones. All the refuse odds and ends of Creation—the pieces left after the rocks and mountains of the rest of the world were fashioned—have been thrown together here. It was a sea of black stone-mounds, out of which rose occasional peaks of still blacker stone. Through this we passed into a region of gray stone and then into another of red stone, journeying for four hours up one mound and down another, by paths and no paths, which were most laborious for our camels. I began to be fearful we should never get out of the geological labyrinth into which the hadji conducted us, but the majestic range of Djebel El-Lamool, beyond the Nile, served him as a guide. He looked occasionally towards a bastion-like projection in the sheer walls of porphyry, and at last, when I was quite tired and famished, took us up a ridge whence I saw the river again below us. The road into the valley was next to impracticable, but our camels stumbled and scrambled and slid till they reached the ledge of halfeh overhanging the river. Below us was a square mass of burnt brick, about ten feet in height—part of a building long since destroyed. "Here is the bath," said the hadji. We dismounted, and he conducted us to the foot of the ruin, where, in a hole in the earth, a spring of water bubbled up profusely, and trickled away, through a trough of stones. There was an end of my anticipations of a refreshing bath, for which I had come prepared. The water was hot enough, in truth (131°), and I could not bear my hand below the surface. Under the bank, a dozen springs with a smaller flow of water, oozed through the soil, which was covered with a whitish deposit in places. To atone for my disappointment, I took breakfast in the shadow of the ruined wall, while my camel-men bathed themselves in the water, with many exclamations of "*Bismillàhi!*" (In the name of God). The hadji then left us, and we followed the Nile past the cataracts of Song and Tangoori, which latter we heard all night, roaring grandly between the gusts of wind.

During the night the wind blew violently, and I had great fears that my tent would come down about my ears. I heaped the sand against it on the outside, for further protection, but every thing within was so covered that its original color could no longer be discerned. The moon shone between wild and stormy clouds, and all signs betokened a gust of rain. We took more than ordinary precautions in the disposition of our baggage, as this part of the road was much infested with marauding bands of Kababish, who came from the side of Dar-Fūr and plundered the inhabitants along the river, as well as small caravans. I trusted in the protection afforded by my tent, which, from its appearance, would be taken as belonging to an officer of the government.

On the eighth day we rose—for the first time in all my African travel—in a cold, raw and cloudy dawn. Fortunately for us, a company of merchants, bound for Wadi-Halfa, passed at daybreak, for we entered on an *akaba* of unknown length, and the wind had blown so violently within the last few days that the old caravan trail was not to be found. The country was a wilderness even more drear than those we had passed. On climbing the long stony surges, I sometimes flattered myself with the hope of seeing beyond the Desert; but no—I had only a more extended horizon. Long, shadowy streaks of rain swept along the eastern horizon, and the mountain-chains which lay against them were colored the darkest and intensest shade of violet—precisely that of the lower leaves of the pansy. As we advanced, the air grew colder, and a shower of large, scattering drops passed over us. The camels shrank and trembled, and my men crept behind them for shelter. Though it was a satisfaction to know that those African skies *can* rain sometimes, I was soon so benumbed as to need my capote. The temperature was perhaps not lower than 60°, yet I felt it severely. About ten o'clock, the shekh's camel, which had before shown symptoms of fatigue, lay down and refused to go further. As it was impossible to stop in the Desert, I distributed its load among the other four, and ordered him to drive it loose behind us. This, however, was of no avail, and at last he concluded to wait till it had rested a little. I gave him the water-skin, and we pushed on. Half an hour afterwards, when I was eating breakfast under the lee of a sand-hill, Ali, who had remained behind with him, came up, saying they had examined the camel and decided that it was sick. The shekh thereupon wept most vehemently, fearing it would die, and turned about with it to make his way home. Ali lent him a dollar and promised to take him the rest of the money due him. The other men were quite downcast by the shekh's misfortune. There was nothing to be done, however, but to push ahead, as the other camels were well nigh worn out.

We kept on all the afternoon, with the cold wind blowing in our faces, and occasionally a shower of colder rain dashed upon us. The road ascended until towards noon, when we passed through a gateway between two peaks of granite, whose loose masses threatened to topple down the sides and crush us. Then for three or four hours we travelled over more elevated ranges, from the crests of which we had wide glimpses over the terrible tract, yet could see nothing but sand and stones—stones and sand. In the east a long mountain-range lay dark and distant, under the shadow of the rain-clouds, and it was some comfort to know that it was beyond the Nile. As night approached, I feared we should be obliged to camp in the akaba, and without water, but after ten hours of most wearisome travel, we reached a ridge, whence we looked into a vast basin of rocky hills, between us and the mountains, whose long chain of jagged peaks, touched with the full yellow light of the setting sun, stood against the black gust that rolled away beyond them into the Great Nubian Desert. The Nile was not to be seen, yet deep in the centre of this landscape, I caught a glimpse of some thorny bushes, which our further descent showed to be near the village and cataract of Samneh. The bed of the river was filled with masses of black rock, and the cataract, just below the village, roared magnificently all through the night. The wind blew again, and so violently, that I awoke with my ears, mouth and nostrils filled with sand.

The morning was cold, with a violent wind, but I strengthened my camels with an abundant feed of bean-vines and dourra, and set off early. I walked ahead to the temple of Samneh, which stands on a rocky eminence above the cataract. The hill is surrounded with the remains of a massive brick wall, and there are traces of a road leading to the summit. The temple is quite small, and of simple though graceful design, containing only one chamber, at the end of which a headless statue lies on its back. From the little portico in front there is a fine view of the gorge through which the river breaks. A broad stratum of porphyry crosses his bed, broken only in the centre by a gap or flood-gate, not twenty yards across. Through this the whole force of his current is poured, and at the time of my visit, when the water was low, he seemed but a pigmy flood. In fact, for a mile or two below this cataract, there is scarcely any point in all his tortuous and difficult course where one might not throw a stone across. After leaving the temple, our road led over the desolate stony hills, high above the river's bed. We looked down into the deep and narrow defile through which he flows, and which his waters scarcely brightened or cheered, for there was no vegetation on his banks except now and then a bunch of halfeh grass or a few stunted thorns. The air was so bracing that I felt nc more fatigue, but only regret, that the journey was so near its close. Old Mohammed walked ahead, singing his accustomed song: "*Koolloo nasee fee djennatee, tefoddhel, ya er-rakhman!*" (O Most Merciful, grant that all my people may enter thy Heavens!) Thus we travelled all day, and towards evening came down to the Nile again at the little village of Meersheh.

This place is a beautiful little oasis in the midst of the savage Belly of Stone. The Nile has a more gentle current, and his banks have room enough for some groves of luxuriant date-trees, and fields of wheat and cotton. My tent was pitched beside the rustling palms, and I sat down with a glad heart and a full pipe, on the last night of my long and toilsome journey by land. During the evening one of the natives took a fancy to my Abou-Sin, and made numerous small offers for the purchase of him. I refused, preferring to send him on to Assouan, but in the morning the man came again, and at last, with many struggles, raised his price to one hundred and ninety piastres, whereupon I thought it best to sell and so avoid all further trouble. I stipulated, however, that Abou-Sin was to be delivered to him at Wadi-Halfa, and that he should accompany us thither on the morrow. The night was intensely cold, although the air was probably not below 60°. I could hardly bear the coldness of the water in the morning. It stung my burnt face like fire, and increased the pains of my unfortunate cracked nose. The Barabras brought me some milk for my coffee in a basket of closely-plaited grass, smeared with grease on the inside. It precisely resembled those baskets made by the Indians of California, which will carry water

The milk, however, had a taste of the rancid grease, which prevented me from drinking much of it.

We arose shivering in the early dawn, and for the last time put the loads on our fagged and unwilling camels. Soon after starting, I saw ahead, through a gateway of black porphyry rocks, the long, yellow sand-hills of the Libyan Desert, like those which line the western bank of the Nile, from Assouan to Korosko. This was a joyful token that we had reached the end of the savage Batn El-Hadjar. As we were travelling over the rolling upland of yellow sand, enjoying the view of the wild frontier of the Belly of Stone, out of which we had just issued, a large caravan of Kababish Arabs, returning towards Dar-Fūr with empty camels, met us. There were upwards of fifty camels and thirty men—half-naked savages, with projecting features, wild eyes, and a wilderness of hair on their heads. The Kababish were easily distinguished by their long plaits, laid close to the head, and smeared with fat. The others, who had enormous masses of wool, standing out in all directions for a foot or more, were probably Howoweet, from the side of Dar-Fūr. We asked the distance to Wadi Halfa, and were answered with the universal "*hassa*," (just now!) whereby these people designate any indefinite period of time.

After three or four hours, I began to look out for Abou-Seer, a lofty cliff to which travellers repair for a bird's-eye view of the Second Cataract—to them the turning point of their Nile journey, to me the termination of my long mid-African rambles, and the commencement of my return to the living world. Our road was a mile or two behind the river, and as Achmet had only visited the mountain from the side of Wadi Halfa, he could not serve as a guide. I turned into the hills, taking him, Mohammed and Ali, and leaving the other man to go on with the baggage camels. We wandered for some time over the rough ridges, and at last reached a spur of the hills which Achmet took to be Abou-Seer, but which was not it. I was so hungry that I stopped for breakfast, and before I had finished, Ali, who was overflowing with joy at the idea of reaching Wadi Halfa, came to me with the news that he had been climbing a high point, whence he could see the end of the mountains. The Nile, beyond, he said, was broad and smooth, and there were more date-trees than he had seen since leaving Sukkôt. I left him to ride my Abou-Sin, and walked on to the peak he had climbed. As I reached its base, however, I saw that the true headland projected still further beyond, terminating in a cone-like summit. As I came out from among the hills behind it, the view suddenly opened before me far to the north and east, and I saw the long date-groves of Wadi Halfa apparently at my feet.

Abou-Seer is a cliff of calcareous rock, and its base is completely covered with the names of tourists who have visited it. Achmet wanted me to add my name to theirs, but as I had brought no hammer and chisel from Cairo, like most travellers, I could not gratify him. A few steps took me to the summit of the cliff, which drops on the eastern side in a sheer precipice to the water's edge. It is at least three hundred feet in perpendicular height, and as it forms the corner of the range, the view on three sides is uninterrupted for many leagues. The panorama is truly grand, and probably unlike any other in the world. To the south the mountains of the Batn El-Hadjar rise like a black wall, out of which the Nile forces its way, not in a broad sheet, but in a hundred vexed streams, gurgling up amid chaotic heaps of rocks as if from subterranean sources, foaming and fretting their difficult way round endless islands and reefs, meeting and separating, seeking every where an outlet and finding none, till at last, as if weary of the long contest, the rocks recede, and the united waters spread themselves out, sluggish and exhausted, on the sands below. It is a wonderful picture of strife between two material forces, but so intricate and labyrinthine in its features, that the eye can scarcely succeed in separating them, or in viewing it other than as a whole. The streams, in their thousand windings, appear to flow towards all points of the compass, and from their continual noise and motion on all sides, the whole fantastic wilderness of rock seems to heave and tug, as it is throttled by the furious waters. This is the last great struggle and triumph of the Nile. Henceforth, his tortured waters find repose. He goes down to Egypt as a conquerer, crowned with a double majesty after all his toils. Is it to be wondered at, that the ancient race which existed by his bounty, should worship him as a God?

But by this time we saw our baggage-camels, like specks on the sand, approaching Wadi Halfa. Ali, unable to contain himself, started off on a run, and we soon lost sight of him. I mounted my faithful big dromedary, Abou-Sin, and after two more hours on his lofty hump, dismounted at the ferry-place, opposite Wadi Halfa, never, alas! to mount him again. A boat with a company of merchants from Cairo had just arrived, and the sailors were unloading their packages of merchandise. The merchants came up and saluted me, and could scarcely believe that I had been so far as the White Nile. They were bound for Dongola, and one of them, learning that my brown dromedary was for sale, offered to buy it. Achmet conducted the business for me, for the bargaining lasted at least two hours, before the purchaser succeeded in slowly struggling up to a decent price. The Barabra who had bought Abou-Sin was also on hand, to ratify the bargain, and I was thus saved from the necessity of sending the animals to the markets of Assouan. I must do both the men the justice to say that they afterwards made every exertion to cheat me, in the way of counting money and offering bad pieces, and at last gave a large pile of copper coin, which, when it was counted, lacked two piastres of the right amount. When all was finished, I delivered Abou-Sin into the hands of his rascally new master, with a sorrowful heart, for the old fellow and I were good friends. Had he known we were to be separated, I am sure those large black eyes of his would have dropped a few tears, and that capacious throat gurgled out a sound of lamentation. Achmet threw his arms around the beast's big head and kissed him tenderly. I was about to do the same thing, when I remembered that the never-sweating skin of a dromedary exhales not the freshest of odors, and preferred caressing him with my hand rather than my lips. So farewell to Abou-Sin, and may he never want dourra and bean-vines, nor complain under too heavy loads: and should he die soon (for he is waxing in years), may some son of his strong loins be there to carry me, when next I visit Central Africa!

My arrival at Wadi Halfa terminated the journey of thirty-four days from Khartoum. In that time my little caravan had travelled between eight and nine hundred miles, and at least half of it as rough travelling as can be found in Africa. Now we were beyond danger and done with fatigue, and could look forward to seeing Cairo in another month. Not until we were all seated in the ferry-boat, crossing from the opposite bank, did I fairly realize that our severe journey was over. The camels were left behind, the baggage piled up on board, and as we were rowed slowly across the river, it suddenly flashed through my mind that the same gentle motion of oars and waves was thenceforth to rock me all the way to Cairo. I drew a long breath, and fervently ejaculated: "*el hamdu lillàh!*" to which the others, as in duty bound, responded. Achmet, who usually postponed his prayers until he reached home, recited a chapter from the Koran, and Ali, who never prayed, broke into sailor-songs by starts, and laughed continually, from inward delight.

After my tent was pitched on the beach, I called my camel-men, Ali and Mohammed, who had crossed with me, and gave them each the forty piastres still due, with a Maria Theresa dollar—*abou-zeràr*, or the Father of Buttons, as this coin is called in Central Africa, from the button which clasps the drapery on the Empress's shoulder—as backsheesh. The men were delighted, and kissed my hand, in token of gratitude. I gave them also the money for the shekh, and took leave of them with the exclamation: "May God grant you a prosperous return to your country!" They replied, warmly: "May God prolong your days, O Effendi!" and as they moved away I overheard old Mohammed again declare to Achmet: "Wallah, but this is a good Frank! He certainly has Islam in his heart!"

CHAPTER XXXVII

THE ROCK TEMPLES OF ABOU-SIMBEL.

Wadi Halfa—A Boat for Assouan—We Embark on the Nile Again—An Egyptian Dream—The Temples of Abou-Simbel—The Smaller Temple—The Colossi of Remeses II.—Vulgarity of Travellers—Entering the Great Temple—My Impressions—Character of Abou-Simbel—The Smaller Chambers—The Races of Men—Remeses and the Captive Kings—Departure.

WADI HALFA is an ordinary Arab village, and noted only for being the head of navigation on the Nubian Nile. There were six or seven boats in port, some of them loaded with gum and ready to start for Assouan. They were all *nekkers*, or trading boats, built of heavy wood, and not to be moved down stream against a strong head-wind. I therefore engaged the ferry-boat in which I had crossed—a light, open boat, manned by two Nubian boys. The raïs made a frame of sticks near the stern, and covered it with palm-mats, to serve as a cabin. The open hold was turned into a kitchen, and taken possession of by my two men. There was barely room enough for all of us and our baggage, and a fat sheep I bought, as provision for the voyage, but as I proposed being gloriously lazy, to make up for the foregone toils, I needed no more.

The morning after my arrival at Wadi Halfa all was ready. A few children came down to greet me with the hate-ful word "backsheesh," which I had not heard for three months and hoped never to hear again; but a few Arabic exclamations soon put them to flight. We shoved away from the beach, followed by the cries of a dozen lazy sailors, who also wanted backsheesh for saying "*salaam*" at parting. I stretched myself out on my bed, on deck, and lay looking on the receding shore, where my camel-men and camels (Abou-Sin still among them) were encamped. Abou-Sin's head was turned towards the river, as if looking for his master, for the hapless creature certainly thought I should go over to mount him on the morrow. Alas, my brave old dromedary! we shall never again play friendly tricks upon each other. Raïs Ramadan took his station at the helm, and the boys plied their oars actively, so that we soon lost sight of Wadi Halfa. All the afternoon we glided slowly down the stream between rich palm-groves and grain-fields. The appearance of thrift and fertility, which the country presented, was most agreeable after the waste fields of Dongola, and the unproductive rocks and sands of the intermediate districts. The mountains behind were lower and rounder in their outlines, and the landscapes softer an richer tha any I had seen since leaving beautiful Dar Shygheea. By sunset we had made such good progress, that there was every hope of reaching Abou-Simbel in the morning.

There was no wind during the night, and the boys worked bravely. About two hours after midnight I was awakened from a deep sleep by the shock of the boat striking the shore. I opened my eyes and saw, as I lay, without moving my head, a huge wall of rock before me, against which six enormous statues leaned as they looked from deep niches cut in its front. Their solemn faces were touched by the moon, which shone full on the cliff, and only their feet were wrapped in shadow. The lines of deep-cut hieroglyphics over the portal of this rocky temple were also filled with shadow and painted legibly on the gray, moonlit rock. Below them yawned the door—a square of complete darkness. A little to the left, over a long drift of sand that sloped from the summit of the cliff nearly to the water's edge, peered the mitred head of a statue of still more colossal proportions. I gazed on this broad, dim, and wonderful picture for a moment, so awed by its majesty that I did not ask myself where nor what it was. This is some grand Egyptian dream, was my first thought, and I closed my eyes for a few seconds, to see whether it would vanish. But it stood fast and silent as ever, and I knew it to be Abou-Simbel. My servants all slept, and the raïs and boys noiselessly moored the boat to the shore, and then lay down and slept also. Still I lay, and the great statues looked solemnly down upon me, and the moon painted their kingly nomens and banners with yet darker distinctness on the gray rock. The river made no sound below, the long grass stirred not a blade at the foot of the crags, and the slopes of sand were white and dumb as snow. I lay in too deep a repose for thought, and was not then conscious how grateful was such a silence in Nature, while the moon held up that picture before me. It might have been two minutes or twenty, before the current slowly swung the stern of the boat around, and the picture as slowly shifted from my view, leaving instead the Southern Cross in its shrine of stars.

In the morning, I found that we lay at the foot of the smaller temple. I quietly waited for my cup of coffee, for the morning reality was infinitely less grand than my vision of the night. I then climbed to the door and entered. The interior is not large nor imposing, after one has seen the temples of Egypt. The exterior, however, is on such a colossal scale, that, notwithstanding the want of proportion in the different statues, the effect is very striking. The largest ones are about thirty-five feet high, and not identical, as are those of the great temple. One, who stands with one leg advanced, while he holds a sword with the handle pressed against his breast, is executed with much more spirit than is usually met with in statues of this period. The sculptures of the interior are interesting, and being of the time of Remeses the Great, whose history they illustrate, are executed with much skill and labor. The head of the goddess Athor, on the face of the columns in the hall, is much less beautiful than that of the same goddess at Dendera. It is, in fact, almost broad and distorted enough to represent the genius Typhon.

The front of the great temple is not parallel to that of the other, nor does it face the river, which here flows in a north-east course. The line of the cliff is broken between the two, so that the figures of the great Remeses, seated on each side of the door, look to the east, the direction of the line of the face being nearly north. Through the gap in front, the sands have poured down from the Desert behind, almost wholly filling up the space between the two cliffs; and though since the temple was first opened, in 1817, it has been cleared nearly to the base more than once, the rapid accumulation of sand has again almost closed the entrance The southern colossus is only buried about half way to the knee, but of the two northern ones there is little else to be seen except the heads. Obscured as is the effect of this grand front, it is still without parallel in the world. I had not thought it possible that in statues of such enormous magnitude there could be such singular beauty of expression. The face of Remeses, the same in each, is undoubtedly a portrait, as it resembles the faces of the statues in the interior and those of the King in other places. Besides, there is an individuality in some of the features which is too marked to represent any general type of the Egyptian head. The fullness of the drooping eyelid, which yet does not cover the large, oblong Egyptian eye; the nose, at first slightly inclining to the aquiline, but curving to the round, broad nostrils; the generous breadth of the calm lips, and the placid, serene expression of the face, are worthy of the conqueror of Africa and the builder of Karnak and Medeenet Abou.

The statue next the door, on the southern side, has been shivered to the throne on which it is seated, and the fragments are not to be seen, except a few which lie upon the knees. The ridiculous vanity of tourists has not even spared these sublime monuments, and they are covered wherever a hand can reach, with the names of noble and ignoble snobs. The enthusiastic antiquaries who cleared away the sands have recorded the fact in modest inscriptions, near the door, where they do not offend the eye; and one readily pardons the liberty the writers have taken. But there are two Germans (whose names I will not mention, since it would help give them the very notoriety they covet), who have carved their names in letters a foot long, on the thigh of one of the statues, and afterwards filled them with black paint. I should like to see them subjected to a merciless bastinado, on the same part of their own bodies. Certainly, to have one of the statues seated on their breasts as a nightmare, every night of their lives, would not be too much punishment for such a desecration.

The great doorway of the temple is so choked up with sand that I was obliged to creep in on my knees. The sun by this time had risen exactly to the only point where it can illumine the interior, and the rays, taking a more yellow hue from the rock and sand on which they fell, shone down the long drift between the double row of colossal statues, and lighted up the entrance to the second hall of the temple. I sat down in the sand, awed and half frightened by the singular appearance of the place. The sunshine, falling obliquely on the sands, struck a dim reflection against the sculptured roof, and even lighted up the farthest recesses of the grand hall sufficiently to show its imposing dimensions. Eight square pillars—four on either side of the central aisle—seem to uphold the roof, and on their inner sides, facing each other, are eight statues of the King. The features of all are preserved, and have something of the grace and serenity, though not the majesty of the great statues outside. They look into each other's eyes, with an eternal question on their fixed countenances, but none can give answer. There was something so stern and strange in these eight faces, that I felt a shudder of fear creep over me. The strong arms are all crossed on their breasts, and the hands hold various sacred and regal symbols, conspicuous among which is something resembling a flail, which one sees often in Egyptian sculpture. I thought of a marvellous story I once read, in which a genie, armed with a brazen flail, stands at the entrance of an enchanted castle, crushing with the stroke of his terrible weapon all who come to seek the treasure within. For a moment the childish faith in the supernatural was as strong as ever, and I looked at the gloomy entrance beyond, wishing to enter, but fearing the stony flails of the terrible Remesi on either hand. The faces were once partially colored, and the black eyeball, still remaining on the blank eye of stone, gives them an expression of stupor, of death-in-life, which accounted to me for the nervous shock I experienced on entering.

There is nothing in Egypt which can be likened to the great temple of Abou-Simbel. Karnak is grander, but its grandeur is human. This belongs rather to the superhuman fancies of the East—the halls of the Afrites—or to the realm of the dethroned Titans, of early Greek mythology. This impression is not diminished, on passing the second hall and corridor, and entering the adytum, or sacred chamber of the temple. There the granite altar yet stands in the centre, before the undestroyed figures of the gods, who, seated side by side, calmly await the offerings of their worshippers. The peculiar individuality of each deity is strikingly shown in these large statues, and their attitude is much less constrained than in the sitting statues in the tombs of Thebes. These look as if they *could* rise, if they would. The walls are covered with sculptures of them and of the contemplar deities, in the grand, bold style of the age of Remeses. Some visitors had left a supply of dry palm branches near the entrance, and of these I made torches, which blazed and crackled fiercely, flaring with a rich red light on the sculptured and painted walls. There was sufficient to enable me to examine all the smaller chambers, of which there are eight or nine, cut laterally into the rock, without any attempt at symmetry of form, or regularity of arrangement. Several of them have seats running around three sides, exactly like the divans in modern Egyptian houses. They were probably designed for the apartments of the priests or servants connected with the temple.

The sculptures on the walls of the grand hall are, after those of Medeenet Abou, and on the exterior wall of Karnak, the most interesting I have seen in Egypt. On the end wall, on either side of the entrance, is a colossal bas-relief, representing Remeses slaying a group of captive kings, whom he holds by the hair of their heads. There are ten or twelve in each group, and the features, though they are not colored, exhibit the same distinction of race as I had previously remarked in Belzoni's tomb, at Thebes. There is the Negro, the Persian, the Jew, and one other form of countenance which I could not make out—all imploring with uplifted hands the mercy of the conqueror. On the southern wall, the distinction between the Negro and the Egyptian is made still more obvious by the coloring of the figures. In fact, I see no reason whatever to doubt that the peculiar characteristics of the different races of men were as strongly marked in the days of Remeses as at present. This is an interesting fact in discussing the question of the unity of origin of the race. Admitting the different races of men to have had originally one origin, the date of the first appearance of Man on the earth, must have been nearer fifty thousand than five thousand years ago. If climate, customs, and the like have been the only agents in producing that variety of race, which we find so strongly marked nearly four thousand years ago, surely those agents must have been at work for a vastly longer period than that usually accepted as the age of Man. We are older than we know; but our beginning, like our end, is darkness and mystery.

The sculptures on the side walls of the temple represent the wars of Remeses, who, as at Medeenet Abou, stands in a chariot which two horses at full speed whirl into the ranks of the enemy. The king discharges his arrows against them, and directly in front of him a charioteer, mortally wounded, is hurled from his overthrown chariot. The groups are chiselled with great spirit and boldness; the figures of the king and his horses are full of life. Towering over all, as well by his superior proportions as by the majesty and courage of his attitude, Remeses stands erect and motionless amid the shock and jar and riot of battle. There is no exultation in his face; only the inflexible calmness of Destiny.

I spent some time contemplating these grand and remarkable memorials of the greatest age of Egypt, and left with my feeling for Egyptian art even stronger than before. I watched the giant figures of the portico, as the swift current carried my boat down stream, reluctant to lose sight of their majestic features. But the yellow of the cliff turned to purple, and at last other crags passed before it.

CHAPTER XXXVIII.

RETURN TO EGYPT.

I Lose my Sunshine, and Regain it—Nubian Scenery—Derr—The Temple of Amada—Mysterious Rappings—Familiar Scenes—Halt at Korosko—Escape from Shipwreck—The Temple of Sebooa—Chasing other Boats—Temple of Djerf Hossayn—A Backsheesh Experiment—Kalabshee—Temple of Dabôd—We reach the Egyptian Frontier.

THE distressing coldness of the temperature the night before reaching Wadi Halfa, affected me more painfully than all the roastings I had endured in Soudân. My nose after losing six coats of skin, became so hard and coppery, that like Anthony Van Corlear's, the reflected rays from it might have pierced even the tough skin of a crocodile. My frame was so steeped in heat, that had our fuel fallen short, I might have "drawn" my tea, by hugging the kettle in my arms. I had been so bathed and rolled in light, the sun had so constantly, with each succeeding day, showered upon me his burning baptism, that I came to regard myself as one of his special representatives, and to fancy that, wherever I went, there was a sort of nimbus or radiation around me. But those few drops of rain, among the stony mountains of the Batn El-Hadjar, quenched at once the glow of my outer surface, and the cold winds which followed, never ceased blowing till they extinguished even the central fires. I was like an incipient comet, snuffed out of existence and made satellite to some frozen planet. My frame was racked with pains, which turned into misery the refreshing indolence of the Nile. I had no medicines, but put my philosophy into practice: the climate of Nubia, I said, has given me this infliction, therefore the country must supply the remedy. So I sent the raïs ashore in search of it. He came back with a cup of oil which a shining daughter of the land was about bestowing upon her crispy tresses, and I drank it with a heroic faith in the efficacy of my theory. I was not disappointed, and on the third day sat once more in the sun, in the bow of my boat, trying to regain the effluence I had lost.

The scenery of the Nile below Abou-Simbel is very beautiful. The mountains recede again from the bank, and show themselves occasionally in picturesque peaks. The shores are low and rich and the groves of date-trees most luxuriant. The weather was delightfully calm and warm, and the Nile, though swift, ran smooth and shining as the oil of his own castor bean-fields. During the sweet, quiet hour before and after sunset, we floated down through the lovely region about Bostàn and Teshka. Three tall peaks of dark-brown rock rose inland, beyond the groves of the beautiful Ibreemee palm, whose leaves, longer and more slender than those of the Egyptian date-tree, are gracefully parted at the sides—half of them shooting upward in a plumy tuft, while the other half droop around the tall shaft of the tree. The boys worked during the second night with unabated force. I awoke as the moon was rising through black clouds, and found the lofty crags of

Ibreem overhanging us. We swept silently under the base of the heights, which in the indistinct light, appeared to rise four or five hundred feet above us. By sunrise, the date-groves of Derr, the capital of the Nuba country, were in sight, and we were soon moored beside the beach in front of the town. Derr stretches for some distance along the shore, and presents an agreeable front to the river. A merchant, from a boat near ours, brought me two small loaves of delicious Egyptian bread. He had been in Soudân, and knew how such bread would relish, after the black manufacture of that country.

An hour afterwards my boat ran to the eastern bank, to allow me to visit the little temple of Amada. This temple stands on a slight rise in the sands, which surround and entirely overwhelm it. It consists only of a low portico, supported by eight pillars, a narrow corridor and the usual three chambers—all of very small dimensions. The sculptures on the walls are remarkable for the excellent preservation of their colors. The early Christians, who used this temple for their worship, broke holes in the roof, which admit sufficient light for the examination of the interior. Without knowing any thing of the hieroglyphic inscriptions on the temple, I should judge that it was erected by some private person or persons. The figures making the offerings have not the usual symbols of royalty, and the objects they present consist principally of the fruits of the earth, which are heaped upon a table placed before the divinity. The coloring of the fruit is quite rich and glowing, and there are other objects which appear to be cakes or pastry. While I was examining the central chamber, I heard a sound as of some one sharply striking one of the outside pillars with a stick. It was repeated three times with an interval between, and was so clear and distinct that I imagined it to be Achmet, following me. I called, but on receiving no answer, went out, and was not a little surprised to find no person there or within sight. The temple stands at a considerable distance from any dwelling, and there is no place in the smooth sands on all sides of it where a man could hide. When I mentioned this circumstance, on returning to the boat, Achmet and the raïs immediately declared it to be the work of a *djin*, or afrite, who frequently are heard among the ruins, and were greatly shocked when I refused to accept this explanation. I record the circumstance to show that even in the heart of Nubia there are mysterious rappings.

Beyond Derr I entered the mountain region of granite, sandstone and porphyry, which extends all the way to Assouan. As I approached Korosko, which is only about twelve miles further, the south-wind increased till it became a genuine *khamseen*, almost blotting out the landscape with the clouds of sand which it whirled from the recesses of the Biban. We were obliged to creep along under the bank till we reached Korosko, where we ran up to the same old landing-place at which I had stopped in December. The bank was eight feet higher than then, the river having fallen that much in the mean time. There was the same house, open on the river-side, the same old Turk sitting within, the dark sycamores shading the bank, the dusty terrace with the familiar palms tossing their leaves against the wind, the water-mill, the white minaret at the foot of the mountain, and, lastly, the bold, peaked ridge of Djebel Korosko behind. There was the very spot where my tent had stood, and where I first mounted a dromedary for the long march through the Nubian Desert. There was also the corner by which I turned into the mountain-pass, and took leave of the Nile. I recognized all these points with a grateful feeling that my long wandering in Central Africa was over, without a single untoward incident to mar my recollection of it. I had my pipe and carpet brought under the shade of the sycamore, while Achmet went up to the Governor's house, with the raïs and one of the boys. Before long, the latter appeared with his shirt full of pigeons (for I had not forgotten the delicious roast pigeons we took from Korosko into the Desert), then the raïs with my sack of charcoal, the Governor having only used about one-third of it during my absence, and finally the Governor himself. Moussa Effendi shook me cordially by the hand and welcomed me many times, thanking God that I had returned in safety. We sat on my carpet, talked for an hour about my journey, took coffee, and I then left the worthy man and his wretched village, more delighted at having seen them again than I can well express.

The same evening, the wind veered to the north-west, nearly at right-angles to our course, and just at dusk, as the raïs and Ali were rowing vigorously to keep the boat on the western side of the river (the other being full of dangerous reefs), the rope which held the long oar in its place broke, and Ali tumbled heels over head into the wooden cooking bowl of the raïs. The wind carried us rapidly towards the opposite shore, and while Ali and Lalee were trying to fix the oar in its place, we heard the water roaring over the rocks. "O Prophet!" "O Apostle!" "Prophet of God, help us!" were the exclamations of the raïs, but little black 'Med Roo mee, who sat at the helm, like Charlemagne on a similar occasion, said nothing. He looked keenly through the gloom for the reef, and at last discerned it in time for the boat to be sculled around with the remaining oar, and brought to land just above the dangerous point. A shipwreck in the Nile is a more serious matter than one would imagine, who has never seen the river during a strong wind. Its waves run as roughly and roar as loudly as those of a small sea.

We reached Seboo a during the night, and I walked up to the temple as soon as I rose. Early as it was, several Arabs descried me from a distance, and followed. The temple, which is small and uninteresting, is almost buried under drifts from the Desert, which completely fill its interior chambers. Only the portico and court, with three pillars on each side, to which colossal caryatides are attached, remain visible. Before the pylon there is an avenue of lion-headed sphinxes, six of which, and a colossal statue of sandstone, raise their heads above the sand. I was followed to the vessel by the men, who importuned me for backsheesh. When I demanded what reason they had for expecting it, they answered that all strangers who go there give it to them. This was reason enough for them; as they knew not why it was given, so they knew not why it should be refused. The crowd of travellers during the winter had completely spoiled the Barabras. I said to the men: "You have done nothing for me; you are beggars,"—but instead of feeling the term a reproach, they answered: "You are right—we are beggars." With such people one can do nothing.

For the next two days we lagged along, against a headwind. My two boys did the work of two men, and I stimulated them with presents of mutton and tobacco. Three English boats (the last of the season), left Wadi-Halfa three days before me, and by inquiring at the village, I found I was fast gaining on them. I began to feel some curiosity concerning the world's doings during the winter, and as these Englishmen were at least three months in advance of the point where I left off, they became important objects to me, and the chase of them grew exciting. I prepared for my encounter with them and other belated travellers on the Nile, by making an American flag out of some stuff which I had bought for that purpose in Dongola. The blue and white were English muslin, and the red the woollen fabric of Barbary, but they harmonized well, and my flag, though I say it, was one of the handsomest on the river.

The temple of Djerf Hossayn is excavated in the rock, near the summit of a hill behind the village. A rough path, over heaps of stones, which abound with fragments of pottery, denoting the existence of an ancient town, leads up to it. When I reached the platform in front of the entrance I had a convoy of more than a dozen persons, mostly stout, able-bodied men. I determined to try an experiment, and so told them at the start to go back, for they would get nothing; but they were not to be shaken off. I avoided with the greatest care and patience all their endeavors to place me under obligations to them; for these cunning Barabras are most assiduous in their efforts to render some slight service. If it is only kicking a stone out of your path, it constitutes a claim for backsheesh, and they represent their case in such a way that it would be the most glaring ingratitude on your part not to give it.

On entering the temple, the vast square pillars of the hall, with the colossal figures attached to them, produce a striking impression. The effect of these pillars, which fill nearly half the space of the hall itself, is to increase its apparent dimensions, so that the temple, at the first glance, seems to be on a grander scale than is really the case. I had some curiosity regarding this place, from the enthusiastic description of Warburton, and the disparaging remarks of Wilkinson. After seeing it, I find them both correct, in a great measure. The colossal statues of the grand hall are truly, as the latter observes, clumsy and badly executed, and the sculptures on the walls are unworthy the age of Remeses; but it is also true that their size, and the bulk of the six pillars, which are lofty enough to be symmetrical, would have a fine effect when seen at night, by the light of torches, as Warburton saw them. All the chambers have suffered from smoke and bats, and the bigotry of the old Christians. The walls are so black that it is difficult to trace out the figures upon them. This, however, rather heightens the impression of a grand, though uncouth and barbarous art, which the temple suggests. I made but a brief visit, and marched down the hill with the population of Djerf Hossayn in my train. The boat had gone ahead, as the only approach to the shore was a mile or two beyond, but they insisted on following me. I ordered them to leave, fearing lest the very fact of their walking so far in the hot sun would induce me to break my resolution. It would have been, indeed, a satisfaction to give ten piastres and be freed from them, and I took no little credit to myself for persisting in refusing them. They all dropped off at last, except two, who came almost to the spot where the boat was moored, and only turned back because I was in advance and ordered the raïs to move on as soon as I got on board. I should like to know their opinion of me. I have no doubt the people considered me the most eccentric Frank who ever came among them.

The next morning we reached Kalabshee, and before sunrise I was standing on the long stone platform before the temple. The pylon of hewn sandstone rises grandly above the spacious portal, and from the exterior the building has a most imposing air. Its interior once, probably, did not diminish the impression thus given; but at present it is such an utter mass of ruin that the finest details are entirely lost. The temple is so covered with the enormous fragments of the roof and walls that it is a work of some difficulty to examine it; but it does not repay any laborious inspection. The outer wall which surrounds it has also been hurled down, and the whole place is a complete wreck. I know of no temple which has been subjected to such violence, unless it be that of Soleb, in Dar El-Màhass.

Below the temple we passed the Bab (Gate) El-Kalabshee, where the river is hemmed in between enormous boulders of granite and porphyry. The morning was cold and dark, and had there been firs instead of palms, I could have believed myself on some flood among the hills of Norway. I urged on the boys, as I wished to reach Dabôd before dark, and as Ali, who was anxious to get back to Egypt, took a hand at the oar occasionally, our boat touched the high bank below the temple just after sunset. There is a little village near the place, and the reapers in the ripe wheat-fields behind it were closing their day's labor. One old man, who had no doubt been a servant in Cairo, greeted me with "*buona sera!*" Achmet followed, to keep off the candidates for backsheesh, and I stood alone in the portico of the temple, just as the evening star began to twinkle in the fading amber and rose. Like Kalabshee, the temple is of the times of the Cæsars, and unfinished. There are three chambers, the interior walls of which are covered with sculptures, but little else is represented than the offerings to the gods. Indeed, none of the sculptures in the temples of the Cæsars have the historic interest of those of the Eighteenth Egyptian dynasty. The object of the later architects appears to have been merely to cover the walls, and consequently we find an endless repetition of the same subjects. The novice in Egyptian art might at first be deceived by the fresher appearance of the figures, their profusion and the neatness of their chiselling; but a little experience will satisfy him how truly superior were the ancient workmen, both in the design and execution of their historic sculptures. In Dabôd, I saw the last of the Nubian temples, in number nearly equal to those of Egypt, and after Thebes, quite equal to them in interest. No one who has not been beyond Assouan, can presume to say that he has a thorough idea of Egyptian art. And the Nile, the glorious river, is only half known by those who forsake him at Philæ.

After dark, we floated past the Shaymt-el-Wah, a powerful eddy or whirlpool in the stream, and in the night came to a small village within hearing of the Cataract. Here the raïs had his family, and stopped to see them. We lay there quietly the rest of the night, but with the first glimpse of light I was stirring, and called him to his duty. The dawn was deepening into a clear golden whiteness in the East, but a few large stars were sparkling overhead, as we approached Philæ. Its long colonnades of light sandstone glimmered in the shadows of the palms, between the dark masses of the mountains on either hand, and its tall pylons rose beyond, distinct against the sky. The little hamlets on the shores were still in the hush of sleep, and there was no sound to disturb the impression of that fairy picture. The pillars of the airy chapel of Athor are perfect in their lightness and grace, when seen thus from a boat coming down the river, with the palm-groves behind them and the island-quay below. We glided softly past that vision of silence and beauty, took the rapid between the gates of granite, and swept down to the village at the head of the Cataract. The sun had just risen, lighting up the fleet of trading boats at anchor, and the crowds of Arabs, Egyptians and Barabras on the beach. The two English dahabiyehs I had been chasing were rowed out for the descent of the Cataract, as I jumped ashore and finished my travels in Nubia.

CHAPTER XXXIX

VOYAGE DOWN THE NILE.

Assouan—A Boat for Cairo—English Tourists—A Head-wind—Ophthalmia—Esneh—A Mummied Princess—Ali Effendi's Stories—A Donkey Afrite—Arrival at Luxor—The Egyptian Autumn—A Day at Thebes—Songs of the Sailors—Ali leaves me—Ride to Dendera—Head-winds again—Visit to Tahtah—The House of Rufaä Bey.

I reached the Egyptian frontier on the morning of the sixteenth of March, having been forty days in making the journey from Khartoum. Immediately upon our arrival, I took a donkey and rode around the Cataract to Assouan, leaving Ali to take care of the baggage-camels. I went directly to the beach, where a crowd of vessels were moored, in expectation of the caravans of gum from the South. An Egyptian Bey, going to Khartoum in the train of Rustum Pasha, had arrived the day before in a small dahabiyeh, and the captain thereof immediately offered it to me for the return to Cairo. It was a neat and beautiful little vessel, with a clean cabin, couch, divan, and shady portico on deck. He asked twelve hundred piastres; I offered him nine hundred; we agreed on a thousand, and when my camels arrived there was a new refuge prepared for my household gods. I set Achmet to work at getting the necessary supplies, sent the raïs to bake bread for the voyage, and then went to see the jolly, flat-nosed Governor. He received me very cordially, and had a great deal to say of the unparalleled herd of travellers on the Nile during the winter. Ninety-six vessels and eleven steamboats had reached the harbor of Assouan, and of these the greater number were Americans. "Mashallah! your countrymen must be very rich," said the Governor.

When I left the divan, the firing of guns announced the safe arrival of the English boats below the Cataract. Very soon I saw two burnt-faced, tarbooshed individuals, with eye-glasses in their eyes, strolling up the beach. For once I threw off the reserve which a traveller usually feels towards every one speaking his own language, and accosted them. They met my advances half-way, and before long my brain was in a ferment of French and English politics. Europe was still quiet then, but how unlike the quiet of the Orient! The Englishmen had plenty of news for me, but knew nothing of the news I most wanted—those of my own country. Had our positions been reversed, the result would have been different. They left at sunset for the return to Thebes, but I was detained until noon the next day, when I set off in company with the boat of Signor Drovetti, of Alexandria, who left Khartoum a few days after me. I had six men, but only two of them were good oarsmen.

In the morning, when I awoke, the broken pylon of Ombos tottered directly over the boat. I rushed on deck in time to catch another sight of the beautiful double portico, looking down from the drifted sands. The wind blew very strongly from the north, but in the afternoon we succeeded in reaching

Djebel Silsileh, where the English boats were moored. We exchanged pistol salutes, and I ran up to the bank to visit some curious sculptured tablets and grottoes, which we did not see on the upward voyage. During the night the wind increased to such an extent that all the boats were obliged to lay to The morning found our four dahabiyehs floating slowly down in company, crossing from side to side transversely, in order to make a little headway. After three or four hours, however, the wind grew so strong that they were driven up stream, and all ran to the lee of a high bank for shelter. There we lay nearly all day. The Englishmen went ashore and shot quails, but I lounged on my divan, unable to do any thing, for the change from the dry, hot desert air, to the damp Nile blasts, brought on an inflammation of the eyes, resembling ophthalmia. I was unable to read or write, and had no remedies except water, which I tried both warm and cold, with very little effect.

Towards evening the wind fell; after dark we passed the pylon of Edfoo, and at noon the next day reached Esneh. I went at once to the temple, so beautiful in my memory, yet still more beautiful when I saw it again. The boys who admitted me, lifted the lids of the large coffin and showed the royal mummies, which are there crumbling to pieces from the neglect of the Egyptian authorities, who dug them up at Goorneh. The coffins were of thick plank and still sound, the wood having become exceedingly dry and light. The mummies were all more or less mutilated, but the heads of some were well preserved. In form, they differ considerably from the Arab head of the present day, showing a better balance of the intellectual and moral faculties. On one of them the hair was still fresh and uncorrupted. It was of a fine, silky texture and a bright auburn color. The individual was a woman, with a very symmetrical head, and small, regular features. She may have been a beauty once, but nothing could be more hideous. I pulled off a small lock of hair, and took it with me as a curious relic. Esneh appeared much more beautiful to me than on my upward journey; possibly, by contrast with the mud-built houses of Soudân. I went to a coffee-shop and smoked a *sheesheh*, while the muezzin called down from the mosque in front: "God is great; there is no God but God; Mohammed is the Prophet of God."

Ali Effendi, the agent of the *Moodir*, or Governor, came to see me and afterwards went on board my vessel. As the wind was blowing so furiously that we could not leave, I invited him to dinner, and in the meantime we had a long talk on afrites and other evil spirits. I learned many curious things concerning Arabic faith in such matters. The belief in spirits is universal, although an intelligent Arab will not readily confess the fact to a Frank, unless betrayed into it by a simulated belief on the part of the latter. Ali Effendi informed me that the spirit of a man who is killed by violence, haunts the spot where his body is buried, until the number of years has elapsed, which he would otherwise have lived. He stated, with the greatest earnestness, that formerly, in passing at night over the plain between Embabeh and the Pyramids, where Napoleon defeated the Mamelukes, he had frequently heard a confusion of noises,—cries of pain, and agony, and wrath—but that now there were but few sounds to be heard, as the time of service of the ghosts had for the most part expired.

One of his personal experiences with an afrite amused me

exceedingly. He was walking one night on the road from Cairo to Shoobra, when he suddenly saw a donkey before him. As he was somewhat fatigued, and the donkey did not appear to have an owner, he mounted, and was riding along very pleasantly, when he was startled by the fact that the animal was gradually increasing in size. In a few minutes it became nearly as large as a camel; and he thereby knew that it was no donkey, but an afrite. At first he was in such terror that the hairs of his beard stood straight out from his face, but suddenly remembering that an afrite may be brought to reveal his true nature by wounding him with a sharp instrument, he cautiously drew his dagger and was about to plunge it into the creature's back. The donkey-fiend, however, kept a sharp watch upon him with one of his eyes, which was turned backwards, and no sooner saw the dagger than he contracted to his original shape, shook off his rider and whisked away with a yell of infernal laughter, and the jeering exclamation: "Ha! ha! you want to ride, do you?"

We had scarcely left Esneh before a fresh gale arose, and kept us tossing about in the same spot all night. These blasts on the Nile cause a rise of waves which so shake the vessel that one sometimes feels a premonition of sea-sickness. They whistle drearily through the ropes, like a gale on the open sea. The air at these times is filled with a gray haze, and the mountain chains on either hand have a dim, watery loom, like that of mountains along the sea-coast. For half a day I lay in sight of Esneh, but during the following night, as there was no wind, I could not sleep for the songs of the sailors. The sunrise touched the colonnade of Luxor. I slept beyond my usual time, and on going out of the cabin what should I see but my former guide, Hassan, leading down the beach the same little brown mare on which I had raced with him around Karnak. We mounted and rode again down the now familiar road, but the harvests whose planting I had witnessed in December were standing ripe or already gathered in. It was autumn in Egypt. The broad rings of clay were beaten for threshing floors, and camels, laden with stacks of wheat-sheaves paced slowly towards them over the stubble fields. Herds of donkeys were to be seen constantly, carrying heavy sacks of wheat to the magazines, and the capacious freight-boats were gathering at the towns along the Nile to carry off the winter's produce.

It was a bright, warm and quiet day that I spent at Thebes. The great plain, girdled by its three mountain-chains, lay in a sublime repose. There was no traveller there, and, as the people were expecting none, they had already given up the ruins to their summer silence and loneliness. I had no company, on either side of the river, but my former guides, who had now become as old friends. We rode to Karnak, to Medeenet Abou, to the Memnonium, and the Colossi of the Plain. The ruins had now not only a memory for me, but a language. They no longer crushed me with their cold, stern, incomprehensible grandeur. I was calm as the Sphinx, whose lips no longer closed on a mystery. I had gotten over the awe of a neophyte, and, though so little had been revealed to me, walked among the temples with the feelings of a master. Let no one condemn this expression as presumptuous, for nothing is so simple as Art, when once we have the clue to her infinite meanings.

White among the many white days of my travel, that day

at Thebes is registered; and if I left with pain, and the vast regret we feel on turning away from such spots, at least I took with me the joy that Thebes, the mighty and the eternal, was greater to me in its living reality than it had ever been in all the shadow-pictures my anticipation had drawn. Nor did the faultless pillars of the Memnonium, nor the obelisks of Karnak, take away my delight in the humbler objects which kept a recognition for me. The horses, whose desert blood sent its contagion into mine; the lame water-boy, always at my elbow with his earthen bottle; the grave guides, who considered my smattering of Arabic as something miraculous, and thence dubbed me "Taylor Effendi;" the half-naked Fellahs in the harvest-fields, who remembered some idle joke of mine,—all these combined to touch the great landscape with a home-like influence, and to make it seem, in some wise, like an old resting-place of my heart. Mustapha Achmet Aga, the English agent at Luxor, had a great deal to tell me of the squabbles of travellers during the winter: how the beach was lined with foreign boats and the temples crowded day after day with scores of visitors; how these quarrelled with their dragomen and those with their boatmen, and the latter with each other till I thanked Heaven for having kept me away from Thebes at such a riotous period.

Towards evening there was a complete calm, and every thing was so favorable for our downward voyage that I declined Mustapha's invitation to dine with him the next day, and set off for Kenneh. The sailors rowed lustily, my servant Ali taking the leading oar. Ali was beside himself with joy, at the prospect of reaching his home and astonishing his family with his marvellous adventures in Soudân. He led the chorus with a voice so strong and cheery that it rang from shore to shore. As I was unable to write or read, I sat on deck, with the boy Hossayn at my elbow to replenish the pipe as occasion required, and listened to the songs of the sailors. Their repertory was so large that I was unable to exhaust it during the voyage. One of their favorite songs was in irregular trochaic lines, consisting of alternate questions and answers, such as "*ed-dookan el-liboodeh fayn?*" (where's the shop of the cotton caps?) sung by the leader, to which the chorus responded: "*Bahari Luxor beshwoytayn.*" (A little to the northward of Luxor). Another favorite chorus was: *Imlăl-imlăl-imlălee!*" (Fill, fill, fill to me!) Many of the songs were of too broad a character to be translated, but there were two of a more refined nature, and these, from the mingled passion, tenderness and melancholy of the airs to which they were sung, became great favorites of mine.*

* I give the following translations of these two songs, as nearly literal as possible:

I.

Look at me with your eyes, O gazelle, O gazelle! The blossom of your cheeks is dear to me; your breasts burst the silk of your vest; I cannot loose the shawl about your waist; it sinks into your soft waist. Who possesses you is blessed by heaven. Look at me with your eyes, O gazelle, O gazelle! Your forehead is like the moon; your face is fairer than all the flowers of the garden; your bed is of diamonds; he is richer than a King who can sleep thereon. Look at me with your eyes, O gazelle, O gazelle!

II.

O night, O night—O darling, I lie on the sands. I languish for the light of your face; if you do not have pity on me, I shall die.

O night, O night—O darling, I lie on the sands. I have changed color

Before sunrise we reached Kenneh. Here I was obliged to stop a day to let the men bake their bread, and I employed the time in taking a Turkish bath and revisiting the temple of Dendera. My servant Ali left me, as his family resided in the place. I gave him a good present, in consideration of his service during the toilsome journey we had just closed. He kissed my hand very gratefully, and I felt some regret at parting with, as I believed, an honest servant, and a worthy, though wild young fellow. What was my mortification on discovering the next day that he had stolen from me the beautiful stick, which had been given me in Khartoum by the Sultana Nasra. The actual worth of the stick was trifling, but the action betrayed an ingratitude which I had not expected, even in an Arab. I had a charming ride to Dendera, over the fragrant grassy plain, rippled by the warm west wind. I was accompanied only by the Fellah who owned my donkey—an amiable fellow, who told me many stories about the robbers who used formerly to come in from the Desert and plunder the country. We passed a fine field of wheat, growing on land which had been uncultivated for twenty years. My attendant said that this was the work of a certain Effendi, who, having seen the neglected field, said that it was wrong to let God's good ground lie idle, and so planted it. "But he was truly a good man," he added; "and that is the reason why the crop is so good. If he had been a bad man, the wheat would not have grown so finely as you see it."

from my longing and my sorrow; you only can restore me, O my darling.

O night, O night—O darling, I lie on the sands. O darling, take me in: give me a place by your side, or I must go back wretched to my own country.

For three days after leaving Kenneh, a furious head-wind did its best to beat me back, and in that time we only made sixty miles. I sighed when I thought of the heaps of letters awaiting me in Cairo, and Achmet could not sleep, from the desire of seeing his family once more. He considered himself as one risen from the dead. He had heard in Luxor that his wife was alarmed at his long absence, and that his little son went daily to Boulak to make inquiries among the returning boats. Besides, my eyes were no better. I could not go ashore, as we kept the middle of the stream, and my only employment was to lounge on the outside divan and gossip with the raïs. One evening, when the sky was overcast, and the wind whirled through the palm-trees, we saw a boy on the bank crying for his brother, who had started to cross the river but was no longer to be seen. Presently an old man came out to look for him, in a hollow palm-log, which rolled on the rough waves. We feared the boy had been drowned, but not long afterwards came upon him, drifting at the mercy of the current, having broken his oar. By the old man's assistance he got back to the shore in safety.

On the fourth day the wind ceased. The Lotus floated down the stream as lightly as the snowy blossom whose name I gave her. We passed Girgeh, Ekhmin; and at noon we brushed the foot of Djebel Shekh Hereedee and reached the landing-place of Tahtah. I had a letter from Rufaā Bey in Khartoum to his family in the latter town, and accordingly walked thither through fields of superb wheat, heavy with ripening ears. Tahtah is a beautiful old town; the houses are of burnt brick; the wood-work shows the same fanciful Saracenic patterns as in Cairo, and the bazaar is as quiet, dim and spicy as an Oriental dream. I found the Bey's house, and delivered my letter through a slave. The wife, or wives, who remained in the hareem, invisible, entertained me with coffee and pipes, in the same manner, while a servant went to bring the Bey's son from school. Two Copts, who had assisted me in finding the house, sat in the court-yard, and entertained themselves with speculations concerning my journey, not supposing that I understood them. "Girgos," said one to the other, "the Frank must have a great deal of money to spend." "You may well say that;" his friend replied, "this journey to Soudân must have cost him at least three hundred purses." In a short time the Bey's son came, accompanied by the schoolmaster. He was a weak, languid boy of eight or nine years old, and our interview was not very interesting. I therefore sent the slave to bring donkeys, and we rode back to the boat.

CHAPTER XL.

THE RETURN TO CAIRO—CONCLUSION.

Siout in Harvest-time—A kind Englishwoman—A Slight Experience of Hasheesh—The Calm—Rapid Progress down the Nile—The Last Day of the Voyage—Arrival at Cairo—Tourists preparing for the Desert—Parting with Achmet—Conclusion.

We reached Siout on the morning of the twenty-eighth of March, twelve days after leaving Assouan. I had seen the town, during the Spring of an Egyptian November, glittering over seas of lusty clover and young wheat, and thought it never could look so lovely again; but as I rode up the long dyke, overlooking the golden waves of harvest, and breathing the balm wafted from lemon groves spangled all over with their milky bloom, I knew not which picture to place in my mind's gallery. I remained half a day in the place, partly for old acquaintance sake, and partly to enjoy the bath, the cleanest and most luxurious in Egypt. I sought for some relief to my eyes, and as they continued to pain me considerably, I went on board an English boat which had arrived before me, in the hope of finding some medicine adapted to my case. The travellers were a most innocent-faced Englishman and his wife—a beautiful, home-like little creature, with as kind a heart as ever beat. They had no medicine, but somebody had recommended a decoction of parsley, and the amiable woman spoiled their soup to make me some, and I half suspect threw away her Eau de Cologne to get a bottle to put it in. I am sure I bathed my eyes duly, with a strong faith in its efficacy, and fancied that they were actually improving, but on the second day the mixture turned sour and I was thrown back on my hot water and cold water.

While in Egypt, I had frequently heard mention of the curious effects produced by *hasheesh*, a preparation made from the *cannabis indica.* On reaching Siout, I took occasion to buy some, for the purpose of testing it. It was a sort of paste made of the leaves of the plant, mixed with sugar and spices The taste is aromatic and slightly pungent, but by no means disagreeable. About sunset, I took what Achmet considered to be a large dose, and waited half an hour without feeling the slightest effect. I then repeated it, and drank a cup of hot tea immediately afterwards. In about ten minutes, I became conscious of the gentlest and balmiest feeling of rest stealing over me. The couch on which I sat grew soft and yielding as air; my flesh was purged from all gross quality, and became a gossamer filagree of exquisite nerves, every one tingling with a sensation which was too dim and soft to be pleasure, but which resembled nothing else so nearly. No sum could have tempted me to move a finger. The slightest shock seemed enough to crush a structure so frail and delicate as I had become. I felt like one of those wonderful sprays of brittle spar which hang for ages in the unstirred air of a cavern, but are shivered to pieces by the breath of the first explorer.

As this sensation, which lasted but a short time, was

gradually fading away, I found myself infected with a tendency to view the most common objects in a ridiculous light. Achmet was sitting on one of the provision chests, as was his custom of an evening. I thought: was there ever any thing so absurd as to see him sitting on that chest ? and laughed immoderately at the idea. The turban worn by the captain next put on such a quizzical appearance that I chuckled over it for some time. Of all turbans in the world it was the most ludicrous. Various other things affected me in like manner, and at last it seemed to me that my eyes were increasing in breadth. "Achmet," I called out, "how is this ? my eyes are precisely like two onions." This was my crowning piece of absurdity. I laughed so loud and long at the singular comparison I had made, that when I ceased from sheer weariness the effect was over. But on the following morning my eyes were much better, and I was able to write, for the first time in a week.

The calm we had prayed for was given to us. The Lotus floated, sailed and was rowed down the Nile at the rate of seventy miles a day, all hands singing in chorus day and night, while the raïs and his nephew Hossayn beat the tarabooka or played the reedy zumarra. It was a triumphal march; for my six men outrowed the ten men of the Englishman. Sometimes the latter came running behind us till they were within hail, whereupon my men would stand up in their places, and thundering out their contemptuous chorus of "*hê tôm, tôm, koosbarra!*" strike the water so furiously with their long oars, that their rivals soon slunk out of hearing. So we went down, all excitement, passing in one day a space, which it had taken us four days to make, on our ascent. One day at Manfaloot; the next at Minyeh; the next at Benisooef; the next in sight of the Pyramids; and so it came to pass that in spite of all my delays before reaching Siout, on the sixteenth day after leaving Assouan, I saw the gray piles of Dashoor and Sakkara pass behind me and grow dim under the Libyan Hills.

And now dawns the morning of the first of April, 1852—a day which will be ever memorable to Achmet and myself, as that of our return to Cairo. When the first cock crowed in some village on shore, we all arose and put the Lotus in motion. Over the golden wheat-fields of the western bank the pyramids of Dashoor stand clear and purple in the distance. It is a superb morning; calm, bright, mild, and vocal with the songs of a thousand birds among the palms. Ten o'clock comes, and Achmet, who has been standing on the cabin-roof, cries: "O my master! God be praised! there are the minarets of Sultan Hassan!" At noon there is a strong head-wind, but the men dare not stop. We rejoice over every mile they make. The minaret of old Cairo is in sight, and I give the boat until three o'clock to reach the place. If it fails, I shall land and walk. The wind slackens a little and we work down towards the island of Roda, Gizeh on our left. At last we enter the narrow channel between the island and Old Cairo; it is not yet three o'clock. I have my pistols loaded with a double charge of powder. There are donkeys and donkey-boys on the shore, but Arabian chargers with Persian grooms were not a more welcome sight. We call them, and a horde comes rushing down to the water. I fire my pistols against the bank of Roda, stunning the gardeners and frightening the donkey-boys. Mounted at last, leaving Achmet to go on with the boat to Boulak, I dash at full speed down the long street leading into the heart of Cairo. No heed now of a broken neck: away we go, upsetting Turks, astonishing Copts and making Christians indignant, till I pull up in the shady alley before the British consulate. The door is not closed, and I go up stairs with three leaps and ask for letters. None; but a quantity of papers which the shirt of my donkey-boy is scarcely capacious enough to hold. And now at full speed to my banker's. "Are there any letters for me?" "Letters?—a drawer full!" and he reaches me the missives, more precious than gold. Was not that a sweet repayment for my five months in the heat and silence and mystery of mid-Africa when I sat by my window, opening on the great square of Cairo, fanned by cool airs from the flowering lemon groves, with the words of home in my ears, and my heart beating a fervent response to the sunset call from the minarets: "God is great God is merciful!"

I stayed eight days in Cairo, to allow my eyes time to heal. The season of winter travel was over, and the few tourists who still lingered, were about starting for Palestine, by way of Gaza. People were talking of the intense heat, and dreading the advent of the *khamseen*, or south-wind, so called because it blows fifty days. I found the temperature rather cool than warm, and the *khamseen*, which blew occasionally, filling the city with dust, was mild as a zephyr, compared to the furnace-like blasts of the African Desert. Gentlemen prepared themselves for the journey across the Desert, by purchasing broad-brimmed hats, green veils, double-lined umbrel las, and blue spectacles. These may be all very good, but I have never seen the sun nor felt the heat which could induce me to adopt them. I would not exchange my recollections of the fierce red Desert, blazing all over with intensest light, for any amount of green, gauzy sky and blue sand. And as for an umbrella, the Desert with a continual shade around you, is no desert at all. You must let the Sun lay his sceptre on your head, if you want to know his power.

I left Cairo with regret, as I left Thebes and the White Nile, and every other place which gives one all that he came to seek. Moreover, I left behind me my faithful dragoman, Achmet. He had found a new son in his home, but also an invalid wife, who demanded his care, and so he was obliged to give up the journey with me through Syria. He had quite endeared himself to me by his constant devotion, his activity, honesty and intelligence, and I had always treated him rather as a friend than servant. I believe the man really loved me, for he turned pale under all the darkness of his skin, when we parted at Boulak.

I took the steamer for Alexandria, and two or three days afterwards sailed for fresh adventures in another Continent. If the reader, who has been my companion during the journey which is now closed, should experience no more fatigue than I did, we may hereafter share also in those adventures.

FINIS.

www.ingramcontent.com/pod-product-compliance
Lightning Source LLC
LaVergne TN
LVHW021308110826
845150LV00003B/522

* 9 7 8 1 4 2 5 5 5 9 4 3 4 *